D1101529

HITLER'S DEATH

Published in 2005 by Chaucer Press
20 Bloomsbury Street
London WC1B 3JH

© 2005 Chaucer Press

Designed and produced for Chaucer Press
by Open Door Limited, Rutland, UK
Editors: Josephine Bacon, Emily Romanowska and Stephen Chumbley

Russian Editorial board:
J. F. Pogonyi (chairman)
V. K. Vinogradov (deputy chairman)
A. A. Zdanovich (deputy chairman)
G. V. Zaitsev, N. P. Mikheikin,
N. V. Teptzov (chief secretary)
Authors: V. K. Vinogradov, J. F. Pogonyi, N. V. Teptzov

Title: Hitler's Death
ISBN: 1-904449-13-1

A collection of hitherto top-secret material from the Central Archive of the Federal Security
Service debunks the myths surrounding the last days of Hitler and Goebbels, and tells the story
of what happened to their corpses, destroyed on the instructions of the KGB of the Soviet
Union in 1970.

The book is based on records of interrogations and on statements written by General Field
Marshal F. Schörner, Hitler's personal security chief SS Gruppenführer H. Rattenhuber, Head of
the central defence region of Berlin General Wilhelm Mohnke, the Führer's doctor Professor
Werner Haase, a member of the Chancellor's bodyguard Harry Mengershausen, intelligence
officer K. Janke and others. The book includes the full text of Martin Bormann's diary and some
unique illustrations.

© Zvonnitsa Publishing House, 2000

HITLER'S DEATH

Russia's Last Great Secret from the Files of the KGB

Foreword by
ANDREW ROBERTS

CHAUCER PRESS

CONTENTS

CONTENTS

CONTENTS

HITLER'S DEATH

Based on declassified documents provided by the Russian Federal Security Service, many of them published for the first time:

Secret operations by the SMERSH, the Soviet Security Service in the search for Hitler, Goebbels and other high-ranking Nazis

Records of the interrogations of members of the Führer's innermost circle

Material from forensic experts

The diary of Martin Bormann

Speculation and rumours about Hitler's end

FOREWORD

The Nazi Götterdamerung of late April 1945 has never been more closely forensically examined than in this definitive collection of documents from the KGB's own archives. The eerie atmosphere in the Berlin Reichschancellery at the time of the suicide of Adolf Hitler has long fascinated historians and laymen alike; now there is a single source book that brings together every imaginable aspect of that defining moment in the history of the modern world. The authors – V.K. Vinogradov, J.F. Pogonyi and N.V. Teptzov – deserve high commendation for placing the entire record in the public domain in this very scholarly and accessible way.

The booming of the Red Army's constantly advancing guns; Dr Goebbels reading Thomas Carlyle's *Frederick the Great* to his despondent Fuhrer down in the bunker; farcical military conferences where units are deployed which have in reality long since surrendered or deserted; the shotgun wedding of Hitler and Eva Braun, with the Fuhrer being formally asked whether he was of Aryan racial origin; the poisoning of the couple's German shepherd dog Blondi by cyanide capsule; the utterly cold-blooded murder by Joseph and Magda Goebbels of their six young children, to save them from the horror of growing up in a post-Nazi world; the breathtaking wait outside Hitler's room to hear the shot that signalled that Civilisation had at last triumphed over Barbarism – these are only some of the morbid yet utterly compelling images that we all have of *Der Untergang* ('The Downfall'). This book comprehensively shows us which are accurate and which the product of our collective false consciousness about that final scene.

A central paradox of World War II – or The Great Patriotic War as the Russians call it – was that in order for the pathological murderers of the Third Reich to be defeated, Civilisation had to call in aid from Joseph Stalin and a Bolshevik regime that had massacred innocents on a similarly vast scale ever since grabbing power in 1917. The work of the three Russian authors in the KGB archives proves beyond doubt what Western scholars such as Antony Beevor, Richard Pipes, Norman Stone and Simon Sebag Montefiore have long been alleging – that Stalin knew perfectly well that Hitler had died by his own hand in the bunker, but that he encouraged doubt about the Fuhrer's fate for his own Cold War propaganda ends. Such cynicism and disregard for veracity on the part of Stalin and the Soviet leaders will hardly come as a great revelation, but these documents clearly establish that they knew the truth many years before they publicly acknowledged it.

Germany's attempt at world conquest had to end the way it did – with Hitler's suicide in the bunker on the Wilhelmstrasse in the centre of the capital city of the Reich – for there to be any closure in the long, sad story of Prussian and then Nazi aggression. Between 1864 and 1939, a period of only 75 years, Prussia and its successor Reichs were involved in five wars of expansion, only one of which – the Franco-Prussian War of

1870-71 – was not initiated by them. To burn this craving for continental conquest out of the German national psyche, it was necessary to have the leader of the Fatherland shoot himself in the bombed-out ruins of the Prussian capital. Any demise less total and self-inflicted might have created a new *Dolchstosslegende* ('stab-in-the-back myth'), such as that which had pertained after the Great War, when the defeat was blamed on socialists, Jews, bankers – indeed anyone except the German High Command. Part of the reason why Germany has been such a successful, pacific, liberal democracy for the past sixty years is precisely because of the way that Hitler met his end in the manner described in such mesmerising detail in this book. Germany needed Year Zero in order to be reborn.

Of course, as with any contemporaneous document-based evidence, the testimonies contained here need to be evaluated through the prism of the circumstances prevailing at the time. Most of the Germans whom the Soviets interrogated who had been close to Hitler in the bunker were captives of indefinite duration in whose interests it was to tell their captors what they wanted to hear. Many of them were (understandably) frightened, possibly undernourished, probably nerve-wracked and fearful of the future. Moreover some were shell-shocked and suffering from all the demoralising psychological traumas associated with national destruction and defeat. Their reminiscences cannot thus be viewed as having the objectivity of, say, an affidavit in a court of law. Yet with that important caveat being borne in mind, what the Germans told the Russians about life in the bunker was incredibly comprehensive, as these enthralling pages bear witness.

When Winston Churchill was told on 1 May, 1945 of the German official broadcast that Hitler had died 'fighting with his last breath against Bolshevism', his comment was: 'Well, I must say that he was perfectly right to die like that'. Lord Beaverbrook, who was dining with him at the time, observed that it was obviously untrue. As *Hitler's Death* proves so conclusively, Beaverbrook was right. Before the discovery of DNA it was difficult, if not impossible, conclusively to ascertain that the charred remains found under a layer of soil in the bomb-crater ten feet from the garden entrance to the *Fuhrerbunker* were the corpses of Adolf Hitler and Eva Braun. Yet the work of the Soviet intelligence services (principally SMERSH) in piecing together all the evidence for the couple's final moments – as well as the incontrovertible dental evidence set out in pages 95-107 – put the established historical record beyond any reasonable doubt.

What will intrigue readers, apart from the details of life in the bunker from SMERSH's German interviewees, and the first-class photographs reprinted here, are the various rumours about Hitler's fate that circulated in the immediate post-war period. Was he hiding in a cave somewhere in the Alps; did he get to South America by submarine; had he somehow secretly managed to fly out of Berlin while his capital was being reduced to ashes? The Soviets did nothing to quash such speculations, appreciating that they redounded to Russia's political interest by keeping Germany in view as a potentially *revanchist* enemy. Indeed the great Marshal Zhukov himself fuelled such speculations in June 1945 by mentioning that there had been runways available to the Luftwaffe right up until the actual fall of central Berlin.

Rumours have a tangible power and value in times of great unrest, and the story that Hitler had a son (see pages 296-7) was circulated by the Reuters and TASS news agencies on New Year's Day 1946, only to be denied – at least by Reuters - the following day. Denials never have quite the same power of penetration as the initial story, however, which necessarily remains in the public arena. The belief that a twelve-year-old son of Adolf Hitler and Eva Braun had escaped to Czechoslovakia under the name Friedrich Schulz simply added grist to the Soviet propaganda mill. 'It is supposed that [Martin] Bormann's aide-de-camp Friedrich Wilhelm Paustin tried to deliver Hitler's last will and the boy's photograph to Eva Braun's family', recorded TASS about Hitler's son. Such footnotes to history are intriguing, even though what they report is utterly untrue, because they reveal the state of mind of the victors in the immediate aftermath of the greatest struggle of modern history. As well as laying bare the pathology of the Third Reich on its autopsy slab, these pages tell us much about the Allies too. Overall, it must be said that the Soviet investigators were painstakingly thorough, and the questions they posed to Hitler's entourage in 1945 were much the same as we might have done today. It was not the investigators but the Soviet propagandists who kept alive the myth of Hitler's escape.

The authors are also to be commended for adding some invaluable appendices, including a series of reports about the way that the corpses of Hitler, Eva Braun and the Goebbels family were finally physically destroyed during the night of 4 April, 1970. The bodies had been buried at a KGB base in Magdeburg, East Germany in February 1946, which 24 years later was about to be turned over to the locals as surplus to requirements. So potent a symbol to neo-Nazis were the mortal remains thought to be – even though the 'skulls, shin-bones, ribs, vertebrae and so on' were in 'an advanced state of decay, especially those of the children' – that the Chairman of State Security, Yuri Andropov, ordered that they be burned with charcoal, crushed to dust, collected up and then thrown into a river. It was another potent example of Soviet thoroughness when it came to the necrosis of Nazism.

In one sense, of course, this entire book is a series of appendices to the authors' impressive and comprehensive Preface. It is fitting that it should have been compiled by three Russians, since it must never be forgotten – especially not on this sixtieth anniversary of the victory over Hitlerism – that 80% of all Wehrmacht casualties in the Second World War were inflicted by the Red Army on the Eastern Front. The blood-sacrifices made by Mother Russia between 1941 and 1945 were primarily what destroyed Hitler's dreams for global mastery, although the contributions made by the English-speaking peoples and others were, of course, considerable.

This book represents a real contribution to the available evidence of a momentous world-historical event: it also recalls how occasionally in the course of human affairs, Evil can succumb.

Andrew Roberts
July 2005

PREFACE

For many years, the circumstances of Adolf Hitler's death, or his mysterious disappearance, have been one of the great mysteries of World War II. The world had been in ignorance, possessing only some information from a few witnesses which was unconfirmed by any material evidence.

As the fierce fighting approached the capital of the Third Reich, Soviet military counter-espionage officers had the serious task of searching for and capturing the leading Nazi war criminals. Naturally, the Soviet Secret Service was primarily interested in information about Hitler and his closest circle, where, according to intelligence, feverish activity had begun to enable them to evade responsibility for their crimes by any means. The day was inexorably approaching when just punishment would be meted out both to those who had formulated the Nazis' inhuman plans and to those who had put them into practice.

Meanwhile some of the faithful servants of Hitler's regime were already testifying before the investigators of 'Smersh', the General Counter-Espionage Department, or had already been sentenced for crimes they had committed in the USSR and other countries of Europe liberated from the Occupation.

The initial information about what had been happening in the territories under the Nazi jackboot had come from the captured generals and other officers of Field Marshal Friedrich von Paulus's army which had capitulated at Stalingrad in early 1943. More information was accumulated as other occupied countries were liberated. Commissions were set up especially to investigate the Nazi atrocities and the first trials were held to expose and punish the leading Nazi conquerors and their collaborators. The Gauleiter of Byelorussia, Wilhelm Kube, did not escape justice, being liquidated by NKVD special task groups in Minsk. Reinhard Heydrich, Reich Protector of Bohemia and Moravia and the right-hand man of Reichsführer-SS Heinrich Himmler, had been assassinated by the Czech resistance in 1942.

Closer to Berlin, 'bigger fish' were being caught in the net spread by the Soviet intelligence service. Among those arrested were Kurt Janke, an experienced German spy, General Heinrich Vert, Chief of Staff of the Hungarian Army, Walter Wolf, Chief of the German Police in Poland, and Erich Gunzen, Head of the German Military Mission in Romania. But the top war criminals remained in Berlin and other areas as yet unoccupied by Allied forces.

According to available information, Russian intelligence officers knew that the chief war criminal, Hitler himself – who had arrived in Berlin with his entourage by special train from Frankfurt-on-Main on 17 January, 1945 – was now residing permanently in a special bunker under the old Reich Chancellery at 77–78 Wilhelmstrasse. The war was approaching the Nazi den much more quickly than Hitler had expected, however. That is why, on 20 April, he sent the majority of his staff to the Berghof, one of his residences in the south of Germany, himself moved into a new reinforced-concrete bunker with an exit into the garden of the Reich Chancellery. At the time, air raids on the capital of the Third Reich were intensifying.

During the capture of Berlin, Soviet military counter-espionage officers and men were operating in 'Smersh' task-groups of formations of the 1st Byelorussian Front. They directly participated in the battle for the capture of the administrative buildings and government offices, showing exemplary courage, fortitude and persistence in accomplishing their mission. They were among the first to storm the Reichstag and the Reich Chancellery, capturing many of those close to Hitler, Goebbels and Bormann, and saving many important documents.

On 30 April, during street-fighting in Berlin, a naval NCO named Paul Marzers was captured, a man who had been with an SS composite battalion. Acting on information received from him that, as of 28 April, Hitler, Goebbels and others were still in the Reich Chancellery, Lieutenant-Colonel I. I. Klimenko, Chief of the 'Smersh' Section of the 79th Infantry Corps, immediately gave orders to task-groups under his command to start searching for the Nazi leaders, accompanied by German prisoners who were to identify them. To establish the exact whereabouts of Hitler and those of his retinue who had remained in Berlin, their captured colleagues, acquaintances and relatives were questioned. They were asked about the fate of the leading Nazis and about the atmosphere in the bunker before and during the battle of Berlin.

On 3 May, Erich Haberman, an officer of the guard, was captured in civilian clothes in the basement of the Reich Chancellery's hospital, and he confirmed that Hitler was dead. He also stated that he had seen Elisabeth Lyndhurst, a nurse at the hospital, wearing around her neck a locket containing a portrait of Hitler's mother and that she had the Führer's gold Party badge in her hand. Lyndhurst was detained by Soviet intelligence officers who found the following items which had actually belonged to Hitler: his gold pocket watch, a portrait of his mother, his Party badge, a World War I Iron Cross and a medal for a minor wound.

Another nurse from the Reich Chancellery hospital – Erna Flegel – stated that, on the night of 29/30 April, she was summoned to Hitler together with all the medical staff and that the Führer shook hands with everyone. Along with this, other members of Hitler's staff who had been detained said that Bormann and other top SS officers left the bunker to break out of Berlin and escape to the West, and that Dr Goebbels and his family committed suicide in the bunker.

Locating the top Nazis and solving the mystery of their disappearance called for immediate and decisive action, unambiguous decisions and professional investigative procedures. Right from the final days of the war, it was very important to get to the truth, as the fate of the Nazi war criminals was already starting to be surrounded by myths and legends, rumours and speculations, which were often contradictory. From a political and historical perspective, it was necessary to ensure that the truth was made known to future generations, and to remove the halo of mystery surrounding Hitler and his followers, who during their lifetime had sincerely believed in horoscopes, mysticism and a sort of divine providence. Typical of this was Goebbel's belief, seriously discussed with Hitler, that the sudden death of US President Roosevelt would result in the break-up of the Allied coalition.

The Führer's last retreat was occupied by Soviet forces on 2 May. On the same day, at 17.00, 'Smersh' officers Lieutenant-Colonel Klimenko, Chief of the Counter-Espionage Section of the 79th Infantry Corps, Major B. A. Bystrov, Chief of Sub-Section of Counter-Espionage Section of the 3rd Assault Army and Major I. G. Hazin, Deputy Chief of the Counter-Espionage Section of the 207th Infantry Division, while searching for Hitler's remains in the garden of the Reich Chancellery accompanied by the witnesses Karl Schneider, Hitler's garage mechanic and the Reich Chancellery's cook Wilhelm Lange, discovered the burnt corpses of a man and a woman. The Germans recognised them as those of Goebbels and his wife Magda.

On 3 May, Lieutenant L. A. Ilyn, commander of a platoon of the 'Smersh' Counter-Espionage Department of the 207th Infantry Division, discovered a horrible scene in one of the rooms of the bunker: six children looking as if they had just fallen asleep. These were Goebbel's children who had been poisoned by their parents before they took their own lives.

On the same day, Vice-Admiral Hans-Erich Voss, a prisoner-of-war, and the above-mentioned Lange and Schneider, were assembled to officially identify the corpses. Without hesitation they all identified them as the Goebbels family.

Given the significance of the first discovery of the remains of a leading Nazi, the record of identification was signed, along with other immediate participants in the 'discovery', by Lieutenant-General A. A. Vadis, Chief of the 'Smersh' Counter-Espionage Department of the 1st Byelorussian Front, his Deputy Major-General G. A. Melnikov, Lieutenant-General V. K. Gvozd, Chief of the Intelligence Department of the 3rd Assault Army Staff, and other army counter-espionage officers. The opinion of the witnesses was confirmed at the time by another German prisoner – the Reich Chancellery's chief technician, Wilhelm Tziem.

After the remains of Goebbels and his wife had been exhumed, Colonel A. S. Miroshnichenko Chief of 'Smersh' Counter-Espionage Department of the 3rd Assault Army, taking into account information about the Führer's suicide, reinforced the search parties and ordered them to search thoroughly in the grounds of the Reich Chancellery and to detain anyone who could provide information about Hitler's fate.

On 5 May, not far from where the corpses of Goebbels and his wife had been found, Privates I. D. Churakov, E. O. Oleynik and I. E. Seroukh, lead by Lieutenant of the

PREFACE

Guards A. A. Panasov, commander of a platoon of the 'Smersh' Counter-Espionage Department of the 79th Infantry Corps, discovered the badly-burnt corpses of a man and a woman that had been covered with soil in a bomb crater.

Several days later, on the orders of the High Command, a Reich Chancellery guard officer, Harry Mengershausen, was invited to examine the place of the burial. He recounted all he knew about the deaths and the attempts to destroy the corpses of Hitler and his wife Eva Braun. Intelligence officers made a 'field sketch' at the site and the Chief of the Topographical Service, Major of the Guards G. E. Gabelok, also performed a topographical survey of the site at which the corpses had been discovered. The statement of the German guard concerning what he had seen while on duty was verified by discovery in the crater of the corpses of the Führer's poisoned pet dogs. The discovery was made on 5 May by a group of 'Smersh' officers headed by Captain A. G. Deriabin, Assistant Chief of the Counter-Espionage Section of the 79th Infantry Corps. The first report of the examination of the burial site of Hitler and his wife, compiled on 13 May, was signed by everyone who had participated in discovery of the corpses, from Lieutenant-Colonel Klimenko himself down to the private soldiers and the witness Mengershausen.

The remains of the Goebbels family and the Hitlers, as well as those of both dogs, were taken to the 'Smersh' Counter-Espionage Section of the Department of the 79th Infantry Corps for examination. It was very important to confirm or refute the visual identification of the corpses by using the most reliable scientific methods. As early as 3 May, on the orders of Lieutenant-General K. F. Telegin, a member of the War Council of the 1st Byelorussian Front, a special group of military doctors was formed, headed by Leading Pathologist of the Red Army I. A. Kraevsky and Leading Forensic Medicine Expert of the 1st Byelorussian Front F. I. Shkaravsky. Once the corpses had been discovered, these experts did all the work needed to identify them.

Intelligence officers also took the necessary measures to search for documents and new witnesses. In Professor Blaschke's dental surgery in the Reich Chancellery, they discovered notes concerning dental treatment and the making of dentures for Hitler, Goebbels and other Nazi leaders and their families. Counter-espionage officers identified Germans who had worked as dental technicians and had assisted the Führer's dentist, and enlisted their co-operation in the identification process.

As early as 10 May, important evidence was provided by Professor Blaschke's assistant, Käthe Heusemann, who had frequently assisted him during Hitler's dental treatment. The information provided by her concerning the peculiarities of Hitler's teeth and those of his wife and their dentures turned out to be significant proof of the Nazi leader's death. The teeth remaining in the bodies were quite sufficient for official examination. On 19 May, Heusemann was questioned by Lieutenant-General Vadis and Colonel Miroshnichenko of 'Smersh'. She was asked about her direct participation in dental treatment and about the distinctive features of Hitler and Eva Braun's teeth and dentures. On receiving detailed answers, the officers showed her the surviving teeth and dentures that had been recovered and, without hesitation, she positively identified them as being those of Hitler and his wife. Further information received from her, after this initial interrogation, was compared with evidence obtained from others and from re-examination of the remains. Similar procedures were applied to the remains of Goebbels and his family, General Hans Krebs and even of Hitler's dogs, which had been recovered from the garden of the Reich Chancellery.

In addition to the involvement of military counter-espionage officers, the search for the former inhabitants of the bunker and the leading Nazis also involved officers of the NKVD departments set up in Soviet-occupied Germany by the Military Administration. In Berlin, these task forces operated under the command of Major-General A. M. Sidnev. On his orders, on 18 September, 1945 the chief of the 17th Task Group, A. V. Arkhipenkov, began to identify, detain and question people who were spreading rumours about Hitler (information about them had been provided by the British).

Aside from those who spread the most absurd rumours about the fate of the Nazi leaders, the search for the Nazi regime's VIPs continued, using those who had worked for them. Security officers of the Berlin Task Sector had to study and check multiple reports on the possible whereabouts of persons close to top-ranking SS officers and Hitler's immediate circle. This stream of information also contained data about Hitler's personal driver, Erich Kempka, about Bormann's brother who was living in the vicinity of Treptov Park, about the Führer's cloakroom attendant, 30-year-old Freda Ivert, about a Metropolis theatre dancer named Hilda Martsilevsky (the mistress of Hitler's chief aide-de-camp SS Brigadenführer Julius Schaub), about the personal driver of Hitler's aide-de-camp SS Brigadenführer Albrecht Homke, about 'Sepp' Dietrich, head of Hitler's bodyguard before 1933, about Hitler's brother Alois and many others.

Thus, for example, on 2 October, 1945, on the basis of evidence from Max Schultze, an arrested Gestapo officer, the following persons were declared wanted: Gestapo Chief Heinrich Müller, Johann Rattenhuber, head of Hitler's bodyguard, the Chief of Berlin Police Department Bock, Hitler's personal photographer Heinrich Hoffmann and others.

To regularise the search operations, concentrate efforts and resources of task forces and collate the vast amount of information about the Third Reich leader's retinue, the Berlin NKVD Task Department opened an operational search file on Adolf Hitler, case No. 300919. Operative and investigative documents were collected in it as well as correspondence from counter-espionage departments and units, copies of reports from foreign news agencies, information bulletins produced by the Allies and other material.

As a result, unique documents were preserved that day-by-day reflected the difficult investigative work performed by all the official institutions involved in the difficult situation of the first months after the end of the war.

Thanks to these efforts, during the said period, the following persons were arrested: Hans Piekenbrock and Franz von Bentivegny, Chiefs of Abwehr Departments 1 and 2, Kurt Gerum, Chief of Police of Berlin, Martin Muchmann, Gauleiter of Saxony, Gustav Martenn, of the Poltava District (during its occupation), and Wilhelm Mohnke, commander of the SS Division 'Leibstandarte Adolf Hitler', as well as the wanted Rattenhuber, Hitler's personal servant Heinz Linge, his SS aide-de-camp Otto Günsche, and his personal pilot Hans Baur. These last were with Hitler in the bunker until the day of his suicide. Investigators were able to trace some contacts of the photographer Hoffmann but neither he nor his archive were found.

In the course of this extensive search, the diaries of Goebbels and Bormann were recovered. These historically significant prizes shed light not only on the ideas of Nazism and its crimes, but also provide an interesting chronicle of the last agonising days of those who were with Hitler to the end.

As stated in a letter of 2 June, 1945 from Lieutenant-General Vadis to V. A. Abakumov, the Chief of the Headquarters of 'Smersh', Goebbels' diary was discovered in Hitler's bunker at the Reich Chancellery. However, the story of the search for Bormann's diary is more complex. Although a number of accounts of its discovery exist in the literature, the authors feel there are still questions to be answered. The Central Archive of the FSB contains a document connected with this story. It consists of a note, sent by high frequency transmitter on 29 June, 1945 from the 'Smersh' Department of the 5th Assault Army to Major-General Melnikov, Chief of 'Smersh' of the Group of the Soviet Occupation Forces in Germany, claiming that the diary had been handed over to counter-espionage officers of the Military Council of the Army. The counter-espionage service conducted an investigation into the circumstances of the diary's discovery and found that it had been taken from a French forced labourer named André by Ernst Otto, the manager of a Berlin car plant. André had been repatriated soon after. According to the Germans who brought this diary to the City Commandant's Office, André had reportedly discovered the document in the pocket of a leather coat that had been given to him by some Soviet soldiers in the central district of Berlin. In order to be sure, 'Smersh' officers interrogated prisoners from Hitler's bodyguard who stated that Bormann had been in the bunker until 30 April but that he wore a grey siren suit, not a leather coat. The investigation was consequently unable to fully discover the circumstances in which the diary had left the bunker nor its travels before it ended up in Soviet hands. The text of the document (21 pages in the original German, 15 pages when retyped in Russian) was translated into Russian by Lieutenant Midovolkina and

Sergeant-Major Waitner (the daughter of a German political refugee). By 9 June, it was already on the desk of Lieutenant-General Vadis, who gave orders for it to be copied to the NKVD representative for the Soviet Occupation Forces, I. A. Serov. It should be stated that the authorship of the diary is not in question, even though Bormann wrote it in the third person.

Similar searches were undertaken in the other Allied occupation zones, the British and American intelligence services being particularly active. Of those detained by them, the most important information about the fate of Hitler and his followers came from the driver Kempka, Bormann's secretary Frau Krüger, and Hitler's bodyguards Hermann Karnau, Erich Mansfeld and Hilco Poppen.

One great achievement was the interception of all three copies of Hitler's 'political testament' along with his instructions to Grand Admiral Karl Dönitz on the formation of Germany's new government – without Himmler and Hermann Göring, whom Hitler had expelled from the Party for treason. These historical documents were taken from couriers who had left the bunker on the morning of 30 April, 1945. They had managed to get through the Soviet forces surrounding Berlin and reach relatives and friends. The first to be detained was Heinz Lorenz, who produced forged identification documents. He had been a liaison officer on Goebbels' staff. Under interrogation, he confessed his mission and provided the names of the other two couriers. As a result, the Allies were able to arrest Major Willi Johannmeier and Bormann's aide, Wilhelm Zander, to whom the other two copies had been entrusted.

In late 1945, American military intelligence agents questioned Professor Blaschke, who revealed his 'description of the dental peculiarities' of his high-ranking Nazi patients.

On 1 November, 1945, British counter-espionage published a special report that included the statement that 'there is no evidence to support some of the theories that are circulating that Hitler is still alive'.

Soviet counter-espionage officers and their Western colleagues liaised through the Allied Control Commission in Germany, to which representatives of the intelligence and counter-espionage services of the victorious countries were attached. Thus, in June, 1946, at the request of the Head of the Soviet Mission Colonel K. V. Dubrovsky, the Chief of the British Intelligence Service, Brigadier M. B. Jennings, provided details of the interrogation of Hitler's former aide-de-camp von Below concerning Hitler's last days in the bunker and the circumstances of the deaths of the leading Nazis, in order to help locate those still unaccounted for.

Some 'Smersh' officers from Moscow who had good command of German were entrusted to sort out the captured materials found in Goebbels' flat and in the bunker. These included numerous books, documents, photos, Party and military jackets and uniform caps of the leading Nazis. There were also celebratory greetings to Hitler, letters from loyal subjects, greeting cards, Martha Goebbels' diploma for her services in arranging the 1936 Olympic Games and so on. There was even a medicine chest and a portable gas-detector because the bunker residents were afraid that the Russians would 'smoke them out' with chemical weapons. This booty was supplemented by personal belongings discovered with the remains of Hitler, Goebbels and their relatives, including weapons, Party badges, and a gold cigarette-case, probably presented by Hitler to Goebbels' wife.

Counter-espionage officers had to sort through these items thoroughly and describe them in detail. In this work, Captain D. G. Kopeliansky, an officer of Section 4 of 'Smersh' showed his worth; later, along with other specialists, he participated in the preparations for the Nuremberg Trials. In the identification and interrogations connected with the discovery of the fate of the Nazi leaders, the following persons also participated as interpreters: Senior Lieutenant N. A. Katyshev, senior investigator of CED 'Smersh' of the 79th Infantry Corps, Captain M. S. Alperovich, Chief of the Investigation Unit of the Intelligence Department of the Staff of the 3rd Assault Army, Private Oleinik, Sergeant Gorelik, investigator-interpreter Senior Lieutenant N. A. Vlasov, and Captain of the Guards V. A. Shirokov, Assistant to the Chief of the Investigation Section of the Intelligence Department of the Red Army General Staff.

An interpreter of CED 'Smersh' of the 3rd Assault Army, E. M. Kagan, was the first to publish her account of these events (under the name of Rzshevskaya) in the USSR in 1961. In 1968, the writer Leo Bezymensky – one of the historical researchers involved in the search for the remains of Hitler – published photographs in the West of Hitler and Eva Braun's dentures. Lieutenant of the Guards Lieutenant Kalashnikov, a photographer with the 79th Infantry Corps, had been present at the identification of the Führer's remains and it is highly likely that these photographs were taken by him.

Only in late May, 1945 were documents confirming Hitler's death sent from Berlin through 'Smersh' and NKVD channels to the Soviet leadership. On 16 June, Soviet police chief, Lavrentii Beria reported the Records of Identification of the Führer's remains to Stalin and Molotov as well as the results of examinations and witness statements from German prisoners. The Soviet Government's statement on the results of the work on locating Hitler and his closest officials, however, and the dental and other research records used to identify the corpses of the leading Nazis were not publicly released. This could be due to political considerations but there were also some doubts on the part of the State Security Agency and the Ministry of Interior officials as to the results of tests and identification of the Nazi leaders' remains.

It is no coincidence that at a press conference given by Marshal G. K. Zhukov and A. J. Vyshinsky, reported in Pravda on 10 June, 1945, when a reporter, A. Vert, asked the

Marshal *'Do you have any idea or opinion as to what happened to Hitler?'*, Zhukov answered: *'The situation is very mysterious. From the diaries of aides-de-camp of the German Commander-in-Chief it is known that two days before the fall of Berlin, Hitler married a film actress [sic], Eva Braun. We have failed to discover a body confirmed as Hitler's. I cannot say anything definite about Hitler's fate. At the last moment, he could had flown out of Berlin because there were runways available for that.'*

In January, 1946, Lieutenant-General A. Z. Kobulov, Chief of the General Department of Prisoners-of-War and Internees (GDPWI) NKVD USSR, signed an analytical report concerning a version of Hitler's suicide. Some doubts, based on a number of contradictions in the evidence of witnesses, were emphasised in it. In particular, the following questions were raised: why had none of the sources stated what had happened to Hitler's remains after they were burned; why was there no information that a doctor had been called to certify death; why were there contradictions in statements about carrying the bodies out into the Reich Chancellery's garden and about who participated (i.e. who actually carried the bodies and who merely accompanied them); why were there discrepancies in witness statements concerning the external appearance of the bodies; about whether the corpses of the Nazi leaders were burned completely; why the remains were discovered by soldiers of a 'Smersh' platoon before the location had been indicated by the guard Mengershausen and so on. It is interesting that, in relation to Mengershausen, the report stresses: 'He was the only person to give evidence about the burial of the corpses that proved to be correct'.

On the basis of what the authors of this report considered these 'serious contradictions', it was decided to consolidate all available material from the Operational Department of (GDPWI) NKVD, CED 'Smersh' of the USSR Defence Ministry and Serov's office in Berlin for 'detailed and rigorous verification of the whole body of the facts'. It could be that Kobulov and his staff were confused, not only by contradictions stressed by them in their report, but also by the fact that after the Reich Chancellery was captured on 4 May, 1945 the corpse of Hitler's double – Gustav Veler – was discovered (this was recorded by a film crew).

As a result of the GDPWI initiative, in 1946 a commission was especially set up to conduct further excavations at the site at which Hitler and Eva Braun's corpses had been discovered. A fragment of skull was then discovered. In the statement, it was described as follows: 'The left sincipital portion of a skull with an exiting bullet hole'. It should be noted that in the report of 8 May, 1945 upon examination of the burned corpses, it was stressed that 'the top of the skull is partially absent'. During this further examination, traces of blood were discovered on the upholstery of the sofa in the bunker in which, according to Linge, the Führer had committed suicide.

Due to the relocation of the 'Smersh' Counter-Espionage Department of the 3rd Assault Army, the corpses that had been examined in May, 1945 were re-buried in a forest near the city of Rathenow, Brandenburg, at the beginning of June. On the orders of Lieutenant-General P. V. Zelenin, the Chief of 'Smersh' CED of the Group of the Soviet Occupational Force in Germany, on 21 February, 1946 the remains were re-buried in the grounds of a military base in Magdeburg where the 'Smersh' Counter-Espionage Section of the 3rd Assault Army was based. The results of this re-examination were not made public at the time. Clearly, Hitler's death and the circumstances surrounding the event immediately became an important factor in political intrigue between the Anti-Hitler Coalition Allies. It seems that Stalin quite clearly understood this and skilfully used it in his relations with the West. Numerous witness statements and the results of identification and medical examinations had proved the fact of Hitler's death, but Stalin was in no hurry to publish these conclusions. He planned his moves for many years ahead, especially as there was a historical precedent: the last Russian Tsar, Nicholas II, had been shot without trial, though there had been demands to hold a public trial. What is more, the body of the dead Tsar had been thoroughly concealed. The Bolsheviks believed that this would cause monarchist forces to lose their symbol, which might have been a unifying factor in their fight against the Soviets.

Stalin had learned of the Nazi leader's death when at 03.50 on 1 May, General Krebs, Chief of Staff of the German Army, had been brought to the headquarters of the 8th Guard Army. He stated that he had authority to establish contact with the Supreme Command of the Red Army to negotiate a cease-fire. At 04.00 General V. I. Chuikov reported to Zhukov by telephone that Krebs had informed him of Hitler's suicide. Zhukov immediately called Stalin. According to the Marshal's account, Stalin said the following: '*So, he's caught it at last, the rascal. It's a pity we couldn't take him alive. Where is Hitler's corpse?*' According to General Krebs, Hitler's body had been burned.

The rest of the world heard of it through the German radio. Only a day after the Führer's death, on the evening of 1 May, an obituary was broadcast, disclosing the following information: 'It is reported from Hitler's Chief Headquarters that our Führer Adolf Hitler, today in the afternoon at his Command Post in the Reich Chancellery, fighting against Bolshevism until his last breath, died for Germany.'

However, these were only words, unconfirmed by solid evidence, and gave rise to much rumour and speculation that spread wider and wider every day. Different versions of Hitler's death appeared, as well as accounts of his escape or imprisonment. In one instance, based on a German radio broadcast, it was stated that he had died 'heroically' in street-fighting and his corpse was reportedly hidden by his faithful followers. According to another version, Hitler was killed by his own officers in Berlin. The most popular story was that of Hitler's escape from besieged Berlin, the rumour being that he was hiding somewhere in Paraguay or Argentina. Whether he had made his escape by aircraft or by submarine became the subject of serious discussion.

Stalin was playing a waiting game. On 26 May, 1945, at a meeting with the American President's representative, Harry L. Hopkins, he stated that presumably '*Bormann, Goebbels, Hitler and probably Krebs escaped and are in hiding now*'. This version was repeated by Stalin more than once, though he had received the reports on the results of the identifications and medical examinations. Two weeks later, on 9 June, Marshal Zhukov made the above-mentioned statement concerning the last days of the Nazi leaders in the Reich Chancellery. As for Hitler's death, he repeated Stalin's version. To this day, no official documents explaining why the Soviet leadership adopted such a position in public have ever been published.

In 1948, 'trophies' from the bunker in the form of material evidence (burnt items, Goebbels' dentures, and most importantly parts of the jaws and teeth that were used to identify the corpses of Hitler, Eva Braun and others) were sent from Germany to Moscow, to the Investigation Section of the 2nd General Department of the USSR Ministry of State Security, which had the task of summarising all the facts connected with the circumstances of deaths of the leaders of the Reich.

In 1954, on the orders of I. A. Serov, the Chairman of the KGB attached to the USSR Council of Ministers, all these items and materials were archived in a special storage room in the KGB archives. In 1996, the Central FSB Archives were opened to the public, including documents concerning a secret KGB operation codenamed Operation 'Archive' that describe how, in 1970, on the initiative of KGB Chairman Y. V. Andropov, the remains of Hitler and the others were totally destroyed. As a just punishment and retribution for the atrocities they had committed, their ashes disappeared into the waters of the River Ehle, near the East German village of Biederitz.

This book, compiled on the basis of the documentation, scientific medical research and other reliable information, provides the final answer to one of the greatest mysteries of the twentieth century.

The majority of these documents, including material from the Central FSB Archive of Russia, have never before been published, not even in Russian, although some have been paraphrased in other accounts or appeared only in short extracts. The documents are presented in chronological order, except for certain sections linked by subject-matter. The Russian text has been translated from their originals, only obvious errors in the Russian have been corrected without explanation. Where the original omitted words or parts of words, these have been added in square brackets.

V. K. **Vinogradov**
J. F. **Pogonyi**
N. V. **Teptzov**

The editorial board and the group of the authors of this book would like to express their gratitude to the specialists of the Central FSB Archive of Russia J. L. Berezhanski, N. N. Voyakina, A. M. Kalganov, M. V. Kutzenko, O. K. Matveev, N. M. Peremyshlennikova and J. M. Razboev; Chief of FSB Department of the Omsk Region V. V. Toloknov, journalist V. A. Mironov; and V. A. Filippov for their work in locating archive materials and preparing the texts of the documents, commentaries and illustrations.

PART I

ESTABLISHING THE TRUTH

SPECIAL REPORT BY G. K. ZHUKOV AND
K. F. TELEGIN TO I. V. STALIN

3 May, 1945
Top secret
To Supreme Commander
Marshal of the Soviet Union

Comrade I. Stalin

On 2 May, 1945 in the city of Berlin in the grounds of the Reich Chancellery of the Reichstag in the Wilhelmstrasse, where Hitler's headquarters were lately situated, burned bodies were discovered that were identified as those of Reichsminister of Propaganda Dr **Goebbels** and his wife.

On 3 May this year in the same area, at **Goebbels'** headquarters (a bunker about 80 metres deep) the six corpses of **Goebbels'** children were discovered and removed.

All indications on the children's corpses were that they had been killed by powerful poisons.

The Chief of 'Smersh' Counter-Espionage Department of the 1st Byelorussian Front Lieutenant-General Comrade **Vadis** personally showed the corpses to the prisoners: Vice-Admiral **Voss**, Grand-Admiral **Dönitz's** representative at Hitler's headquarters, **Schneider**, in charge of the Reich Chancellery's garage, the cook **Lange**, and the chief technician of the Reich Chancellery **Tziem** [in the original text, the name is wrongly given as 'Tzien']. They recognised the corpses as those of **Goebbels**, his wife and their children.

In the process of examining the corpses of **Goebbels** and his wife, gold NSDAP badges, two 'Browning No 1' pistols and a cigarette case bearing Hitler's monogram were discovered. According to **Voss**, only one woman in Germany – **Goebbels'** wife – had such a gold badge which had been presented to her by Hitler three days before his suicide. Voss also identified Hitler's signature on the cigarette case.

Near the Reich Chancellery, in the courtyard of the Ministry of Propaganda, a corpse was discovered wearing a uniform of a general, who was identified by **Voss** as Lieutenant-General **Krebs**, the Chief of the General Staff of the German Army. Furthermore, in the lining of his uniform jacket near the left side pocket a strip of cloth was discovered bearing the name 'Krebs'.

On 1 May this year, **Krebs** visited the 8th Guard Army of our Front as an emissary to hold talks about capitulation. Examination of the body revealed a bullet hole in the right side of the chin with an exit wound in the back of the head, which proves his suicide.

The corpses of **Goebbels** and his family as well as that of **Krebs** are in the custody of 'Smersh'.

Commander of the Forces of
the 1st Byelorussian Front
Marshal of the Soviet Union

Zhukov

Member of the Military Council
of the 1st Byelorussian Front
Lieutenant-General

Telegin

3 May, 1945
Berlin
Information
1. Received through High Frequency Transmitter – Lieutenant-Colonel Penin at 21.30
3 May, 1945
2. Sent – Lieutenant-Colonel Vasilev – 3 May, 1945 at 21.30

Ф. К-1 ос; оп. 4; д.9; л. 176-178
(КОПИЯ)
(a copy)

DOCUMENTS IDENTIFYING THE CORPSES OF GOEBBELS, HIS WIFE AND THEIR SIX CHILDREN

2–22 May, 1945
REPORT
2 May, 1945 Berlin

We, the undersigned – Chief of the 'Smersh' Counter-Espionage Section of the 79th Infantry Corps Lieutenant-Colonel **Klimenko**, Chief of the 4th Sub-Section of the 'Smersh' Counter-Espionage Section of the 3rd Assault Army Major **Bustrov** and Deputy Chief of the 'Smersh' Counter-Espionage Section of the 207th Infantry Division Major **Hazin** – make the following declaration:

On 2 May, we, with the German witnesses – **Lange**, Wilhelm and **Schneider** Karl – arrived in the area of the Reichstag, where at 17.00 on the same date near Goebbels' bunker, several metres from the entrance door, two burnt corpses were discovered – one of a man and one of a woman.

The witnesses Lange and Schneider after a thorough examination of the corpse of the man identified it as the corpse of German Reichsminister of Propaganda – Dr **Goebbels**.

To secure it from any outside interference and to save it for further confirmation of Goebbels' identity, the corpse was taken to 'Smersh' Counter-Espionage Section of the 79th Infantry Corps. This declaration is confirmation thereof.

Chief of the 'Smersh' CES
of the 79th Infantry Corps
Lieutenant-Colonel   **Klimenko**

Chief of the 4th Sub-Section of the
'Smersh' CES
of the 3rd Assault Army Major   **Bystrov**

Deputy Chief of the 'Smersh' CES
of the 207 Infantry Division Major   **Hazin**

*Ф.К-1 ос; оп. 4; д.6; л. 19-20
(ПОДЛИННИК)*
(original)

IDENTIFICATION REPORT

3 May, 1945
City of Berlin

We, the undersigned, Chief of 'Smersh' Counter-Espionage Department of the 1st Byelorussian Front Lieutenant-General **Vadis**, Deputy Chief of 'Smersh' Counter-Espionage Department of the 1st Byelorussian Front Major-General **Melnikov**, Chief of 'Smersh' Counter-Espionage Section of the 3rd Assault Army Lieutenant-General **Miroshnichenko**, Chief of Section of 'Smersh' Counter-Espionage Department of the 1st Byelorussian Front Lieutenant-Colonel **Barsukov**, Chief of Section of 'Smersh' Counter-Espionage Department of the 79th Infantry Corps Lieutenant-Colonel **Klimenko**, Chief of Political Section of the 79th Infantry Corps Colonel **Krylov**, Chief of Intelligence Section [of the Staff] of the 3rd Assault Army Lieutenant-Colonel **Gvozd**, Chief of 'Smersh' Counter-Espionage Section of the 207th Infantry Division Major **Aksenov**, Deputy Chief of 'Smersh' Counter-Espionage Section of the 207th Infantry Division Major **Hazin**, Chief of Squad of 'Smersh' Counter-Espionage Section of the 3rd Assault Army Major **Bystrov**, Senior Investigator of the 'Smersh' Counter-Espionage Department of the 1st Byelorussian Front Captain **Helimsky**, Corps Physician of the 79th Infantry Corps Medical Service Lieutenant-Colonel **Grachev**, a German language interpreter, Chief of Investigation unit of the Intelligence Section [staff] of the 3rd Assault Army Captain **Alperovich**, make the following declaration:

On 2 May, 1945, in the centre of the city of Berlin, in the bomb-shelter of the German Reich Chancellery, several metres from the entrance door, Lieutenant-Colonel **Klimenko**, Majors **Bystrov** and **Hazin** in the presence of the citizens of Berlin, the Germans **Lange**, Wilhelm – a cook at the Reich Chancellery – and **Schneider,** Karl – a Reich Chancellery garage mechanic, discovered at 17.00 the burnt corpses of a man and a woman, the man's body being short, with a twisted right foot (lame) with a burnt metal brace on it, and the burnt remains of an NSDAP uniform jacket and a gold Party badge; near the burnt body of the woman there was a burnt gold cigarette-case, and on the body a gold NSDAP member's badge and a burnt gold brooch.

Near the heads of both corpses there were two 'Walther No 1' (burnt). On 3 May this year, the Commander of a squad of the 'Smersh' Counter-Espionage Section of the 207th Infantry Division, Lieutenant **Ilyin**, discovered six corpses of children aged from 3 to 14, five girls and one boy, with indications of poisoning, dressed in light night-clothes, in beds in a separate room of the Reich Chancellery's bomb-shelter.

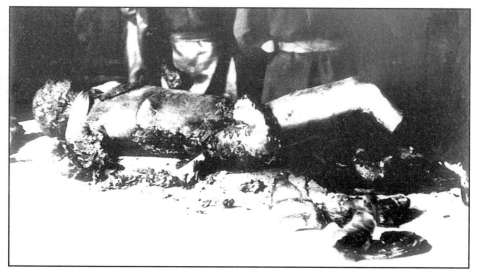

The burnt corpse of Goebbels

Due to the fact that the said corpses were recognised as Dr Goebbels, his wife and children, all the bodies were taken to the headquarters of the 'Smersh' Counter-Espionage Section of the 79th Infantry Corps of the 1st Byelorussian Front for examination and identification by persons who knew them intimately.

The following prisoners-of-war, who had known Goebbels, his wife and their children personally, were brought to where the bodies were found: Grand-Admiral **Dönitz's** personal representative at Hitler's headquarters Vice-Admiral **Voss**, Hans Erich, born in 1897, Reich Chancellery garage mechanic **Schneider**, Karl-Friedrich-Wilhelm, and the Reich Chancellery cook **Lange**, Wilhelm.

As a result of questioning and having the corpses shown to them, Vice-Admiral **Voss**, **Lange,** and **Schneider** positively identified the bodies as those of Goebbels, his wife and their children. Vice-Admiral **Voss**, being asked how he recognised the people as **Goebbels**, his wife and children, explained that he recognised the burnt body of the man as the former Reichsminister of Propaganda Dr Goebbels by the following signs: the burnt corpse has an obvious resemblance to Goebbels, from the shape of the head, the line of the mouth, the metal brace that Goebbels had on his right leg, his gold NSDAP badge and the burnt remains of his Party uniform. **Voss** also explained that during the last days (3 weeks) until 1 May this year he was constantly at **Hitler's** headquarters and personally met Hitler, Goebbels and other persons close to them. On 30 April this year, **Voss** heard about **Hitler's** suicide and about the appointment of Dr Goebbels [as Reich Chancellor] before Hitler's death.

On 1 May this year **Voss** saw **Goebbels** for the last time at 20.30 in the bunker in which **Hitler**'s headquarters were located. In his conversation with **Voss**, **Goebbels** stated that he would follow Hitler's example, i.e. he would commit suicide.

Voss supported his identification of the woman's burnt body as that of **Goebbels**' wife by her height (above average) and by the burnt gold NSDAP badge on the body, the only such badge given to a woman, presented to her by **Hitler** three days before his death.

Besides, while examining a cigarette-case discovered beside the woman's corpse, a monogram in German 'Adolf Hitler, 29.10.34.' was found inside it. According to **Voss**, Goebbels' wife had used it for the last three weeks.

When examining the corpses of the children **Voss** identified all of them without exception as **Goebbels**' children because he had seen all of them many times. He called one of the girls – **Goebbels**' daughter about 3 years old – by her name, Heide, because she had visited **Voss**'s flat more than once.

Asked to identify the corpses, the above-mentioned cook, **Lange**, and the garage mechanic, **Schneider**, positively stated that they recognised the burnt corpse as that of Dr **Goebbels**, supporting their statement by the face, the height of the corpse, the shape of the head and a metal brace on the right leg.

Additionally, the cook **Lange,** in the presence of the military officers mentioned above in this Report, also recognised the children's corpses as those of **Goebbels**' children, giving the names of two of them, a girl Hilde and a boy Helmut, whom he had personally known for a long time.

From an external examination of the children's bodies, the Corps Physician Lieutenant-Colonel of Medical Service **Grachev** established that the death of the children was the result of injections of carboxyhaemoglobin, which caused poisoning.

Based on these facts we, the undersigned, come to the conclusion that the burnt corpses we examined – that of a man, a woman and six children – are the corpses of German Reichsminister of Propaganda Dr Josef **Goebbels**, his wife and children.

We make this declaration accordingly.

The statements of **Voss**, **Lange** and **Schneider** identifying the corpses were provided in German through a German-language interpreter – Chief of Investigation Sub-Section of the Intelligence Section of the Staff of the 3rd Assault Army Captain **Alperovich**.

Chief of 'Smersh' Counter-Espionage Department
of the 1st Byelorussian Front

Lieutenant-General **Vadis**

Deputy Chief of 'Smersh' Counter-Espionage Department
of the 1st Byelorussian Front

Major-General **Melnikov**

Chief of 'Smersh' Counter-Espionage Section
of the 3rd Assault Army

Lieutenant-General **Miroshnichenko**

Chief of Section of 'Smersh' Counter-Espionage
Department of the 1st Byelorussian Front

Lieutenant-Colonel **Barsukov**

Chief of Section of 'Smersh' Counter-Espionage
Department of the 79th Infantry Corps

Lieutenant-Colonel **Klimenko**

Chief of 'Smersh' Counter-Intelligence Section
of the 207th Infantry Division

Major **Aksenov**

Deputy Chief of 'Smersh' Counter-Espionage
Section of the 207th Infantry Division

Major **Hazin**

Chief of Political Section of the 79th Infantry Corps

Colonel **Krylov**

Chief of Intelligence Section of the Staff of the 3rd Assault Army

Lieutenant-Colonel **Gvozd**

Chief of Squad of 'Smersh' Counter-Espionage
Section of the 3rd Assault Army

Major **Bystrov**

Senior Officer of 'Smersh' Counter-Espionage Department
of the 1st Byelorussian Front

Captain **Helimsky**

The Corps Physician of the 79th Infantry Corps
                    Medical Service Lieutenant-Colonel **Grachev**

Commander of 'Smersh' CES platoon of the 207th Infantry Division
                    Lieutenant **Ilyin**

German language interpreter – Chief of Investigation office
of Intelligence Section of the 3rd Assault Army Staff
                    Captain **Alperovich**

We confirm that we have understood the contents of this Report translated (orally) to us from Russian into German by interpreter **Alperovich** and we authorise this by our signatures.

The corpses presented were identified by:

a prisoner-of-war Vice-Admiral
of the German Navy
                    Voss

Reich Chancellery cook
                    Lange

Reich Chancellery garage mechanic
                    Schneider

Ф. 4 ос; оп. 3; д. 36; л. 8-11
(ПОДЛИННИК)
(original)

RECORD OF IDENTIFICATION

3 May, 1945
Army in the Field

I, Senior Investigator of 'Smersh' Counter-Espionage Section of the 79th Infantry Corps Lieutenant **Katyshev** with the participation of a German language interpreter Private **Oleinik**, on this day questioned as an witness **Lange**, Wilhelm*, born 1891 in Westphalia, Altenas district, Halfer, a German, from a workers' family, a cook at the German Reich Chancellery, an NSDAP member since 1937, married, address: 18, Shtubnitzstrasse, Berlin-Pankow.

The witness was warned that for giving false evidence he is liable to punishment under Article 95 of the RSFSR Criminal Code. [Signed] Wilhelm **Lange**

The interpreter – Private Oleinik – was informed of liability for incorrect translation under Article 95 of the RSFSR Criminal Code. [Signed] **Oleinik**.

Question: You have examined the burnt body of a man. Whom do you identify this corpse as?

Answer: Yes, I examined the corpse very thoroughly and I recognised it as the Reichsminister of Propaganda Dr Josef **Goebbels**.

----

* On 28 August, 1951 Lange was arrested by the USSR Ministry of State Security on charges that 'being a member of the Nazi Party and serving in Hitler's Reich Chancellery, he was serving Hitler's close circle'. By ruling of a Special Judicial Council attached to the Ministry of State Security as of 17 November, 1951 he was put into corrective labour camp for 10 years. In a the ruling of the Prosecutor-General's Office of the Russian Federation as of 29 May, 1992 he was rehabilitated under the Law of the Russian Soviet Federative Socialist Republic 'On Rehabilitation of Victims of Political Repression' of 18 October, 1991.

Question: On the basis of what features do you recognise the corpse as that of Dr **Goebbels**?

Answer: I recognise the corpse as Reichsminister Dr Goebbels by the following features:

1. For the last eight days Dr Goebbels was in the Reich Chancellery with his family – I insist on this because I personally saw him coming into the dining-room. Berlin was encircled by Russian forces and there was no way out. I suppose that Dr Goebbels, seeing no way out of the situation, committed suicide. Who set fire to him, I don't know.

2. The shape of the body, head and legs of the corpse examined by me was absolutely identical to the appearance of the body of Dr **Goebbels**. I have no doubt that the corpse is that of the late Dr **Goebbels**, because it was found in the grounds of the Reich Chancellery near **Goebbels**' personal bunker.

3. Dr Goebbels was of short stature, one (the right) leg was shorter than the other – he had a brace on the right leg. The corpse has all these characteristics.

4. Dr Goebbels wore a light jacket and black trousers. On his jacket there was the badge of a member of the National-Socialist Party of Germany. The burnt remains of the clothes on the corpse are identical to Dr Goebbels' clothes.

Based on these characteristics, I identified the corpse as that of Reichsminister of Propaganda, Dr Josef **Goebbels**.

Question: Who else can confirm your statement?

Answer: Those who were patients in or who worked in the hospital in the Reich Chancellery could identify Dr **Goebbels**' corpse and confirm my evidence, of their number I can name:

1. Professor **Haase**
2. Electrician **Hentschel**

Both should now be in the vicinity of the Reich Chancellery.

From my statement everything was written down correctly and read aloud to me in German.

Wilhelm Lange

Interpreter: **Oleinik**

Interrogator: Senior Investigator 'Smersh' CES
of the 79th Infantry Corps

Lieutenant Katyshev

Ф. 4 ос; оп.3; д. 36; л. 17-18
(заверенная копия)
(certified copy)

RECORD OF IDENTIFICATION

3 May, 1945
Army in the Field

I, Senior Investigator of 'Smersh' Counter-Espionage Section of the 79th Infantry Corps Lieutenant **Katyshev** with the participation of a German language interpreter Private **Oleinik**, on this day questioned as a witness **Schneider**, Karl-Friedrich-Wilhelm, born 1899 in the city of Berlin, a German, from a workers' family, a mechanic in the garage of the German Reich Chancellery, an NSDAP member, married, address: 16, Hermann-Göring-Strasse.

The witness and the interpreter were warned that for supplying false evidence and for incorrect translation they were liable under Article 95 of the RSFSR Criminal Code.

Karl Schneider   Oleinik

Question: You have examined the burnt body of a man, whom do you identify as this corpse?

Answer: I examined the corpse very closely and I recognise it as that of the Reichsminister of Propaganda Dr Josef **Goebbels**.

Question: On what characteristics do you base your identification of the corpse as being that of Dr **Goebbels**?

Answer: I saw the Reichsminister of Propaganda Dr **Goebbels** several times. Although I did not see him myself during the time that the Russian forces were surrounding Berlin, I heard from others that, during this desperate time, Adolf **Hitler** and Dr **Goebbels** and his family were still in Berlin and were in their personal bunkers in the grounds of the Reich Chancellery. Proceeding from this, I state that the corpse I examined was that of Dr **Goebbels**.

1. Dr **Goebbels** is of short stature, physically weak, one (the right) leg is shorter than the other, and on his right leg he has a metal brace: the corpse has all these characteristics.

2. The build of the body, and the shape of the head of the corpse are identical to those of Dr **Goebbels**.

3. The corpse was discovered near Dr **Goebbels**' personal shelter in the grounds of the Reich Chancellery, where only members of the government were allowed.

4. I learnt of the suicide of Dr **Goebbels** as well as that of Adolf **Hitler** on the evening of 1 May, 1945. This news was spread by word of mouth; everyone was talking but no one knew the details.

Based on the characteristics mentioned above I state that the corpse I examined is that of the Reichsminister of Propaganda Dr Josef **Goebbels**.

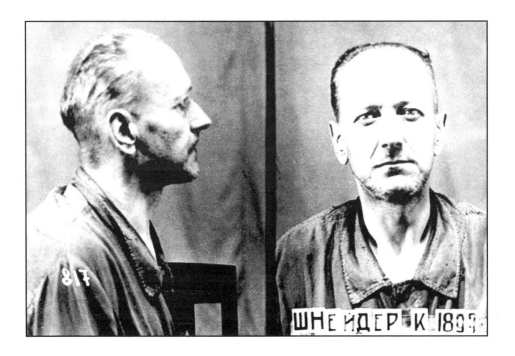

Photograph of Karl Schneider from the investigation file.

On 28 August, 1951, Schneider was arrested by agents of the USSR State Security Service on charges that 'as a member of the Nazi Party and serving in the SS Leibstandarte Adolf Hitler regiment with the rank of SS Hauptsturmführer, he served in the Reich Chancellery and by being in charge of a vehicle repair workshop, he provided for Hitler's security'. In a judgement by the USSR Ministry of State Security's Special Judicial Council dated 8 December, 1951, Schneider was sentenced to 15 years in a labour camp. Under a ruling of the Praesidium of the USSR Supreme Council dated 28 September, 1955, he was released early and was handed over to the GDR authorities on 20 January, 1956.

Question: Who, apart from yourself, can identify the corpse of Dr Goebbels and confirm your statement?

Answer: I suppose that Professor **Haase** and **Tziem**, who should now be in Berlin in the vicinity of the Reich Chancellery, could identify Dr **Goebbels** and at the same time confirm my statement.

My statement was written down correctly and read aloud to me in German.

Karl Schneider*

Interpreter: Oleinik

Interrogator: Senior Investigator 'Smersh' CES of the 79th Infantry Corps

Lieutenant **Katyshev**

Participated in questioning:

Chief of 'Smersh' Counter-Espionage Section of the 79th Infantry Corps

Lieutenant-Colonel **Klimenko**

Ф. 4 ос; оп 3; д. 36; л. 19-20
(заверенная копия)
(an authorised copy)

----

* Schneider's arrest was recorded for legal purposes on completion of his case investigation. The same procedure was applied to other prisoners-of-war.

RECORD OF INTERROGATION

19 May, 1945

I, Senior Investigator of the 2nd Sub-Section of the 4th Section of 'Smersh' Counter-Espionage Department of the 1st Byelorussian Front Captain **Terioshin** with participation of German language interpreter **Gorielik** questioned the prisoner **Schneider**, Karl, born in 1899, in the city of Berlin, a German national, a citizen of Germany, eight years of education, a car mechanic, worked as head of the vehicle repair workshop at the garage of the German Reich Chancellery in Berlin, an NSDAP member, married, address: 16, Hermann-Göring-Strasse.

The German-language interpreter was warned that for incorrect translation she was liable for prosecution under Article 95 of the RSFSR Criminal Code.

Questioning started at 22.30 on 19 May this year.

Questioning ended at 03.50 on 20 May this year.

Question: From what date did you work as the head of vehicle repair workshop at the garage of the Reich Chancellery?

Answer: I worked as the head of vehicle repair workshop at the garage of the Reich Chancellery from 1937.

Question: When did you see **Hitler** for the last time?

Answer: I saw Hitler only once, in 1941. After that I did not see him.

Question: What do you know about Hitler's fate?

Answer: I cannot say anything about Hitler's fate.

I heard on the evening of 1 May, 1945 from the head of the Reich Chancellery garage and from Hitler's personal driver SS Obersturmbannführer **Kempka**, Erich that Hitler was allegedly dead.

Rumours were circulating among the soldiers of the guard that Hitler had committed suicide.

I don't know if Hitler was in Berlin before 1 May, 1945. I did not happen to see him.

I should like to stress the following facts:

On 28 or 29 April this year, I received an order by phone from Hitler's secretariat through the telephone operator on duty (I do not know his name) to send all available petrol to the Führer's bunker. To fulfil this order I sent eight tanks (20 1-litre cans) of petrol to the Führer's bunker.

On the night of the 28th or 29th, I received an order by phone from Hitler's secretariat through the telephone operator on duty (I don't know who personally) to send blow-torches to the Führer's bunker, and I sent 8 available blow-torches there.

On the evening of 1 May, 1945, I received an order by phone through the telephone operator on duty (whose name I do not know) to send to the Führer's bunker all available petrol, and I sent four tanks of petrol to the Führer's bunker.

Comparing these facts with the rumours of Hitler's death I came to the conclusion that the petrol I sent to the Führer's bunker was used to burn Hitler's corpse.

Question: When did you last see the Reichsminister of Propaganda **Goebbels**?

Answer: I saw the Reichsminister of Propaganda **Goebbels** only once, in 1934, at the Berlin car plant where Goebbels was buying a car for himself. I talked to Goebbels then and showed him how to handle the car.

Question: What do you know of the fate of **Goebbels** and his family?

Answer: On approximately 21 April this year, when heavy shelling of Berlin started, rumours circulated among the staff of the garage that **Goebbels** had moved into the Führer's bunker with his family.

On 1 May of this year, I heard that **Goebbels** had committed suicide (I do not remember from whom).

In the evening of 2 May after the Red Army units seized Berlin, a Soviet officer and I searched the Reich Chancellery garden for Hitler's corpse or the place in which his corpse was burned.

Near the Führer's bunker, we discovered two corpses, that of a man and a woman. I recognised the man's body as that of Reichsminister of Propaganda Josef **Goebbels** judging by the figure, height, the shape of the head, and mostly by his right leg which was shorter than the left and turned inwards.

I failed to recognise the corpse of the woman, [but] I supposed that it was the body of **Goebbels'** wife.

This Record is a correct account of my statement and was read aloud to me in German.

Interrogator: Senior Investigator of the 2nd Sub-section of
the 4th Section of the 'Smersh' Counter-Espionage Division
of the 1st Byelorussian Front

Captain **Terioshin**

Translated from German into Russian: **Gorielik**

Арх. Н-20855; л. 30-31 Об.
(ПОДЛИННИК)
(original)

RECORD OF IDENTIFICATION

3 May, 1945
Army in the Field

I, Senior Investigator of the 'Smersh' Counter-Espionage Section of the 79th Infantry Corps Senior Lieutenant **Katyshev** with the participation of a German language interpreter Private **Oleinik**, questioned on this day as a witness **Tziem***, Wilhelm Ernst Karl, born in 1900 in the city of Burgh (near Magdeburg), a German national, from a workers' family, an engineer, chief technician of the Reich Chancellery, married, address: 36, Rosekastrasse, Berlin-Neunköln.

The witness and the interpreter were informed of their liability under Article 95 of the RSFSR Criminal Code for, respectively, giving false evidence or an incorrect translation.

Question: You have examined the burned body of a man. Who do you identify as this corpse?

Answer: Yes, I have examined the corpse very closely and I identify it as the German Reichsminister of Propaganda Dr Josef **Goebbels**.

Question: What characteristic features of Dr **Goebbels** do you know and how do they match those of the corpse?

Answer: I was not personally acquainted with Dr Goebbels, but due to my official position I saw Goebbels often. The last time I saw him was on 30 April, 1945. Dr **Goebbels** was living with his family in the so-called 'Führer's bunker', i.e. in his personal shelter in the grounds of the Reich Chancellery.

Characteristics of **Goebbels**: of short stature, physically weak, he limped while walking, one leg was shorter than the other, the face was narrow, the forehead sloped back. He often wore a light-coloured jacket and black trousers.

All of these characteristic features of Goebbels' are absolutely identical to those of the corpse. What is more, I recognised the suit you showed to me and I state that it belonged to Dr **Goebbels**.

I have no doubts and state that the corpse I have examined is the corpse of the Reichsminister of Propaganda Josef **Goebbels**.

This Protocol is a correct transcription of my statement and was read aloud to me in German. **Tziem**

----

* In the original the name is incorrectly given as 'Tzien'.

Interpreter: **Oleinik**

Interrogator: Senior Investigator
'Smersh' Counter-Espionage Section
of the 79th Infantry Corps
                              Senior Lieutenant **Katyshev**

  Also participated in the interrogation: Chief of 'Smersh' Counter-Espionage Section
of the 79th Infantry Corps
                              Lieutenant-Colonel **Klimenko**

Ф. 4 ос; оп. 3; д. 36; л. 21-22
(заверенная копия)
(an authorised copy)

RECORD OF INTERROGATION

3 May, 1945

I, Senior Investigator of the 2nd Sub-Section of the 4th Section of the 'Smersh' Counter-Espionage Department of the 1st Byelorussian Front Captain **Terioshin**, with participation of a German language interpreter Private **Gorelik**, questioned the prisoner **Tziem**, Wilhelm, born in 1900 in the city of Burgh (near Magdeburg), a German by nationality, a German citizen, higher education, heating engineer, married, according to him not a member of the Party, worked as a technical manager of the Reich Chancellery building, address: 36, Rosekastrasse, Berlin-Neunköln.

The German language interpreter Gorelik was warned of liability for incorrect translation under Article 95 of the RSFSR Criminal Code.

Interrogation started at 04.00

Interrogation finished at 06.20

Question: State your name.

Answer: My correct name is **Tziem**. In the Protocol of Identification of the corpse of the Reichsminister of Propaganda **Goebbels**, compiled according to my evidence on 3 May, 1945 there is a mistake – instead of my name **Tziem**, **Tzien** is written there, which is wrong.

Question: Since what date have you worked as technical manager of the Reich Chancellery building?

Answer: I have worked as technical manager of the Reich Chancellery building since 1939. My job gave me access to all the rooms of the Reich Chancellery building.

Question: Did you meet members of the family of the Reichsminister of Propaganda **Goebbels**?

Answer: I met the wife of the Reichsminister of Propaganda Goebbels in mid-April, 1945 in the garden of the Reich Chancellery. She was a woman of about 40, of medium height, thin, with dark blond hair.

I also saw **Goebbels**' children – five girls aged from 3 to 13 years old and one boy 8 years old – playing in the garden of the Reich Chancellery, near the Führer's bunker in late April, 1945.

Question: When did you see the Reichsminister of Propaganda **Goebbels** for the last time?

Answer: The last time I met the Reichsminister of Propaganda **Goebbels** was during the day of 29 April, 1945 in the Führer's bunker where I had been summoned to check the ventilators. I met **Goebbels** in the lobby of the bunker, as he was going to **Hitler's** study.

Question: What do you know about the fate of Reichsminister of Propaganda **Goebbels** and his family?

Answer: On the evening of 1 May, 1945, I was visited by the electrician of the Führer's quarters **Gentsche,** Hans (40 years old, of medium height, lean, with round face) who informed me that **Goebbels** was dead. He did not disclose any details of **Goebbels**' death.

When Red Army units entered Berlin, I was detained at the Reich Chancellery by a Russian officer. During one of the interrogations on 3 May, 1945 at Plotzensee I was invited to examine (identify) a number of corpses.

Eight corpses were displayed for identification: that of a man, a woman, five girls and one boy.

After thorough examination, I recognised the man's corpse as that of Reichsminister of Propaganda Josef **Goebbels** by a crooked and shortened right leg, by his build, by the shape of the head and by the remains of his half-burnt suit (yellow jacket and black trousers).

In outward appearance, the corpse of the woman resembled **Goebbels**' wife. The children's corpses I recognised as Goebbels' six children: five girls aged from 3 to 13 years old and a boy of 8 years old. I knew their faces by photos in newspapers.

Question: When did you last see **Hitler**?

Answer: I saw Hitler for the last time at 12 midnight on 29 April, 1945. As I stated before, I had been summoned to the Führer's bunker to check the ventilators. While fixing the ventilators, I saw Hitler through the open door to the study, sitting at the table in his study talking to a young woman, possibly his secretary.

Question: What do you know about Hitler's fate?

Answer: On 30 April, 1945 at 6 p.m., workers **Vernika** (sewerman) and **Gunner** (electrician), who were returning from their work in the Führer's bunker told me and other employees that they had heard of **Hitler**'s death.

They disclosed no other details. I did not receive any information about this matter from other sources.

This Record was written down correctly and read aloud to me in German. **Tziem**
Interrogator: Senior Investigator
of the 4th 'Smersh' Counter-Espionage Department
of the 1st Byelorussian Front Captain **Terioshin**
Translated from German into Russian by **Gorelik**

Ф.К-1 ос; оп. 4; д. 8; л 142-144
(заверенная копия)
(certified copy)

RECORD OF IDENTIFICATION OF THE CORPSES

18 May, 1945

We, the undersigned, Chief of 'Smersh' Counter-Espionage Department of the 1st Byelorussian Front Lieutenant-General **Vadis**, Chief of 'Smersh' Counter-Espionage Section of the 3rd Assault Army Lieutenant-General **Miroshnichenko**, Chief of the 2nd Sub-Section of the 4th Section of 'Smersh' Counter-Espionage Department of the 1st Byelorussian Front Major **Gershgorin**, Chief of the 4th Sub-Section of the Section of 'Smersh' Counter-Espionage Department of the 3rd Assault Army Major **Bystrov** with a German language interpreter of 'Smersh' Counter-Espionage Section of the 3rd Assault Army Guard Lieutenant **Kagan**, make the following declaration:

On 18 May, 1945 at 16.00, in presence of the persons mentioned above, one corpse of a man and six children's corpses were shown to **Heusemann**, Käthe, who worked in the dental surgery of the Reich Chancellery as an assistant to Prof. **Blaschke**.

Heusemann, after thorough examination of all the corpses, said that she recognised the bodies as those of Reichsminister of Propaganda Dr **Goebbels** and his six children, stating that she identified the corpses by the following characteristic features:

Goebbels' corpse she identified by the characteristic form of the head with strongly protruding occiput, notably protruding upper jaw and teeth, by the shape of his face, and by his height as well as by his crooked leg (lame).

Among children's corpses Heusemann identified:

1. **Goebbels'** daughter – Hilde.
2. **Goebbels'** son – Helmut.
3. **Goebbels'** daughter – Helga
4. **Goebbels'** daughter – Heide
5. **Goebbels'** daughter – Hedda
6. **Goebbels'** daughter – Holde

After she had examined the children's corpses, Heusemann stated that she identified them as Goebbels' children by their faces, heights and ages, adding that the corpses were still in good condition, and thus she was absolutely positive and she stated that they were definitely the corpses of **Goebbels'** children.

Answering the question as to whether she was positive in her identification of the corpses, **Heusemann** said that she had no doubts that she had seen the corpses of **Goebbels** and his six children.

This Record of Identification is correctly compiled on the basis of my general evidence, and read aloud to me in German.

I put my signature to this. **Heusemann**

This Record was written in German by the interpreter of the 'Smersh' Counter-Espionage Department of the 3rd Assault Army Guard Lieutenant **Kagan**.

The Report was produced by:
Chief of the 'Smersh' Counter-Espionage Department
of the 1st Byelorussian Front

Lieutenant-General A. **Vadis**

Chief of the 'Smersh' Counter-Espionage Section
of the 3rd Assault Army

Lieutenant-General **Miroshnichenko**

Also present:
Chief of the 2nd Sub-Section of the
4th Section of the 'Smersh' Counter-Espionage Department
of the 1st Byelorussian Front

Major **Gershgorin**

Chief of the 4th Sub-Section of the Counter-Espionage
Section 'Smersh' of the 3rd Assault Army

Major **Bystrov**

Correct:
Chief of the 4th Section of the 'Smersh' Counter-Espionage Department
of the 1st Byelorussian Front

Lieutenant-Colonel **Vasiliev**

Ф. К-1 ос; оп. 4; д. 8; л. 13-14
(заверенная копия)
(certified copy)

RECORD OF IDENTIFICATION

22 May, 1945
The City of Finov

We, Deputy Chief of the 4th Section of the 'Smersh' Counter-Espionage Department of the 1st Byelorussian Front, Lieutenant-General of the Guards **Chernykh**, Chief of the 4th Sub-Section of the 'Smersh' Counter-Espionage Section of the 3rd Assault Army Major **Bystrov** and investigator 'Smersh' CES of the 1st Byelorussian Front Senior Lieutenant **Vlasov**, state that on this date, at 7.10 Moscow time in normal visibility, we showed the prisoner – the former head of **Goebbels'** personal guard **Eckold**, Wilhelm – seven corpses, one the corpse of a man and six corpses of children, for identification.

For identification purposes the bodies were exhumed and displayed in wooden coffins.

As a result of examination of the corpses presented to him, **Eckold** said that he identified the man's body as that of the former German Reichsminister of Propaganda and Gauleiter of Berlin, Dr **Goebbels**, by the following characteristic features: a very distinctive occiput, high, sloping forehead, large ugly front teeth in the upper jaw, and the physical defect of the right leg (lame).

Eckold identified the six children's corpses shown to him as those of **Goebbels'** children: son **Helmut**, 8–9 years old, daughter **Helda** approximately 12 years old, and daughter **Hilda** approximately 10 years old. He also identified the other three bodies as Goebbels' children, but he could not identify them by name as he used to confuse them when they were still alive.

Repeatedly asked if he was positive that the corpses presented to him for identification were the corpses of Dr **Goebbels** and his children, **Eckold** categorically stated that there was no doubt about it, in view of which which this Record is compiled.

The Record of Identification was read to me in German translation, and the circumstances of identification are stated correctly. **Eckold**

Deputy Chief of the 4th Section of the
'Smersh' Counter-Espionage Department
of the 1st Byelorussian Front
                    Lieutenant-General of the Guards **Chernych**

Chief of the 4th Sub-Section of the 'Smersh' Counter-Espionage Section
of the 3rd Assault Army

Major **Bystrov**

Investigator of 'Smersh' CES of the 1st Sub-Section
of the 4th Section of the 1st Byelorussian Front

Senior Lieutenant **Vlasov**

Ф. К-1 ос; оп. 4; д. 8; л. 15-16
(ПОДЛИННИК)
(original)

RECORD OF DISCOVERY OF TWO
CORPSES NEAR HITLER'S BUNKER

5 May, 1945
The City of Berlin, Army in the Field

I, Senior Lieutenant of the Guards **Panasov**, Alexey Alexandrovich, and Privates **Churakov**, Ivan Dmitrievich, **Oleinik**, Eugeny Stepanovich and **Seroukh**, Ilia Efimovich, in the city of Berlin, in the grounds of Hitler's Reich Chancellery, where corpses of Goebbels and his wife were discovered near Hitler's personal bunker, report that two burned bodies of a woman and a man were found and recovered.

The crater in which the corpses of Hitler and Eva Braun were discovered

The corpses were badly burnt and could not be identified without additional information.

The corpses were in a bomb-crater 3 metres away from the entrance to Hitler's bunker and they were covered with a layer of soil.

The corpses are held at the 'Smersh' Counter-Espionage Section of the 79th Infantry Corps.

Commander of
the 'Smersh' CES platoon of the 79th Infantry Corps   **Panasov**

Private of the 'Smersh' CES
of the 79th Infantry Corps   **Churakov**

Private of the 'Smersh' CES
of the 79th Infantry Corps   **Oleinik**

Private of the 'Smersh' CES
of the 79th Infantry Corps   **Seroukh**

Ф. 4 ос; оп. 3; д. 36; л. 23
(ПОДЛИННИК)
(original)

RECORD OF INTERROGATION OF THE REICH CHANCELLERY PHYSICIAN HELMUT KUNZ

7 May, 1945

Chief of the 4th Section of the 'Smersh' Counter-Espionage Department of the 1st Byelorussian Front Lieutenant-Colonel **Vasiliev**, through the German language interpreter-investigator Senior Lieutenant **Vlasov**, questioned the German prisoner-of-war **Kunz**, Helmut, born in 1910 in the city of Etlingen, province of Baden, a dentist, who had until recently worked in SS Medical Department of Berlin as a junior scientific assistant of the Dentist-General. When the Department was disbanded he went to work at a hospital. On 23 April the hospital was evacuated from Berlin and he was transferred to the Reich Chancellery. At that time it had no dentist.

Question: Did you have any connection with the Reich Chancellery before 23 April?

Answer: Before that time I had no connection with the Reich Chancellery.

Question: What rank did you have?

Answer: SS Sturmbannführer.

Question: Who personally did you treat while working at the Reich Chancellery?

Answer: I personally treated **Goebbels**' wife and later treated soldiers who were at the Reich Chancellery.

Question: How long had you known **Goebbels** and his family?

Answer: I became acquainted with **Goebbels** on 1 May this year [through] his wife. Before that I knew him by his appearances in parades. I saw **Goebbels** for the first time around 1922 when he spoke in public in the People's House in Vienna.

Question: How was it that you had no access to the Reich Chancellery, but on 1 May were introduced to Goebbels and were immediately allowed into his quarters?

Answer: I suppose because I was acquainted with **Goebbels**' wife whom I treated.

Question: Have you been in Goebbels' flat?

Answer: I was in **Goebbels**' bunker in the Reich Chancellery, where his family – the wife and children – also lived.

Question: What physical defects do you know of in **Goebbels**, his wife and children?

Answer: The wife and the children were absolutely normal, but **Goebbels** was lame in the right leg.

Question: Specify more precisely what happened with **Goebbels** and his family.

Answer: On 27 April this year before supper, at 8–9 p.m., I met **Goebbels**' wife in the lobby at the entrance to Hitler's bunker, where she said to me that she wanted to speak to me on a very important matter and added: '*Now the situation is such that we*

55

obviously must die' – and because of that she asked me to help to kill her children, and I agreed.

After this, **Goebbels'** wife invited me into the children's bedroom and showed me all her children. At the time the children were going to bed and I did not speak to any of them.

At that moment, when the children were going to sleep, Goebbels himself entered, said good night to them, and left.

Often spending 10–15 minutes in the room I said good night to **Goebbels'** wife and went to my post at the hospital which was in the bunkers some 500 metres from the bunkers of **Hitler**, Goebbels and other persons who were at Hitler's headquarters.

On 1 May this year, at approximately 4–5 p.m., Goebbels' wife telephoned me at the hospital and said that a lot of time had already passed and asked me to come to the bunker immediately. After that I went to her, not having any medicines with me.

When I reached **Goebbels'** bunker I saw Goebbels himself in his study with his wife and the State Secretary of the Minister of Propaganda **Naumann**, who were discussing something.

After some 10 minutes of waiting at the door to the study, when **Goebbels** and **Naumann** left, **Goebbels'** wife invited me into the study and said that the decision had already been taken (i.e. to kill the children), because the Führer was dead and about 8–9 o'clock in the evening the troops would try to break out, so we should die. There was no other way out for us.

During our talk, I suggested to Goebbels' wife that she should send the children to the hospital and put them under the protection of the Red Cross, but she refused stating that it was better to let the children die . . .

About 20 minutes later, during our talk, **Goebbels** returned to the study and addressed me thus:

'Doctor, I'd be very grateful to you, if you would help my wife to kill the children.'

I suggested to Goebbels, as I had to his wife, that he should send the children to the hospital under protection of the Red Cross, but he answered: *'It is impossible, because they are still the children of Goebbels.'*

After that **Goebbels** left and I stayed with his wife, who spent about an hour playing patience.

About an hour later, **Goebbels** returned again with **Schach**, the Deputy Gauleiter for Berlin, and because **Schach**, as I gathered from their talk, was going to break out with the troops, he said goodbye to **Goebbels**. **Goebbels** presented him with a pair of dark-coloured horn-rimmed spectacles saying: *'Take them as a memento, the Führer always wore them.'* After that **Schach** said goodbye to Goebbels' wife, as well as to me, and left.

After **Schach's** departure **Goebbels'** wife said: *'Our troops are leaving now, the Russians could come here at any moment and interfere with our plans, so we should hurry up and finish things.'*

Photograph of Helmut Kunz from the investigation file.

On 6 June, 1945, Kunz was arrested by the 'Smersh' CED of the 1st Byelorussian Front on the charge that 'after Germany's aggression against the Soviet Union, from June to September, 1941, he participated in fighting against Red Army troops in the vicinity of the city of Demyansk in the ranks of a detached engineer combat battalion of the SS Totenkopf [Death's Head] Division. On 23 April, 1945, as a dedicated and loyal Nazi, he was employed as a doctor in the hospital at the Reich Chancellery; working at the said hospital, he treated members of German Government and their families. In its judgement of 13 February, 1952, the War Tribunal of the Moscow Military District sentenced Kunz to 25 years' imprisonment. Under a Decree of the USSR Supreme Council of 28 September, 1955 he was released early. On 29 October of that year he was handed over to the government of the GDR.

When we, i.e. Goebbels' wife and I, left the study, in the lobby there were two soldiers who were unknown to me, one in the uniform of the Hitler Youth, the uniform of the other I don't remember. While **Goebbels** and his wife were saying goodbye, the strangers asked: '*And what about you Herr Minister, what did you decide?*' **Goebbels** said nothing, but his wife stated: '*The Gauleiter of Berlin and his family will stay in Berlin and die here.*'

After saying goodbye to these men, **Goebbels** went to his study and his wife and I went to their quarters (bunker) where in the front room Goebbels' wife took a syringe filled with morphine and gave it to me, then we went into the children's bedroom. At that time the children were already in their beds, but were not asleep.

Goebbels' wife announced to the children: '*Children, don't be afraid, the doctor will give you a vaccine, which is now being given to children and soldiers.*' With these words she left the room and I stayed there alone and started to administer morphine, first to the two older girls, then to the boy and to the other girls. Injections of 0.5ml. were given in the arms below the elbow. To give the injections took approximately 8–10 minutes. After that I again went out into the lobby where I met **Goebbels**' wife who I told we should wait about 10 minutes for the children to fall asleep. At the time I looked at my watch – it was 20.40 (1 May).

Ten minutes later, **Goebbels**' wife, accompanied by me, entered the children's bedroom where she stayed for about 5 minutes putting crushed ampoules of cyanide in their mouths. (The cyanide was in 1.5ml glass ampoules.) When we returned to the lobby she said: '*All is finished.*' Then we went downstairs to Goebbels' study where we found him very nervous, pacing the room. Entering the study Goebbels' wife said: '*Everything is finished with the children, now it is time to think about ourselves.*' **Goebbels** answered:

'*We should hurry, because we have little time.*'

Then **Goebbels**' wife said: '*We shall not die here in the basement*', and **Goebbels** added: '*Certainly not, we'll go out to the garden.*' His wife replied: '*We won't go to the garden but to Wilhelmplatz, where you worked all your life.*' (Wilhelm Square – the square between the buildings of the Reich Ministry of Propaganda and the Reich Chancellery.)

During this conversation, **Goebbels** thanked me for making their fate easier and, saying goodbye to me, wished me success in life and good luck.

After that I went to my hospital (it was about at 9.15 or 9.20 at night).

Question: Where could Goebbels' wife have obtained poison (potassium cyanide)?

Answer: Goebbels' wife said to me that she had got morphine and a syringe from Hitler's second physician, **Stumpfegger**, but I don't know where she got the ampoules of cyanide.

Question: When you left them, what were **Goebbels** and his wife wearing?

Answer: At the moment of our parting with **Goebbels** he was wearing a Party uniform – a brown jacket, black trousers and boots. On the left sleeve he had a simple red armband with a black swastika in a white circle. I cannot confirm if he wore a gold Party badge because I do not remember it.

Goebbels' wife was dressed in a suit (a striped dark grey jacket and a skirt), without a hat. On her left breast there was a silver medal, the 'Mother's Cross', which was given to mothers who gave birth to seven children. If she had a Party badge I don't remember it.

I must also add that on 24 April this year when Goebbels' wife visited me as a dentist, in a private conversation she said that she also had a son by her first husband Quant [unclear], by name who served in the German Army with the rank of Leutnant or Oberleutnant. While on the Italian front in 1944 he was taken prisoner by Anglo-American forces and sent to Algeria from where he contacted the Goebbels by letter through the Red Cross.

Question: Specify the ages of Goebbels' children and how they were dressed.

Answer: All in all, there were six children whose killings I assisted: five girls and one boy. The elder girl was about 12–13 years old, the second girl was 10–12, the boy was 8–9, the third girl was 6–8, the fourth was 4–6 and the fifth was about 4 years old.

The elder girl was dressed in light-blue pyjamas, consisting of a short-sleeved jacket and trousers. All the other children, as far as I can remember, wore white night-gowns.

Question: From whom and when did you hear about the death of Goebbels and his wife?

Answer: I know absolutely nothing about that.

Question: Specify who from the medical staff of the hospital was invited to Hitler's bunker, when he decorated them, and how did you get there?

Answer: On the night of 29/30 April of this year I was in the officers' mess, which was above Hitler's bunker. At approximately 01.30 Professor Haase, chief physician of the hospital, called me on the telephone and said that the Führer invited me and all the medical staff of the hospital to visit him in the bunker. Twenty minutes later when all the employees were on their way to Hitler's quarters, I joined them. In this group there were:

1. Chief Physician of the hospital – Obersturmführer Professor Dr Haase.
2. Senior Physician of the hospital – Standartenführer Professor Dr Schenck.
3. The second physician of the hospital – Sturmbannführer, Dr Kunz.
4. Surgical nurse Erna Flegel.
5. Surgical nurse Liselotte Chervinska.
6. Surgical nurse Rut (full name unknown)

We assembled in the lobby near the Führer's quarters and after 10 minutes Hitler himself came to us. Haase introduced me and Dr Schenck to him. After that, on behalf of those who had been decorated, nurse Lyndhurst gave a short speech on loyalty to the Führer. Hitler thanked all those decorated for their service and went to his study and we went back to our posts.

Magda Goebbels with her children.

Among those decorated there were: Professor **Haase** – he was decorated with the Cross 'Kriegsferdienst Kreuz 1st Class' (for exceptional service) – and four nurses, Erna **Flegel**, Liselotte **Chervinska**, Elisabeth **Lyndhurst** and Rut (surname not known), who were given the 'Kriegsvendienst Kreuz 2nd Class', that had been presented by Hitler's aide-de-camp Günsche in the hospital before the audience with Hitler.

Question: Tell in detail what happened to **Hitler**.

Answer: I first heard of **Hitler's** death at 9 a.m. on 1 May when the Red Army troops had already surrounded Berlin. I went to **Goebbels'** quarters, where his wife was crying and saying that she had gone on her knees before **Hitler** and asked him not to do this and then she added: '*but there was no other way out*'.

Goebbels' wife did not say anything definite about what Hitler had done to himself.

Question: How can this be? You were there all the time and you do not know the circumstances of Hitler's death?

Answer: At the actual time I was not there and I can only repeat what I have heard. I believed what **Goebbels'** wife was saying. She said that Germany was like a flock without a shepherd, because **Hitler** was dead.

Question: It is impossible that you do not know how Hitler died because you were at the headquarters. We demand that you tell us the whole truth.

Answer: I do not know the details of **Hitler's** death and I can tell only what I heard from **Goebbels'** wife. Also, there were rumours among the staff that **Hitler** had committed suicide and that his corpse would be burnt in the garden of the Reich Chancellery.

Question: From whom did you hear that **Hitler's** corpse would be burnt?

Answer: I heard about it from **Rattenhuber**, SS Gruppenführer, who was in charge of security at the Führer's headquarters. He said: '*Father has left us alone and now we must take his corpse upstairs.*'

Question: Did Hitler commit suicide alone or was there anyone else?

Answer: **Hitler** committed suicide with his wife **Braun**, whom he married several days before his death.

Question: What have you heard about it?

Answer: I know that on the evening of 30* April, **Goebbels'** children ran up to Frau **Braun** and called her 'Aunt Braun'. She replied to them: '*Now I am not Aunt Braun, but Aunt Hitler*'. Braun spoke about this in the presence of Dr **Haase** in the following circumstances: Professor **Haase** and I were dining, and Frau **Braun** entered the room with the children. Passing the table she spoke to Professor **Haase**, saying that today the children had called her 'Aunt Braun'. She told them to call her 'Aunt Hitler'.

----

*In fact it could have been on 29 April.

Question: How do you know that **Braun** must have committed suicide together with **Hitler**?

Answer: On the evening of 30 April, **Braun** invited me, Professor **Haase** and two female secretaries for a cup of coffee. She told us that **Hitler** had written his last will and that **Hitler** would die when he received confirmation that the will had reached the person it had been sent to.

She also said: '*All betrayed us – even Göring and Himmler*', and it would not be difficult to die because the poison had already been tested on a dog, and death would come quickly.

Question: Who tested this poison on a dog?

Answer: **Braun** said that the poison had already been tested, but she did not say who personally had done it.

Question: You stated that several days before his death **Hitler** married Eva **Braun**. Specify where Braun was before her marriage and what she was doing.

Answer: From the accounts of Gruppenführer **Rattenhuber**, chief of Hitler's bodyguard, and **Hitler**'s personal pilot Gruppenführer **Baur**, I know that before her official marriage Eva **Braun** was with **Hitler**. I know no further details.

Question: From what sources did you learn that **Himmler** was going to hold talks with the Allies and with whom exactly?

Answer: As I have already stated, on 30 April of this year between 10 and 11 o'clock at night I was in the mess with Professor **Haase** and **Hitler**'s secretaries Frau **Junge** and Frau **Christian**. Eva Hitler, **Hitler**'s wife, came there, and invited us into one of the rooms of the mess where we were for about 20 minutes.

During our conversation, Eva Hitler said to us that **Göring** was not reliable, which we had always known, that **Himmler**, instead of moving troops from the West to defend Berlin, was holding talks with the Allies (with America and Britain, I suppose) on a cease-fire without Hitler's approval. She did not tell us anything more detailed on this matter.

Question: When and with whom did you leave the bunker and where did you go?

Answer: I was in the bunker of the hospital until 2.00 a.m. on 3 May this year, i.e. until the moment of capture. Professor **Haase** and nurses **Flegel** and **Chervinska** stayed with me in the hospital.

Professor **Schenck** and a nurse named **Rut** (I don't know her surname) took part in an attempt to break through the encirclement, and their fate is unknown to me.

(Questioning suspended)

My testimony was read to me in German translation and was transcribed correctly from my words. **Kunz**

Investigators:

Chief of the 4th Section of the 'Smersh' Counter-Espionage Department
of the 1st Byelorussian Front

Lieutenant-Colonel **Vasiliev**

Interpreter:

Senior Lieutenant **Vlasov**

Testimony was written in shorthand:

Medical Service Junior Lieutenant **Hrusheva**

Арх. Н-21092; л. 12-20
(ПОДЛИННИК)
(original)

Hans Baur, *born on June 19, 1897 in Ampfing, decorated World War I pilot, commercial pilot between the wars (one of Lufthansa's first six pilots), became Hitler's pilot shortly after flying his one millionth kilometre, in the bunker until 1 May 1945. He remained in Soviet captivity until 1955, returned to Germany, published his memoirs 'Mit Mächtigen zwischn Himmel unde Erde' in 1971, and died on February 17, 1993 in Neuwiddersberg.*

Gerda Christian, *née Daranowski, born on 13 December, 1913 in Berlin, wife of Air Force General Christian, Hitler's Secretary from 1937 until the end, escaped to West Germany, died of cancer in Dusseldorf in 1996.*

Gertrude (Traudl) Junge, *née Humps, born 1920 in Munich, Hitler's secretary from January 1943 to the end, died of cancer in February 2002. Her memoirs 'Until the Final Hour: Hitler's Last Secretary' were published posthumously in 2003.*

REPORT OF EXAMINATION OF THE SITE OF THE BURIAL OF THE CORPSES OF ADOLF HITLER AND EVA BRAUN

13 May, 1945
Berlin

We, the undersigned, Chief of 'Smersh' Counter-Espionage Section of the 79th Infantry Corps Lieutenant-Colonel **Klimenko**, Senior Investigator of 'Smersh' Counter-Espionage Section of the 79th Infantry Corps and serving also as an interpreter Senior Lieutenant **Katyshev**, Chief of the Topographical Service of the 79th Infantry Corps Major of the Guards **Gabelok**, Photographer of the 79th Infantry Corps Junior Lieutenant of the Guards **Kalashnikov**, privates of a detached infantry platoon with the 'Smersh' Counter-Espionage Section of the 79th Infantry Corps **Oleinik, Churakov, Novash, Mialkin** with participation of a witness **Mengershausen** Harry, on this day examined the place of burial of the corpses of Reichschancellor of Germany Adolf **Hitler** and his wife.

The witness **Mengershausen**, Harry said that from 10 to 30 April, while serving in an SS unit under the command of **Mohnke**, he took part in the defence of the Reich Chancellery and guarded Adolf Hitler.

At noon on 30 April, 1945, **Mengershausen** was on guard in the new Reich Chancellery, patrolling the lobby and passing **Hitler**'s study next to the Blue Dining-room.

Mengershausen stopped at the last window of the Blue Dining-room, the one nearest to the entrance door to the garden and began to watch the movements in the garden of the Reich Chancellery.

At that moment, Sturmbannführers **Günsche** and **Linge** carried the bodies of Adolf Hitler and Eva **Braun**, his former personal secretary* out of the emergency exit of the 'Führerbunker'. This excited **Mengershausen**'s curiosity and he watched what was going on with great attention.

Hitler's personal secretary **Günsche** poured petrol over the bodies and set fire to them. In half an hour, the bodies of **Hitler** and his wife were burnt, and then put in the bomb crater, approximately 1 metre away from the aforementioned emergency exit, and buried.

The entire process of the carrying-out of the bodies of Adolf **Hitler** and his wife, and of their burning and burial was watched by **Mengershausen** from a distance of 60 metres.

----

* *Sic.*

The emergency exit from Hitler's bunker.

In the same crater, on 2 April, 1945, **Hitler's** own dog was buried, **Mengershausen** went on. Its characteristic features: a big German Shepherd with long ears, a black back, and light-coloured flanks. **Mengershausen** knows that the dog was poisoned because Paul **Feni**, who was looking after Hitler's dog, told him so.

Examination of the places indicated by the witness **Mengershausen**, verified the truthfulness of his evidence. Being on duty on 30 April, 1945 **Mengershausen** could easily watch what was going on at the emergency exit of the 'Führerbunker'. Witness **Mengershausen's** evidence is still more valid because the burnt corpses of a man and a woman were recovered by us on 5 May, 1945, as well as those of two poisoned dogs which were identified by other witnesses as belonging to **Hitler** and his personal secretary Eva **Braun**.

Field sketches of the place in which the corpses of Hitler and his wife were discovered and photographs of the places indicated by the witness **Mengershausen** are enclosed with this Report.

Chief of 'Smersh' Counter-Espionage Section of the 79th Infantry Corps
Lieutenant-Colonel **Klimenko**

Senior Investigator of 'Smersh' Counter-Espionage Section
of the 79th Infantry Corps and interpreter
Senior Lieutenant **Katyshev**

Chief of the Topographical Service of the 79th Infantry Corps
Major of the Guards **Gabelok**

Photographer of the 79th Infantry Corps
Junior Lieutenant of the Guards **Kalashnikov**

Privates of the 'Smersh' Counter-Espionage Section of the 79th Infantry Corps:
Oleinik
Churakov
Novash
Mialkin
Witness   **Mengershausen**

Ф.К-1 ос; оп. 4; д. 6; л. 1-2
(ПОДЛИННИК)
(original)

MAP OF THE SITE OF THE DISCOVERY OF THE CORPSES OF HITLER AND EVA BRAUN

Scale 1:1000 (1cm = 10m)
Field sketch by Guard Major Gabelyok

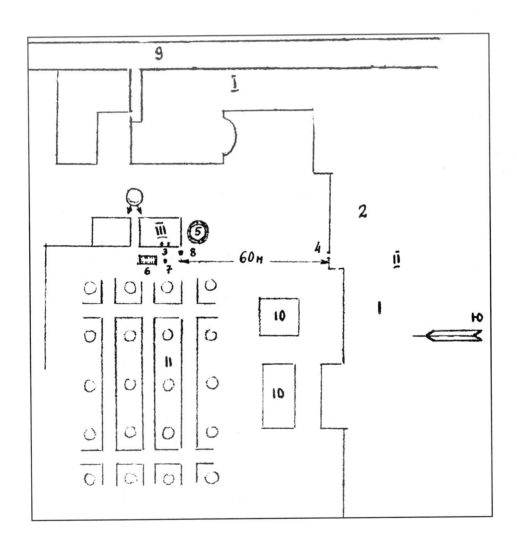

KEY TO THE PLAN

I. Old Reich Chancellery.

II. New Reich Chancellery.

III. Hitler's bunker.

1. Hitler's study.

2. Blue Dining-room.

3. Emergency exit from Hitler's bunker.

4. The last window of the Blue Dining-room.

5. Watch tower.

6. Bomb-crater.

7. The place where the corpses of Goebbels and his wife were burned.

8. The place where the corpses of Hitler and his wife were burned.

9. Wilhelmstrasse.

10. Ornamental pools.

11. Park.

Major of the Guards **Gabelyok**

13 May, 1945

Ф. 4 ос; оп. 3; д. 36; л. 24-25

(подлинник)

(original)

RECORD OF ADDITIONAL INTERROGATION
OF REICH CHANCELLERY GUARD
HARRY MENGERSHAUSEN

18 May, 1945

Mengershausen Harry, born 1915 in the city of Bremen, German national, from a businessman's family, a officer of the police guard of the Reich Chancellery, with the rank of Oberscharführer, education 8 years of people's school.

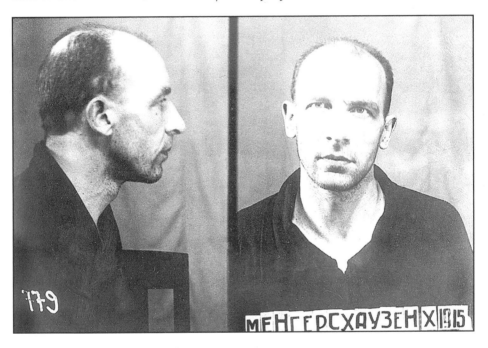

Photograph of Harry Mengershausen from the investigation file.

On 10 August, 1951, Harry Mengershausen was arrested by the USSR Ministry of State Security on charges that he 'was a member of the SS, a criminal organisation, and took part in punitive actions against civilians in German-occupied countries'. In a judgement of the Special Judicial Council attached to the USSR MSS dated 26 December, 1951 Mengershausen was sentenced to 15 years' imprisonment in a corrective labour camp. Under a Decree of the Praesidium of the Supreme Council of the USSR of 28 September, 1955 he was released early and 12 January, 1956 handed over to the GDR authorities

Interrogation began at 17.00, and ended at 24.00

Interpreter Kagan is warned of his liability under Article 95 of the USSR Criminal Code. **Kagan**

Question: Do you confirm your evidence of 13 May, 1945 about **Hitler**'s fate?

Answer: Yes, I completely confirm my evidence of 13 May, 1945 about **Hitler**'s fate.

Question: Recount in detail what you know of **Hitler**'s fate.

Answer: In late April, 1945 when Red Army troops entered Berlin, the Reich Chancellery was under artillery fire. Besides, the city was constantly being bombarded by the Soviet Air Force.

Many of the Reich Chancellery's personnel and guards were under great stress: there was talk that the war was lost and that the only way out was surrender.

On 30 April, 1945 fighting had reached the Alexanderplatz, near the Reichstag. On that day the defence of the Reich Chancellery was entrusted to the elite SS officers. The shelling was intensifying by the moment, and the staff and guards of the Reich Chancellery were panicking and, seeing that there was no hope, were changing out of their uniforms and into civilian clothes and escaping.

Hitler, **Goebbels** and their staff stayed in the bunkers all the time and did not go out, all knowing that Berlin would fall in a few hours. Escape from the Reich Chancellery was impossible because it was surrounded by Red Army units. The situation for all who remained in the Reich Chancellery was critical.

On this day, 30 April, 1945 I was on duty in the Reich Chancellery from 10.00 a.m., patrolling the hall in which a kitchen and the Green Dining-room were situated. I was also watching the garden bunker because some 80 metres from the green dining-room was Hitler's bunker.

While patrolling the lobby I approached the kitchen and met an acquaintance of mine, **Hitler**'s orderly **Bauer**, who was going to the kitchen. He told me that Hitler had shot himself in his bunker. I asked where the Führer's wife **Braun** was, but he replied that she was also lying dead in the bomb-shelter but he did not know if she had taken poison or had shot herself.

My conversation with **Bauer** lasted for only a few minutes, because he was hurrying to the kitchen where food had earlier been cooked for Hitler's suite; later he returned to the bunker. The kitchen was 1.5 metres * from the bunker.

----

* *Sic.*

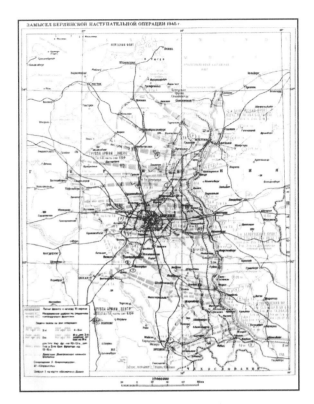

Russian map of the plan for the attack on Berlin, 1945.

I did not believe what **Bauer** had said about **Hitler** and his wife being dead and I continued on guard.

No more than an hour after my meeting with **Bauer**, on my way to the terrace, which was 60–80 metres from the bunker, I saw Hitler's aide-de-camp Sturmbannführer **Günsche** and his servant Sturmbannführer **Linge** come out with Hitler's corpse in their arms and lay it down 1.5 metres from the entrance. Then they went back inside and several minutes later carried his wife, Eva **Braun**, out of the bunker and put her near Hitler's corpse on the left. Beside the corpses there were two 20kg cans of petrol from which **Günsche** and **Linge** started to pour petrol on the corpses and then both set fire to them.

When the bodies were burnt, two men from **Hitler**'s personal guard, whose names I don't know, came from the bunker, took the burnt corpses and put them in a bomb crater which was 2 metres from the bunker. When the hole was filled with soil and the ground was levelled they returned to the bunker.

When they had all gone, I went to the place where the bodies were burnt and saw ashes there.

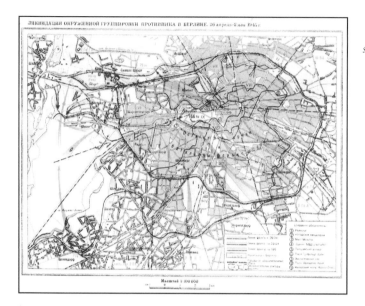

Destruction of the surrounded enemy forces in Berlin. 25 April– 2 May, 1945.

Question: How did you recognise the corpses being carried out of the bunker as being those of **Hitler** and his wife **Braun**?

Answer: The bodies that were carried from the bunker were definitely those of **Hitler** and his wife, Eva **Braun**.

I knew **Hitler** by his face and his clothes. He had black trousers worn over high boots and grey-green uniform jacket. Under the uniform jacket, I could see a white shirtfront and a necktie. None of the Nazi Party leaders except for **Hitler** wore such a uniform, and I had seen him in this uniform several times, [that's why] I remembered it exceptionally well.

When **Hitler** was being carried out I clearly saw his face in profile – his nose, hair and moustache. So I confirm that it was definitely **Hitler**.

Hitler's wife **Braun**, when she was being carried out of the bunker, was dressed in a black dress, with several pink flowers made of cloth on the breast. I saw her several times wearing this dress in the bunker. Besides, I saw her face – it was oval, thin, with a straight, narrow nose and fair hair. Thus, knowing **Hitler**'s wife **Braun** very well, I state that it was definitely her body that was carried out of the bunker.

Question: Who else from the Reich Chancellery's guards saw the burning of **Hitler** and **Braun**'s corpses?

Answer: I don't know if there was anyone else who saw the burning of **Hitler** and **Braun**'s corpses. Of all the guards of the Reich Chancellery on duty, I was the closest to **Hitler**'s bunker.

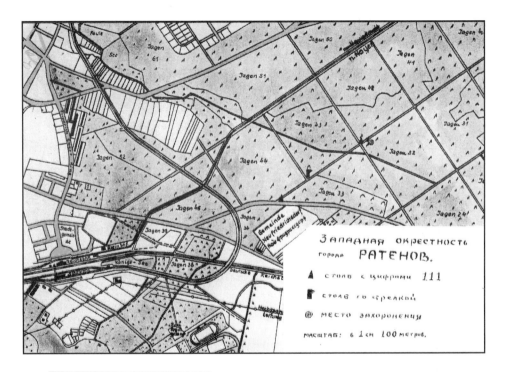

Above: Russian map of the burial site of Hitler, Goebbels and members of their families near the city of Rathenow, June, 1945.

Left: Assault on the central section of the Berlin defence.

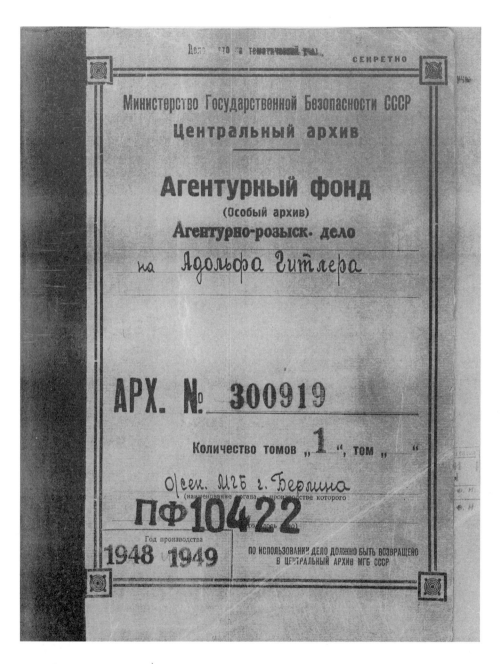

The cover of the USSR Ministry of State Security's investigation file on Adolf Hitler.

Left: Adolf Hitler's military uniform jacket and service cap.

Below: Adolf Hitler's gold Nazi Party badge.

Right: Adolf Hitler's military uniform jacket.

Below: Pistol belonging to Hitler's successor, Grand-Admiral Dönitz.

Above: Adolf Hitler's Party uniform jacket.

Above: Signet ring discovered at Hermann Göring's residence.

*Right: Josef Goebbels' Party
uniform jacket.*

*Below: Partially burnt gold Nazi
Party badges found on the bodies
of Goebbels and his wife.*

Above: Josef Goebbels' burnt orthopaedic boot.

Left: Parts of Magda Goebbels' jaw.

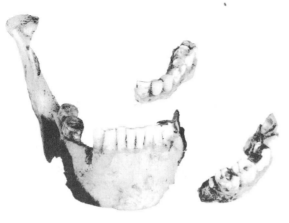

*Right: Josef and Magda Goebbels'
burnt pistols.*

*Below: Outside and inside of gold cigarette-
case, partially destroyed by fire, found
on the body of Magda Goebbels.
It contains Hitler's signature and
the date '29. X. 1934'.*

Right: Gas detection device found in Hitler's bunker.

Below: Medicine chest found in Hitler's bunker.

Question: Were any of **Hitler's** followers present at the burning and burying of the corpses of **Hitler** and **Braun**?

Answer: Except for **Günsche** and **Linge**, no one was present during burning of the corpses of **Hitler** and his wife, and the burial was performed by two men of Hitler's guard.

Question: Who apart from **Hitler** did you see in the Reich Chancellery on 30 April, 1945?

Answer: After Hitler's suicide I saw **Goebbels** leave **Hitler's** bunker several times. Also, while on duty, I saw Reichsleiter **Bormann**, Chief of the General Staff General **Krebs**, General **Burgdorf**, and Vice-Admiral **Voss**.

Site of the burning (x) and burial (xx) of Hitler's corpse near
the emergency exit from the bunker (xxx).

Question: Where did **Günsche** and **Linge** disappear to after they had burnt the corpses of Hitler and his wife?

Answer: After Günsche and Linge burnt Hitler and his wife, I did not see them again because the same day, 30 April this year, I changed into civilian clothes and hid in a basement.

Question: Did **Günsche** and **Linge**, as well as the others who were in the Reich Chancellery on 30 April of this year, have the chance to leave Berlin?

Answer: They had no chance because the Reich Chancellery was surrounded by Red Army troops. On the morning of 2 May, 1945, I heard from some German soldiers that all those who were in the Reich Chancellery, together with the troops, tried to break through the encirclement to get to Friedrichstrasse, but whether they succeeded I don't know.

Question: You are being shown photograph No 1. Tell us what you see in this photograph.

Answer: In photograph No 1 shown to me there is the emergency exit of **Hitler**'s bunker. I know this place very well and I can show where the corpses of **Hitler** and his wife **Braun** were burnt as well as where they were buried.

On the photo, the place where **Hitler** and **Braun** were burnt is marked 'x', the place where they were buried is marked 'xx', and the emergency exit from **Hitler's** bunker is marked 'xxx'.

Question: Do you state that you personally saw the corpses of **Hitler** and his wife **Braun** being carried out, and saw them being burnt and buried?

Answer: All that I have already told about **Hitler**, I confirm now and state once again that I personally saw the corpses of **Hitler** and his wife **Braun** carried out of the bunker, burnt and buried.

The Record of Interrogation was read to me in German, and it is a correct record of my statement, which I confirm with my signature.

Mengershausen

Interpreter: **Kagan**
Interrogation by: Chief of 'Smersh' Counter-Espionage Department
of the 1st Byelorussian Front

Lieutenant-General A. **Vadis**

Chief of 'Smersh' Counter-Espionage Section of the 3rd Assault Army

Colonel **Miroshnichenko**

Also present were: Chief of the 2nd Sub-Section of the 4th Section
of the 'Smersh' Counter-Espionage Department of the 1st Byelorussian Front

Major **Gershgorin**

Chief of the 4th Sub-Section of 'Smersh' Counter-Espionage Section
of the 3rd Assault Army

Major **Bystrov**

Correct: Chief of the 4th Section of 'Smersh' Counter-Espionage Department
of the 1st Byelorussian Front

Lieutenant-Colonel **Vasiliev**

Арх. Н-21092; л. 12-20
(ПОДЛИННИК)
(original)

RECORD OF INTERROGATION OF HITLER'S PERSONAL DOCTOR PROFESSOR WERNER HAASE

18 May, 1945

I, investigator of the 1st Sub-Section of the 4th Section of 'Smersh' Counter-Espionage Department of the 1st Byelorussian Front Senior Lieutenant **Vlasov,** questioned prisoner-of-war SS Reserve Obersturmbannführer **Haase,** Werner.

Interrogation began at 23.00 and was conducted in German.

Haase Werner, born in 1900 in the city of Kuten, Anhalt province, a salaried employee, a doctor, academic rank Professor of Medicine, education – higher, member of the Nazi Party since 1933, SS officer since 1941.

Question: Were you personally acquainted with the Reichsminister of Propaganda Josef **Goebbels?**

Answer: Working from 1935 to 1945 as **Hitler's** deputy personal doctor, I repeatedly met **Goebbels** in **Hitler's** quarters and exchanged greetings with him. I did not have any closer relations with **Goebbels.**

I was similarly acquainted with Goebbels' wife – Magda **Goebbels.**

Question: When and where did you last see **Goebbels** and his wife?

Answer: When the fighting reached Berlin, **Goebbels** and his family (his wife and six children) moved into Hitler's bunker, situated under the Reich Chancellery, where I last saw him at approximately 11–12 a.m. on 1 May, 1945 when I passed him talking to Reichsleiter Martin **Bormann** in the hall on my way to the dining-room.

I also saw **Goebbels'** wife for the last time there, in **Hitler's** bunker approximately two days before that, again in passing.

Question: What do you know of the fate of **Goebbels** and his family?

Answer: From **Hitler's** senior personal doctor, SS Standartenführer **Stumpfegger,** and Goebbels' dentist, Dr **Kunz,** I know that **Goebbels** and his wife committed suicide on the evening of 1 May, 1945, by taking poison, which one I cannot say. In an operating room of the Reich Chancellery hospital, at approximately 19.00–20.00 on 1 May, 1945 **Stumpfegger** told me the following: '*Goebbels and all his family are dead.*' **Stumpfegger** said nothing about the circumstances of their deaths.

As early as 30 April, 1945 Dr **Kunz** was depressed and, answering my questions reluctantly, said that he was troubled because he might have to participate in killing Goebbels' children with poison.

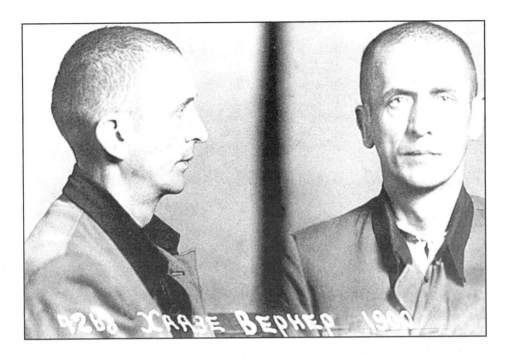

Photo of Werner Haase from the investigation file.
The photograph is marked '4268 Haase Werner, born in 1900'.

On 6 June, 1945, Haase was arrested by 'Smersh' CED of the 1st Byelorussian Front on charges that he 'was a personal doctor of the former Reichschancellor of Germany, Hitler, and also treated other leaders of Hitler's government and of the Nazi Party and members of Hitler's SS guard'. He died on 30 November, 1950 in the Butyr prison hospital.

On 1 May, 1945 at approximately 14.00–15.00, **Kunz** was summoned by telephone from the hospital to **Goebbels'** quarters, which were in Hitler's bunker some 500 metres from the hospital.

Kunz returned to the hospital between 19.00–20.00 on 1 May, 1945 in a very depressed state. He came into my room, sat on the bed and held his head in his hands. In Answer to my question: 'Are Goebbels and his family dead?', he said: 'Yes'. On my asking if he had been alone, **Kunz** answered: 'Doctor Stumpfegger helped me.' I failed to get any more information from him.

Question: Describe Goebbels and his wife.

Answer: **Goebbels** looks about 50, below average height, skinny, frail, with his right leg crippled from birth, as a result of which he had to wear a brace and a special right boot with a thicker sole.

Werner Haase's military identity card.

Goebbels' wife looks about 45, a little taller than her husband, thin, fair with very blonde hair. **Goebbels**' wife has no physical defects.

Question: Did you know the children of Goebbels?

Answer: No, I did not know Goebbels' children personally. I know that **Goebbels** had six children: five girls and a boy, aged between 4 and 14.

I also know that **Goebbels**' wife had another son by her first husband who served in the German Army.

Question: On 6 May, 1945 you were shown the corpses of a man, a woman and six children for identification. Did you identify them?

Answer: From the corpses shown to me I quite confidently identified the body of the man as **Goebbels**. Though the corpse was so badly burnt that the facial features were disfigured, I was still able to identify **Goebbels** by the shape of his head, his height, his build, by his crippled right leg (club foot) and by the boot from his right leg, made to special order so as to fit his deformity. I do not know of any other person with features resembling the features of **Goebbels** described by me.

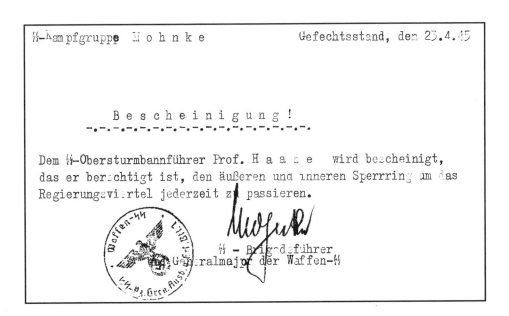

Above: Photocopy of the Führer's telegram to Professor Werner Haase: 'Accept my most profound congratulations on your birthday. Adolf Hitler'. 2 August, 1943.

Below: Professor Haase's pass for the government district, 23 April, 1945.

As for the corpse of the woman shown to me, I couldn't determine if it was the corpse of Goebbels' wife, because the corpse was badly burnt, but the size and the stature of the corpse were identical to that of **Goebbels'** wife.

From the six children's corpses shown to me I couldn't identify anybody, because, as I stated earlier, I did not know Goebbels' children.

Interrogation ended at 03.00.

The Record of Interrogation was read to me in German translation, and my evidence was written down from my words correctly.

Haase

Interrogation by:

Investigator of the 'Smersh' Counter-Espionage Department

of the 1st Byelorussian Front

Senior Lieutenant **Vlasov**

Verified:

Chief of the 4th Section of the 'Smersh' CED

of the 1st Byelorussian Front

Lieutenant-Colonel **Vasiliev**

Ф. К-1 ос; оп. 4; д. 8; л. 133-135

(заверенная копия)

(an authorised copy)

RECORD OF INTERROGATION OF
THE HEAD CHEF OF THE REICH CHANCELLERY
WILHELM LANGE

18 May, 1945

I, Senior Investigator of the 2nd Sub-Section of the 4th Section of the 'Smersh' Counter-Espionage Department of the 1st Byelorussian Front Captain **Terioshin** with the participation of the German language interpreter **Gorelik** questioned the prisoner **Lange,** Wilhelm, born in 1891 in the village of Halfer, (district of Altina), Westphalia (Germany), German national, citizen of Germany, pastry-cook by profession, working as a chef in the kitchen of Hitler's personal dining-room at the Reich Chancellery, married, 8 years of school, a member of the NSDAP since 1937, living in Berlin – 18, Netzestrasse, Pankow Stub.

The German language interpreter **Gorelik** was warned of his liability for incorrect translation under Article 95 of the USSR Criminal Code.

Questioning began at 12.10
"   "   ended at 22.30

Question: For how long did you work as a chef in the kitchen of Hitler's household at the Reich Chancellery?

Answer: I worked as a chef in the kitchen of Hitler's household from 1935 until the Red Army's entry into Berlin.

Question: Did you happen to meet leaders of the German government during your work in the Reich Chancellery?

Answer: Yes, during my work in the Reich Chancellery I met the leaders of the German government repeatedly, namely the Führer, Adolf **Hitler**, Reichsminister of Propaganda Dr Josef **Goebbels** and members of their immediate circle.

Question: For how long have you known members of the family of the Reichsministry of Propaganda Josef **Goebbels**?

Answer: Of the members of Reichsminister of Propaganda Josef **Goebbels**' family I used to see his wife and his children.

Goebbels' wife (I don't know her name) I met at the parties in the Reich Chancellery in 1938.

Then (i.e. in 1938), as far as I remember, **Goebbels**' wife looked like a lady of about 30, of medium height, with regular features, slender and slim with blonde hair.

In later years I did not meet **Goebbels**' wife and I cannot describe her appearance now.

On approximately 24–25 April, 1945 in the kitchen of the Reich Chancellery, I saw all six children of Dr **Goebbels** when they passed the kitchen of the Reich Chancellery on their way to the Führer's bunker.

Question: Describe the appearance of Goebbels' children.

Answer: The Reichsminister of Propaganda Goebbels had six children: five girls and one boy. Their names and appearance are known to me from newspapers, magazines and photos.

Goebbels' elder daughter – **Helga**, 13 years old, approximately 1m 30cm in height, thin, with an oval face and fair hair.

Goebbels' second daughter – **Hilde**, 12 years old, about 1m 20cm, thin, with an oval face and fair hair.

Goebbels' third daughter – **Holde**, 10 years old, about 1m 1cm, thin with an oval face and fair hair.

Goebbels' son – **Helmut**, 8 years old, about 1m 10cm, sturdily built, with an oval face and fair hair.

Goebbels' fourth daughter – **Hedda**, 5 years old, approximately 1m, thin, with an oval face, fair hair.

Goebbels' fifth daughter – **Heide**, 3 years old, about 80cm, thin, oval face, fair hair.

Question: When did you last see the Reichsminister of Propaganda Goebbels?

Answer: I last saw Goebbels on 27 or 28 April, 1945 in the garden of the Reich Chancellery. I was going from the kitchen through the garden to the pantry to get some provisions and saw Goebbels standing near the door to Hitler's bunker. Goebbels was talking to a man in military uniform whom I did not know.

Question: What do you know of the fate of Goebbels and his family?

Answer: At 8.00–9.00 p.m. on 1 May, 1945 Sergeant-Major **Tornow**, who looking after Hitler's dogs, came to the kitchen and told me that Goebbels and his wife had committed suicide in the garden near the Führer's bunker. No details were disclosed to me by Sergeant-Major **Tornow**.

Question: What do you know of Sergeant-Major **Tornow**?

Answer: Sergeant-Major **Tornow**, who looked after Hitler's dogs, was about 40 years old, born in Silesia, a German national. Distinguishing features: of medium height, average build, oval face, dark blond hair, with a small moustache, he has white false teeth in his upper jaw.

On the evening of 1 May, 1945 Sergeant-Major **Tornow** was going to leave the Reich Chancellery and break out of the Red Army encirclement. I don't know if he managed to do it.

Question: Continue with your evidence as to the fate of **Goebbels** and his family.

Answer: During the day of 2 May, 1945, when the Red Army took Berlin, I was in the grounds of the Reich Chancellery in the hospital (in the bomb-shelter under Hitler's study). I was summoned from there by a Soviet officer (whose name and rank I do not know) to identify the corpses discovered in the garden of the Reich Chancellery.

Near the entrance to the Führer's bunker, approximately 2 metres from the door, there were two corpses, those of a man and of a woman.

After thorough examination of these burnt bodies, I recognised the man's body as the corpse of the Reichsminister of Propaganda Dr Josef **Goebbels**, and the woman's body as that of his wife.

I recognised **Goebbels**' corpse by the following features: by his height, the shape of his head and his body as well as by the remains of the orthopaedic boot on his right foot, because **Goebbels**' right leg was shorter than the left one and he had a club foot.

Besides there were some parts of a suit (a light-coloured jacket and black trousers) that were not completely burnt, that **Goebbels** had been wearing when he was alive.

As for the corpse of the woman I examined, I was not as certain in recognising it as the corpse of **Goebbels**' wife, because I could identify her only based on photos in newspapers and magazines. As I have already stated before, I had only fleeting encounters with her in 1938 at parties in the Reich Chancellery, and in 7 years she had changed a little. Notwithstanding that, by its height and build the corpse of the woman found near Goebbels' corpse resembled **Goebbels**' wife.

As for the fate of **Goebbels**' children, I did not know anything about that until 3 May, 1945 when I was invited by Soviet officers to examine the children's bodies (five girls and boy) aged from 3 to 13 years.

After thorough examination of these corpses I identified them as the corpses of **Goebbels**' six children: Helga, Hilde, Holde, Helmut, Hedda, Heide, whom I met in the Reich Chancellery on 24 or 25 April, 1945.

When and how **Goebbels**' children were killed I do not know, but because of the lack of wounds on the bodies one can suppose they were poisoned.

Question: When did you last see **Hitler**?

Answer: I last saw Hitler at the beginning of April, 1945 in the garden of the Reich Chancellery, where he was walking his dog, a German shepherd named **Blondi**.

Question: What do you know of **Hitler**'s fate?

Answer: I don't know anything definite about **Hitler**'s fate.

On the evening of 30 April, 1945 Sergeant-Major **Tornow**, who looked after Hitler's dogs, came to my kitchen to get food for the puppies. He was upset about something and said to me: *'The Führer is dead and there is nothing left of his corpse.'*

Rumours were spreading among the personnel of the Reich Chancellery that **Hitler** either took poison or shot himself and that his corpse was burnt. I do not know if this is true.

This Record was written down from my words correctly and read to me in German.

Lange

Interrogator:
Senior Investigator of the 4th Section 'Smersh' of CED of the 1st Byelorussian Front
Captain **Terioshin**

Translated from Russian into German:
Gorelik

Арх. Р-45945; л. 30-34
(ПОДЛИННИК)
(original)

DOCUMENTS CONCERNING THE DOGS IN THE FÜHRER'S BUNKER

5–22 May, 1945

REPORT

5 May, 1945
The City of Berlin Army, in the Field

We, Deputy Chief of the 'Smersh' Counter-Espionage Section of the 79th Infantry Corps Captain **Deriabin**, Platoon Commander and Senior Lieutenant of the Guards **Panasov**, sergeants and privates of the platoon: **Tsibochkin, Alabudin, Kirilov, Korshak** and **Guliaev**, in the vicinity of Hitler's Reich Chancellery, 100m to the south-east of the building, in the place where earlier the corpses of Goebbels and his wife had been discovered, found and dug up two dead dogs.

Characteristic features of the dogs:

1. A German shepherd (female) with dark-grey coat, tall, with a small link-chain dog-collar. No wounds or blood were discovered on the corpse.

2. A small dog (male) with black coat, without a collar, no wounds, but bone of the upper jaw was broken, and there was blood in the mouth.

The dogs' corpses were in a bomb-crater, 1.5m from each other and were covered with a thin layer of soil.

It could be supposed that the killing of the dogs was done 5–6 days previously, because there was no smell and the hair could not easily be pulled out.

In order to discover items that could indicate the owner of the dogs and the cause of their death, we thoroughly dug up the soil where the dogs were discovered and examined it. We discovered:

1. Two dark-coloured glass medicine vials.

2. Separate burnt lists of books issued by a printing-house and small pieces of paper with handwriting on them.

3. Metal elliptical pendant on a thin ball-chain 18–20cm long, on the back of which there was an engraved inscription 'Keep me with you forever.'

4. 600 marks in German currency in 100-mark notes.

5. Elliptical metal badge No. 31907.

The corpses of the dogs and the items discovered at the site were photographed and are held at 'Smersh' CES of the Corps as certified in this Report.

Deputy Chief of the 'Smersh' CES of the 79th Infantry Corps
Captain **Deriabin**

The 'Smersh' CES Platoon Commander of the 79th Infantry Corps
Senior Lieutenant of the Guards
Panasov

Sergeant of the 'Smersh' CES platoon of the 79th Infantry Corps
Tsibochkin

Privates of the 'Smersh' CES of the 79th Infantry Corps:
Alabudin
Kirilov
Korshak
Guliaev

Ф. 4. ос; оп. 3; д. 36; л. 28-29
(подлинник)
(original)

DOCUMENT No 3
POST-MORTEM OF THE CORPSE OF
THE GERMAN SHEPHERD DOG

7 May, 1945, Berlin-Buch,
Morgue of SHY* 496

Medical board, consisting of Leading Forensic Medicine expert of the 1st Byelorussian Front Lieutenant-Colonel of the Medical Service **Shkaravsky F. I.**, Leading Pathologist of the Red Army Lieutenant-Colonel of the Medical Service **Kraevsky K. A.**, Acting Leading Pathologist of the 1st Byelorussian Front **Marantz A. J.**, Army Forensic Medicine Expert of the 3rd Assault Army Major **Boguslavsky Y. I.** and Army Pathologist of the 3rd Assault Army Medical Service Major **Gulkievitch J.**, on the orders of Member of the War Council of the 1st Byelorussian Front Lieutenant-General **Telegin** performed a post-mortem on the corpse of a **German Shepherd Dog**.

---

* Surgical Field Hospital.

In the course of the investigation it was established that:

A. External examination

The corpse of a large dog (female), German Shepherd breed. The colour of the coat – dark-grey on the back, light-grey on the belly. There are black hairs around the mouth. The tail is of medium furriness. The length of the body from the occipital bone to the beginning of the tail – 91cm. The teeth are white, upper parts of the fangs are slightly worn down.

Nipples of greyish colour, well formed, when squeezed do not show any discharge.

In the mucous membrane of the tongue, 2 pieces of a thin glass ampoule were discovered, one part of the bottom, the other part of the side.

In the mucous membrane of the palate there are small abrasions with smooth edges, and mucus in the mouth containing blood. The abrasions are surrounded with haemorrhaging.

Other injuries were not discovered on the corpse of the dog, the long bones were found, through manual examination, to be unbroken.

B. Internal examination

Position of internal organs is correct, the quantity of blood is moderate. Cardiotomy showed friable red blood clots – the same was found in the major blood vessels.

On dissection, the corpse produced a strong smell of bitter almonds.

Intestines contain significant quantities of half-digested food with an unpleasant acid smell.

Examination of internal organs does not reveal any obvious symptoms of disease.

For chemical analysis 10cc of blood was taken and put in a glass test-tube as well as samples of the lungs, heart, liver, kidneys, spleen, stomach and intestines, all being placed in glass vessels.

The said objects, without preservation, were sent to the Front Epidemiological laboratory no. 291 for forensic chemical examination to detect cyanide compounds and the principal poisons . . .*

*Signatures of members of the commission follow.

FINDINGS OF THE COMMISSION

Based on the results of the post-mortem on the corpse of a German Shepherd dog and forensic chemical tests of its internal organs, the commission comes to the following conclusions:

1. The post-mortem examination did not find any injuries or pathological symptoms that could have caused the death of the dog.

2. In the mucous membrane of the palate and the tongue, pieces of a thin glass ampoule were discovered and on dissection the corpse produced a strong smell of bitter almonds. Forensic chemical tests showed cyanide compounds in the internal organs.

3. Thus, it can be stated that the death of the German Shepherd dog was the result of poisoning with a cyanide compound.

Commission:

Leading Forensic Medicine expert of the 1st Byelorussian Front Lieutenant-Colonel of the Medical Service **Shkaravsky**

Leading Pathologist of the Red Army Lieutenant-Colonel of the Medical Service **Kraevsky**

Acting Leading Pathologist of the 1st Byelorussian Front Medical Service Major **Marantz**

Army Forensic Medicine Expert of the 3rd Assault Army Medical Service Major **Boguslavsky**

Pathologist of the 3rd Assault Army Medical Service Major **Gulkievitch**

22 May, 1945

Ф. 4 ос; оп. 3; д. 36; л. 40-41
(ПОДЛИННИК)
(original)

TESTIMONY BY THE DENTIST OF HITLER AND EVA BRAUN

19 May, 1945 and 24 July, 1947

RECORD OF ADDITIONAL INTERROGATION

The prisoner Heusemann, Käthe, born in 1909 in the city of Liegnitz (Silesia), a German national, secondary education, not a member of the Party. Before the Red Army took Berlin, she worked in a dental surgery as an assistant to Professor Blaschke. Address: 39-40, Flat 1, Pariserstrasse, Berlin.

19 May, 1945

Questioning began at 01.15

"   "   finished at 06.00

Interpreter Kagan was warned of liability under Article 95 of the USSR Criminal Code.

Question: Do you confirm the evidence given by you in the interrogation of 10 May, 1945?

Answer: Yes, I completely confirm my evidence of 10 May.

Question: Specify when you worked in the dental surgery of the Reich Chancellery and what your job was.

Answer: I did not complete special dental school but from April, 1937 I had practical experience at Professor Blaschke's, in his private dental surgery in Kurfürstendamm, 213. He had been Hitler's personal dentist since 1932 and he had a dental surgery in the Reich Chancellery as well.

From December, 1944 until 20 April, 1945, I was an assistant to Professor Blaschke in the dental surgery of the Reich Chancellery.

Question: Who exactly of the leaders of the German government was treated by Professor Blaschke in the dental surgery at the Reich Chancellery?

Answer: In the dental surgery of the Reich Chancellery Professor Blaschke treated Reichschancellor **Hitler**, his lover **Braun**, Eva, Reichsminister **Goebbels**, his wife Magda Goebbels and all their six children, Reichsführer-SS **Himmler**, Reichsleiter Dr **Ley**, Reich Press Chief Dr **Dietrich** and other Reich leaders.

Question: What was your exact role in assisting Professor Blaschke in treating the leaders of the German government?

Answer: My assistance to Professor Blaschke in treating the leaders of the German Government was that I handed instruments and medicines to him during treatment. My duties also included watching Professor Blaschke's work in the mouth and promptly handing him the necessary instruments and medicines without his having to ask for them. Because of that, I knew the state of every patient's teeth very well, and those of such state leaders as Hitler, Goebbels, Himmler and others especially well.

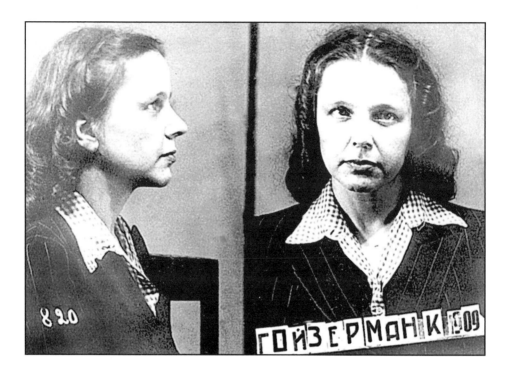

Photo of Käthe Heusemann, born 1909, from the investigation file.

On 28 August, 1951 Heusemann was arrested by USSR MGB officials on charges that 'being an assistant of Hitler's private dentist Professor Blaschke she, together with the latter, treated Hitler, Himmler and other Nazi leaders until April, 1945'. According to the statement of the Special Judicial Council attached to the USSR MGB as of 17 November, 1951 she was interned in a corrective labour camp for 10 years. In an order of the Russian Federal General Prosecutor's Office of 28 April, 1992, she was 'rehabilitated' as of 18 October, 1991, on the basis of the Russian Soviet Federal Socialist Republic Decree Concerning the Rehabilitation of the Victims of Political Repression.

Question: What kind of dental treatment was given to **Hitler**, particularly on the last occasion?

Answer: The majority of the teeth in **Hitler's** mouth were false, many of them having been fitted by Professor **Blaschke** in 1932. Since then, Professor **Blaschke** had constantly monitored the condition of **Hitler's** teeth and cared for them.

From 1944 to 1945, I assisted Professor **Blaschke** in examining **Hitler's** teeth six times, removing tartar and lubricating the gums.

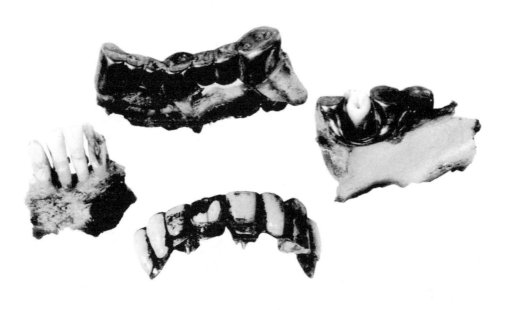

Above: parts of Hitler's jaw used for the identification of his body.

In the autumn of 1944, I participated in the extraction of **Hitler**'s sixth tooth in the left part of the upper jaw (1 molar 6). To do this, Professor Blaschke and I went to **Hitler**'s Headquarters near the city of Rastenburg (East Prussia). To extract this tooth, Professor Blaschke, using a dentist's drill, cut the gold denture between the 4th and 5th teeth in the left upper jaw while I was holding a mirror in the mouth and watching the whole procedure with great attention. Thus, in the left upper jaw, the 5th false gold tooth and the 6th natural one with a gold crown were extracted. As a result, the last tooth that remained in the left upper jaw was the 4th one.

Question: Describe the state of the teeth in Hitler's upper and lower jaw.

Answer: Hitler's upper jaw had a gold bridge which rested on the 1st left tooth with a fenestrated crown, on the root of the 2nd left tooth, on the root of the 1st right tooth and on the 3rd right tooth with a gold crown. The upper jaw had 4 teeth to the left and 5 to the right. The false teeth were made of gold with porcelain facets.

Above: Eva Braun's teeth used for identification of her body.

The lower jaw contained 14 teeth and consisted of two bridges. There were 8 teeth in the left side of the jaw and 6 teeth in the right. On the right side there were 5 natural teeth: 1st, 2nd, 3rd, 4th, 5th, and the 6th one was false, made of gold with a porcelain facet, connected by a gold bridge with the 3rd and 5th ones.

There were 8 teeth in the left side, 6 of them natural: the 1st, 2nd, 3rd, 5th, 8th and 4th, while the 6th and 7th ones were made of gold and were connected by gold bridges to the 3rd, 5th and 8th ones.

Question: Do you remember the peculiarities of the teeth and characteristics of **Hitler**'s dentures?

Answer: Yes, I clearly remember the structure of **Hitler**'s teeth and gold dentures as well as all their peculiarities.

Question: Before you are a lower jaw with gold bridges and teeth as well as a gold bridge with teeth from an upper jaw. Can you say who they belong to?

Answer: I recognise the gold bridges and teeth from upper and lower jaws shown to me because they belong to the Reichschancellor of Germany, Adolf **Hitler**.

Question: On what evidence do you base your assertion that the gold bridges and teeth presented to you are Hitler's?

Answer: I state that the gold bridges and teeth shown to me belong to Hitler on the basis of the following evidence: in the upper jaw shown to me I see a clear mark, left when the gold bridge was cut by a dental drill behind the 4th tooth. I remember this mark clearly because it was made by Professor Blaschke with my assistance to remove Hitler's 6th tooth in the autumn of 1944.

Besides there are all the peculiarities of Hitler's teeth, that I had described earlier.

Question: So, you still insist that the bridges and teeth shown to you belong to Hitler?

Answer: Yes, I say definitely once again that the gold bridges and teeth shown to me belong to Hitler.

Question: Do you know the peculiarities of the teeth of Hitler's mistress – Eva **Braun**, and what exactly they were?

Answer: Yes, the peculiarities of the teeth of Eva Braun are very well known to me, because I assisted Professor Blaschke more than once in her dental treatment. Braun was missing two teeth, the 6th and 7th, in her right lower jaw. In the summer of 1944, Professor Blaschke's technician – **Echtmann**, Fritz – made a gold and resin bridge for her, which Professor **Blaschke** fitted, with my assistance. The denture rested on a gold, cemented crown, attached to the 8th tooth to the right and on a gold clasp on the 5th tooth to the right. Besides, a month ago we extracted one tooth in the upper jaw, the 6th one on the left.

Question: Before you are a gold bridge and teeth. Can you say who they belong to?

Answer: The bridge and teeth shown to me belong to Hitler's mistress – Eva **Braun**.

Question: On what evidence do you base your statement that the gold bridge and teeth shown to you belong to Hitler's mistress – Eva Braun?

Answer: I well remember the gold bridge with teeth for the right part of the lower jaw from the 5th to the 8th teeth with false 6th and 7th teeth because I held this bridge in my hands, and washed it with alcohol before it was inserted. If the gold bridge is shown to Echtmann, who personally made it, he will obviously recognise it as the one he made for Eva Braun.

Question: What do you know about the fate of Hitler and his lover Eva Braun?

Answer: On 2 May, 1945 in the city of Berlin in the Pariserstrasse, I heard from different persons whom I knew that Hitler had shot himself and his corpse had been burnt. As for Braun, I did not hear anything about her and I know nothing about her fate.

Question: When did you last see Hitler and his lover Braun?

Answer: I saw Hitler for the last time at the beginning of April, 1945 in the Reich Chancellery, when I went there to get cigarettes.

The Record of Interrogation has been read to me in German, and is correct. This I verify by my signature.   **Heusemann.**

Interpreter of 'Smersh' CED of the 3rd Assault Army
                    Lieutenant of the Guards **Kagan**

Questioning was done by:
Chief of 'Smersh' Counter-Espionage Department of the 1st Byelorussian Front
                    Lieutenant-General A. **Vadis**

Chief of 'Smersh' Counter-Espionage Section of the 3rd Assault Army
                    Colonel **Miroshnichenko**

There also were present:
Chief of the 2nd Sub-Section of the 4th Section of the 'Smersh' Counter-Espionage Department of the 1st Byelorussian Front
                    Major **Gershgorin**

Chief of the 4th Sub-Section of 'Smersh' Counter-Espionage Section of the 3rd Assault Army
                    Major **Bystrov**

Арх. Р-41512; л. 17-24
(подлинник)
(original)

SIGNED STATEMENT OF KÄTHE HEUSEMANN

No earlier than 23 July, 1947

Description of teeth of **Hitler** and Eva **Braun**

Adolf Hitler's lower jaw

single teeth 4 2 11 2

3 – gold denture on its own root

4 – gold clasp

5 – gold crown on its own root

6, 7 – gold clasps

8 – gold crown on its own root

3 – natural tooth with gold filling inside

5 – gold crown with natural root

6 – gold bridge with porcelain facet

The 4th tooth surrounded from the inside by a gold clasp that fastened the 3rd and 5th teeth.

The upper jaw:

Gold bridge with nine intermediate links and 4 abutments.

1 – natural tooth with a fenestrated crown and porcelain filling

2 – Richmond crown with natural root and porcelain facet

3 – gold crown

4 – gold clasp with porcelain facet

5 – gold clasp

3 – gold clasp with porcelain facet

4 – gold clasp with porcelain facet

Upper jaw of Frau Braun:

In the upper jaw all natural teeth, except for the 6th.

5 – gold filling

2 1 1 2 3 – jacket crowns.

Lower jaw:

In the lower jaw all teeth natural except for 7, 6.

Gold bridge with false tooth 8, 7, 6, 5

5 – gold filling

6 – gold clasp with false tooth

8 – gold crown

Арх. Р-41512; л. 44-45

(ПОДЛИННИК)

(original)

INFORMATION ABOUT THE TEETH OF
ADOLF HITLER

24 July, 1947
Top secret

On 23 July, 1947, in the presence of German language interpreter Senior Lieutenant **Potapova** I questioned a witness – dentist **Echtmann**, Fritz, who confirmed the evidence given by him during questioning of 11 May, 1945 concerning the teeth of Eva **Braun**, as well as during additional questioning of May the same year.

Photograph of Fritz Echtmann taken from the file.

On 30 August, 1951, Echtmann was arrested by the USSR MGB officials on charges that 'as a dental technician specialist to Hitler's dentist, Blaschke, he assisted Hitler and his circle'. According to the statement of the Special Judicial Council attached to the USSR MGB as of 17 November, 1951 he was interned in a corrective labour camp for 10 years. In an order of the RF General Prosecutor's Office as of 28 April, 1992, he was 'rehabilitated' as of 18 October, 1991, on the basis of the RSFSR Decree Concerning the Rehabilitation of the Victims of Political Pepression.

Echtmann stated that he considered it necessary to supplement his statement with new facts concerning **Hitler's** teeth which were important to the investigation. Below is the statement of **Echtmann, Fritz:**

'In January, 1945, in Berlin, **Hitler's** personal dentist Professor **Blaschke** gave me several X-ray photographs of Hitler's upper and lower jaws and suggested that I make a gold bridge for **Hitler's** upper jaw.

Basing on the X-ray photographs of **Hitler's** upper jaw and other data I established that until the autumn of 1944 Hitler's upper jaw had a gold bridge, which consisted of 11 segments and links, as shown in picture no.1.

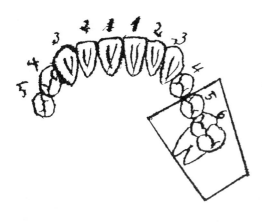

Left: Pic 1. – The cut part of the denture consisting of two links and the root of the 6th tooth, which was extracted.

Below: Pic 2. – Diagram showing normal upper jaw.

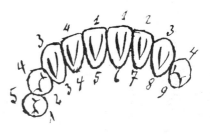

In the autumn of 1944, Professor **Blaschke** cut one part from this bridge, which consisted of two links, and extracted the root of the sixth tooth. Blaschke gave me the piece of the bridge to use as material for making gold false teeth.

Thus, as a result, in his upper jaw Hitler had a gold bridge consisting of 9 links, as shown in picture 2.

The said two links were removed from **Hitler's** mouth by cutting through the bridge with a dentist's drill. I did not make a gold bridge for **Hitler** later, as he felt that the military situation was very grave and there was no time to do it properly.

Thus, by examining the evidence, it is easy to see the drill marks on the 4th tooth, because the operation was conducted between the 4th and 5th teeth in the upper jaw.

The gold bridge, consisting of 9 links in the upper jaw, which remained in **Hitler's** mouth, was based on 3 natural tooth roots and one natural tooth, while 3 gold teeth of the bridge were fastened to 3 natural teeth by gold fasteners and one fenestrated crown of the denture was attached to a natural root. The remaining 5 gold teeth were on abutments. (see picture no. 3)

Below is a sketch of the gold bridge in the form that I wanted to make it (see picture no. 4)

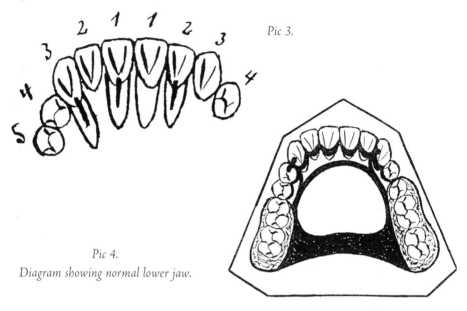

Pic 3.

Pic 4.
Diagram showing normal lower jaw.

As for Hitler's lower jaw, based on X-ray photographs I can conclude that Hitler's lower jaw had gold false teeth – one to the left, one to the right and in the middle part of the jaw there were natural teeth with the whole lower jaw having a complete set of teeth.'

Deputy Chief of Sub-Section of the 4th Section of the 3rd
General Department of the USSR MSS
Major **Vaindorf**

Interpreter of the 4th Section of the 3rd General
Department of the USSR MSS
Senior Lieutenant **Potapova**

24 July, 1947

Ф. К-1 ос; оп. 4; д. 12; л. 40-42
(ПОДЛИННИК)
(original)

INFORMATION ABOUT EVA BRAUN'S TEETH

24 July, 1947
Top secret

On 23 July, 1947 in the presence of German language interpreter Senior Lieutenant **Potapova**, I questioned a witness, – dentist **Echtmann,** Fritz, who confirmed the evidence concerning Eva Braun's teeth, given by him during questioning on 11 May, 1945 as well as during additional questioning in May the same year.

Echtmann stated that he considered it necessary to supplement his evidence with new facts important to the investigation. The following is Echtmann's statement:

'In 1941, for the first time, I made 4 porcelain jacket crowns for the upper jaw of Eva Braun, consisting of German-made "Vita" brand porcelains, as shown in picture no. 1.

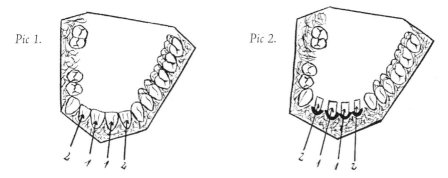

Pic 1.   *Pic 2.*

Jacket crowns were made corresponding to the shape of her own teeth, which were attached after drilling, as shown in figure no. 2.

Because Eva **Braun** was a very demanding patient, in 1943 I had to make two new jacket crowns for her and two more in mid-1944 to replace a total of four old crowns, as shown in picture no. 3.

In autumn 1944, I made a gold bridge for the right side of Eva Braun's lower jaw, connecting the 5th and 8th teeth. Between the 5th and 8th teeth, false 6th and 7th teeth made of Palopont, man-made resin, held by 2 golden half-clasps, made in such a way that they did not show. These half-clasps were soldered to a gold backplate, which connected the gold crowns on the 5th and 8th teeth, thus making a 4-link bridge. The construction of this bridge is unique, my own invention, which I made for the first and only time for Eva Braun's lower jaw. In any case in all my practice I have never seen a bridge of similar construction.

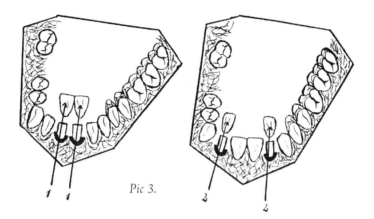

Pic 3.

The most important proof that the golden denture described by me belongs to Eva Braun is the following:

Because the space in the lower jaw between the 5th and 8th teeth was too small to insert 6th and 7th teeth of normal size, instead of a big 6th molar I had to make a small pre-molar the same size as the 5th and 4th teeth.

Crowns and bridgework on Eva Braun's jaw.

Thus, in the right lower jaw Eva **Braun** had 3 similar pre-molars of which one was artificial, made of "Palopont" (usually a person has only two).

The two crowns in the bridge last mentioned were attached to the wisdom tooth and the 5th pre-molar tooth.

At the beginning of April, 1945, Professor Blaschke asked me to make a small bridge for Eva **Braun**'s right upper jaw.

The denture consisted of a crown for the 7th tooth and one false tooth, the sixth, which Eva Braun lacked. For that, Professor Blaschke did the drilling of the 7th tooth, where the crown was to be fitted and put a fenestrated gold filling on the 5th tooth, to which the 6th artificial tooth would be fastened with a pin.

On 19 April, 1945, I called Professor **Blaschke** and told him that the small bridge was ready. He told me it would be sent to Berchtesgaden if Eva **Braun** was there.

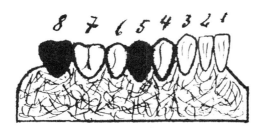

Premolars and crowns in Eva Braun's jaw.

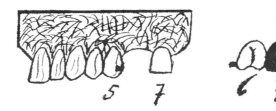

Crowns and missing tooth in Eva Braun's jaw.

On the same day, 19 April, I sent the small denture to Professor Blaschke at the Reich Chancellery.

Later, in a talk with his assistant **Heusemann** I learnt that Professor **Blaschke** had flown to Berchtesgaden on 20 April and had not fitted the small denture in Berlin.'

Deputy Chief of Sub Section of the 4th Section of the
3rd General Department of the USSR MSS
Major **Vaindorf**

Interpreter of the 4th Section of the 3rd General
Department of the USSR MSS
Senior Lieutenant **Potapova**

24 July, 1947

Ф. К-1 ос; оп. 4; д. 12; л. 35-39
(ПОДЛИННИК)
(original)

A LETTER FROM I. A. SEROV TO L. P. BERIA CONCERNING THE FATE OF HITLER AND GOEBBELS

31 May, 1945
Top secret

To the Peoples' Commissar of the Interior of the Council of SSR

Comrade BERIA L. P.

Attached to this letter I refer to you to Documents* of forensic medical examination and Reports of identification of the presumed corpses of **Hitler, Goebbels** and their wives as well as Records of Interrogation of persons close to them, along with photographic evidence.

The said documents and photographs support our assumption that **Hitler** and **Goebbels** committed suicide.

Previously we were not certain as to which of **Goebbels'** legs had a physical deformity, but now this is established from **Goebbels'** photograph where it can be clearly seen that his right leg was deformed.

Similarly, there is no doubt that the supposed corpse of **Hitler** is really his. It was possible to establish this on the basis of evidence provided by a dentist and a dental nurse who had treated **Hitler**. Their evidence was supported by forensic examination.

Besides, State Security Captain **Kuchin,** who was sent by us with a group of the Staff at the Front to the Allies, was present during the arrest of **Dönitz's** so-called 'government'.

Comrade Kuchin reported that, on the premises of the German Military Command, they discovered an original telephonogram from the Chief of the Party's Chancellery **Bormann** to Grand-Admiral **Dönitz**, in which he pronounced **Hitler's** death on 29th April of this year, and he informed **Dönitz** that **Hitler's** last will was to come into effect, and accordingly all power passed into the hands of **Dönitz** as his successor.

This telephonogram has an incoming reference number, and also the names of those who transmitted and coded it.

----

* Copies of the Documents sent to I. V. Stalin and V. M. Molotov from USSR NKVD with no. 702/b 31.V.45/

The documents included the text of Grand-Admiral **Dönitz**'s order, in which he says that under the current conditions there was no other way out for **Hitler** apart from suicide, by which he wanted to free the German leadership to conclude a cease-fire.

In this appeal, **Dönitz** calls for continued fighting for **Hitler**'s ideas, and he calls Hitler's death 'Hitler's last service to the German people'.

Enclosures: as per the text.*

I. SEROV

31 May, 1945

Decision of L. P. Beria: 'Send to Comrades Stalin and Molotov. L. Beria. 7.VI.45.'

Ф. 4 ос; оп. 3; д. 46; л. 1-2
(ПОДЛИННИК) (original)

----

*A reference to the records of the forensic examination and identification of corpses of the families of Hitler and Goebbels.

REPORT
ON THE BURIAL OF THE CORPSES OF HITLER, GOEBBELS AND OTHER PERSONS

Top Secret
4 June, 1945
the 3rd Assault Army

On 4 June, 1945, the commission including Chairman of the Commission – Chief of 'Smersh' Counter-Espionage Section of the 3rd Assault Army Colonel **Miroshnichenko** and the members of the Commission, Deputy Chief of the 'Smersh' Counter-Espionage Section of the 3rd Assault Army Colonel **Gorbushin**, Chief of the 4th Sub-Section of the 'Smersh' Counter-Espionage Section of the 3rd Assault Army Major **Bustrov**, Commander of the 5th detached company Senior Lieutenant **Gorokhov**, Commander of a platoon of the 5th detached company Senior Lieutenant **Byelobragin**, Sergeant-Major **Bakalov** and Privates **Hyretdinov** and **Teriaev**, of the 5th detached company, compiled the following report:

On 2 May, 1945, a group of officers of the 'Smersh' Counter-Espionage Section of the 3rd Assault Army in the city of Berlin, discovered in the grounds of Reich Chancellery, several metres from the emergency exit of Hitler-Goebbels' bunker, the corpses of German Reichsminister of Propaganda of Dr Josef **Goebbels** and his wife Magda **Goebbels**, and in the course of the examination of the interior of the bunker, the corpses of **Goebbels'** children were found in a bedroom: daughter Hilde, son Helmut, daughter Helga, daughter Hedda, daughter Heide and daughter Holde.

At the same time, the body of the Chief of the German General Staff General **Krebs** was found in the courtyard of the Ministry of Propaganda.

All these corpses were delivered to the 'Smersh' Counter-Espionage Section of the 3rd Assault Army in the city of Buh (Berlin).

In a further search on 5 May, 1945, several metres from the place where the corpses of Goebbels and his wife had been discovered, two badly-burnt bodies were discovered in a bomb-crater these were the corpse of the Reichschancellor of Germany Adolf **Hitler** and the corpse of his wife **Braun**, Eva. These two corpses were also taken to the 'Smersh' Counter-Espionage Section of the 3rd Assault Army – the city of Buh (Berlin).

All the bodies brought to the 'Smersh' Counter-Espionage Section of the 3rd Assault Army were subjected to the following procedures: forensic medical examination and identification by persons who knew them when alive.

After the forensic medical examination and all operations to identify them were completed, all the corpses were buried near the city of Buh.

Because of the relocation of the 'Smersh' Counter-Espionage Section of the Army, the corpses were exhumed and moved first to the region of the city of Finov, and later, on 3 June, 1945, to the region of the city of Rathenau, where they were finally buried.

The corpses were in wooden coffins in a 1.7 metre deep grave, laid out in the following order:

From east to west: **Hitler**, Eva **Braun**, **Goebbels**, Magda **Goebbels**, **Krebs** and **Goebbels**' children.

Hitler's corpse, removed from a bomb crater.

At the western end of the grave there is also a basket containing the bodies of two dogs, one of which belonged to Hitler personally and the other to **Braun,** Eva.

The location of the burnt bodies: Germany, province of Brandenburg, the vicinity of the city of Rathenau, forest to the east off the city of Rathenau, along the road from Rathenau to Schtechow, before reaching the village of Neu Friedrichsdorf, 325 metres from a railway bridge, along a forest road, from a milestone numbered 111 northeastwards 4-side marker bearing the same number 111, a distance 55 metres. From this 3rd pole due east it is a distance of 26 metres.

The grave was filled in and smoothed over and small pine trees planted on it forming the number 111.

A map with the layout is attached. The Report is compiled in three copies.

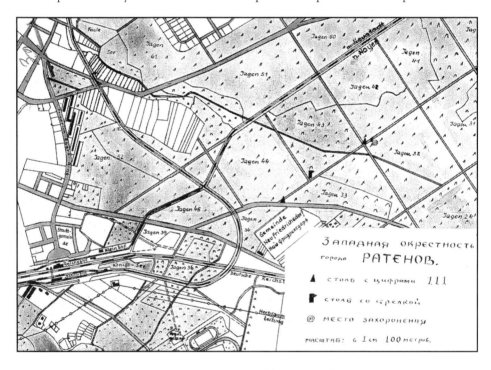

Russian map showing the site of the burial of the corpses of Hitler, Goebbels and the members of their families in the vicinity of the city of Rathenau. June, 1945

Chairman of the Commission
    Colonel **Miroshnichenko**

The members of the Commission:
    Colonel **Gorbushin**
    Major **Bustrov**
    Senior Lieutenant **Gorokhov**
    Senior Lieutenant **Byelobragin**
    Sergeant-Major **Bakalov**
    Red Army Private **Hyretdinov**
    Red Army Private **Teriaev**

Ф. К-1 ос; оп. 4; д. 9; л. 143-144
(ПОДЛИННИК)
(original)

CONCERNING THE RE-BURIAL OF THE REMAINS

21 and 23 February, 1946
Covering letter 'Smersh' CES of the 3rd Assault Army
on 23 February, 1946
Top secret
Personal
To the Chief of the 'Smersh' Counter-Espionage Department of the Group of the
Soviet Occupation Forces in Germany to Lieutenant-General
Comrade Zelenin

I enclose herewith the Report on the new location of the grave containing the corpses
of members of the German government – Hitler, Goebbels and others.

Enc. according to the text on 2 t/l
Chief of the 'Smersh' Counter-Espionage Section
of the 3rd Assault Army

Colonel **Miroshnichenko**

A piece of Hitler's skull showing a bullet hole at the back.

DOCUMENT
21 February, 1946
3rd Assault Army of the Soviet Occupation Forces in Germany

The Commission consisting of the Chairman of the Commission – Chief of the 'Smersh' Counter-Espionage Section of the 3rd Assault Army Colonel **Miroshnichenko** and the members of the Commission: Deputy Chief of the 'Smersh' Counter-Espionage Section of the 3rd Assault Army Colonel **Gorbushin**, Commandant of the 'Smersh' Section of the Army Senior Lieutenant **Bormashov**, Assistant Commander of a platoon of the 5th detached infantry company Senior Sergeant **Spiridonov** and Sergeant-Major **Ivanov** make the following statement, that on this day, according to orders of the Chief of the 'Smersh' Counter-Espionage Department of the Group of the Soviet Occupational Forces in Germany – Lieutenant-General Comrade **Zelenin**, we opened up the grave containing the corpses in the vicinity of the city of Rathenau:

of Reichschancellor of Germany Adolf **Hitler**

of his wife **Braun**, Eva

of the Minister of Propaganda of Germany – Dr Josef **Goebbels**, his wife Magda Goebbels and their children – son Helmut and daughters Hilde, Helga, Hedda, Holde and [Heide]

of the Chief of the German General Staff – General **Krebs**

Hitler's skull discovered in the Soviet archives. The bullet hole is clearly visible.

All the corpses mentioned are in a state of partial decay in wooden coffins and were delivered in this condition to the city of Magdeburg, to the headquarters of the 'Smersh' Counter-Espionage Section of the Army and again buried in a grave 2 metres deep in the yard of a building at no. 36 Westendstrasse, near the southern stone wall of the yard, 25 metres due east of the wall of the garage of the house.

The grave was filled in and smoothed over, blending in with the surrounding terrain.

Chairman of the Commission:

Colonel **Miroshnichenko**
Colonel **Gorbushin**

Members of the Commission:

Senior Lieutenant **Bormashov**
Senior Sergeant **Spiridonov**
Sergeant-Major **Ivanov**

Ф.К-1 ос; оп. 4; д. 9; л. 142-144
(ПОДЛИННИК)
(original)

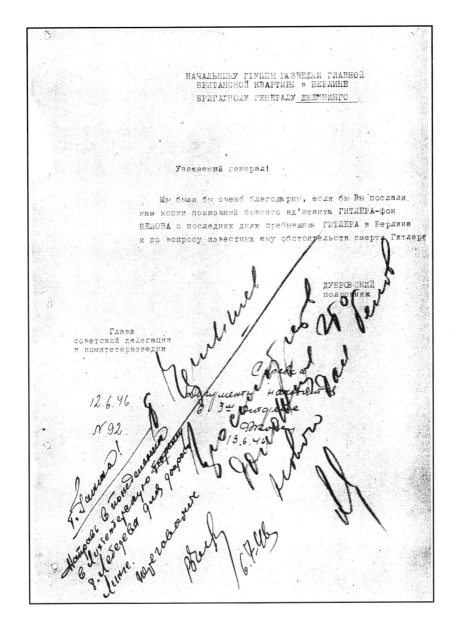

НАЧАЛЬНИКУ ГРУППЫ РАЗВЕДКИ ГЛАВНОЙ
БРИТАНСКОЙ КВАРТИРЫ в БЕРЛИНЕ
БРИГАДНОМУ ГЕНЕРАЛУ ДЖЕННИНГС

Уважаемый генерал!

Мы были бы очень благодарны, если бы Вы послали
нам копии показаний бывшего ад'ютанта ГИТЛЕРА-фон
БЕЛОВА о последних днях пребывания ГИТЛЕРА в Берлине
и по вопросу известных ему обстоятельств смерти Гитлера

ДУБРОВСКИЙ
полковник

Глава
советской делегации
в комитетеразведки

12.6.46
№ 92

*Facsimile of a letter from Colonel K. V. Dubrovsky, Deputy Chief of Operative Section NKVD
of the Group of the Soviet Troops in Germany to Brigadier-General Jennings, Chief of British
Intelligence in Berlin. It is a request to provide a copy of evidence from the former Führer's
aide-de-camp von Below about Hitler's last days in the bunker
and his knowledge of the events of his death: 12 June, 1946*

117

SECRET *Bx w 294*
29.6.46.

Berlin Military
Ext: 86-5180

Intelligence Bureau,
Adv. H.Q., Control Commission for
Germany (British Element),

Ref: CIB/Pers.

BERLIN,
B.A.O.R.

From: Brigadier M. B. Jennings, CBE.   26th June, 1946.

Dear Colonel,

        I have much pleasure in enclosing a report of
the interrogation of Von BELOW for which you asked in your
letter of the 12th June.

                        Yours sincerely,

Colonel DUBROVSKI,
Soviet Delegation Intelligence Committee.

Facsimile of the reply to the request, received on 26 June, 1946.

PART II

THE LAST DAYS OF THE DOOMED

MARTIN BORMANN'S DIARY

Chief of Hitler's Office, Deputy Führer
of the National-Socialist Party

1 January–1 May, 1945
Name and Address: M. Bormann, Obersalzberg
Berchtesgaden 2443,
or Berlin 117411

In case of accident inform: Munich 70261 or Blankenzee/Mekl. 66

Bormann, Martin, born in 1900 in Halberstadt, Germany. Reichsleiter, Hitler's personal secretary. After 30 April, 1945, he disappeared from the bunker.
In 1946, the International War Crimes Tribunal at Nuremberg tried Bormann in absentia and sentenced him to death. In April, 1973, a West German court officially proclaimed Bormann dead, on the basis of the identification of a skeleton, discovered near one of the Berlin metro stations. The Court ordered all other supposedly available evidence to be expunged and any reports of alleged meetings with a living Bormann to be ignored in future.

Hitler's General Headquarters, Adlerhorst

Monday, 1st January
Führer's dinner with Göring, Keitel, M.B. (Martin Bormann), Rundstedt, Scherf, Dönitz, Jodl, Ribbentrop, Burgdorf, Guderian and Speer.
Rudel received diamonds to add to his gold 'Knights Cross'.

Tuesday, 2nd January
Ribbentrop visiting the Führer, after that he visited M.B.

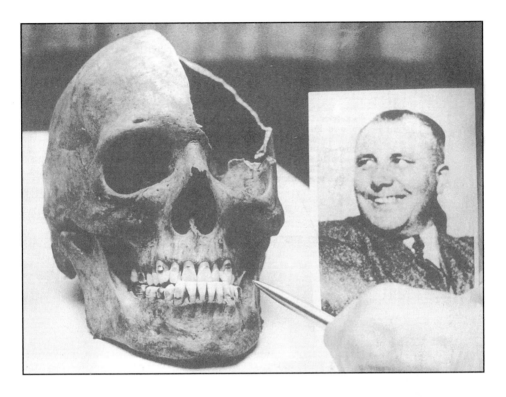

Hitler's personal secretary, Martin Bormann, pictured alongside the skull excavated near the Lehrt metro station in Berlin in 1972. The pointer indicates the fragments of glass found between the teeth, hinting at the fact that Bormann committed suicide, probably after being identified in the street while attempting to flee.

Wednesday, 3rd January

At 13.00, a meeting took place at M.B.'s with Dr Goebbels, Dr Naumann, Speer, Saur and Ganzenmüller about the problem of workers and employees of the war industries and Reich railways being called up to the Army.

After dinner there was a meeting in the Führer's quarters.

Thursday, 4th January

Speer and Saur with the Führer, after them came Ganzenmüller.

Friday, 5th January

Reichsmarschall (Göring) summoned to Hitler to discuss the problems of the war in the air. M.B. to report to Führer.

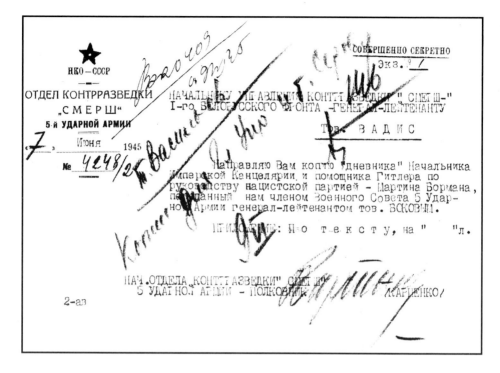

Covering letter accompanying the copy of Bormann's diary, sent on 7 June, 1945 to Lieutenant-General A. A. Vadis from 'Smersh' CES of the 5th Russian Assault Army.

Sunday, 7th January

This evening at 22.00 M.B. departed by car to Munich.

Repeated heavy air raids on Munich.

To arrive in Munich at 8 o'clock.

In the morning visited Fegelein.

Tuesday, 9th January

M.B. visited his wife and children in Obersalzberg.

Wednesday, 10th January

After dinner there was a meeting with Klopfer, Friedrichs and Hummel.

Then there was a conference with the leader of the Hitler Youth, Axmann.

Thursday, 11th January
Inspection of all mines. M.B. met H. Shenck.

Friday, 12th January
M.B. spoke to Weingart, Preiss and Dr von Hummel.
Dinner with Weingart, Josefa, Fraulein Zilberhorn, Fraulein Funk, Frl. Lazetski,
Frau Tresemer, Frl. Bauriedl, Dr Schtoll, Dr von Hummel, Mullerbuch, Post,
Schenk, Greiderer and others.

ADLERHORST

Saturday, 13th January
After dinner, M.B. was with his wife and children in Raihenhalle to inspect mushroom
farm (field mushrooms) of the gardener Volmark.
In the evening M.B. talked to Party Comrade Treisch.
In the morning, the Bolsheviks began an offensive.

Sunday, 14th January
Visit to Auntie Heschen.

Monday, 15th January
Due to the major offensive in the East – at 16.30 departure of the Führer's train
to Berlin, arrival on 16. 1. at 11.30.
M.B. must remain in Obersalzberg!

Thursday, 18th January
18.10/ 19.10 departure for Berlin.
My wife and I were with Eva Braun, Frau Fegelein and Bredow.

Friday, 19th January
Arrived in Berlin at 14.55. At noon the wife left for Stolpe.

Saturday, 20th January
At noon – the situation in the East is becoming ever more threatening. We have
abandoned the district of Wartegau. Enemy's leading tank units are near Katowice.
At night, at 22.00, wife returned from Stolpe.

BERLIN

Sunday, 21st January
At 13.00 M.B. with Terboven reports to Führer. Afterwards, meeting with Lammers. At 15.00 the Führer receives Quisling with Lammers, M.B. and Terboven. In the evening with the wife at Fegelein's.

Monday, 22nd January
At 15.00, continuation of the Führer's meeting with Terboven, Quisling, Lammers and with M.B.

Tuesday, 23rd January
Meeting at Führer's with Ribbentrop, M.B., Lammers, Keitel, Jodl, Dönitz and Reichsmarschall (Göring).

Friday, 26th January
At 4 o'clock in the morning the wife and driver Kinkel left Berlin. At 15.00 they will be in Munich, at 16.00 they will leave Munich, and at 20.00 they will be in Obersalzberg.

M.B'.s second meeting with Greiser.

Sunday, 28th January
After dinner the Führer had a conference with Quisling, Lammers, Ribbentrop and M.B.

Monday, 29th January
15.15–16.20. Seyss (Seyss-Inquart) and M.B. were at the Führer's. In the morning M.B. had a talk with von Hummel.

Tuesday, 30th January
At noon, M.B. as usual made a short report to the Führer. After dinner, Dr Naumann made a report to the Führer. In the evening – Dr Ley. At 19.15 the Führer addressed the German people.

Wednesday, 31st January
In the morning, the Russian tanks were near Grossen. They crossed the Oder between the cities of Küstrin and Wriezen.

Thursday, 1st February
In the morning M.B. had a meeting with Party Comrade Stehr. In the evening the Führer received Stehr and appointed him Gauleiter.

Friday, 2nd February
At noon, M.B. spoke to General Reinecke, and at 18.00 with Axmann, later with von Hummel.

Saturday, 3rd February
Before noon, there was a heavy air raid on Berlin (bombing damaged the new Reich Chancellery, the anteroom of Hitler's headquarters, the dining-room, the winter garden and the Party Chancellery).
Fighting for the Oder River crossing.
Bombing damaged the facade of the Party Chancellery.

Monday, 5th February
Talk with Schirach about Freisler.
At 14.45, bombing.
Air raids on the cities of Villach (4 times), Salzberg (5 times), Regensburg, Strasbourg, Traunstein, Rosenheim and others.
In the evening after M.B'.s discussion of the current situation with Lammers and Seyss at the Führer's, spoke to Goebbels.

Tuesday, 6th February
Eva Braun's birthday.
At 13.15 Dr Goebbels and Dr Lammers met M.B.
In the evening M.B. was visited by Kaltenbrunner.

Wednesday, 7th February
Führer spoke to Gauleiter Koch, Guderian and Wenck. After that he talked to Obergruppenführer Wolf.
In the evening M.B. was with the Reichsführer-SS at Fegelein's.
Discussion and dinner.
After that meeting with Eva Braun and Fegelein.

Thursday, 8th February
At noon, M.B. discussion with Count Gessler and Standartenführer Becher, then with Burgdorf about security service.
At night was invited with Gessler, Speer, Fegelein and the Führer to Eva Braun.

Friday, 9th February
Noon. Enemy's assault on the city of Weimar.
In the evening, departure of Eva Braun and Frau Fegelein.

Saturday, 10th February
Dinner at Fegelein's with Reichsführer-SS Himmler and General Burgdorf.
After dinner, talk with Himmler, later with Lammers.
Supper with Himmler, Sepp Dietrich, Berger and Fegelein.
After supper, there was a discussion.

Sunday, 11th February
In the morning, M.B. talked with Kaltenbrunner.

Monday, 12th February
The same.

Tuesday, 13th February
Together with Fegelein M.B. was at Maibach (Zossen) camp at Colonel Zitrat's.
In the late evening and at night there were heavy air raids on the centre of Dresden.

Wednesday, 14th February
At noon as usual report to the Führer.

Thursday, 15th February
At noon again an air raid on Dresden.
After dinner M.B. spoke to Hummel, Lammers, and after them with Kaltenbrunner.

Friday, 16th February
M.B. spoke to Party Comrades Friedrichs and Klopfer.

Saturday, 17th February
M.B. spoke to Ruder, Lammers and Axmann.

Sunday, 18th February
M.B.'s talk with Dr Hummel and Dr Schmidt-Remer about what they have in common.
In the evening M.B. went to Zossen.

General 'Sepp' Dietrich – a high-ranking Nazi, whose meetings with Bormann were briefly noted by Bormann in his 'historic' diary.

Monday, 19th February
With Fegelein in Zossen camp.

Tuesday, 20th February
Müller and two officers of State Security Service went to the North [to Bormann's estate in Mecklenburg].
In the morning, M.B. was at the Party Chancellery and met Friedrichs, Walkenhorst, Zander, Klopfer and Schmidt-Remer.

Wednesday, 21st February
Müller returned from the North. Talked to Müller at Zossen camp, later with Zander.
Heavy daylight air raids on Vienna, Erfurt and Nuremberg.

129

HITLER'S MAIN HEADQUARTERS

Thursday, 22nd February
At noon M.B. was at the Führer's, after dinner Forster was at the Führer's.
M.B. spoke to Dr Naumann, Ruder and Friedrichs.

Friday, 23rd February
M.B. spoke to Admiral Voss, Klopfer, Dr Stoll, Lammers.
In the evening with Backe, Rieke and with Klopfer.

Saturday, 24th February
At 14.00, reichsleiters, gauleiters, and liaison officers were at the Führer's in the Reich
Chancellery. Congratulations on the occasion of awarding of a German decoration to
Konstantin Hierl who was 70 years old on 24 February.
Dinner – speech by the Führer.
At night at Goebbels' from 20.00, invitation on the occasion of Hierl's 70th birthday.

Sunday, 25th February
Heavy daylight air raids on Linz and Munich.
In the evening Fegelein and Burgdorf to supper with M.B.

Monday, 26th February
Heavy air raid in Berlin. Second hit on the Party Chancellery (heavy).
Spoke to Obergruppenführer Steiner. Reichsminister Backe and State Secretary Rieke
were at the Führer's to report on the problem of shortages.

Tuesday, 27th February
At noon, M.B.'s meeting with Burgdorf about Gen. von Alfen. Spoke to Jenom about
Norway. At 16.30 spoke to Dr Ley. In the evening with Fegelein and Bredow.
Intensive air raids on Augsburg, Halle and Salzburg.

Wednesday, 28th February
As usual, Zander to report to the Führer about the situation.

Thursday, 1st March
After dinner, M.B. spoke to Obergruppenführer Prutzmann, in the evening with
Sepp Dietrich and Kaltenbrunner.

Friday, 2nd March

In the morning, intensive air raids on Magdeburg, Dresden, Chemnitz, Plauen and Cologne.

In the morning spoke to Party Comrades Friedrichs and Dotzler.

Saturday, 3rd March

With the Führer at headquarters of the 'Berlin' and 'Döberitz' divisions.

The Anglo-Americans are in Neuss and Krefeld.

Russians based at Kozlin and Slawa.

Sunday, 4th March

M.B. spoke to Dr Ley, Werner Lorenz, Admiral Voss and Admiral Matiss.

Again with Ley. Report to Führer. Spoke to Ruder.

In the evening with Fegelein and Burgdorf.

Deep penetrations into Pomerania. Tanks at Kolberg, Schlave and Dramburg.

In the West, only one bridgehead is left.

Monday, 5th March

In the morning, a new heavy air raid on Chemnitz.

Tuesday, 6th March

In the morning M.B. spoke to Dr von Hummel. Report to Führer, spoke to Lammers, Schmidt-Remer.

Hummel in Dresden at Frau Hammitsch.

M.B. with the Vosses at Pum.

Wednesday, 7th March

M.B. in the morning visited a sauna.

At 16.30 M.B. spoke to Dr Glassmaier and Florian.

After that M.B. spoke to Dr Naumann.

In the evening, Eva Braun took an express train to Berlin.

Thursday, 8th March

In the morning M.B. spoke to Klopfer, Friedrichs, Müller and Zander.

The British have entered Cologne!

The Russians are in Altdam!

Friday, 9th March
In the morning, spoke to Hummel, who came from Stolpe.
Führer's meeting with Kesselring, Manteuffel and Hubner.
M.B. spoke to Freiling, Zander and others.

Sunday, 10th March
M.B. spoke to Ruder, Eberlein, Hewel, Geiger.
M.B. spoke to Dönitz.
M.B. to report to Führer daily.

Sunday, 11th March
M.B. spoke to Geiger and Dr Ley.
15.50 M.B. to report to Führer.
16.00 Spoke to Lammers, Schirach and Dr Haffner, Gen. State Prosecutor in the People's Court.
In the evening M.B. at General Winter's, Bule, Colonel Polek and others in the mess.

Monday, 12th March
Noon – M.B. spoke to Schmidt-Remer, Geiger, Keitel (Bodevin, Field-Marshal's brother), Sturmbannführer Zander and Dr Tratt.

Thursday, 13th March
M.B. has daily meetings with Geiger.
With Burgdorf at the Führer's.
In the evening with Prof. Buchner at the Führer's!
At 22.00, an air raid by high-speed bombers on Berlin.
The first major damage to the Ministry of Propaganda.

Wednesday, 14th March
M.B. spoke to Ruder and Frau Forster, with Field-Marshal Keitel, Dr Pavlitsky, Müller.
In the evening spoke to Gruppenführer Frank.

Thursday, 15th March
In the morning M.B. went by Kondor plane to Salzburg (Beetz*).
Spoke to Dr Hummel.
*Ed note: name of the pilot

Friday, 16th March
M.B'.s meeting with Schenk and Bredow in Obersalzburg, with Miss Josefa.

Saturday, 17th March
Kaufman and Dönitz received by the Führer.
M.B. visits the Gutshof and Durrec mines.
Noon – visit of Frau Hanke.

Sunday, 18th March
M.B. inspects the mines and so on.

Monday, 19th March
At 17.00 M.B. goes from Salzburg via Munich to Berlin.
At 1.50 at night with Forster at Führer's until 3.30, then air raid alert.
An air raid on Hagen, Zossen at 5.30.

Tuesday, 20th March
With Fegelein in sauna.
At noon M.B. met Party Comrades Friedrichs, Schmerbeck and Geiger.

Wednesday, 21st March
M.B. to report to Führer, after that a meeting with Klopfer.

Thursday, 22nd March
At 13.00, M.B.'s meeting with Waiblinger. Spoke to Walkenhorst, Lammers, Schutte, Geiger, Prof. Blaschke.

Friday, 23rd March
M.B. spoke to Walkenhorst, Geiger, Zander and Hauptsturmführer Eckhardt.

Saturday, 24th March
Noon: the first attack from the south (Italy) on Berlin. The weather being favourable, air raid on Wesel at 3.00 in the morning. At 15.00 M.B. with Gauleiter Koch at Führer's.
M.B. met Pavliysky, Walkenhorst, Steineker, Dr Schmidt-Remer.

Sunday, 25th March
With Fegelein in sauna.
To report to the Führer with Sauckel.
Tanks at Aschaffenburg.

Monday, 26th March
Spoke to Air Force General Schumacher.
Discussions with General von Hengel.
At 17.00 a meeting with Sauckel.
Because Zander is ill, M.B. participated in situation report.

Tuesday, 27th March
In the morning a meeting with Hilgenfeld, Walkenhorst, Hummel.
Situation conference.
In the evening spoke to Bühle about transport.

Wednesday, 28th March
9.45 a meeting with Gen. Gercke about transport.
Noon – discussing the situation with Rosenberg and Walkenhorst.
Spoke to Dr Ley about 'Adolf Hitler Volunteer Corps', with Dr Kaltenbrunner
and others.
Tanks in Marburg and Gissen.

Thursday, 29th March
Leading tanks in Korbach!
Artillery shelling of Rechnitz (Styria).
The situation in the south-east is very tense.
M.B. with General Reinecke, Ley, Admiral Matiss.
Situation conference.
With Axmann in the evening. Guderian is sacked.

Friday, 30th March
M.B. talks to Grand-Admiral Dönitz.
Situation conference.
Dr Dietrich removed by Hitler.
At noon tanks at Beverungen (Weser).
At night tanks at Hersfeld.

Saturday, 31st March
M.B'.s meeting with Geiger, Muller.
Situation conference.
A telephone conversation with Frau Scholtz-Klink.
In the evening Krebs, Scherf, Bühle come to M.B.'s.

Sunday, 1st April
M.B. meeting with Party Comrades Friedrichs, Keitel and Ruckschedel.
Situation conference.
Artillery shelling of Eisenach.
Russian tanks near Weiner-Neustadt.

Monday, 2nd April
In the morning spoke to Cap. Assman.
In the evening – the enemy broke through into Thuringia near Untermasfeld,
in Herschel, Eisenach and Weimar.

Tuesday, 3rd April
A talk with Sturz and Kreisleiter Kerner.
Situation conference.

Wednesday, 4th April
M.B'.s meeting with Axmann.
Situation conference.
Spoke to Zunderman.

Thursday, 5th April
The Bolsheviks are near Vienna!
Anglo-Americans are in the Thuringian region. They are advancing at Langensalz
and Mainingen.
Spoke to Zander.

Saturday, 7th April
In the evening Krebs, Vinter, Burgdorf, Fegelein, Maisel and Wenck at M.B'.s.
Situation conference.

Sunday, 8th April

M.B.'s meeting with engineer Lesty (262).

Situation conference.

Führer's meeting with Kaufmann and Field-Marshal Busch.

Monday, 9th April

M.B.'s meeting with Friedrichs.

After dinner, the Führer met Gauleiter Hofer, with M.B., Jodl and General Winter.

In the evening – met Obergruppenführer Frank, after that there was a discussion with Hubner about Keitel.

Tuesday, 10th April

M.B. spoke to Frau Scholtz-Klink.

    " "   with Gen. Wenck.

    " "   with Walkenhorst and Hess.

    " "   with Hofer.

Wednesday, 11 April

Engagement day!

M.B. spoke to Lauterbacher and Eggeling.

Enemy's tanks at Magdeburg, Ostersleben, Hamburg, Aachen and Scharnebeck (on the Elbe).

Thursday, 12th April

M.B'.s talk with Schmidt-Remer.

Report to Führer.

Situation conference!

In the evening Kesselring was there as usual, there was a long talk.

Roosevelt died.

Friday, 13th April

M.B. spoke to Gerland, Metzner, Hilgenfeld and Walkenhorst.

Enemy tanks are near Seehausen (on the Elbe), Wittenberg, near Stendal and Tangermünde.

Enemy tanks entered the cities of Dortmund and Kettwig, Gummersbach and Arnsberg.

The enemy's tanks are near Magdeburg, Nordhausen, Claustal, Halle, Zeitz, Saalfeld and Kronach.

Saturday, 14th April
Our Krenzi D.* (birth sign).
The enemy has captured Rausformwald, Kalbe, in Garz – Guntersberg, Hohenstein, Ennstal, Kronach, Steinach, Bamberg, Wildbad and Rastatt.
In the evening, attack on Potsdam.
Deputy Gauleiter Metzner is dead.

Sunday, 15th April
M.B. spoke to Rekman.
After dinner, on the Führer's order, spoke to Eva Braun, Dr Malz and Dr Stumpfegger about the case of Professor Brandt.
Situation conference at night. (M.B. stayed in Berlin).
The enemy occupied the cities of Arnheim, Ketten, Andreasberg (in Gartz), Chemnitz, Meran, Berneck, Bayreuth and Bühl (Baden).

Monday, 16th April
The enemy occupied the cities of Leverküsen, Iserlohn, Mittweide, Crimmitshau, Weida, Schlitz, Erlangen and Offenburg (Baden).
Heavy fighting on the Oder!

Wednesday, 18th April
Heavy fighting on the Oder!
Dinner with General Krebs and Hilpert.
In the evening – arrival of Bredow.

Thursday, 19th April
Heavy fighting on the Oder!

Friday, 20th April
The Führer's birthday, but, unfortunately, the mood is not festive. The advance party was ordered to fly to Salzburg.

Saturday, 21st April
In the morning, Puttkamer and his people flew out.
After dinner, shelling of Berlin started.

*Ed. note: see page 139

Sunday, 22nd April
The Führer will stay in Berlin!
In the evening Schörner arrived in Berlin.

Tuesday, 24th April
General Weidling appointed the Commandant of Berlin.

Wednesday, 25th April
Göring expelled from the Party!
The first massive attack on Obersalzberg.
Berlin is surrounded!

Friday, 27th April
Himmler and Jodl prevent quick arrival of the divisions sent to us!
We'll fight and we'll die with our Führer – devoted unto the grave.
Others think they are acting from 'higher considerations', they sacrifice their Führer –
pah, what sons of bitches! They have lost all their honour!
Our Reich Chancellery is turning into ruins.
'The world is now hanging by a thread'.
The Allies demand our unconditional surrender – that would mean high treason!
Fegelein is disgraced – he tried to escape from Berlin in civilian clothes.

Sunday, 29th April
The second day begins with overwhelming fire. On the night of 28/29th April the
foreign press reported Himmler's surrender proposal.
Adolf Hitler and Eva Braun's wedding. Führer dictates his political and personal
testaments.
Traitors Jodl, Himmler and the Generals leave us to the Bolsheviks.
Again overwhelming fire!
According to the enemy's reports, the Americans have stormed Munich.

30.4.45
Adolf Hitler D.*
Eva H. (Hitler) ^

*Ed note: See page 139

(Theodor Bormann):
   Born 1.7.1862 D*.
   Died 8.7.1903 ^
   Bormann may have used the letter "T" (Tod).

Tuesday, 1st May
Attempt to break out from the encirclement!

The diary was translated into Russian from German by
               Senior Lieutenant **Midovkina**
               Sergeant-Major **Waitner**

Correct:
Officer of the 2nd Sec. of the 'Smersh' CED of the 5th Assault Army
Senior Lieutenant   **Zheludkov**

7 June, 1945

Ф. К-1 ос; оп. 4; д. 9; л. 146-160
(машинописная копия)
(photocopy)

*Ed. note: The sign "У" in Russian (which stands for "umerl" = died) as does the sign ^ also used by Bormann to mean death, proved by the following extract from Bormann's diary.

MANUSCRIPT EVIDENCE FROM THE HEAD OF INTELLIGENCE DEPARTMENT 'EAST'

14 April, 1945

I, **Janke**, Kurt, during my work in the German intelligence service, had the opportunity to meet the current leaders of the German government – **Hitler, Himmler, Göring, Goebbels, Ribbentrop, Hess**, and the former Chief of German Military Intelligence Admiral **Canaris**.

I consider it necessary to reveal further facts known to me concerning these persons.

ABOUT HITLER

I met **Hitler** as long ago as 1921 in Munich, when **Ludendorff** entrusted me with the task of meeting **Hitler** and finding out the nature of the National-Socialist Party, which at that time was being organised by **Hitler**.

In Munich, I first met **von Pfeffer** (later the head of the SA), whom I knew. Together we found **Hitler** in one of the cafés and asked him to tell us about the basics of National-Socialism.

Hitler delivered a lecture to both of us, accompanying it with exclamations and unnatural gesticulations. This meeting left an impression on me that Hitler was not quite normal.

Later **Pfeffer**, based on what he had heard from **Hitler**'s aide-de-camp Colonel **Schmundt**, told me that **Hitler** was often in an abnormal state. **Pfeffer** gave an example of how, when talking to Schmundt and his personal photographer Hoffmann, **Hitler** would hop about, rubbing his hands and giggling as he confidently predicted the defeat of the Russians.

Pfeffer, who had been close to Hitler earlier, told me also that he often gave way to depression, throwing himself on the floor and biting the carpet in an hysterical fit.

Hitler is not married. In 1936–37, **Goebbels** made attempts to persuade Hitler to marry the daughter of the Duke of **Mecklenburg** – a beautiful young woman. My agent **Petrow** once witnessed a visit by **Hitler** and **Goebbels** to the Duke of Mecklenburg's hunting lodge. **Petrow**, renowned as one of the best hunters in Germany, was a guest of the **Mecklenburgs**, when **Hitler** and **Goebbels** suddenly arrived, accompanied by a retinue of SS officers. Due to their arrival, all the guests, including **Petrow**, were locked up by the SS officers in two small rooms. For unknown reasons the marriage of **Hitler** and the daughter of the Duke of **Mecklenburg** never happened.

Kurt Janke's identity card, 1934.

At present, I suppose, **Hitler** is at his residence at Berchtesgaden. In September, 1944, my agent, Dr **Markus**, informed me that large quantities of ammunition and food were being taken to Berchtesgaden and stored in a special bomb-shelter. In January, 1945, the Chief of the Foreign Policy Department of the German Information Bureau **Ritten** told me that rapid construction of defensive installations was under way in the mountains of South Germany near Berchtesgaden. In answer to my questions, **Ritten** stated that the works in Berchtesgaden were kept strictly secret and he did not know any details.

Hitler's intimate circle includes his deputies in the leadership of the National-Socialist Party **Bormann**, **Goebbels**, **Himmler**, **Hoffman** and a doctor named **Mulok** [*sic*]. The latter, although he is not a good doctor, enjoys Hitler's complete confidence.

Of those who opposed **Hitler**, I am personally acquainted with Professor Ludwig **Nohe** and **Sauerbruch**. **Nohe** is a renowned shipbuilding specialist, who lived with his family in Danzig, where he was the Director of the Danzig Shipyard. During the German occupation of France, **Nohe** was the head of all shipyards on the French Atlantic coast.

Nohe, as I know, was closely connected with **Churchill** and a member of **Vansittart's** Imperial Security Council. Before the war, **Nohe** visited **Churchill** frequently as his guest, and I suppose he could have been enlisted to work for Britain or for the Soviet Union. At one time, **Heydrich** wanted to take action against **Nohe**, because **Nohe's** wife was Jewish, but after I told **Heydrich** of **Nohe's** English connections, he abandoned the idea.

Sauerbruch is a well-known German doctor who was once invited to treat the British **King George**. As early as before the war, the Abwehr and the SD tried to employ **Sauerbruch** for intelligence work against Britain but he flatly refused. **Sauerbruch**, like **Nohe**, is a staunch opponent of **Hitler** and only his international reputation has saved him from arrest in Germany.

CONCERNING GOEBBELS

Goebbels, though one of those closest to **Hitler**, in my opinion will support him only until he sees that **Hitler's** defeat is inevitable. Then he'll join **Hitler's** adversaries.

Goebbels had already made such an attempt in 1933. The then leader of the East German SA, Captain **Stennes**, heading the opposition to **Hitler** among the stormtroopers, was planning a revolt against **Hitler**. At the time, **Goebbels** had contacts with **Stennes** and tried to reach an agreement with him for joint action against **Hitler**.

Later, when **Hitler's** position improved, **Goebbels** cut his ties with **Stennes** and the latter was sent to China.

Because I was aware of **Goebbels'** attempts to ally himself with **Stennes**, **Goebbels**, being afraid of exposure, was hostile to me and tried hard to force me out of the Intelligence Service.

In his personal life, **Goebbels**, as far as I know, is an unscrupulous man. He is married, but in Berlin his intimate relations with actresses are well known. In 1939–1940 **Goebbels** had a affair with a Czech film actress, Lida **Baarova**, who got to know some highly secret information from **Goebbels** and was telling it to her acquaintances.

The Abwehr, upon receiving information of **Baarova's** knowledge of secret information, arrested her, but when it became evident that **Baarova** had received this information from Goebbels, the case was abandoned and she was expelled from Germany.

After this incident, according to what **Ritgen** told me, **Goebbels** ceased his affairs with film stars and changed to 'nurturing young talent'.

Transport pass of Dr Josef Goebbels, Reichstag Deputy 1938

CONCERNING GÖRING

In 1933, and later in 1936, I visited **Göring** in one of his Berlin palaces. This palace is furnished in oriental luxury. By the way, when I was there, **Göring's** wife (a former actress) was holding a lion cub on her lap.

Göring's private apartment was literally piled high with flowers like that of a theatrical prima donna.

Göring is ill and he constantly takes morphine. His rapid mood swings were very evident – one moment he is lively and the next sad, with his eyes absolutely dead.

Before the war, **Göring** enjoyed great influence and authority, but latterly his power waned because he failed to provide **Germany** with adequate defence against the Allied air raids.

In one of his public speeches, **Göring** once said that if a single enemy bomb were dropped on Germany, he should have been called not **Göring** but **Meier***. Since then, in Germany, **Göring** has been called **Meier**.

*Ed note: a Jewish name, hence a term of derision.

CONCERNING HIMMLER

Schellenberg, who was a close ally of Himmler, often characterised him to me as very persistent in reaching his goals, and totally loyal to Hitler. Himmler is married but his wife plays no role in public life.

CONCERNING RIBBENTROP

Ribbentrop is married to the daughter of Henkel, the famous owner of champagne vineyards. Ribbentrop lives in Hindenburg's palace, which he redecorated.

CONCERNING CANARIS

Canaris is married, with two daughters aged 18 and 19. I suppose that Canaris' wife and daughters have been arrested as family members of a participant in the conspiracy against Hitler. Canaris also has a brother, also called Canaris, a prominent industrialist.

I had very good relations with Canaris. Among ourselves we called each other by nicknames. I called him 'Kiku' and he called me 'Father Janke'. Canaris was rather critical of current events. With Hitler, he had strictly official relations. I often heard Canaris say in indignation: 'This craziness will never end'. But generally, he was very careful, and mistrustful of people. In intelligence, Canaris was an expert, choosing his agents with great care. Canaris had several of his own agents, called in the terms of the British intelligence service 'freelance hunter stringers'. These agents were in his exclusive service and were kept secret from the other agents. One such 'freelance hunter', under an appropriate cover, was sent to the country that was being targeted by the intelligence service, where he selected the most interesting figures for recruitment. After studying a candidate for recruitment, another 'freelance hunter' was sent to him to perform the recruitment. After recruitment, the recruiter handed over the new agent to the resident and ceased his own contacts with him. From Ritten, I know that during the war a number of such 'freelancers' defected to the British, which was another reason for Canaris' arrest.

I advised Canaris that when recruiting influential agents he should recruit them to work as if for some other country. In 1924, I used this kind of recruitment in my own work. Ellis, an officer of the Intelligence Service worked at the British Embassy in Vienna, in the guise of a mechanic. My agent, Petrov, became acquainted with Ellis through a Mrs. Fassner who was used by us as a contact. We knew that Ellis was in need of money, so Petrov offered him a considerable sum and so recruited him allegedly for the Japanese intelligence service. Because the Japanese intelligence service had a reputation among intelligence officers of being one of the most conspiratorial, Ellis easily agreed to be recruited.

After the outbreak of war in 1939, our connection with **Ellis** was lost, but **Petrov** hoped that **Ellis** would appear somewhere in a neutral state and it might be possible to re-establish contact with him.

Of the officers of the German intelligence service, the leading roles today are played by **Kaltenbrunner, Skorzeny, Schellenberg** and **Marwede.**

Kaltenbrunner is an SS Obergruppenführer and is Chief of the SD and the German Intelligence Service. I don't know him personally. I know that he was once a lawyer, then joined the ranks of the National-Socialist Party. **Kaltenbrunner** was an enemy of **Heydrich**, but I don't know the reason for their conflict.

SS Obersturmführer **Skorzeny** is the man who organised Mussolini's kidnapping from the British. He is a prominent officer of the German Intelligence Service and is under the direct command of **Kaltenbrunner**. In January, 1945, I visited **Schellenberg** in Berlin, from whom I heard that **Skorzeny** had contacts with Vlasov's army, but I do not know the nature of these contacts. **Skorzeny** is an Austrian, about 33–34 years old.

Schellenberg Walter – Brigadeführer and Chief of the 6th Section of the Reich General Department of Security. He now has the German intelligence department – Abwehr-1 and Abwehr-2 – under his direct command. **Schellenberg** is a member of the National-Socialist Party, but I greatly doubt his loyalty to National-Socialism. In my view he is a careerist he would serve not only the Nazis but any other political system that might be established in Germany. **Schellenberg** is married and has three children.

Marwede – a Lieutenant-Colonel, who earlier worked in Abwehr-2 performing espionage against France. For the last two years, he has been at the Russian Front spying on the Soviet forces. **Marwede** is a clever man, but of low morals, being an intriguer and a sycophant.

Kurt Janke.

Evidence received by:
Senior Investigator of the 'Smersh' General Department
Captain **Grishaev**

Translated from German by:
Task Officer of the 'Smersh' General Department
Captain **Kopeliansky**

Ф. К-1 ос; оп. 4; д. 16; л. 91-97
(ПОДЛИННИК)

THE APPEAL BY GRAND-ADMIRAL DÖNITZ

2nd SS Panzer Division 'Das Reich'

1-a
2 May, 1945

The Appeal by Grand-Admiral Dönitz
to the German people should be
brought to the notice of the Staff

It is signed on behalf of the Division Command by
the 1st officer of the General Headquarters

The Appeal
German men and women!
Soldiers of the German Army!
Our Führer, Adolf Hitler, has fallen. The German people bow their heads in deepest mourning and reverence.

He saw the terrible dangers of Bolshevism early on and he devoted all his life to the struggle against it. This struggle and his unshakeably straight path was ended by his heroic death in the capital of the Reich. Until the very end, his life was devoted to the good of Germany. His struggle against Bolshevism was for Europe and the whole civilised world.

The Führer appointed me as his successor. With full responsibility, I assume the leadership of the German people at this difficult hour that will decide our fate. My first task is to save the German people from the attacking Bolshevik enemy. The armed struggle is being continued only for this aim. And as long as the British and the Americans are preventing it we will have to continue our defence against them. In this case, the British and the Americans continue fighting, not in the interest of their own people but for the dissemination of Bolshevism in Europe. What the German people suffered during the war on the battlefield, as well as on the home front, is unmatched in history. In this trying time of need and hardship, I shall try my best to support tolerable living conditions for our heroic men, women and children. To do this I need your help. Believe me, because your path is my path. Support order and discipline in towns and villages. Each of you must perform your duties at your assigned post. In this way, we should be able to lessen the suffering that will confront all of us in the near future. If we do our best, God will not abandon us after all this suffering and sacrifice.

Signed by: Dönitz

Verified:

SS Hauptsturmführer (the signature is illegible)

Translated by:

Senior Interpreter of the Investigation Section of the 2nd General Department of the USSR Ministry of State Security

Senior Lieutenant **Shilova**

Арх. Н-21138; т. 2; л. 252
(перевод с подлинника)

---

2. SS-Panzer-Division   Div.Gef.St., 2. 5. 45   253
    "DAS REICH"
          Ia

Nachstehenden Aufruf des Grossadmirals Dönitz an das Deutsche Volk zur Bekanntgabe an die Truppe.

Für das Divisionskommando
Der 1. Generalstabsoffizier

[signature]

A u f r u f.

Deutsche Männer und Frauen,
Soldaten der-Deutschen Wehrmacht !

Unser Führer Adolf H i t l e r ist gefallen. In tiefster Trauer und Ehrfurcht verneigt sich das Deutsche Volk. Frühzeitig hat er die furchtbare Gefahr des Bolschewismus erkannt und diesem Ringen ist sein Dasein geweiht. Am Ende dieses seines Kampfes und seines unbeirrbaren geraden Lebens steht sein Heldentod in der Hauptstadt des Deutschen Reiches. Sein Leben war ein einziger Dienst für Deutschland. Sein Einsatz im Kampf gegen die bolschewistische Sturmflut galt darüber

erträgliche Lebensbedingungen zu verschaffen. Zu allem brauche ich Euere Hilfe. Schenkt mir Euer Vertrauen, dem Euer Weg ist auch mein Weg. Haltet Ordnung und Disziplin in Stadt und Land. Aufrecht tue jeder an seiner Stelle seine Pflicht. So werden wir die Leiden, die die kommende Zeit jedem Einzelnen von uns bringen wird, mildern und verhindern können. Wenn wir tun, was in unserer Kraft steht, wird auch der Herrgott nach soviel Leid und Opfer uns nicht verlassen.

gez. D ö n i t z

Part of Grand-Admiral Dönitz's appeal to the German People.

GRAND-ADMIRAL DÖNITZ'S ORDER

SS 2nd Panzer Division
Divisional Headquarters
'Das Reich' 1-a

On the occasion of the Führer's heroic death, on 2 May, all units will parade to hear the Appeal of Grand-Admiral Dönitz to the German people, the order to the troops and the Appeal of the Commander-in-Chief of Army Group Centre.

Signed for the Commander of the Division [signature]
1st Officer of the General Headquarters
Soldiers of the German Army!
Assuming command of all the armed forces of Germany, I fully intend to continue with the struggle against the Bolsheviks until all the fighting troops and the hundreds thousands of families living in the eastern regions of the Reich are saved from enslavement and annihilation.

I have to continue the fight against the British and Americans only because and insofar as they are hindering my struggle against the Bolsheviks.

The current situation demands discipline and obedience from you, who have already performed such historic deeds and who are now longing for an end to the war. Only unquestioning obedience to my orders will avoid chaos in this critical situation. Anyone who would now shirk his duty and thus betray German women and children to enslavement and death is a traitor and a coward.

The loyalty and allegiance that every one of you swore to the Führer is now due to me as his successor.

German soldiers! Fulfil your duty!
This means life or death for our people.
Signed by: **Dönitz**

Verified: SS Hauptsturmführer (the signature is illegible)
Translated by:
Task Officer of the Investigation Section of the 2nd General Department of the USSR Ministry of State Security
Senior Lieutenant **Kush**

Арх. Н-21138; т. 2; л. 252
(перевод с подлинника)

Facsimile of the order from Grand-Admiral Dönitz.

Karl Dönitz, born 16 September, 1891 in Grünau near Berlin. Despite never joining the Nazi party, he attained the high rank of Grand Admiral and later became Commander-in-Chief of the German navy. He also served as president of Germany for twenty days following Adolf Hitler's suicide. Arraigned as a war criminal at Nuremburg, he was sentenced to ten years imprisonment for war crimes. Dönitz's memoirs, entitled 'Ten Years and Twenty Days', were published in 1958 and a second volume covering his early years 'My Ever-Changing Life' in 1968. Dönitz died on 24 December, 1980 in Aumühle.

THE APPEAL BY FIELD-MARSHAL SCHÖRNER

2nd SS Panzer Division 'Das Reich' Divisional Headquarters 1-a
2 May, 1945

This Appeal by the Commander of the 'Centre' Army Group is intended for information and for being taken into consideration by the staff of the Unit.

Signed for the Commander of the Division

1st Headquarters officer Schiller

Soldiers of 'Centre' German Army Group!

As a martyr for his ideas and his faith, Adolf Hitler died as a soldier of European civilisation, fighting against Bolshevism until his last breath.

His cause and his mission are a sacred legacy for our descendants.

It is the duty of all of us, who are still alive, to continue with the fight, following his will and accomplishing his mission.

The fight for the freedom and future of Germany continues.

Grand-Admiral Dönitz has taken over the leadership of the German people and the command of the German Army.

Let us unite around him, let us be obedient and loyal to him!

We know that after this bloody battle, the survival of our people will be ensured.

The heroic death of our Führer is the best example for us.

Let everyone prove by his deeds that he can live up to the example of our Führer, who died in battle.

Heil Adolf Hitler!

Signed by:

Schörner, Field-Marshal General

Verified:

SS Hauptsturmführer (the signature is illegible)

Translated by:

Task Officer of the Investigation Section of the 2nd General Department of the USSR Ministry of State Security

Senior Lieutenant **Kush**

Арх. Н-21138; т. 2; л. 218
(перевод с подлинника)

2. SS-Panzer-Division   Div.Gef.St., 2. 5. 45   **219**
   "DAS REICH"
      Ia

   Nachstehenden Aufruf des O.B. der Heeresgruppe Mitte
zur Kenntnisnahme und Bekanntgabe an die Truppe.

                  Für das Divisionskommando
                  Der 1. Generalstabsoffizier

        A b s c h r i f t.

       Soldaten der Heeresgruppe Mitte !
    Als Märtyrer seiner Idee und seines Glaubens und als
Soldat der europäischen Sendung ist Adolf Hitler bis zum
letzten Atemzug gegen den Bolschewismus kämpfend gefallen.
    Sein Werk und seine Mission werden den kommenden Ge-
schlechtern heiliges Vermächtnis sein. Wir Lebenden haben
die Pflicht, in seinem Sinne weiterzukämpfen und sein Werk
zu vollenden. Der Kampf um Deutschlands Freiheit und Zukunft
geht weiter. Grossadmiral D ö n i t z hat den Befehl über
das Deutsche Volk und die Deutsche Wehrmacht übernommen.
Treu und gehorsam scharen wir uns in dieser Stunde um ihn.
Wir wissen, dass am Ende dieses blutigen Ringens das Leben
unseres Volkes dennoch gesichert sein wird. Der Heldentod
des Führers ist für jeden anständigen Soldaten höchste Ver-
pflichtung. Jeder setze sich so ein, dass er vor seinem gefalle-
nen Führer bestehen kann.

               Heil A d o l f H i t l e r

                 gez. S c h ö r n e r
                 Generalfeldmarschall

F. d. R. :

SS-Hauptsturmführer

Facsimile of the appeal to the troops by Field-Marshal Schörner

151

RECORD OF INTERROGATION OF FÜHRER HEADQUARTERS LIAISON OFFICER VICE-ADMIRAL HANS-ERICH VOSS

6 May, 1945

I, Deputy Commander of the 1st Sub-Section of the 4th Section of 'Smersh' Counter-Espionage Department of the 1st Byelorussian Front – Major **Bandasov**, through interpreter Sergeant **Gorielik**, questioned a prisoner-of-war, Vice-Admiral Voss, Hans-Erich, born in 1897 in the town of Argemunde, province of Brandenburg, living in the city of Berlin-Dalhem, Bieterstrasse 14-17, a German national, education secondary, vocational – finished naval college in 1917 in the town of Murvek, graduated from military anti-aircraft artillery college in 1923 in the town of Wilhelmshaven, attended the Naval Officers School in 1934, married, naval liaison officer to Hitler's headquarters with the rank of Vice-Admiral.

Interrogation started at 11.20 on 6 May, 1945.

Interpreter **Gorielik** was warned of liability for incorrect translation under Article 95 of the USSR Criminal Code.

Question: Do you know the Reichsminister of Propaganda, Dr **Goebbels**?

Answer: Yes, I know the German Reichsminister of Propaganda Dr **Goebbels**, Josef very well.

Lately **Goebbels**, in addition to the post of Reichsminister of Propaganda, held the post of Defence Commissioner of Berlin, that of Berlin Party Leader (Gauleiter) and the post of Reichschancellor.

Question: When and under what circumstances did you meet **Goebbels**?

Answer: In the summer of 1942, when I was commander of the heavy cruiser *Prinz Eugen*, my ship was visited by Dr **Goebbels** as a representative of the top Party and government circles, along with journalists who were there to acquaint themselves with the life and actions of the crew, to write up the crew in the press as the crew of one of the best ships. During this visit I had the opportunity to become personally acquainted with **Goebbels**.

Question: What kind of relationship existed between you and **Goebbels**?

Answer: After the said meeting on board my ship in the summer of 1942, I did not meet **Goebbels** again until I was appointed naval liaison officer to Hitler's headquarters in March, 1943.

After my arrival in Berlin from my ship, I often met **Goebbels** at the Headquarters. He knew me as one of the best battleship commanders and invited me to the Ministry of Propaganda where we had discussions on a variety of civil as well as military matters.

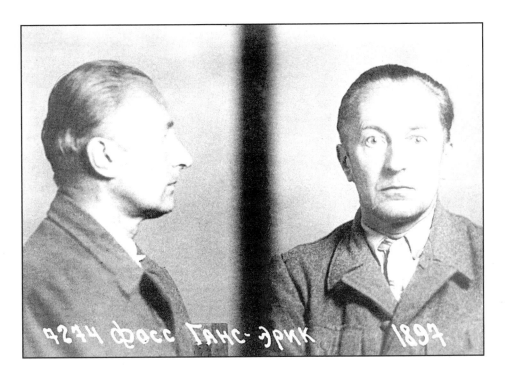

*Photograph of Hans-Erich Voss, taken from his file. The caption reads
'9274 Foss Hans Erich [born] 1897'.*

On 10 August, 1951 the MGB USSR officials arrested Voss on charges that 'he held a command
post in Hitler's war fleet, that was involved in an aggressive war in breach of international laws
and treaties'. By the decision of a Court Martial of the Moscow Military District of 16 February,
1952 he was sentenced to 25 years' imprisonment. Based on the Decree of the Praesidium of the
USSR Supreme Council of 22 December, 1954, he was released early and handed over to the
GDR authorities. Died on 18 November 1969 in Berchtesgarden.

During my time at the Headquarters in East Prussia, I met **Goebbels** less often, these
meetings being more by chance and only semi-official.

In February this year, Headquarters moved to Berlin and, in the same month, **Goebbels**
with his wife were invited by Grand-Admiral **Dönitz** to his residence for a house party.

No one was present at the party except **Goebbels**, his wife, myself and **Dönitz** with
his wife. No political or military questions were discussed.

Correction: at the party **Goebbels**, **Dönitz** and I discussed whether the defence of
Berlin could be organised and in what way.

We spoke of the necessity of building stronger street fortifications and involving youths from the Volkssturm to a greater extent in the defence of the city, but all these questions were touched upon only fleetingly and superficially.

I have been personally acquainted with **Goebbels'** wife since February, 1945. My relationship with **Goebbels** and his wife became especially close from approximately 7 April, 1945 when Hitler's Headquarters moved to the bunker under the Reich Chancellery.

Question: Were all of Hitler's Headquarters in this shelter or only part of them?

Answer: The bunker under the building of the Reich Chancellery contained **Hitler** with his wife Eva **Braun**, **Goebbels** with his family, the Deputy Chief of the General Staff General **Krebs**, Hitler's Chief aide-de-camp General **Burgdorf**, Reichsleiter **Bormann**, the Foreign Ministry representative **Hewel**, the Deputy Reich Press Chief (I don't know his name) and I – **Voss**. Along with those named there were technical personnel and domestic staff.

As for the Headquarters, at the beginning of the Soviet offensive, it was situated in Berlin's Dahlem district. Later it was moved to the Zossen district and then, in view of the danger of Berlin being surrounded, it moved to the city of Chemnitz. I have no information as to where the Headquarters are now.

Question: How did your close relations with **Goebbels** and his wife manifest themselves during your stay in the bunker?

Answer: In the bunker, I had the most intimate contact with both **Goebbels** and his wife. **Goebbels** often talked to me about the trying situation that had arisen for Germany and for us personally, but he wouldn't entertain the idea of our surrender to the Soviets, saying: '*I was the Reichsminister of Propaganda and led the fiercest propaganda activity against the Soviet Union, for which they would never pardon me*'. He couldn't escape also because he was Berlin's Defence Commissioner and he considered it would be disgraceful for him to abandon his post.

Goebbels' wife treated me as a close confidante. She also saw that there was no way out of the situation and often lamented that there was no hope of survival for herself, her husband and their children and obviously they would have to die.

Question: What do you know about **Goebbels'** personal life and his family?

Answer: I know the following about **Goebbels'** personal life and his family:

His family consists of 9 persons – himself, his wife (her first name and surname I do not know) and 7 children, 6 of them (1 boy and 5 girls aged from 3 to 13 years old) his own, and the 7th – Harold, 19–20 years old – is not his own son, but from his wife's first marriage. Harold serves as a private in the German army. Goebbels got on very well with his family.

One of the many photographs of Goebbels addressing the troops.

Question: Describe **Goebbels** and his wife.

Answer: **Goebbels**, Josef is about 48 years old, of medium height, slim, oval face, high forehead, black hair combed back, the right leg slightly shorter than the left, and crooked. He was lame in the right leg and wore specially-made boots.

His wife (I don't know her first name and surname) is about 40–43, of medium height, slim, a very beautiful blonde, blue eyes, nice figure, looks very young, has no particular distinguishing features. I don't know her relatives.

Question: How do you explain **Goebbels'** failure to evacuate his family from Berlin?

Answer: **Goebbels**, being the Minister of Propaganda and NSDAP Gauleiter of Berlin, in his broadcasts repeatedly encouraged the citizens not to lose heart, and to stay at their posts until the end. To show that the German government adamantly believed in our victory he spoke of his family which he had not and would not evacuate from the city.

Question: Was **Goebbels'** wife a member of the NSDAP and what position did she hold?

Answer: **Goebbels'** wife was a member of the NSDAP, but I do not know what position she held in the Party.

Question: When and under what circumstances did you last see **Goebbels** and his wife?

Answer: The last time I saw **Goebbels** and his wife was on 1 May, 1945 at approximately 20.00 hours under the following circumstances:

The commander of the Reich Chancellery guard and Hitler's personal bodyguard, SS Brigadeführer **Mohnke**, who was responsible for the defence of the Reich Chancellery, seeing that further resistance was senseless, on the orders of the Berlin Commandant assembled what was left of his troops, about 500 men. He was joined by the remaining officers in an attempt to break out of the encirclement.

All these people were gathered near shelter No 3 under the Reich Chancellery.

Before the breakout began, about 10 generals and officers, including myself, went down individually to **Goebbels'** shelter to say goodbye.

While saying goodbye I asked **Goebbels** to join us. But he replied: '*The captain must not leave his sinking ship. I have thought about it all and decided to stay here. I have nowhere to go because with little children I will not be able to make it, especially with a leg like mine. I shall only be a burden to you. I'll stay here until the end*'. Then I said goodbye to his wife, who was in the next room. In parting, she said to me: '*We are tied to the children, with whom we couldn't go anywhere*'.

At that, I left the **Goebbels** family and I never saw them again.

Question: How were **Goebbels** and his wife dressed at your last meeting with them?

Answer: **Goebbels** was dressed as always in Party uniform – black trousers, shoes, brown jacket, the shirt and tie of the same colour, without a cap. His wife wore a dark blue dress.

Question: What was **Goebbels**' reaction to **Hitler**'s death?

Answer: When **Goebbels** learnt that **Hitler** had committed suicide, he was very depressed and said: *'It is a great pity that such a man is not with us any longer. But there is nothing to be done. For us, everything is lost now and the only way out left for us is the one which Hitler chose. I shall follow his example'.*

Question: Who was **Hitler**'s personal doctor during the final days?

Answer: Standartenführer **Stumpfegger** was Hitler's personal doctor from November, 1944 to the end.

Question: Where was he at the moment of **Hitler**'s death?

Answer: At the moment of Hitler's death **Stumpfegger** was in the bunker, but I don't know if he was at **Hitler**'s side. After **Hitler**'s death I met him but we did not discuss the death.

Question: Where is **Stumpfegger** now?

Answer: He participated in the breakout with the survivors of **Mohnke**'s brigade, but the attempt failed and I don't know where he is.

Interrogation suspended at 4.00 on 7 May, 1945.

The Record was read to me in German: it is written down correctly.

Voss

Questioned by:
Deputy Commander of the 1st Sub-Section of the 4th Section of 'Smersh'
Counter-Espionage Department of the 1st Byelorussian Front
Major **Bandasov**

German language interpreter – Sergeant **Gorielik**

Арх. Н-21134; л. 19-24 об.
(ПОДЛИННИК)

RECORD OF INTERROGATION OF
PROFESSOR KARL VON AIKEN

Mid-May, 1945
Ninth Day of Army in the field

I, Chief of military unit 44400-YA Colonel Miroshnichenko, on this day questioned as a witness Professor von **Aiken**, Karl, born in 1873 in the town of Mulheim in the Ruhr, university education, a German national, not a Party member. Director of the Berlin Central Clinic of Otolaryngology. Lives in Berlin-Dahlem, Schweinfurtstrasse, 17.

Professor **Aiken** was warned of liability for committing perjury. **Aiken.**

Question: How long have you worked at the Berlin Central Clinic?

Answer: I have worked uninterruptedly at the Berlin Central Clinic of Otolaryngology since 1922.

Question: Did you provide medical treatment to members of the German government?

Answer: Yes, I was allowed into the Reich Chancellery and as a professor, I frequently provided medical treatment to members of the German government.

Question: Which German government leaders did you actually treat and what was the nature of that treatment?

Answer: I frequently provided medical treatment to the following leading figures in the German government:

1. I treated Reichsmarschall Göring's throat from the end of July, 1944 until September, 1944.

2. In May, 1935, I operated on Reichschancellor Hitler's throat for ablated polyps. I again provided medical treatment to Hitler between July and December, 1944, after the attempt on his life on 20 July, 1944 when a bomb explosion caused a rupture of the tympanic membranes and significant loss of hearing. I did not operate on his ears because Hitler's hearing began to recover, so I only monitored his progress.

In the same period, I treated Hitler for follicular tonsillitis. Later, as an after-effect of the follicular tonsillitis, a polyp again formed in his throat. I removed this polyp in November, 1944. Six weeks after the operation, on 30 December, 1944 I again visited Hitler to check the state of his throat after the operation.

Question: What other medical treatment did you provide to Hitler?

Answer: No other medical treatment was provided by me to Hitler and after 30 December, 1944, I did not meet him again.

Question: Can you name other doctors who provided medical treatment to Hitler?

Answer: Hitler received medical treatment from Professor Morell, who was his personal physician and was based at the Reich Chancellery. The dentist who treated

Hitler was a dentist of the Reich Chancellery, whose name I don't know. He also worked at the Reich Chancellery.

This doctor's name should be known to Professor Steiner – a deputy director of the Dental Department of Charité Polyclinic.

Question: Did Hitler have any physical defects?

Answer: While operating on his throat and treating his follicular tonsillitis, I noticed that the majority of the teeth in both Hitler's upper and lower jaws were false, but without a removable bridge. As I recall, some of the false teeth were gold and others were natural tooth colour. I do not know of any other of Hitler's distinguishing physical deformities.

The record is correctly transcribed, translated for me from Russian into German. signature of von Aiken.

Questioned by:

Chief of military unit 44400-YA

Colonel **Miroshnichenko**

Deputy Chief of military unit 44400-YA

Colonel **Gorbushin**

Interpreter of military unit 44400-ß

Ф.К-1 ос; оп. 4; пор. 7; л. 60-61 об.
(ПОДЛИННИК)

MANUSCRIPT STATEMENT BY HITLER'S AIDE-DE-CAMP OTTO GÜNSCHE

17 May, 1945

At 10.00 on 22 April, 1945, in my flat at 17, Hermann-Göring-Strasse, Berlin, I was awoken by a loud explosion. At first I thought that a bomb had exploded nearby, but later I found out that it was an artillery shell. I got dressed and took the shortest route to get to the Führer Adolf **Hitler**'s concrete bunker. There, I found many officers of the SS Guard Command, the Reich Security Command, the Führer's kitchen staff, and so on.

They were loudly discussing the fact that the first artillery shells had fallen on Berlin itself. I quickly went to the lobby near the Führer's living-room, where I met General **Burgdorf**, Gruppenführer **Schaub**, the Führer's adjutant, Colonel von **Below**, Major **Johannmeier**, and another of the Führer's adjutants, Gruppenführer Albert **Bormann**.

These people were also discussing the shelling of Berlin. At 12.30, the Führer emerged from his room and inquired about the calibre of the shells landing in Berlin. Then I listened to a report of Major **Johannmeier** on the situation on the Eastern Front. At 14.30, the Führer lunched with his wife (née Eva **Braun**). At 16.30, there were several lengthy situation reports. Grand-Admiral **Dönitz**, Field-Marshal **Keitel**, General **Model**, General **Krebs**, General **Burgdorf** and Luftwaffe General **Kolbe** took part in the discussion that followed. The main focus of this discussion was the situation in the vicinity of Berlin and the 'Vistula' Army Group. The Führer intended the 9th Army to attack in a north-westerly direction and for an SS Army Group, under General **Steiner**, to attack southwards; through these offensives, he wanted to repel what he considered to be the weak Russian forces, enabling our main forces to reach Berlin and thus to set up a new front line. This new front line would then have been deployed approximately as follows: from Stettin in the north, along the River Oder to Frankfurt-on-the-Oder and then turning west through Furstenwalde, Zossen and Treuenbritzen to the Elbe.

The following preconditions were necessary for this:
1) The line on the lower Oder had to be held.
2) The Americans had to be kept on the west bank of the Elbe.
3) The left flank of the 9th Army, on the Oder, had to hold.

Otto Günsche, *born on 24 September, 1917 in Jena, SS Major who became Hitler's Personal Adjutant from 1944. Captured and imprisoned by the Soviets until 1956 when he was handed over to the GDR authorities, became a successful businessman and died of heart failure on 2 October, 2003.*

Otto Günsche's soldier's book.

After Chief-of-Staff General **Krebs** reported that the Russians had broken through the front line south of Stettin in great force, it should have been obvious to the Führer that his planned new front could not be set up and he expressed an opinion that consequently Mecklenburg would also be besieged by the Russian forces in a few days. Nevertheless, the 9th and the 12th Armies, as well as Steiner's army group, were given orders to attack in the direction of Berlin. At the time, some of the leading officers in the Headquarters advised the Führer to leave Berlin. The Führer replied that he did not think of leaving at all and in any case he would stay in the city, saying: *'If Berlin is fated to fall, before it happens I'll shoot myself'*.

Upon hearing the situation report, the Führer summoned Dr **Goebbels** and when the latter came he had a long talk with him. After some time, **Goebbels'** wife also entered the Führer's room.

During the final days, the enemy shelling intensified. Grand-Admiral **Dönitz** and his Staff, the Chief-of-Staff of the Armed Forces, Supreme Command Field-Marshal **Keitel**, the Chief of the Department of Operative Combat Planning, Colonel **Model** and his staff, as well as Luftwaffe Chief-of-Staff General **Koller** and his staff, left Berlin and were to go to any part of Germany not occupied by the enemy. Their actual destinations are not known to me.

Those reporting on the situation were:

General **Krebs** – the Army Chief-of-Staff,

General **Burgdorf** – the Führer's senior aide-de-camp from the Armed Forces,

Reichsminister Dr **Goebbels**,

Reichsleiter **Bormann** – Chief of the Nazi Party Chancellery,

The former Commandant of Berlin (I have forgotten his name),

Colonel von **Below** – Air Force adjutant,

Major **Johannmeier** – senior Army adjutant

Sturmbannführer **Günsche** – SS adjutant.

On 26 April, 1945, the last telephone lines connecting the city with the outside world were cut. Communication was only possible by radio. But because of the constant artillery fire, the antennas were damaged, are to be precise, they were completely out of action. Reports of the movements or progress of the offensive of the three armies mentioned above were very scarce, and often reached Berlin by roundabout routes. On 28 April, 1945, Field-Marshal Keitel reported the following by radio:

1) The attack by the 9th and 12th Armies petered out due to strong Russian counter-attacks, and any further attack is impossible.

2) SS General Steiner's army group has still not arrived.

After that, it became clear to everyone at Headquarters that this sealed the fate of Berlin. On 27 April, 1945, SS Gruppenführer **Fegelein**, the Reichsführer-SS's liaison officer, left the Führer's Headquarters, i.e. the bunker, without permission. He was found in his flat in civilian clothes and arrested. It was proved that he wanted to flee Berlin disguised as a civilian. On the evening of 28 April, 1945, he was sentenced to death by court-martial and shot.

As early as 22 April, 1945, the Führer ordered me to form a combat group from the guard battalions and the remaining personnel of the defunct SS units. SS-Brigadeführer **Mohnke** was to command this group in the government district. The command post of the combat group was set up in the concrete bomb-shelter of the Reich Chancellery. The task of the combat group was to guard and defend the government district. Brigadeführer **Mohnke** assumed his duties in the evening of 22 April, 1945 and from that day on he attended the situation conferences.

On the night of 28 April, 1945, the Führer dictated his last testament to his secretaries, Christian and Junge. This was typed up in three or four copies. Its contents are known only to Reichsleiter **Bormann** and, of course, to those who typed it. On the morning of 29 April, 1945, copies were entrusted to Major **Johannmeier**, who was to take them to Field-Marshal **Schörner**, commander of 'Centre' Army Group, to Oberreichsleiter **Lorenz** who was to take one to Gauleiter **Giesler** in Munich, and to **Zander**, who was to convey his copy to Grand-Admiral **Dönitz** or Field-Marshal **Kesselring**. **Bormann** ordered these men to change into civilian clothes and escape through the Russian lines.

Colonel von **Below** was similarly tasked to get through the Russian lines and contact the commander of the 12th Army, General **Wenck**. What orders he was carrying I do not know.

Later, we learnt that the Führer had married Eva **Braun**, whom he had known for a long time, on the night of 28/29 April, 1945. On 29 April, 1945, everything was calm in the Führer's bunker. When Russian armoured troops had advanced as far as the Anhalt and Königsplatz railway stations, the Führer was anxious to lose no time in committing suicide. As far as I am concerned, I believe that the Führer took the decision to kill himself on that day because only a few hours were left before the Russian tanks reached the bunker. In the evening, General **Weidling**, the Defence Commander of Berlin, came to the bunker and told the Führer that the situation in the city was hopeless, and that the civilian population, in particular, was in a very bad state. He suggested that the Führer break out of the city with him and the surviving garrison, but the Führer categorically refused. On the evening of 29 April, 1945 the Führer ordered that his dog be poisoned. I believe this was done to test the poison – potassium cyanide. The dog was poisoned by Sergeant-Major **Tornow**, who looked after the Führer's dogs, and he reported that death was instantaneous.

At 3.00 in the morning of 30 April, 1945, I went to my concrete shelter under the Reich Chancellery and went to bed. I left orders to be woken at 10.00. When I woke up, I went for breakfast in the officers' mess in the Führer's bunker, which was next to the Führer's living-room. There I met Reichsleiter **Bormann**, General **Krebs** and General **Burgdorf**. They were discussing the situation in Berlin. I was with them for some time, then I left. When I returned to this room around 12.00–13.00, the three of them were still there in a highly emotional state, and from what they said I understood that the Führer had said goodbye to them. Then they left the room and I was left alone there. After some time, the Commander of the Reich Security Service Gruppenführer and Police Lieutenant-General **Rattenhuber** and the Führer's pilot Gruppenführer and

Police Lieutenant-General **Baur** came in. A little later, the Führer entered the room and said: '*After my death, my corpse must be burnt for I don't want my corpse to be exposed for show later, for an exhibition*'. After that he looked at us steadily and then returned to his room. I went to Major-General **Mohnke** and told him that **Hitler** now intended to take his own life.

At 14.30, I again went into the lobby, and then to the conference room and met Reichsleiter **Bormann**, Dr **Goebbels**, General **Krebs**, General **Burgdorf** and Reich Youth Leader **Axmann**, who in my absence had also arrived at the Führer's bunker. They talked about the Führer's saying goodbye and were in a very agitated state.

At 15.15, I left this room and in another met the Chief of the Führer's SS Guard Sturmbannführer **Schedle** and the Führer's driver Obersturmbannführer **Kempka**. I told them what the Führer had said to me, **Rattenhuber** and **Baur**. After that, we remained in the same room for some time. Suddenly, the door to the lobby half-opened and I heard the Führer's butler, Sturmbannführer **Linge**, say; '*The Führer is dead*'. Though I had not heard a shot, I immediately went through the lobby to the conference room and told the leaders who were gathered there exactly this: '*The Führer is dead*'. They got up and came out with me to the lobby and there we saw two bodies being carried out; one of them was wrapped in a blanket, the other was also wrapped in a blanket but not completely covered. The corpses were carried by Sturmbannführer **Linge**, Hauptscharführer **Kruge**, Obersturmführer **Lindloff** and another SS officer whom I did not recognise. Then Obersturmbannführer **Kempka** and Sturmbannführer **Medle** joined them. From one of the blankets, the Führer's legs were visible. I recognised them by the boots and socks he always wore; out of the other blanket protruded the feet and head of the Führer's wife.

Both corpses were carried out through the emergency exit of the Führer's bunker to the garden. There they were doused with petrol prepared beforehand by Reichsleiter **Bormann** and set alight. That happened at 16.00. Both corpses were accompanied by Reichsleiter **Bormann**, General **Burgdorf**, General **Krebs**, Reich Youth Leader **Axmann**, Dr **Goebbels** and myself. Then I helped to carry the body of the Führer's wife away from the door to the bunker. I am not sure if **Rattenhuber** and **Baur** were present, but it is quite possible that they were there because it was very crowded on the staircase and rather dark.

After the petrol-soaked corpses were set alight, the door to the shelter was closed because of the fierce fire and fumes.

After that, all who were present went to the front room, and from there Dr **Goebbels**, Reichsleiter **Bormann**, General **Burgdorf**, General **Krebs**, Reich Youth Leader **Axmann** and later State Secretary Dr **Naumann** went into the conference room.

A Plan of Hitler's Bunker:

1–4. Diet kitchen.

5–6. Storage rooms.

7–8. Servants' quarters.

9–12. Rooms of Frau Goebbels and her children.

13. Electrical switchboard.

14. Toilets.

15. Private bathroom.

16. Eva Braun's bathroom.

17. Eva Braun's bedroom and living-room.

18. Hitler's study.

19. Lobby to Hitler's flat.

20. Hitler's bedroom.

21. 'Card room' or small conference room.

22. 'The Dog Bunker' or guardroom.

23. Power plant (diesel room).

24. Telephone exchange and guardroom.

25. Emergency telephone switchboard.

26. Sitting room.

27. Goebbels' bedroom (formerly Morell's).

28–29. Stumpfegger's rooms.

30. Lobby and cloakroom.

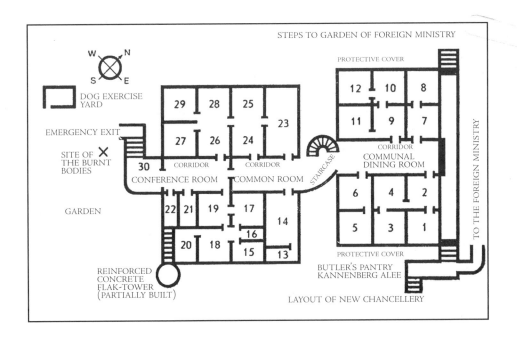

165

The door to the Führer's private room was open and one could smell a very strong smell of almonds (cyanide) coming from there. I looked inside but did not go in, and I then returned to the conference room. SS General **Mohnke** was already there. They discussed the current situation and the Führer's order that after his death they should immediately escape from Berlin in small groups. I heard that Reichsleiter **Bormann** wanted to try to reach Grand-Admiral **Dönitz** by any means, so as to inform him about the Führer's last ideas stated before his death. I don't know what ideas he meant. After that, I again left the room and went next door to have a little rest. Then General **Mohnke** came to me and said that, according to what the Führer had said, now that he was gone, only co-operation with Russia could even partially save Germany. General **Krebs** was ordered to open negotiations with the Russian General **Zhukov** for a cease-fire. Thus, the breakout by the Berlin garrison was postponed. Then I returned to my room and after that went to one of General **Mohnke's** combat groups.

During the night, I learnt that General **Krebs'** terms had been rejected, and on the night of 1 May, 1945 the Berlin garrison was ordered to break out. I was to head north, with **Mohnke's** group and the Führer's secretaries, Frau **Christian** and Frau **Junge**, his diet cook Fraulein **Manzialy** and Reichsleiter **Bormann's** secretary Fraulein **Krüger**.

At 22.00, the breakout began. Our group reached the vicinity of the Wedding railway station without loss, but there we met enemy resistance. After regrouping, we reached the Schultheiss brewery near Monhauseralde railway station by midday on 2 May, 1945.

Among the soldiers who were there, rumours were circulating that Berlin had capitulated and one could see that they were demoralised.

After that, the four women who were with us were dismissed by General **Mohnke** and they immediately left the brewery. I do not know where they went. At 18.00 that evening, General **Mohnke**, the newly-arrived General **Rauch** and his orderly and I went with a Russian interpreter to the commander of one of Russian Corps. Upon our return to the Schultheiss brewery, I was captured as a prisoner-of-war.

SS Sturmbannführer

Günsche

Translated by:
Assistant Chief of Investigation Section
Intelligence Department of the Red Army General Staff
Captain of the Guards **Shirokov**

Ф. К-1 ос; оп. 4; д. 14; л. 3-9
(КОПИЯ)
(copy)

RECORD OF THE INTERROGATION OF THE CHIEF OF GOEBBELS'S PERSONAL GUARD WILHELM ECKOLD

18 May, 1945

I, investigator of the 1st Sub-Section of the 4th Section of 'Smersh' Counter-Espionage Department of the 1st Byelorussian Front, Senior Lieutenant **Vlasov**, questioned a prisoner-of-war Commissar of German Criminal Police – **Eckold**, Wilhelm.*

Interrogation began at 10.30

and was performed in German

Question: Give us a brief biography.

Answer: After finishing secondary school in 1919, for two years I studied to be an accountant, then worked as an accountant in a commercial bank in the town of Grunbach, Bavaria until 1923. In 1924, due to unemployment, I joined the police where I later served in the cities of Weimar, Sondershausen, Mena and Gera in the province of Thuringia, until 1934. My last post in the police was Chief of Police of the city of Gera, with the rank of Polizei-Hauptwachtmeister.

In 1934, in December, on the orders of the Police Commander of Guard in the Gera region, I was sent to the city of Berlin to take up the post of the Chief of the Personal Guard of the Minister of Propaganda **Goebbels** Josef, which I occupied until March, 1939.

In 1939, on the orders of the Chief of the Reich Security Service Police Colonel **Rattenhuber**, I was transferred to the post of Chief of the Personal Guard of the German Protector of Czechoslovakia, Reichsminister Baron von **Neurath**, and at the end of 1942, again on **Rattenhuber's** orders, I was appointed Chief of **Goebbels'** Personal Guard, remaining in that post until the German surrender in Berlin in May, 1945.

----

* **Eckold** Wilhelm – born in 1892 in Hildburghausen, former Criminal Commissar of the Ministry of Propaganda. On 6 June, 1945 was arrested by 'Smersh' CED of the 1st Byelorussian Front on charges that he 'served in German agencies of repression, from 1934 was a member of the SS, a criminal organisation, in the ranks of a police unit that guarded Hitler and from 1935 until the capitulation of Germany was Chief of Goebbels' personal guard'. In a judgement of the Military Tribunal of Moscow District of 23 January, 1952 he was sentenced to 25 years imprisonment. Under a decision of the Military Tribunal of the Moscow Military District, this judgement was allowed to stand. Under a decree of the Praesidium of the USSR Supreme Council of 28 September, 1955, Eckold was handed over to the GDR authorities on 7 January, 1956.

Question: What was the numerical strength of **Goebbels'** Personal Guard?

Answer: There were 12–14 men in **Goebbels'** Personal Guard. An additional eight officers of the 'Berlin' SS Guard battalion were also on permanent guard duty at his flat.

Question: Name all the officers in **Goebbels'** Personal Guard.

Answer: Aside from me as the Chief of the Guard, in the number of **Goebbels'** Personal Guard there were:

1. My deputy **Ostwald**, Johannes, a Kriminalobersekretär, SS Untersturmführer, 43–44 years old, (approximately 180cm tall), athletically built, brown hair, with a clear, oblong face, no special features.

2. **Guntsel**, Hermann, a private, a Kriminalsekretär, SS Untersturmführer, born in 1901, above-average height (170cm), strong build, brown hair, with healthy complexion, and no special features.

3. **Kranzusz**, Hans, a guard, a Kriminalsekretär, SS Untersturmführer, 44–45 years old, above-average height (approximately 175cm), slightly round-shouldered, with grey hair and a thin oblong face.

4. **Jacob**, Friedrich, a guard, a Kriminalsekretär, SS Untersturmführer, about 40, of medium height (up to 170cm), strong build, with brown hair, round, clear face, with no special features.

5. **Reh**, Helmut, a guard, a Kriminalassistent, SS Hauptscharführer, about 30 years old, above-average height (approximately 175cm), slender, with a narrow thin face, dark hair, with no special features.

6. **Harderthauer**, Hans, a guard, a Kriminalobersekretär, SS Sturmscharführer, about 40, above-average height, strong build, with oblong clear face, very fair hair, blue eyes.

7. **Blum**, Hans, a guard, a Kriminalobersekretär, SS Untersturmführer, about 34, above-average height (about 175cm), of strong build, with a clear round face, and very thin dark-brown hair.

8. **Friedrich,** Herbert, a guard, a Kriminalassistent, SS Hauptscharführer, about 30 years old, tall (approximately 180cm), strongly built, slim, brown-haired, with clear narrow face.

9. **Schamal**, Richard, a guard, Kriminalangelstelter, about 45 years old, tall (approximately 189cm), strong build, plump, with a clear round face.

10. **Feucht**, don't remember his first name, a guard, a Kriminalassistent, SS Oberscharführer, 27–28 years old, of medium height (approximately 170cm), slender, blond hair, with a clear narrow face.

11. **Dotsauer**, don't remember his first name, a guard, a Kriminalassistent, SS Oberscharführer, 28–30 years old, above-average height (approximately 175cm), slender, light hair, oblong face.

12. **Petsold**, don't remember his first name, a guard, a Kriminalassistent, SS Hauptscharführer, about 30 years old, above-average height (approximately 175cm), strong build, brown hair, thin oblong face, dark eyes.

13. **Drescher**, don't remember his first name, a guard, SS Hauptscharführer, about 35 years old, tall (approximately 180cm), slender, athletically built, light hair, oblong face, no special features.

Question: What were your duties as Chief of **Goebbels'** Guard?

Answer: My duties included organising the protection of **Goebbels** at his workplace and in his home, and accompanying him on various trips.

Question: When did you last see **Goebbels**?

Answer: I last saw **Goebbels** on 22 April, 1945. From 22 April to the day of my arrest, I lived in my home in the city of Berlin, 20, Hermann-Göring-Strasse, in **Goebbels'** house.

Question: Why were you, the Chief of his Personal Guard, not with **Goebbels** during the final days?

Answer: On 22 April, 1945, the second day after Soviet troops had reached the suburbs of Berlin, **Goebbels** and his family moved into Hitler's bunker. Because this bunker was guarded by Hitler's special SS guard command, my presence was unnecessary and I remained with my men at **Goebbels'** house. **Goebbels** took with him only his personal aide-de-camp, SS Hauptsturmführer **Schwägermann**, Günther.

Question: What do you know of the fate of **Goebbels** and his family after that?

Answer: I don't know anything about **Goebbels** and his family's fate after that. But I want to tell you this: at the end of March of this year, at the time when the Soviet forces had reached the Oder front line, the **Goebbels** family (his wife and children) were at their own estate of Schwanenwerder, 10 kilometres west of Berlin.

On about 31 March, I was summoned there by **Goebbels'** wife to discuss strengthening the security of the estate. While she, her mother and I were talking, she said that if things began to go badly for the German army, they would move to Berlin to live in the Führer's bunker and would stay there to the end, dying there if necessary. She added that she had a powerful poison to take at the critical moment. Her mother supported her decision.

Question: While you were staying at **Goebbels'** house at 20, Hermann-Göring-Strasse, when he and his family were in Hitler's bunker, did you have any communication with him?

Answer: No, we did not have any communication with him. The telephone lines had been cut by air raids and artillery fire, and neither **Goebbels** nor his wife sent any messenger to me, I did not have access to Hitler's bunker.

Question: Describe **Goebbels**, his wife and the children.

Answer: **Goebbels** is about 48–50 years old, below average height, very thin, the head large in proportion to his body, the shape of the head oblong from the forehead to the back of the head. The face is pimpled, the right leg is crippled from birth, because of which he had to wear a leg brace and specially made right boot, with a thicker sole than the left one to make his legs the same length (**Goebbels'** right leg was a little shorter than the left one). **Goebbels** mainly wore civilian dress, but more recently Party uniform – a brown jacket with a red arm-band containing a white circle and black swastika in the centre, and black trousers.

Goebbels' wife, born in 1901, was a little taller than her husband (approximately 167 cm), very slender, with specially dyed blonde hair, the face oblong, narrow, big eyes. She was awarded a Golden Badge of Motherhood (Mutterkreutz) for bringing up seven children.

Only six children lived permanently with **Goebbels** and his wife, five girls and one boy. The girls were aged 12, 10, 9, 7 and 4 years old, and the boy was 8 years old. The girls' names in age order were Helga, Hilde, Holde, Hedda and the name of the fifth one also started with an 'H', but I have forgotten it. The boy's name was Helmut.

Goebbels' wife also had another son named Harald from her first marriage to an industrialist named **Quant**. The latter served as an Oberleutnant in the Airborne Forces of the German Army. He was wounded and taken prisoner by the Anglo-American forces in autumn, 1944, in Italy, and later interned in a prisoner-of-war camp in North Africa. At the same time, in autumn 1944, **Goebbels'** wife received a letter from him through the Swiss Red Cross.

Question: Did **Goebbels'** wife or his children have any physical deformities?

Answer: Neither **Goebbels'** wife nor his children had any physical deformities.

Question: What was the number of **Goebbels'** Party badge?

Answer: I never saw **Goebbels'** Party badge, but from his aide-de-camp SS Hauptsturmführer **Schwägermann** I know that Goebbels had a gold Party badge with a number between 20 and 26. **Schwägermann** told me the exact number but all I can remember now is that it had two digits and the first one was '2'.

Interrogation ended at 17.00

The record was read to me in German translation, and it is correct.

Eckold

Questioned by:

Investigator of the 1st Sub-Section of the 4th Section

of the 'Smersh' Counter-Espionage Department of

the 1st Byelorussian Front

Senior Lieutenant **Vlasov**

Ф. 4 ос; оп. 3; д. 36; л. 128-132

(заверенная копия)

(certified copy)

HANDWRITTEN STATEMENT BY THE COMMANDER OF THE 'ADOLF HITLER' DIVISION, CHIEF OF THE CENTRAL BERLIN DEFENCE REGION WILHELM MOHNKE

Moscow; 18 May, 1945

On the night of 20 or 21 April (I don't remember the exact date) at 2.30 I received an order from Hitler's SS adjutant Major **Günsche** to assemble all SS personnel present in Berlin who were not yet committed to the defence of the city and form them into a combat unit. The staff of the supply and administrative units were to be selected for this, as their work was not so necessary any more. This order, first received by telephone, was delivered to me in writing next morning, giving me authority to act on my own initiative.

When I received this order, I had 850 men of the SS 'Leibstandarte Adolf Hitler' battalion under my command. On 21 April, three companies of men from SS administrative and supply units arrived, totalling 450 men. I formed all of these men initially into 11 companies of 120 men each.

On the same day, I gathered information on the different units available and on the night of 22 April, I selected a further 750 men, who were immediately formed into a combat group. They included:

a) The remaining personnel of the 1st Reserve Training Battalion.

b) Men from the Berlin SS Hospital.

c) Staff of the Army and SS Recruiting Departments.

d) SS Forces' Institute of Hygiene.

e) Men from the Office of the Chief of Long-Range Signals Intelligence and other smaller organisations.

Because the combat experience of these men varied considerably, and some of them were very poorly trained (I mean many of the clerks), I ordered a number of well-trained men from the guard battalion to be brigaded with them. Arms and ammunition for these men were provided from the guard battalion's stores.

The increase in numbers in the units already available required a re-organisation, and this was performed in the afternoon of 22 April. By evening, the unit was finally formed, and named 'Battle Group Mohnke'. It numbered about 2100 and it was armed with 108 light machine-guns, 24 heavy machine-guns and 16 81mm mortars.

At 19.00 that same evening, I received an order through the Führer's aide-de-camp Major **Günsche**, to bring my unit to the government district and report personally to the Reich Chancellery for further orders. After giving all necessary orders for my unit's departure, I drove to the Reich Chancellery, where Major **Günsche** was waiting for me. He ordered me to hold a defensive perimeter around the government district, along the line of the Brandenburg Gate, Potsdammerplatz, the Wilhelmstrasse and the Unter-den-Linden.

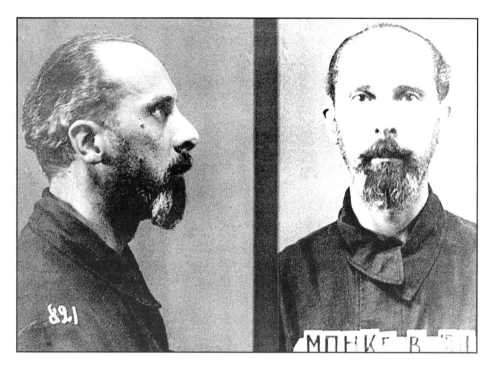

Photo of Wilhelm Mohnke from the investigation file.

Mohnke, Wilhelm was born in 1911 in Lübeck, Germany, a former SS Major-General. On 28 August, 1951 he was arrested by the USSR Ministry of State Security on charges that 'being a member of the Nazi Party and serving in senior command posts in the SS, he participated in an aggressive war in breach of international laws and treaties right up until the German capitulation; also, being a commander of a combat group defending the Berlin Government District, he participated in military action against the Soviet Army, putting up resistance until the final day'. Under a ruling of the Military Tribunal of the Moscow military District of February, 1954 he was sentenced to 25 years' imprisonment in a corrective labour camp. On the basis of a decree of the Praesidium of the USSR Supreme Council of 28 September, 1955 he was released early and on 10 October of the same year handed over to the GDR authorities. Subsequently worked as a dealer in small trucks and died on 6 August, 2001 in Hamburg.

I proposed instead to hold a wider defensive perimeter, and only retreat to the inner circle as a last resort, taking into consideration the need for a special defence of the Reich Chancellery. My proposal was accepted and the perimeter around the government district held by my Battle Group now approximately followed this line: starting in the north from the railway station in the Friedrichstrasse west along the south bank of the Spree to the Krollager, then south through the Tiergarten to the Bendlerstrasse and further, including the Bendler Block, along the eastern bank of the Landwehr canal through the Potsdam bridge to the Hallesches Tor, then north-east through Belle-Allianzplatz along the Lindenstrasse to the square, then north along the western bank of the canal to the Spree and again turning west back to the Friedrichstrasse station. This circle occupied by me nearly coincided with sector 'C' (Centre), provided for in the Berlin defence plan drawn up by its former Commandant Major-General **Reimann**. This sector was occupied by small units, including companies of engineers who were ordered to blow up the bridges, as well as by Volkssturm units.

Once my Battle Group had reached the government district, on the night of 22/23 April, the outer perimeter was occupied and the troops began to fortify their positions.

Small stockpiles of food and ammunition were established at company and battalion level, and we set up our own communications within the unit. Apart from the barricades and preparations for blowing up the bridges, no other defensive work was performed in this area.

All day on 23 April, heavy artillery bombarded the small government district with harassing fire, mainly around the Brandenburg Gate and the Tiergarten.

On 24 April, on the orders of General **Krebs**, I transferred the 1st battalion of my command to sector 'B', because the enemy had managed to break through there. I removed three companies and had to weaken the battle formations. These three companies were transferred to Colonel **Hausen**. I was gradually able to restore the strength of my formations, using soldiers who had become separated from their units and the officers of the State Security Service. During the day of 25 April, a small SS combat group arrived from Furstenberg. It consisted of 14 light tanks, four 38mm anti-aircraft guns and one infantry company.

This group was under my command and for the time being was held in reserve, for use in a counter-attack in case of an enemy breakthrough in my sector. Unfortunately, this group was not under my command for very long. Because of the enemy advance in the northern part of Berlin, as a result of which the Wedding railway station was lost, Krebs ordered me to send the group there immediately. Due to the situation, this group remained in the northern sector and was later placed under the command of Colonel **Hermann**. In the evening of 26 April, a Navy battalion arrived by transport aircraft from Rostock. The planes landed on the airfields to the west of Berlin.

On the following night, the transport of one more battalion was planned, but this proved impossible because, by then, the airfields had been abandoned. The newly-arrived Navy battalion was also placed under my command and to begin with was stationed near the Reich Chancellery as a reserve. Later, on 27 and 28 April, only occasional aircraft landed in Berlin on the East-West axis road. Supplies of ammunition for the troops, primarily for heavy artillery, were brought by parachute drop until the night of 29/30 April, but they were inadequate.

At 15.00 on 24 April, I was summoned to the Führer for the first time. After my report concerning the arrival of the group, I had to report its numbers, structure and how I was deploying it. After that, the situation in Berlin was discussed and then the general situation. General **Krebs**, General **Burgdorf**, Dr **Goebbels**, **Bormann**, Ambassador **Hewel** and State Secretary Dr **Naumann** always participated in these meetings. A representative of the Navy, Admiral **Voss**, was also present, as were representatives from the Army and the Air Force.

The general situation as well as the situation in Berlin was always reported on by General **Krebs** as Chief of the General Staff. Later, after 25 or 26 April, when General **Weidling** had been appointed the Commandant of Berlin, the latter also made a daily report on the situation in the city, and towards the end, after Russian troops had reached some sectors of my outer perimeter, I also had to report about the situation of my unit during daily discussions of the situation in Berlin. So I had a chance to attend the first meeting of 24 April at which the general situation at the front was discussed.

After the report of the Chief of the General Staff, the Führer ordered the 12th Army, under the command of General **Wenck**, to attack from the district between Magdeburg and Brandenburg through Potsdam towards Berlin, and the 9th Army under General **Busse** to attack towards Berlin from Luckenwalde. Simultaneously, the 'Steiner' group, under the command of SS General **Steiner**, should advance towards Berlin from the area to the north of Oranienburg.

If these attacks were successful and the armies were able to join up, after securing Berlin, they were to turn east and form a new front line with Army Group 'Vistula', running north to south, despite some Russian forces having already penetrated beyond it, near Nauen for example.

This order was given by General **Krebs** directly to each of the Armies and he especially stressed that the operation should be performed as quickly as possible. At this time, the advance of the American and British armies was only mentioned in passing. I personally believe that the Führer considered this advance of minor importance but, on the contrary, he took very seriously the expansion of the Russian breach in the fortifications around Stettin and ordered that serious attention be paid to it.

Wilhelm Mohnke's soldier's book.

At the end of this meeting, General **Krebs** spoke to me and repeated my instructions. He said that I was to report to the Commandant of Berlin and should address my reports to him. Notwithstanding that, in the days that followed I received orders from both him and from the Führer himself, for example, as I have already mentioned, concerning the transfer of one of my battalions to some other sector outside my perimeter.

However, in order to speed up communications, my command post was relocated to the Vosstrasse, i.e. near the Führer's bunker. Should there be any important events, I was to report there immediately.

Apart from the people mentioned by me who were present at the meeting of 24 April, there were no other people in the Reich Chancellery right up until the death of Adolf **Hitler**.

On 23 April, Foreign Minister **von Ribbentrop** was there. I saw him during dinner with Ambassador **Hewel**. As I heard later from the Ambassador, the Foreign Minister left the same day for Mecklenburg. I do not know what his mission was or if he went on his own initiative or on Adolf **Hitler**'s orders.

Furthermore, until the evening of 27 April, Air Force General von **Greim** was a guest of the Führer. His leg was broken. On 27 April, the Führer promoted him to Field-Marshal and appointed him Commander-in-Chief of the Air Force. Since this appointment surprised me very much I spoke about it to State Secretary Dr **Naumann** and Major **Günsche**, who told me approximately the following:

On 16 April, **Göring**, without Hitler's permission, had flown to Berchtesgaden and on 23 or 24 April sent a telegram to the Führer, Foreign Minister **Ribbentrop** and Himmler which read roughly as follows:

'*Based on the Führer's speech of 1 September, 1939 and his repeated statements that after the Führer's death I am to be his successor, and proceeding from the fact that the Führer is surrounded in Berlin where he has no freedom and cannot lead the Army and the German people any more, I proclaim myself his successor and assume the functions of the head of government*'.

Because of this telegram, **Göring** was detained in his house in Obersalzberg, and Field-Marshal von **Greim** was appointed to his post.

On 25 and 26 April, I was present at meetings in which the situation in Berlin was discussed. Only the Russian advance from all directions was discussed. In the north, the Russians had seized the Wedding metro station, in the west, they were at the Kaiserdamm and had almost reached the Rhine, in the south they were at the Hallesches Tor, and in the east, the Alexanderplatz. With all his energy, the Führer insisted that the 9th and the 12th Armies should attack as soon as possible, as there was no other hope of saving Berlin.

General **Krebs** answered that he had done everything possible, but, obviously, the armies had to fight against powerful enemy forces. Before the discussion of general situation in the fronts, at which I was not present, the Führer personally dictated a radio message to me. This took place in the afternoon on 26 April. The signal ran as follows:

'*To the Armed Forces Combat Operational Headquarters. Immediately report the situation with the 9th and the 12th Armies and Steiner's group: where are their advance units, how is attack progressing?*'

This telegram was only transmitted late on 27 April due to a damaged antenna and poor radio communications.

In reply, on 28 April the following radio message from Field-Marshal **Keitel** was received, which read as follows:

'*To the Führer's telegram of 26 April:*

1) Wenck's leading forces are fortifying their positions to the south of the Schnielowsee. Along all the eastern flank, there are heavy attacks by Soviet troops.

2) For this reason, the 12th Army cannot continue its advance on Berlin.

3) Main body of the troops of the 9th Army is surrounded. A tank group has advanced to the

West. There are no reports of its whereabouts.

4) The 'Holste' Corps was forced to go on the defensive on the Brandenburg–Retepon–Kremmen line.

All attacks in the direction of Berlin have failed. Along the whole front-line of the 'Vistula' Group, from the region North of Oranienburg and as far as Brandenburg and Anklam, there is heavy defensive fighting. My officers and I spend day and night in trips to the front line, doing everything possible. The importance of the task is explained everywhere, everything possible is being done and everyone proves their loyalty. Keitel'.

In the afternoon of 26 April, during a situation briefing, State Secretary **Naumann** handed the Führer an intercepted American message, saying that **Himmler** had supposedly made a surrender offer to Britain and America. When he heard that, **Hitler** became very grave and at first refused to believe it. But both on that day and the next, information was received from other foreign states, confirming this message. As I heard from the discussion, **Himmler** had supposedly held negotiations through the Swedish Ambassador, **Bernadotte**. After that, on 28 April, the Führer expelled him from the Party.

In the last week of April, **Himmler**'s headquarters were at Lichen near Fürstenberg in Mecklenburg. Where he was after that, I don't know. They said that Himmler supposedly flew out by aircraft but no one could be sure about it. I remember very well that during all these discussions Dr **Goebbels** and **Bormann** spoke particularly forthrightly against **Himmler**.

When I saw the Führer, I came to the conclusion that after receiving this information about **Himmler** and after the radio message received from **Keitel**, which made it clear that there was no hope of relief for Berlin, he understood that his days were numbered and he resolved to commit suicide in the near future.

I became more convinced of it when on 28 April he said after the meeting: *'I cannot live any longer, I am sick of life'*. Exactly by that time the Russians had significantly widened their westward penetration of the fortifications around Stettin.

The situation in Berlin on 29 and 30 April was very serious. On 30 April Russian tanks advanced close to the Reichstag In the north. In the south there was fighting for the Anhalter station and in the surrounding streets. There was also heavy fighting in the vicinity of the Spittalmarkt. As early as the morning of 29 April, the Führer, in presence of General **Krebs**, Dr **Goebbels** and **Bormann** asked me how long I could hold out. I replied that unless I received heavy weapons, principally anti-tank weapons, and sufficient ammunition, I could only hold out for another 2–3 days at most. The Führer simply nodded and went to his quarters. Dr **Goebbels** and **Bormann** pleaded with me to do all I could to hold off the enemy.

The mood of all the leaders was gloomy, and Russian artillery was firing almost constantly at the small government district, which we could do nothing about. None of the leaders made any particular comment on the current situation. All looked to Adolf **Hitler** and felt doomed.

In heavy fighting on the night of 29/30 April and on 30 April I managed to repel all Russian attacks, although suffering heavy losses. At 15.00 I was at my command post when I was summoned by telephone to a meeting. I took my map and went to the Führer's bunker. On the way, I met a distressed Major **Günsche**, who told me that the Führer had just committed suicide. After that, we both hurried to the Führer's bunker and there General **Krebs** in person told me that the Führer had shot himself. With him were General **Burgdorf**, Dr **Goebbels** and **Bormann**. No one said a word.

Dr **Goebbels** and General **Burgdorf** had tears in their eyes. As for me, I was dumbfounded. Though I had expected something like this, I had not thought it would be so soon. None of the leaders could take any decisions for a long time. There was the question on everyone's face: 'What should we do?'

I personally did not see the Führer's body and I don't know what was done to it. During this commotion, I learnt from State Secretary Dr **Naumann** that, not long before his death, the Führer had sent a letter to General **Weidling** ordering him to abandon the defence of Berlin, break out and link up with the nearest German troops. A detailed order in the Führer's name was later given to me by Reichsleiter **Bormann**. The breakout was planned for 23.00 on 30 April, but the start of negotiations with the Russian Army caused it to be cancelled.

At approximately 17.00, General **Krebs** suggested that a decision be taken at last. After that, General **Krebs**, General **Burgdorf**, Dr **Goebbels**, **Bormann** and the State Secretary Dr **Naumann** gathered in the conference room. As I was there, I was also invited.

General **Krebs** took the floor and proposed opening negotiations with the Russians, but first, to enable talks to take place, to secure a cease-fire. He said something like the following (I cannot remember his exact words):

1) Berlin could not be held any longer and it was impossible to believe in any outside help that might save it.

2) As well as it being impossible to win the battle in Berlin, it is likewise impossible to believe in any hope of general victory.

3) Recently, the Führer had told him something like the following: 'The only man with whom Germany could possibly come to an agreement is **Stalin**, because he is self-sufficient and independent; he realises his political and military aims clearly and consistently, while **Churchill** and **Roosevelt** are dependent on their parliaments and capitalism, their policy being shifting and false'. However, he, Adolf **Hitler**, could never enter into negotiations with Stalin.

Thus, it is possible, General **Krebs** went on, that by his suicide the Führer wanted to give us a chance to establish relations with Russia.

4) Therefore he (**Krebs**) proposed first to send a staff officer to the Russians, and then hold talks personally about a cease-fire and its conditions.

During any cease-fire, which might last for 24 hours, it would be necessary to contact Grand-Admiral **Dönitz** and reach an agreement with him about the capitulation of Berlin and later of the whole German Army.

By the end of the day, Colonel **Seifert** was ordered to go to the Russians and make preparations for negotiations. After he had returned with the answer that the Russian Command agreed to talks, on the night of 30 April/1 May, I accompanied General **Krebs** to the Russian positions to the south of the Prinz Albrechtstrasse. I spent the night and the morning of 1 May at my command post among the soldiers of my battle group in order to be able to understand the situation on the front-line at first hand. On my return, I heard that General **Krebs** had returned. I went there immediately and learnt that the cease-fire proposal had been rejected by the Russians and that the Russian Command insisted on the unconditional capitulation of Berlin.

Dr **Goebbels** and **Bormann** argued particularly energetically against capitulation, saying that first Grand-Admiral **Dönitz**, whom the Führer had appointed his successor, should be consulted. I later learnt that the leaders intended to offer surrender only to Russia.

Everyone believed that good relations between Russia and the two capitalist countries – England and America – could not last long, because they had totally different aims. England had already taken steps to keep Russia away from the sea, first through the occupation of Schleswig-Holstein to deny the Russians access to the North Sea, and secondly by occupying Greece and supporting Turkey to close the Dardanelles, i.e. the route from the Black Sea to the Mediterranean. British ambitions for the oil supplies in Persia were also well known. It was emphasised that America's interests lay not in Europe but in Asia, Canada and Australia and that England did not consider itself a European power, merely provoking conflict by setting one state against another. Now that Russia was the major European power, once the war had ended, there could never be a true alliance between them. Russia and Germany were also the two most economically complementary states.

From my own personal experience – as both a regimental and divisional commander in wartime – I would like to add that I never believed in a genuine alliance between Russia and England and America, although I could be mistaken. I am of this opinion because every English or American officer taken prisoner by me, when questioned as to why they were allied to the Russians, said it was only for as long as it took to beat Germany, the only aim of the alliance.

General Hans Krebs (right) at the headquarters of the 8th Army guard. The last commander-in-chief of the Wehrmacht told the world of Hitler's suicide on 1 May, 1945.

At noon on 1 May, a letter was drafted to the Commander of the Russian Forces in Berlin, in which his demand for unconditional capitulation before any talks with Grand-Admiral **Dönitz** was refused. Simultaneously, a request for a cease-fire was made again and we were awaiting a reply. But since by 18.00 we had received no answer, a break-out was fixed for 21.00 on 1 May.

I divided my unit into seven groups and ordered each of them to make their way out separately, because in the current situation I considered a penetration by the whole group to be impossible. My groups had to break through to the north through Pankow and then north-west to the Havel. Then, heading in the general direction of Fehrbellin, they were to try to join up with other German troops.

At 20.00 I had finished all the preparations and went to Generals **Krebs** and **Burgdorf** to say good-bye to them. General **Burgdorf** told me that he did not want to join the break-out because he was too old and had had a similar experience in 1918. He wanted to stay in the Reich Chancellery. General **Krebs** was still not sure what to do. He personally wished me good luck and a successful break-out. I cannot say if the two generals either committed suicide or managed to escape somewhere.

After that, I went to the Führer's bunker to report to **Goebbels** and to say good-bye. I knew that **Goebbels** did not want to leave Berlin. He had already said so earlier. I met **Goebbels** and his wife at the entrance to their rooms. I said good-bye, first to **Goebbels'** wife, who told me that their six children had already died and she and her husband also intended to commit suicide.

Her words to me were: *'My children are already little angels and I, with my husband, will soon follow them'*. I saw that she had a small bottle of poison (potassium cyanide) in her hand. Then I said good-bye to **Goebbels**, and he told me that as Gauleiter of Berlin he would never leave the city and one way or another there would be no life for him after the collapse of Germany. Then he went with his wife to their rooms and I immediately went to my first group, which was under my personal command. It was 21.00.

My group was joined by Ambassador **Hewel** and Admiral **Voss**. At 21.30, I left the Reich Chancellery and, with my group, successfully reached the Friedrichstrasse station. The place was under heavy artillery and rifle fire, so my group was dispersed a little. Crossing the Spree with the remainder of the group I successfully reached the tram line to the Karlstrasse and up the Chausseestrasse to the police barracks near the Wedding station.

Here we met large Russian forces and we could go no further. I was slightly injured, acquiring four contusions, and one of the shots also injured Admiral **Voss**. During the fighting I lost him. (Later I heard that he had been captured.) After that, we turned back and tried to get past the Stettiner railway station. We managed to do it by the morning of 2 May, and at noon I met General **Rauch**, Lieutenant-General **Rattenhuber** and Colonel **Hermann** in the Schönhauser-allee. We decided to set up a joint command post in the Schultheiss-Patzenhofer brewery, to re-order all the troops (by that time soldiers of all units of the Armed Forces and Volkssturm and the police, both armed and unarmed, had been combined) and then, in darkness, we would try to break out again.

During the afternoon, we received more than one demand to surrender from the Russian side. We thoroughly analysed our situation and came to the conclusion that the troops around the brewery had only a very limited fighting capacity. A number of Volkssturm and police had simply scattered and disappeared, and the remaining ones were not all armed and had little ammunition. Besides, there were also several hundred wounded in the brewery. By that time, the brewery was surrounded. When the new demand to surrender was announced, or they would open fire again at 18.00, General **Rauch** and I went to one of the Russian divisions and to avoid unnecessary bloodshed and having received promises of good treatment, laid down our arms. Thus we found ourselves in captivity.

I cannot say anything about the 'Werewolf'* organisation because I know nothing about it except what was reported in the press and on the radio. Among my friends, I once heard that the 'Werewolf' was supposedly set up by **Goebbels**.

As to whether I suppose it possible that the Party would engage in underground resistance, I would like to say the following: I believe that any further resistance by the Party is impossible for the following reasons:

1) After the death of the Führer, **Goebbels** and undoubtedly many other leaders, there are no more Party leaders deserving of loyalty.

2) The Gauleiters – the regional political leaders – with few exceptions had lost the loyalty and support of Party members and the rest of the population because of their extravagant private lives and egotism, even during the war. Sometimes the Party members themselves opposed them. Only the personality of the Führer and the Party discipline imposed by him kept Party members from taking action.

3) In 1942, Adolf **Hitler** began a war on two fronts and in doing so violated his own principle, which he had taught the German people, because in his book *Mein Kampf* he wrote that Germany would never again wage a war on two fronts simultaneously. Although, thanks to initial successes, this concern was not voiced, it nonetheless could be felt.

4) In *Mein Kampf* Hitler also wrote: '*Each government must care about preserving its people. If, during a war, a government sees that the war will not lead to victory, it behaves criminally if it continues with the war even one day longer*'.

This was known in the Party and I believe that the Führer condemned himself with his own words, because it had long been obvious that the war could not be won and I don't believe in miracles.

5) The German people are so tired from the long war and air raids that now they just want to be left in peace. No Party member would dare to make things worse by any rash action.

6) It is possible that the Party members will initially wait and see how any new government acts, but they will come to support any government when they see it behaving justly and honestly, trying to give bread and work to all German citizens, as far as the current situation allows.

Wilhelm Mohnke

Арх. Н-21144; л. 19-28
(ПОДЛИННИК)
(original)

---

*An alleged regrouping of staunch Nazis in the Bavarian Alps who would fight a guerilla war after the surrender. The Allies were concerned about it, but in fact it was a myth created by Goebbels.

EVIDENCE OF THE HEAD OF HITLER'S BODYGUARD
HANS RATTENHUBER

20 May, 1945,
Moscow

I, Hans **Rattenhuber**, former SS Obergruppenführer and Lieutenant-General of German Police, being a witness to **Hitler**'s death, consider it my duty to describe his last days and the circumstances of his death.

This is because, being in Soviet captivity and having had a chance to look through the press, I have seen that in Germany and other countries there is still speculation about **Hitler**'s fate and even rumours that he might be alive.

I was chief of **Hitler**'s bodyguard for 12 years, from 1933 to the day of his death on 30 April, 1945. It is quite natural that, having been close to **Hitler** for such a long time, I should know the details of his life and actions, which could be known only to the limited circle of persons close to him, who enjoyed his greatest confidence.

It is also important for me to state that, following **Hitler**'s death and the collapse of the German Reich, I am no longer bound by my oath of allegiance and I want to speak here of the facts known to me, despite my earlier loyalty to **Hitler** and his closest followers.

First of all, I should briefly describe the situation in Berlin in April, 1945.

As is known, the Russian Spring advance of 1945 on the Oder began on 14 April. The swift Russian thrust through our defences on the Oder took the German Supreme Command completely by surprise, because these fortifications were supposed to be impregnable. **Hitler**'s Headquarters was in confusion. Under the crushing attack of the Red Army the last hopes for salvation of the German capital were collapsing.

Several days later, the enemy had completely encircled Berlin. In a concentrated attack, Russian tank and infantry divisions advanced relentlessly towards the centre of the city, through heavy fighting.

In those dark days of German history, on a small piece of land in the grounds of the Reich Chancellery, all the state, political and military power of Germany was concentrated in **Hitler** in his shelter.

On 21 April, 1945, after the first Russian shell had exploded at the Brandenburg Gate, the Führer moved to a new bunker in the garden of the Reich Chancellery. It was dangerous to stay in the old shelter, situated under the Ceremonial Hall of the Reich Chancellery, because these buildings attracted the attention of the enemy air force and artillery, so the Führer might have been buried, unable to get out from under the rubble.

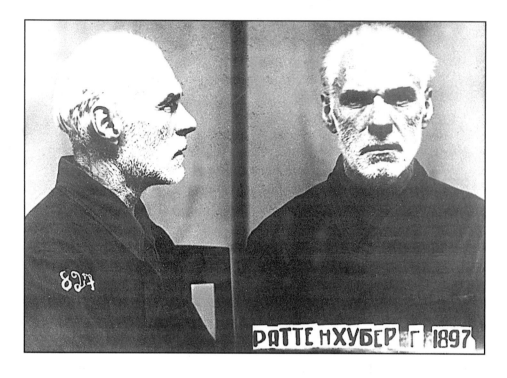

РОТТЕ НХУБЕР Г 1897

Photo of Hans Rattenhuber from the investigation file.

On 28 August, 1951, Rattenhuber was arrested by the USSR Ministry of State Security officers on charges that 'from the early days of the Nazi dictatorship in Germany in 1933 and until the defeat of the latter in 1945, being an SS Gruppenführer, Police Lieutenant-General and the Chief of the Reich Security Service, he ensured the personal security of Hitler and other Reich leaders close to him.' Rattenhuber was sentenced by the Court Martial of the Moscow Military District on 15 February, 1952 to 25 years imprisonment. Based on the Decree of the Praesidium of the USSR Supreme Council of 28 September, 1955 he was released early and on 10 October of the same year handed over to the GDR authorities. Died on 30 June 1957 in Munich.

Hitler's new shelter was a two-level underground concrete structure.

On the lower level, with artificial light and rather poor ventilation, there were the personal rooms of **Hitler** and his wife Eva **Braun**, and a reception room.

By that time, only the most devoted people and a small number of the General Staff officers needed for the military command remained with **Hitler: Goebbels**, who moved into the bunker with his family, the Deputy Chief of the General Staff General **Krebs**, Hitler's senior aide-de-camp General **Burgdorf**, Hitler's Deputy in the Party Martin

Bormann, Ribbentrop's personal representative Ambassador Hewel, the Navy representative Vice-Admiral Voss, the Air Force representative Colonel von Below and the Gestapo Chief Müller. Also in the bunker were Eva Braun, Hitler's bodyguard headed by me, his servants and technical staff.

In those days, Hitler's bunker looked like a front-line command post. Day and night, the officers and generals fighting for Berlin reported there to Hitler as well as to Göring, Ribbentrop, Himmler and others.

Now, what did the Supreme Head of the German State and its Armed Forces Adolf Hitler look like in those critical days for the German people? The physical and moral condition of Hitler in those days was shocking. He was literally a wreck. His face was a mask of fear and confusion, with the wandering eyes of a maniac. An almost inaudible voice, nodding head, stumbling feet and trembling hands. A man who had completely lost his self-control. But he still tried to be the leader and to command. Yet his strange, nervous orders completely disorientated the already confused German Command.

Hitler had not reached such a physical and moral condition suddenly. If Hitler had previously liked to boost his self-esteem by appearing unexpectedly amongst the people or soldiers and officers of the army in the field and watch the effect of his arrival, after 1942 there were great changes.

Hitler was unsettled by the continuous chain of defeats and misfortunes on the Eastern Front, the defeat at Stalingrad being the best example. In this respect, I recall my conversation with Hitler during his stay in Vinnitsa in the autumn of 1942. Hitler, infuriated by the failure of our forces to break through to Stalingrad, after one meeting said in my presence to General Schmundt, aide-de-camp from the Armed Forces General Command, that the German forces had been stopped because the Red Army fought with unsurpassed bitterness and persistence.

According to Hitler, the reason for this was Marshal Stalin's orders. We did not take into consideration – Hitler went on – that the people of Soviet Russia and the Red Army have unlimited trust in Stalin. Several minutes later he called Marshal Stalin a giant.

The well-known attempt on Hitler's life at his headquarters in East Prussia on 20 July, 1944 also played a role in the breakdown of his health. His condition became noticeably worse thereafter, despite the fact that the explosion caused only a nervous collapse and damaged his hearing.

Fear and distrust of people crept over Hitler after the assassination attempt, and the hysterical side of his nature come to the fore. He demanded that I should take the most decisive measures to reinforce his bodyguard. Hitler hated the 'mob', as he called the 'good Germans' among his immediate circle, and feared his own people hardly less than his external enemies.

Hitler's Headquarters in Germany were the equal of the fortifications of the Berlin Wall in the strength of its structure and its defences, and in some ways surpassed it. Multiple layers of electrified barbed wire with booby-traps, large minefields, multi-level guard posts with heavy weapons and flame-throwers surrounded the Headquarters in a triple circle.

The Headquarters and Hitler's shelter were set up in concrete bunkers with walls 6–9 metres thick, connected by a sophisticated network of underground passages. Movement through the grounds of the Headquarters was possible only by specially assigned roads and forest paths, with all the space between them being mined. Camouflaged machine-gun posts were set up beside the roads.

Elite SS armoured units with tanks and artillery were brought there to guard the Headquarters with the 'Leibstandarte Adolf Hitler' Regiment providing internal defence and the 'Hermann Göring' Regiment anti-aircraft defence.

The names of the headquarters, chosen by Hitler personally, were typical of him. I mean such names as 'Felsennest' ('Cliff Nest'), 'Wolfsschlucht' ('Wolf's Gorge'), 'Wolfsschanze' ('Wolf's Lair') and 'Adlerhorst' ('Eagle's Nest').

After the abovementioned attempt on his life, Hitler almost never left his bomb-shelter and stopped his trips to the front. It is clear that his health, already poor, suffered very much without fresh air and sunlight, because as early as 1935–7 Hitler had suffered from a serious stomach complaint and, despite treatment by specialists, there was no visible improvement. Hitler then suffered for a long time and often spoke of his imminent death.

Until the end, Hitler was given daily injections to boost his energy as well as to prevent a sudden stroke. These injections were given so often that Professor Morell was always near him. His right hand had begun to shake after the assassination attempt, and this soon spread to his left hand, and in the last months he was visibly dragging his left leg. Then he completely refused to go outside.

All this caused him to put on weight, his hair turned grey and he aged visibly. In the last days at the Headquarters he trembled more and more and with every new shell burst he used to run out of the room and ask: 'What happened?'

It was hard for me, who had spent so many years with Hitler, to see him in such a state. I could not help remembering the days when Hitler was full of energy and ready to work, when after night-time meetings with ministers by the morning he was already watching documentaries, having his traditional tea in the company of the secretaries on duty, adjutants and even his cook, Manzialy. We were sitting and talking all sorts of nonsense, listening to the radio, the women approaching him with different requests and telling him assorted 'gossip' . . .

But still let us return to grim reality – the end of April, 1945.

Bormann (in front), Hitler and Ribbentrop at Hitler's Headquarter, the 'Wolfsschanze'.

Being a very ambitious and highly stubborn man, Hitler carried on as usual, even under such conditions. When there was still a chance of leaving Berlin and directing the fighting from some safe place, he categorically rejected any such proposal.

On 21 April, 1945, **Hitler** chaired a meeting with the Chief-of-Staff **Keitel**, General **Jodl**, Generals **Bohle, Guderian, Krebs, Koller, Bodenschatz** and Vice-Admiral **Voss**. At the beginning of the meeting, **Göring** reported to **Hitler** that if he wanted to relocate the Headquarters to Berchtesgaden it should be done immediately. All those at the meeting believed that **Hitler** had to leave Berlin because they thought that it was possible to defend Berlin only for a very short time. During the meeting, **Hitler** left the room with **Bormann** and **Keitel** and once more discussed with them whether he should go or not. **Hitler** returned and said that he did not want to leave and would stay in Berlin.

On 26 April, a training aircraft containing General **von Greim** and the pilot Hanna **Reitsch** landed near the Reich Chancellery. **Hitler**'s immediate circle, including **Goebbels**, his wife and others, tried to persuade **Hitler** to leave Berlin in this aircraft. However, on 29 April, Hanna **Reitsch** and General **von Greim** left the Headquarters and supposedly managed to escape from Berlin but **Hitler** stayed in the bunker.

I remember the scene when **Goebbels**' wife – Magda – pleaded with **Hitler,** with tears in her eyes, to leave the bunker. **Hitler** again did not betray his ambition and with a theatrical gesture pushed Magda **Goebbels** away, saying that he would never leave Berlin and would stay there *on everlasting guard*.

In fact, **Hitler** saw no way out of the situation.

I know this because in April, 1945 the Gauleiter of the Tyrol, **Hofer**, came to **Hitler** and proposed that he move to the South Tyrol Fortress, a fortified base in the mountains of the Tyrol that had been well publicised by **Goebbels**.

Hitler waved his hand hopelessly and said: *'I don't see any sense in running from place to place any further'*.

The situation in Berlin at the end of April left no doubt that our days were numbered. Events developed more quickly than we expected. Fire from the Soviet forces was so heavy that first communications outside Berlin, and later within the city, were completely lost.

However, until approximately 25–29 April **Hitler**, being the man he was, still stubbornly hoped for help from troops outside Berlin, especially from General **Wenck**'s 9th Army.

One meeting was followed by another.

Hitler, Göring, Goebbels, Bormann and their high-ranking generals were still planning further combat operations at a time when resistance had become senseless, and when soldiers, deceived and betrayed by their leaders, were dying in the streets of Berlin for **Hitler**'s prestige, and the civilian population of the capital was subject to terrible hardships and suffering.

At the same time, **Hitler** himself clearly understood that his days and the days of Germany were already numbered.

All my life, I shall remember one of the evenings in late April, 1945 when **Hitler** returned jaded from the usual meeting and was sitting at the table examining a map of Berlin with the combat situation marked on it.

I came to him to report about the desperate last measures that had been taken to defend the Headquarters. Despite myself, at that moment, I remembered, not long before, **Hitler** at his Headquarters in East Prussia, together with his marshals and generals, standing over a giant map of Europe, showing where German forces had won victories for him . . . Raising his eyes from the table, **Hitler** looked at me and said: *'The*

Red Army is in Berlin. Only Stalin could do this'.

Thoughtfully **Hitler** returned to the table. I quietly left the room.

Among the political events of that period, it should be emphasised that **Hitler**, as well as his closest assistants, **Bormann**, **Goebbels** and the top military leaders, pinned their hopes on the idea that the alliance between the capitalist countries, Britain and the USA, on the one hand, and the Soviet Union, on the other, must eventually collapse.

I know about this because **Hitler** repeatedly showed me translations of articles published in the American newspaper *The Washington Post* and other publications of the American 'Associated Press', news agency saying that there were supposedly great problems between the leaders of the three powers at the conferences in Teheran and Yalta that prevented them from reaching a joint decision. **Hitler** usually took this news with him to war councils where, with its help, he tried to convince everyone that Germany would be able to reach an agreement with the British and the Americans at the expense of the Russians.

When, on 22–23 April, the Russians broke through the front line and their advance forces were approaching the centre of Berlin, **Hitler** ordered all staff of the Headquarters whose presence in Berlin was not necessary, to fly immediately to Berchtesgaden. **Himmler** had already been away from Berlin for several days. He was at Hohenliden, 70 kilometres north of Berlin.

On 23 April, **Göring** left Berlin, going first to Karinhall and then to Berchtesgaden. On that day, Field-Marshal **Keitel** and General **Jodl** also left Berlin to assume command of the Army Groups to be sent to help the Berlin garrison.

On 25 April, a radio message arrived from **Göring** saying that, according to **Hitler's** speech of 1 September, 1939 in which **Hitler** appointed him his successor, he had assumed the leadership of the state because **Hitler**, being encircled in Berlin, was not in a position to do anything.

When **Hitler** read **Göring's** radio message his face became distorted. He was deeply depressed and only just keeping his self-control, literally shouting: *'Hermann Göring betrayed me and the Fatherland. In the worst moment, he deserted me and the Fatherland. He is a coward. Against my orders, he ran away to Berchtesgaden and established contact with the enemy, producing an outrageous ultimatum to me that if I did not give him an answer by 9.30, he would assume my agreement to it'.*

Hitler ordered **Bormann** to arrest **Göring** immediately and to hold him in custody until the latter sent in his resignation due to ill health. **Hitler** stripped him of all ranks and removed from all his posts.

Bormann gave this order to my Deputy, **Hegel**, who transmitted the corresponding instruction by radio to the chief of **Göring's** bodyguard.

Several hours later, a radio message came that **Göring** was asking to submit his resignation due to 'heart disease'.

As for **Goebbels**, he reacted to **Göring's** betrayal in his own way. He decided to settle a long-standing score with him and made him responsible for all the misfortunes. **Goebbels**, with the affectation and theatricality characteristic of him, spewed out angry accusations against **Göring**. He claimed that **Göring** was responsible for all the current hardships and for the desperate conditions that Germany was experiencing. He also put all the blame on **Göring** for losing the war, which **Goebbels** considered inevitable. **Goebbels** said that, deep down, **Göring** had always been a traitor, never understanding anything, and he was never an expert in anything, he always did stupid things and had ruined Germany. He only pretended to be the Führer's principal helper and was the first to flee as soon as he saw that there was danger.

For all the accusations that **Goebbels** was pouring out against **Göring**, one might have believed that he simply envied the new Führer. This squabble was not new to anyone and it was highly unpleasant to listen to **Goebbels** at this time when German soldiers were shedding their blood for us in the streets of Berlin.

I think it should be emphasised that **Göring's** betrayal was quite logical, because it was the result of all his previous behaviour in his post as second-in-command of the Reich. The war had shown that **Göring** was unable to maintain the combat abilities required of the German Air Force. For a number of years, **Göring** had been exploiting his high status, by engaging mostly in improving his own situation, and after the German Army's success in Europe, this peculiarity was taken to almost incredible lengths.

He mainly used his visits to Italy, France and occupied regions of Russia to shamelessly plunder these countries' valuables. It could be said that the catastrophe that Germany was suffering hardly troubled **Göring**. Just as before the war, he continued hunting in his clownish attire – a red jacket and high green boots – and spent his time with his family in his palaces in Karinhall and Berchtesgaden. At home, he wore a white or pink satin robe with gold fastenings and had his nails manicured.

In autumn 1944, **Göring** cynically said in my presence: *'There is nothing left in life to gain for me, my family is already provided for'.*

By this phrase, he completely revealed his character.

On 27 or 28 April, Deputy Reich Press Chief **Lorenz** reported to **Hitler** that according to the Reuters Press Agency, **Himmler** had approached the governments of the US and Britain with a proposal to conclude a separate peace agreement with them. In despair, **Hitler** threw this telegram on the table and said: *'Now, when even Himmler has betrayed me, I'd better die here in Berlin, rather than lose my life somewhere in a street'.* On the same day, he expelled Himmler from the Party.

Hardly had **Hitler** regained his spirits after **Göring** and **Himmler**'s betrayal, when a telegram from Field-Marshal **Keitel** was received, saying that the 12th Army was under heavy attack by Russian troops and was unable to continue with its offensive to Berlin. The 9th Army was completely surrounded by the Russians and **Holste**'s Corps had gone on the defensive. Thus, all our hopes for salvation collapsed. Our troops' breakthrough had been unsuccessful.

The drama of the situation was aggravated by the fact that **Hitler** received all these reports to the accompaniment of heavy Russian artillery shells bursting in the grounds of the Reich Chancellery.

On that day, **Hitler** looked awful. He could hardly move or speak.

Going from a military meeting to his room **Hitler** said to me: *I can not live any longer, I am sick of life*.

But even on that tragic day **Hitler**, being a superstitious man, played his usual farce, by marrying Eva **Braun**. **Hitler** had had an affair with Eva Braun for 12 years but, for a long time, the name of his 'girlfriend' was not known in Germany.

Eva **Braun** was the daughter of a lecturer at the Munich School of Applied Arts, and when she met Hitler she was working in the photo studio of **Hoffmann**, who later became **Hitler**'s personal photographer. At the beginning of her time as **Hitler**'s 'girlfriend' she was a housekeeper in his residence in Berchtesgaden, where she was the lady of the house. Later, Eva **Braun** lived in the Munich suburbs in a villa bought for her and luxuriously furnished by **Hitler**.

When **Hitler** lived in Munich, where he had his own flat in a private house, he kept his visits to Eva **Braun** secret even from his immediate circle. It should be emphasised that Eva **Braun** played a prominent part in Hitler's private life and influenced him very strongly. Many persons close to Hitler were afraid of her, including even Martin **Bormann**, who was feared and hated by everyone.

Braun did not interfere in politics and never really manifested herself in social life. She was a flighty woman interested only in fine clothes and looking after her appearance. The fate of the German people did not affect her at all. 'Our *Führer*', she used to say, '*is a true sufferer. All have betrayed him, all have left him. Let tens of thousands of Germans die, Hitler's priceless life must be saved*'.

It was 29 April. The whole area around the new Reich Chancellery was under heavy shelling and bombing by the Russians. **Hitler**'s personal garage and the cars in it were destroyed by a direct hit.

The Russian forces advanced towards the Potsdam Station and the Headquarters continued its feverish existence.

Everyone was in confusion. Everyone thought only of saving their own lives. I still remember the treachery of a person very close to **Hitler** – his brother-in-law **Fegelein**, a Gruppenführer and **Hitler**'s SS adjutant. He was married to Eva **Braun**'s sister. On that day, it was discovered that **Fegelein** had gone to his flat, changed into civilian clothes and was planning to flee Berlin. On **Hitler**'s orders, he was arrested and shot in the grounds of the Reich Chancellery.

There was also news of other people's betrayals, but it could not have been any other way, because treachery and hypocrisy had been cultivated among **Hitler**'s associates long before the time I describe. In those critical days for the German people, the ruling clique displayed all its putrid venality, because it consisted of people who had abandoned all their morals. The rich, who had made large fortunes by robbing the German people and later looting the occupied countries, spent their days in drunken orgies, luxuriating off the fat of the land and exploiting their close relationship with **Hitler** only for their own interests.

Hitler was fully aware of the licentious behaviour of his myrmidons because he was repeatedly informed of it by many people, including myself. But his megalomania meant that he averted his eyes from it, as these were the people who hypocritically sang his praises and created the fame he craved. During my long service to **Hitler**, I came to understand the nature of many of the high-ranking officials close to him.

Professor **Hoffmann**, **Hitler**'s personal photographer, was possibly his best friend. Having acquired a monopoly as **Hitler**'s personal photographer, **Hoffmann** amassed such wealth that he became one of the richest men in Germany. **Hoffman** was an alcoholic and when drunk created disturbances that were known to the public. **Hitler** knew of this but went on treating him as his friend.

Hitler's personal aide-de-camp, Obergruppenführer **Schaub**, was his most trusted aide. In 1923, they were in Landsberg prison together. It was no secret that **Schaub** had drunken orgies with ballerinas. It was also known that he used his position close to **Hitler** only for his self-interest.

From 1938, Reichsleiter Martin **Bormann** was one of those closest to **Hitler** – one of the very few people who could influence **Hitler**. He was an exceptionally cruel, artful, hard-hearted and egotistical man. His long drunken parties with **Fegelein**, Admiral **Puttkamer** and others were indescribable.

Others of **Hitler**'s followers did not behave much better, for example **Streicher**, the Gauleiter of Franconia, **Weber**, the Munich District President, and Gauleiter **Kube**, who later became a Reich viceroy in Belorussia, as well as many others. **Kube**'s nightly drunken parties with prostitutes were the talk of Berlin. In Norway, **Terboven** got awfully drunk every night and started drunken brawls. Before the war, all of Munich had talked about 'the nights of the Amazons', organised by **Weber**. In his park, naked women rode horses accompanied by naked SS officers. **Hitler** knew all about it.

At the end of the day on 29 April, in the presence of General **Krebs**, **Goebbels** and

Bormann, **Hitler** asked General **Mohnke**, the commander of the troops defending the government district, how long he could hold out. **Mohnke** replied that with the weapons and ammunition he had, he could hold out for two or three days more. **Hitler** said nothing and went to his room.

In the evening, all those who gathered for the regular meeting were in low spirits. **Hitler**, his face more pinched than before, stared dully at the battle map before him. General **Weidling**, the Commandant of Berlin, repeatedly asked Hitler to permit the breakout from Berlin to begin. **Hitler** replied, with bitter irony: *'Look at my map. Everything marked here is not based on the reports of the Supreme Command but comes from foreign radio station broadcasts. No one reports to us. I can order whatever I want but none of my orders is fulfilled any more'.*

Finally, it was decided that because of the complete failure of airborne resupply, the troops were to be allowed to break out in small groups, on condition that they would continue the fight where possible. Capitulation was impossible.

29 April was really a fateful day!

About 10 o'clock at night, **Hitler** summoned me to his room and ordered me to gather the leading personnel of the Headquarters and his close collaborators in his reception room by 10 o'clock. I remember that at that moment **Hitler** looked like a man who had taken a very significant decision. He sat on the edge of a desk, his eyes fixed on one point. He looked determined.

I went to the door to carry out his order. **Hitler** stopped me and said, as far as I remember, the following: *'You have served me faithfully for many years. Tomorrow is your birthday and I want to congratulate you now and to thank for your faithful service, because I shall not be able to do so tomorrow . . . I have taken the decision . . . I must leave this world'* . . .

I went over to **Hitler** and told him how necessary his survival was for Germany, that there was still a chance to try and escape from Berlin and save his life.

'What for?' **Hitler** argued. *'Everything is ruined, there is no way out, and to flee means falling into the hands of the Russians . . . There would never have been such a moment, Rattenhuber',* he continued, *'and I would never have spoken to you about my death, if not for Stalin and his army. You try to remember where my troops were . . . And it was only Stalin who prevented me from carrying out the mission entrusted to me from heaven'* . . .

Eva **Braun** came in from the next room.

For several more minutes, **Hitler** talked of himself, of his role in history, that had been prepared for him by destiny, and shaking hands with me asked me to leave them alone.

Not withstanding all my loyalty to **Hitler**, it was extremely unpleasant for me to see that even at the last he could not help speaking in a high-flown manner about his 'supreme mission' and so on. He had lost his head from fear.

In **Hitler's** reception room at 10 o'clock there assembled Generals **Burgdorf** and **Krebs**, Vice-Admiral **Voss**, **Hitler's** personal pilot General **Baur**, Standartenführer **Beetz**, Obersturmbannführer **Hegel**, his personal servant Sturmbannführer **Linge**, **Günsche** and myself.

He came out to us and said these words exactly: *'I have decided to abandon this life. Thank you for your good and honest service. Try to escape from Berlin with the troops. I am staying here'.*

Saying goodbye he shook hands with each of us and, dragging his feet and with his head bowed, he went to his room.

Several minutes later, **Hitler** called me, **Linge** and **Günsche** in, and in an almost inaudible audible voice told us to burn his body and that of Eva **Braun**. *'I don't want'*, **Hitler** said, *'the enemy to display my body in a panopticon'.*

That night about 200–300 wounded had gathered at the bunker, where they were cared for by the nurses. Reich Youth Leader **Axmann** came to the bunker and asked **Bormann** to let him introduce to **Hitler** 25 girls, the best nurses in the Reich Chancellery's hospital. **Hitler** agreed. About 2 o'clock that night, the girls were lined up along both sides of the lobby on the lower level of the bunker. Soon **Hitler** arrived. He slowly went up the stairs and shook hands with each of the girls. Then with the traditional raised arm he saluted all the others who were in the bunker and returned to his room.

That night, **Hitler** ordered Professor **Haase**, who was working as a surgeon at the Reich Chancellery's hospital, to be summoned to him. When **Haase** arrived, **Hitler** **showed** him three small glass capsules, each of them in a metal case resembling a rifle cartridge-case. **Hitler** said that these capsules contained an instantaneous deadly poison, adding that he had received the ampoules from Dr **Stumpfegger**.

Hitler asked the Professor how the efficacy of the poison could be tested. He replied that it could be tested on animals, for example on a dog. Then **Hitler** ordered Sergeant-Major **Tornow**, who cared for **Hitler's** favourite dog, Blondi, to be called. When the dog was brought, **Haase** crushed the ampoule with pliers and poured the liquid into the dog's mouth, which was held open by **Tornow**. Several seconds later, the dog started to tremble and 30 seconds later it died. After that **Hitler** told **Tornow** to check if the dog was really dead.

When we left **Hitler's** room, I asked **Haase** what kind of poison there was in the ampoules and if it guaranteed instant death. **Haase** replied that there was cyanide in the ampoules, and that its action was instant and deadly.

That was the last time I saw **Hitler** alive.

It was 30 April. About 10 o'clock in the morning, I went to check the sentries. Going upstairs, I approached the SS guard on duty, **Mengershausen**, who was standing at the exit from the Reich Chancellery to the garden. **Mengershausen** reported to me that about 8 o'clock in the morning Eva **Braun** came up from the shelter, said *'good morning'* and went out into the garden, returning approximately 15 minutes later.

She explained her visit to the garden by saying: *'I want to see the sun for the last time'*. Then she said goodbye to him and, upset, went down into the bunker. At the time the grounds of the Reich Chancellery were already under Russian rifle fire.

I went to **Hitler's** reception room several times and went out to carry out my duties. The situation was very tense and I considered it my duty to provide suitable protection for the bunker by my presence because at any moment we expected the Russians to reach the grounds of the Reich Chancellery.

Between 3 and 4 o'clock that afternoon I returned to Hitler's reception room and was struck by a powerful smell of almonds. My deputy, **Hegel**, reported emotionally that the Führer had just committed suicide.

I must say that although I had expected this, the news still shook me greatly and I slumped into an armchair in despair. At that moment, **Linge** came in and confirmed that **Hitler** was dead, saying that he had had to carry out the hardest order the Führer had ever given him. I looked at **Linge** in surprise. He explained to me that before his death, **Hitler** ordered him to leave the room for 10 minutes, then to return, wait 10 minutes more and then carry out the order. Having said that, **Linge** quickly went to Hitler's room and returned with a Walther pistol, which he placed on the table before me. By its special external finish, I recognised it as the Führer's personal pistol. Now it was clear to me what **Hitler's** order had been. Obviously **Hitler**, doubting the effectiveness of the poison after all the injections he had been given for such a long time, ordered **Linge** to shoot him after he had taken the poison. **Linge** had shot Hitler.

Reich Youth Leader **Axmann**, who was present, took **Hitler's** gun and said that he would hide it for better times.

Nervous stress caused a complete depression and for the time being I was unable to stir myself. My life passed before my eyes as if on a screen. I was shaken out of my stupor by a noise in the room. I saw **Linge**, **Günsche**, Hitler's personal driver **Kempka** and two or three more SS officers, accompanied by **Goebbels** and **Bormann**, carrying the corpses of **Hitler** and Eva **Braun** out of **Hitler's** private room, wrapped in grey military blankets. I pulled myself together and followed them to accompany to his final destination the man to whom I had given 12 years of my life.

Outside the bunker, the SS officers put the bodies in a small hole not far from the bunker entrance. A hail of fire prevented even the most minimal last respects being paid to **Hitler** and his wife. Petrol was poured over their bodies and set alight, but there was no flag to cover **Hitler's** remains. The bodies of **Hitler** and Eva **Braun** were not burning well, as there was not enough fuel, and I went down to order more petrol. When I got back upstairs the corpses were already partially covered with soil. The guard **Mengershausen** told me that it had been impossible for him to stay at his post due to the foul smell of burning corpses, and that they rolled them into the hole where **Hitler's** poisoned dog lay. Upon my return to the bunker, I learnt that **Goebbels** was going to write a letter to the Soviet Supreme Command saying that **Hitler** had committed suicide, appointing Admiral **Dönitz** as his successor, Dr **Goebbels** as Reichschancellor and **Bormann** as Minister for Party Affairs. On the night of 1 May **Goebbels** gave permission for us to try and escape from Berlin, but it was in vain. I was wounded and taken prisoner by the Russians.

As I heard later, after killing their six children, **Goebbels** and his wife committed suicide in the same bunker as **Hitler**.

Ф. К-1 ос; оп. 4; д. 16; л. 63-90
(КОПИЯ)
(copy)

Artur Axmann, *born on 18 February 1913 in Hagen, studied law. In 1940, he became Reich Youth Leader of the Nazi Party. Deployed 16- and 17-year olds to defend Berlin in 1945. Escaped arrest and organised a Nazi underground movement, but was captured by the U.S. army in December, 1945. In 1958, a Nuremberg de-Nazification court sentenced him to thirty nine months imprisonment but he was released immediately as he had served this period while on remand before his trial. In 1958, he was fined 35,000 marks by a West Berlin court for indoctrinating German youth with National Socialism. He subsequently became a businessman in the Canary Islands. Died in Germany on 24 October, 1996.*

Heinz Linge, *born on 23 March, 1913 in Bremen. Former bricklayer became Hitler's personal ordinance officer and valet. He was released from Soviet captivity in 1955, subsequently dealt in property and died in Bremen in 1980.*

RECORD OF INTERROGATION
OF HANS FRITZSCHE,
HEAD OF THE BROADCASTING DEPARTMENT OF
THE GERMAN MINISTRY OF PROPAGANDA

22 May, 1945

I, an investigator of the 1st Sub-Section of the 4th Section of 'Smersh' Counter-Espionage Department of the 1st Byelorussian Front Senior Lieutenant Vlasov, questioned the prisoner Chief of the Broadcasting Department of the German Ministry of Propaganda **Fritzsche**, Hans.

The interrogation began at 18.00 and was conducted in German.

Fritzsche, Hans, born in 1900 in the city of Bochum, province of Westphalia (Germany), living in Berlin, suburb of Steglitz, Beimenstrasse, 13, from an office worker's family, a German national, citizen of Germany, higher education, graduated in 1923 from Berlin University in German History and economics, a member of the Nazi Party since May, 1933.

Question: What post did you hold at the time of the Red Army's entry into Berlin?

Answer: By the time of the Red Army's entry into Berlin I was the Head of the Broadcasting Department in the Reich Ministry of Propaganda, in Berlin. I had held this post since November, 1942.

Question: What relations did you have with members of the government of Germany, and with **Hitler** and **Goebbels** in particular?

Answer: I knew **Hitler** and **Goebbels** personally as well as many other members of the German government. I was received by **Hitler** five or six times on official matters, and as for **Goebbels**, I had constant official contacts with him, being head of one of the eight departments of the Ministry of Propaganda, namely the Head of the Broadcasting Department. I also knew **Hammer** well and until the end of 1944 I was in regular correspondence with him on official matters.

Question: When did you last see **Hitler** and **Goebbels**?

Answer: I last saw **Hitler** in December, 1944 in the New Reich Chancellery. **Hitler** passed by me while I was speaking to State Secretary **Naumann**.

I last saw **Goebbels** on 21 April this year at approximately 11–12 o'clock in his flat in Hermann-Göring-Strasse during a daily official report. On the evening of 22 April, 1945, **Goebbels** went with his family (his wife and 6 or 7 children) to live in **Hitler's** bunker under the Reich Chancellery, and after that I did not see him. All official orders from him were given to me orally by State Secretary **Naumann**.

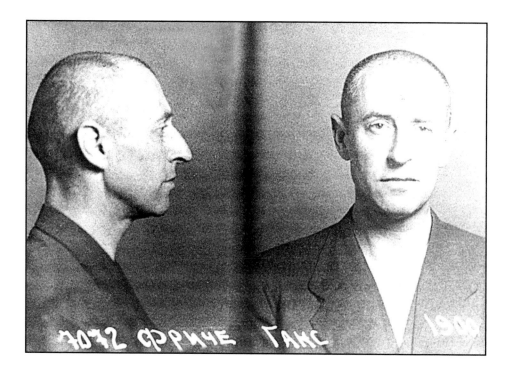

Photo of Hans Fritzsche from the investigation file.

On 6 June, 1945, Fritzsche was arrested by the 'Smersh' Counter-Espionage Department of the 1st Byelorussian Front on charges that 'from 1938 to March, 1942 being the Head of the Press Department in the Reich Ministry of Propaganda and from 1942 until the day of his arrest the Head of the Broadcasting Department at the same Ministry, he controlled the day-to-day general and political content of German press and radio, permeated with lies against the Soviet Union'. He was acquitted by the International War Tribunal in Nuremberg but on 31 January, 1954 he was sentenced by the German De-Nazification Court to nine years in a labour camp.

Question: What do you know of **Hitler** and **Goebbels'** fate?

Answer: On 1 May, 1945, at approximately 20.00, **Naumann** came to my bunker at the Ministry of Propaganda and said: *'24 hours have passed since the Führer's death. Goebbels is close to death'.* I started to ask him about the circumstances of **Hitler** and **Goebbels'** deaths, but he answered me: *'I have no time to tell you about it. Now I have to return because our troops will attempt to escape from Berlin and I want to go with them'.*

Hans Fritzsche's passport, 1944.

The same night, around 22.00, General **Burgdorf**, the Führer's military aide-de-camp came to my office at my request to discuss the question of the Berlin garrison's capitulation. **Burgdorf** told me: '*The Führer has committed suicide. Before his death, he wrote his last will, in which he firmly forbade any capitulation and ordered us to fight to our very last breath*'. For this reason, the tone of the conversation with **Burgdorf** was rather tense.

I know no more details about the circumstances of **Hitler** and **Goebbels**' deaths.

Question: Describe **Goebbels**' appearance.

Answer: **Goebbels** is below average height, of feeble build, had a big nose in comparison with his other facial features, the form of the head was of oblong shape from the forehead to the occiput, big ugly yellow teeth in the middle of the upper jaw, and from birth he had a deformed right leg (lame), to be exact the right foot was slightly turned inwards and his right leg was thinner and a little bit shorter than the left one. Because of that he had to wear a specially made boot on his right foot with the sole thicker than the left one.

Question: Then why in previous interrogations did you state that Goebbels had a deformed left leg, not the right leg?

Answer: I confess that I gave incorrect testimony about **Goebbels'** appearance to the investigation. But it was not done intentionally. Meeting **Goebbels**, I noticed that he was lame in one leg, but I did not notice which one exactly, and because of that I gave incorrect evidence in previous interrogations. Having been shown today, i.e. 22 May, 1945, a number of photos of **Goebbels**, in which he is shown full-length, it is clear which of his legs was lame and I remembered absolutely clearly that Goebbels had a deformed right leg.

Question: Did you know **Goebbels'** wife personally?

Answer: Yes, I knew **Goebbels'** wife personally.

Question: Describe her appearance.

Answer: **Goebbels'** wife was a little taller than her husband, thin, slim, with blonde hair. She had no physical defects as far as I know.

Question: What decorations and badges did you see **Goebbels'** wife wearing?

Answer: I personally did not see **Goebbels'** wife wearing any decorations or badges, but from the press I know that as early as 1940 or 1941 she was decorated with the Maternity Cross (Mutterkreutz), but I do not remember now whether it was gold or silver.

Interrogation ended at 22.00.

The record of the interrogation was read to me in German translation, and is correct.

Fritzsche

Interrogation by:
Investigator of the 4th Section of 'Smersh' Counter-Espionage Department of the 1st Byelorussian Front

Senior Lieutenant **Vlasov**

Арх. Н-17679; т.1; л. 17-22
(ПОДЛИННИК)
(original)

NOTES BASED ON THE EVIDENCE OF
THE GERMAN PILOT HANNA REITSCH

Secret
8 October, 1945

1. Source.

Name: Hanna Reitsch

Rank: Captain (Air Force Captain, honorary rank, awarded for outstanding achievements in aviation)

Born: 29 March, 1912

Marital status: Single

Occupation: Test pilot and expert in aviation research

Citizenship: Germany

Address: Austria, Salzburg, Leopold-Krone castle

Party membership: None

Decorations: Iron Cross 1st Class

2. Introduction.

This report is an account of the last days of the war as seen by Hanna **Reitsch**, famous as a test pilot and an expert in aviation research. Her story will not add any sensational details to what is already known about those days; this is a report of a witness about the real events in high places during the last days. Her account of the flight to Berlin to report to the Führer and of her stay in the Führer's bunker is possibly the most detailed account of all likely to be obtained about those last days. However, as regards the question of **Hitler**'s fate – whether he is dead or not – this report answers it only insofar as it describes his state of mind and general hopelessness, from which one can draw one's own conclusions. As far as she is concerned, the general situation and **Hitler**'s physical state made the very idea of escape impossible.

3. The story of Hanna **Reitsch** is remarkable because she played a small part in the events of the end of the war and because she was personally close to the top Nazis when they were approaching their end. It is also interesting that **Reitsch** was probably one of the last persons, or even the last person, to leave the bunker alive. Her information is believed to be trustworthy and her story could possibly shed some light or could help understanding in detail, what was happening during the last days of Berlin and of the war.

Hanna Reitsch, one of the best pilots in the Luftwaffe.

4. From time to time, she is not very sure about times and names. She forgets names. She may sometimes give the wrong times because the events of those last few days were so intense that it is often impossible for her to remember the strict sequence in which they occurred.

5. It should be emphasised that there is much in this report that should be attributed to the Nazis and their understanding of 'honour'. **Reitsch** makes a fetish of this word in the sense in which they used it, and it characterises her whole philosophy. She constantly repeats this word, understanding it less than her interrogator and using it in a different meaning. Nor did she understand how controversially she used the word. That is why each time she uses the word 'honour', she gives the wrong information.

6. She speaks in colloquial language and this style is partially reproduced here. The information cannot be considered as absolutely accurate: it is given in the way she remembers it. Taking into account that this is her own view and observation of events, the information can generally be considered reliable.

7. **Flight to Berlin.**
On 24 April, **Hitler** telegraphed Lieutenant-General Ritter **von Greim** in Munich ordering him to report to the Reich Chancellery on a very urgent matter. Reaching Berlin at the time was very difficult because the city was practically surrounded by the Russians. However, **von Greim** decided that it was possible to get through to the city with Hanna **Reitsch**'s help as a pilot in an autogyro which could land in the streets or in the gardens near the Reich Chancellery.

8. On the night of 25/26 April, **Reitsch** and **von Greim** arrived at Rechlin and were ready to fly to Berlin immediately. But the only autogyro available had been damaged that day, so it was decided that **von Greim** would be flown by the sergeant-pilot who two days previously had taken Albert **Speer** to **Hitler** and thus had experience of the flight. Out of a sense of responsibility to **von Greim** as his personal pilot and friend, **Reitsch** asked to be taken along. A Foche-Wulf 190 with only one passenger seat behind the pilot's seat was chosen for the flight. **Reitsch** clambered into the fuselage through a small emergency hatchway.

9. Forty fighters were detailed to escort them. Almost as soon as they took off, they encountered Russian fighters. After a low-level flight, they reached Gatow airfield, the only one still held by the Germans. Their plane made it with only a few small hits to the wings, although the escort had suffered heavily.

10. The landing at Gatow took place during a Russian air raid, and the remaining escort fighters engaged the attackers while **von Greim**'s plane landed safely. Immediately, an attempt was made to establish telephone contact with the Reich Chancellery, but all the lines had been cut. It was decided to fly the rest of the way there in a Fieseler-Storch that was at the airfield and land close enough to Hitler's bunker to be able to walk there. **Von Greim** took the pilot's seat, with **Reitsch** as a passenger. The plane took off amid gog-fighting Russian and German aircraft. **Von Greim** managed to clear the airfield and flew at tree-top height to the Brandenburg Gate.

11. There was street-fighting below them, and the sky was full of Russian planes. Several minutes after take-off, the plane's underside was hit and **von Greim** was badly

wounded in the right leg. **Reitsch** took the controls, reaching over **von Greim's** shoulders, and managed to land the plane on the East-West axis road. The moment they landed, heavy Russian artillery and small-arms fire rained down on the landing site. A passing car was commandeered to take them to **Hitler's** bunker. **Von Greim** received first aid on the way.

12. Arrival at Hitler's bunker.
Von Greim and **Reitsch** arrived at the bunker between 6.00 and 7.00 on the morning of 26 April. Frau **Goebbels** was the first to meet them, rushing up to **Reitsch** with tears and kisses, expressing surprise that there still were people of courage and honesty to come to the Führer – unlike all those who had deserted him. **Von Greim** was immediately taken into an operating room where **Hitler's** doctor bandaged his wounded leg.

13. According to **Reitsch**, **Hitler** came to the injured man's room, expressing his deep gratitude to **von Greim** for his arrival. He was saying something to the effect that even a soldier had the right not to obey an order if it was obvious that the fulfilment of such an order was useless and hopeless. After that, **von Greim** made an official report of his arrival.

14. Hitler's denunciation of Göring.
Hitler: *'Do you know why I summoned you?'*
Von Greim: *'No, I don't, my Führer'.*
Hitler: *'Because Hermann Göring betrayed and deserted me and the Fatherland. Behind my back, he established contact with the enemy. His actions were a manifestation of cowardliness. And, contrary to my orders, he escaped to Berchtesgaden. From there, he sent me a disrespectful telegram. He said that some time ago I had appointed him as my successor and that now, when it was impossible for me to govern from Berlin, he was ready to rule instead of me from Berchtesgaden. He concluded the telegram with the statement that if he did not receive a reply from me by 9.30 today by telegraph, he would consider that I had agreed to this'.*

15. This scene is described by **Reitsch** as 'touchingly dramatic'. She says that when the Führer was speaking about **Göring's** betrayal there were tears in his eyes, his head was bowed, his face was deathly white and when he handed this message to **von Greim** the paper shook in his trembling hand.

16. While **von Greim** was reading, the Führer's face was very gloomy. Then its every muscle started to twitch, and his breathing became intermittent. With an effort, he regained enough control to shout:

17. *'An ultimatum! Harsh ultimatum!! Now there is nothing left. Nothing was spared me. There is no one faithful, no honesty left. There is no disillusionment that has not befallen me, no treacheries I have not endured and now – this on top of all. There is nothing left. All the evil has been already been done to me'.*

18. According to **Reitsch**'s description, it was a classical 'Et tu, Brute' scene, full of lamentations and self-pity. For a long time, **Hitler** couldn't continue.

19. With a harsh look in his half-closed eyes and in an unusually low voice he said: *'I shall immediately arrest Göring as a traitor to the Reich. I stripped him of all ranks and removed him from all his positions. That's why I summoned you. By this, I proclaim you the successor to Göring as Air Force Supreme Commander. In the name of the German people, I give you my hand'.*

20. To die for the 'honour' of the Air Force.
Von Greim and **Reitsch** were deeply shocked by the news of **Göring**'s betrayal. As if by some previous arrangement, both of them grabbed **Hitler**'s hands, asking to be allowed to stay in the bunker and to sacrifice their lives for the great sin that **Göring** had committed against the Führer, the German people and the Air Force itself. They asked to be allowed to stay to preserve the 'honour' of the fallen pilots, to restore the 'honour' of the Air Force, profaned by **Göring**, and to guarantee the 'honour' of their Fatherland in the eyes of the whole world. **Hitler** agreed and said that they might stay and that their decision would be remembered in the history of the Air Force for a long time. But back in Rechlin it had been decided that, the next day, a plane would arrive to remove **von Greim** and **Reitsch** from Berlin. Now that they had decided to stay, there was no way to tell anyone that their plans had changed. Aircraft after aircraft was sent from Rechlin but they were shot down one by one by the Russians. At last, on 27 April, a Ju-52 carrying SS personnel and ammunition managed to land on the East-West axis road, but because **von Greim** and **Reitsch** had decided to stay, it was sent away empty. (The order for **Göring**'s dismissal had been issued from the underground Supreme Headquarters on approximately 23 April.)

21. Hitler believes the game is lost.
Later on this first evening, **Hitler** summoned **Reitsch** to his room. She recollects that his face was deeply wrinkled and there was always a misty film over his eyes. He said in a very low voice: *'Hanna, you are one of the people who want to die with me. Each of us has a small bottle of poison like this'.* And he gave her a bottle for herself and another for **von Greim**. *'I don't want any of us to fall into the hands of the Russians and I don't want them to find*

our corpses. Everyone is responsible for the annihilation of their bodies so that nothing is left for identification. Eva and I will burn our bodies. Find your own means for yourself. Would you give it to von Greim?'

22. Reitsch slumped into a chair in tears. Not because – she says – that she now knew she was finished, but because for the first time realised that the Führer considered the game lost. Weeping, she asked: *'My Führer, why are you here? Why are you robbing Germany of your life? If it were known that you were staying in Berlin to the very end, the people would be struck with horror. "The Führer must live to enable Germany to live", the people will say. Save yourself, my Führer, this is the wish of every German'.*

23. *'No, Hanna, if I die, it will be for the honour of our Nation, because being a soldier I must obey my own orders, according to which I would defend Berlin to the end. My dear girl, I didn't expect this. I strongly believed that Berlin would be saved on the banks of the Oder. We sent all we had to hold that position. Believe me, when our greatest effort brought no results, I was more horrified than anyone else. Later, when the city was being surrounded, the thought that there still were 3 million of my compatriots in Berlin made me stay to defend them. Staying here, I believed that all the troops in the country would follow my example and come to save the city. I hoped that they would make a supreme effort to save me and thus save three million of my compatriots. But, my Hanna, I still cherish one hope. General Wenck's Army is coming from the south. He must, and he will, drive the Russians back far enough to save our nation. Then we will rise again'.*

24. It almost seemed as if he believed it himself, and when he had finished he paced the room with long, quick, uneven strides, clenching his hands behind his back, his head shaking with every step. Although his words expressed hope, Hanna says, his appearance showed that the war was ended.

25. Hanna returned to **von Greim** and gave him the poison, and they decided that if the end came, they would quickly drink the contents of the bottles and then each clutch a hand grenade to their chests and pull the pin.

26. Late on the night of 26/27 April the first heavy shelling of the Chancellery began. The explosions of heavy artillery and the crash of collapsing buildings directly above the bunker caused everyone such nervous strain that through the doors someone could be heard crying. Hanna spent the night looking after **von Greim**, who was in considerable pain, and she kept hand-grenades ready in case the Russians reached the Chancellery that morning.

27. Hitler's guests in the bunker.
Next morning, she was introduced to the other people in the bunker and for the first time found out who would be facing death with the Führer.

In the bunker on 27 April were: **Goebbels** and his wife and six children; State Secretary **Naumann**; Hitler's right-hand man Reichsleiter Martin **Bormann**; **Hewel** from Ribbentrop's Chancellery; Admiral **Voss**, Dönitz's representative; General **Krebs** and his aide-de-camp **Burgdorf**; Hitler's personal pilot Hans **Baur**; **Beetz**, another pilot; Eva **Braun**; SS Obergruppenführer **Fegelein**, who was **Himmler's** liaison officer and the husband of Eva **Braun's** sister; Hitler's personal physician Dr **Stumpfegger**; Colonel von **Below**, Hitler's Air Force aide-de-camp; Dr **Lorenz**, the representative of the Press Chief Dr **Dietrich**; two of Hitler's secretaries – Frau **Christian**, the wife of Air Force General **Christian** and Fraulein **Krüger**; and assorted orderlies and SS messengers.

Reitsch says that was everyone.

28. A regular visitor in those last days was Reich Youth Leader **Axmann**, commander of the Hitler Youth Division defending the city. **Axmann** provided current information on the situation which was reflected in his hopelessness which grew with every visit.

29. One more betrayal.
Towards evening on 27 April, Obergruppenführer **Fegelein** disappeared. Soon afterwards, it was announced that he had been arrested in the suburbs of Berlin dressed in civilian clothes, pretending to be a refugee. This news was immediately reported to **Hitler**, who at once ordered his execution. For the rest of the night, **Hitler** was deeply depressed about **Fegelein's** betrayal and he expressed doubts about **Himmler's** loyalty, fearing that **Himmler** had known of **Fegelein's** escape and possibly helped him.

30. Observation on the inhabitants of the bunker.
Reitsch did not have much contact with most of those staying in the bunker, being mainly engaged in looking after **von Greim**. But she had opportunities to talk to many of them and to observe their reactions to the state of affairs in the bunker during those last days. She appears to try to describe her observations truthfully and sincerely. It should be remembered that before **Reitsch** reached the bunker, she had had little contact with the majority of those people and she had rather a low opinion of them. Among those whom she could closely observe, the **Goebbels** couple possibly stand apart.

31. Dr Goebbels.
She describes **Goebbels'** terrible shock at **Göring's** betrayal. He paced his small, luxurious room with long strides like an animal, murmuring malicious accusations

about the Air Force commander and what he had done. The desperate military situation – was **Göring**'s fault. Their current suffering – was **Göring**'s fault. If the war were lost, as seemed inevitable, then it would also be **Göring**'s fault.

32. 'That swine', **Goebbels** said, 'who always presented himself as the Führer's main helpmate, now hasn't the courage to be beside him. Moreover, he wants to replace the Führer as Head of the State. He, who understands nothing, who destroyed the Fatherland by his mistakes and stupidity, now wants to rule the Nation. That is enough to prove that in fact he never was truly one of us, that deep in his heart he was always weak and a traitor'.

33. All this, according to Hanna, was performed theatrically with extravagantly waving hands and complicated gestures. His nervous loping about the room made the spectacle even funnier. When he was not attacking **Göring**, he was addressing the world, praising those who were providing an historic example by staying in the bunker. As if he were on a platform, grasping a chair as if it were a lectern, he declaimed:

34. 'We show to the world how people can die for their honour and our deaths will be an eternal example for all the Germans, both friends and enemies. One day, the whole world will recognise that we were right, that we thought to defend the world from Bolshevism with our lives. Some day this will be written down in history forever'.

35. Obviously, **Goebbels** practised his greatest talent to the end. His room was next to **Reitsch**'s and the doors were usually open. Through them, **Goebbels** could be heard speaking at all hours of the day and night. And all the time he spoke of 'honour', of 'how to die', of 'how to stay loyal to the Führer till the end', of 'the example that will shine as a sacred thing in the tablets of History'.

36. One of the last phrases that **Reitsch** heard from the master of propaganda was: 'We shall die for the glory of the Reich, so that Germany will live forever'. Even **Reitsch** had to come to the conclusion that **Goebbels**' performance, notwithstanding the desperate situation, was a little exaggerated and completely theatrical. She says it seemed to her that **Goebbels** usually behaved as if he were addressing a legion of attentive historians who were writing down his every word. She adds that her own opinion of **Goebbels**' pretentiousness, his superficial knowledge and artificial oratory, was completely confirmed by these tricks. She also says that, having listened to these tirades, she and **von Greim** often asked themselves sadly, shaking their heads: 'And these are the people who ruled our country?' ✓

37. Frau Goebbels.

She described her as a brave woman, who for the most part controlled herself well though sometimes she wept bitterly. Her main concern was for the children, and in their presence she was sweet and lively. She spent most of the day trying to clean and mend their clothes, and, because they had only what they wore, it kept her busy. Often she quickly went to her room to conceal her tears. According to Hanna's description, it could be supposed that Frau **Goebbels** was possibly the ideal woman of Nazi doctrine.

38. If the Third Reich was finished, she wanted to die with it and did not want to let her children outlive her. As proof that she represented a true German woman, **Hitler** presented her, in front of all the inhabitants of the bunker, with his own gold Party badge. '*The solid foundations of honour, on which National-Socialism is built and the German state is based*', those were approximately the words he said, pinning the badge to her dress.

39. Frau **Goebbels** often thanked God that she was alive and could kill her children to save them from any 'evil' which would follow defeat. She said to **Reitsch**: '*My dear Hanna, when the end comes, you must help me with the children if I lack strength. You must help me to leave this life. They belong to the Third Reich and the Führer and if both go, there will be no place here for the children. But you must help me. Most of all, I am afraid that at the last moment I won't have the strength*'.

40. Hanna thinks that at the last moment she did have the strength.

41. Hanna's notes lead us to the conclusion that Frau **Goebbels** was just one of the most convinced listeners to the highly skilful speeches of her own husband and presented the most extreme example of the Nazi influence on German women.

42. Goebbels' children.

Goebbels had six children. Their names and approximate ages were: Helga – 12 years old, Hilde – 11 years old, Helmut – 9 years old, Holde – 7 years old, Hedda – 5 years old, and Heide – 3 years old. They were the only bright spot, making the hard life in the bunker under the veil of death a little easier. **Reitsch** taught them songs, which they sang for the Führer and the wounded **von Greim**. They always said that they were in a 'cave' with their 'Uncle Führer' and though there was bombing outside, nothing could happen to them while they were with him. And 'Uncle Führer' said that soldiers would come soon and drive the Russians away and then tomorrow they would be able to outside again and play in their garden. Everyone in the bunker tried to make their life as pleasant as possible. Frau **Goebbels** thanked **Reitsch** many times for brightening their last days, because **Reitsch** often gathered them around her and told them long stories about her flights and the countries she had visited and the places she had seen.

43. Eva Braun.

According to **Reitsch's** impressions, the Führer's 'girl-friend' was strictly faithful to her ornamental role in the Führer's circle. She spent most of the time polishing her nails, changing her dress every hour and having her hair done etc. She obviously took the prospect of death with the Führer for granted and behaved as if she were saying: *'Has not our affair lasted for 12 years and did I not threaten to commit suicide when Hitler once wanted to get rid of me. It would be a much simpler death and cleaner'.* She repeatedly said: *'Poor, poor Adolf, everyone left him, everyone betrayed him. Better ten thousand others die than he is lost to Germany'.*

44. In **Hitler's** presence, she was always charming and cared for his needs in every way. But only when she was with him did she keep this performance up. Once he had left the room and could not hear her, she would start talking about the ungrateful swine who had abandoned their Führer and that they should all be killed. These remarks sounded childish, and it seemed that at that moment the only 'good' Germans were those in the bunker and all the others were traitors, because they were not here to die with him. The reason for her willingness to die with the others was the same as that of Frau **Goebbels**: after the Third Reich, Germany would not be fit for true Germans to live in. Often she expressed her sorrow that there were people who could not kill themselves and who would have to live without 'honour', like human beings without a soul.

45. Reitsch emphasises **Braun's** obviously limited intellectual abilities, but says that she was a very beautiful woman. **Reitsch** thinks it hardly possible that **Braun** had any wide-ranging influence on **Hitler**. The rumours of a last-minute marriage ceremony **Reitsch** considers highly unlikely not only because, according to her, **Hitler** did not have such an intention, but because the situation in the bunker at the time would have made such ceremony ridiculous. Up to the moment when **Reitsch** left the bunker, only a day before the announcement of **Hitler's** death, there was no talk of such a marriage. She quickly rejects rumours that there were children from the affair as fantastic.

46. Martin Bormann.

Bormann rarely moved from his writing-desk. He was *'putting down events for future generations'*. Every word, every action was recorded on paper. Often, he would approach someone and gloomily ask about the exact contents of the Führer's conversation with a person to whom he had just given an audience. He also meticulously wrote down everything that took place with the others in the bunker. This document was supposed to be removed from the bunker at the last moment so that, according to the modest **Bormann**, it could 'take its place among the greatest chapters of German history'.

47. Adolf Hitler.

During Hanna's stay in the bunker, **Hitler's** behaviour and his physical state deteriorated even further. At first, it seemed that he played his part, defending Germany and Berlin, and at the beginning this was still possible to a certain extent, because communications were still fairly reliable. Information reached them through the telephone in the flak-tower and also from a radio with a portable antenna, attached to a balloon. But each day, it was getting more difficult and finally by the evening of 28 April and all day on the 29th it was almost impossible to maintain communications. Around 20 April, during what seemed to be the last meeting of the War Council held by **Hitler** in Reich Chancellery, the Führer, it was reported, was so depressed by the hopeless situation that he expressed his complete despair in front of the whole Council. In the bunker, Hanna heard that after this, even the greatest optimists in **Hitler's** entourage believed that the war was truly lost. According to **Reitsch**, after this shock in the conference-room, **Hitler** never recovered either physically or morally.

48. Sometimes it seemed that he still counted on the success of General **Wenck**, who was trying to break through from the south. He spoke of little else and throughout the 28th and 29th he was making tactical plans that **Wenck** could use to liberate Berlin. He paced the bunker, waving a road map, which almost disintegrated in his clammy hands, and described plans for **Wenck's** campaign to anyone who would listen. When his excitement reached its peak, he grabbed the map and paced the room with quick, nervous steps, 'directing' the defence of the city with armies that no longer existed (because even **Wenck's** army had been defeated, something that **Hitler** did not know).

49. **Reitsch** describes a pathetic picture of a complete ruin of a man. A tragi-comedy of disillusionment, fruitlessness and futility – to see a man, running blindly from one wall to the other in his last retreat, brandishing papers that shook in his trembling hands or sitting at his table, moving the sweat-slicked counters on the map that showed his non-existent armies, like a boy playing war games.

50. Is it possible that Hitler is still alive?

Reitsch considers the idea that **Hitler** could have left the bunker alive completely impossible. She says she is sure that **Hitler** was physically incapable of escaping when, she left the bunker: 'Even if a way had been cleared for him from the bunker to freedom, even then he would not have had the strength to take it'. She also believes that by the end he had no desire to live and that only his hope of **Wenck** held him back from the fulfilment of a plan for mass suicide. The news that Wenck could not break through, according to her, immediately pulled the trigger of a well-laid plan of liquidation.

51. When she is told about rumours that Hitler could be alive and is in the Tyrol and that her own escape there after leaving the bunker may not be a coincidence, she seems very disturbed by such ideas. She simply says: 'Hitler is dead! The man whom I saw in the bunker could not live. He had nothing to live for, and the tragedy was that he knew it very well, maybe better than anyone else'.

52. Hanna's opinion of the Führer.
Reitsch's account shows that she had great respect for the Führer. What she says about her 'good' opinion of him suffering considerably in the last stages of the war could be true. She described obvious mistakes by the leadership, which she saw or heard about in the bunker. For example, Berlin did not have enough ammunition to secure the German position on the Oder. When this defensive line was penetrated, it turned out that there were no proper plans for the defence of Berlin itself, nor the proper means to command that defence from the bunker. There were no external communications apart from the telephone in the flak-tower. It is possible that **Hitler** only decided at the last moment to command the fighting from the bunker, so he lacked the necessary means to do so. There were no maps, no battle plans and no radio, only hastily-established messenger communications and one telephone. The fact that several days after the defeat of **Wenck**'s army, **Hitler** was unaware of it, is only one example of the results of this poor organisation. Consequently, the Führer of Germany remained helplessly in his bunker, playing war games on the table.

53. **Reitsch** says that 'Hitler the Idealist' died and his country died with him because of the failures of 'Hitler the Soldier' and 'Hitler the Politician'. Still having some loyalty, she says that none of those who knew him can deny his idealistically-motivated intentions, and she also denies that he was simply incapable of ruling the country, saying rather that his main shortcoming was his inability to correctly assess the people around him, which lead him to choose the wrong people for high positions (the most obvious example being **Göring**).

54. She repeats that such a man should never be allowed to rule Germany, or any other nation, again, but strangely she doesn't seem to blame him personally for all the evil that was done, which she completely recognises and readily points out. She says: *The responsibility is largely that of the people who manipulated him, misled him, criminally misdirected and misinformed him. But he can't be forgotten because it was he who chose those who manipulated him*.

55. 'Criminal before the world'.

'Hitler finished his life as a criminal before the world', she says, but is quick to add: *'He began differently. At the beginning, he thought only of how to re-vitalise Germany, how to give his people a life without economic hardship and inadequate social protection. To achieve this, he played a big game, bragging that there was no one who could control the life of his people (except for him?). It was his first big mistake, his first major shortcoming. But when the initial risks brought success, he repeated the mistake of all gamblers – he started to risk more and more, and winning each time, it was easy for him to risk bigger stakes each time'*. According to Reitsch, this all started with the occupation of the Ruhr. It was the first and most difficult gamble of all, and when the world did not respond with war to his Ruhr bluff, all of the subsequent stakes were easily won.

56. Every new success increased the enthusiasm of the people, and that gave him support for the next step. In the end, as Reitsch says, **Hitler** himself changed, turning from an idealistic benefactor into a greedy and cowardly despot. He fell victim to his own megalomania. *'It should never again be allowed in the history of the world'*, she concludes, *'for one man to have such power'*.

57. Suicidal advice.

On the night of 27/28 April, the Russian shelling of the Chancellery reached its peak. The accuracy seemed amazing to those who were underneath. It seemed that every shell landed exactly where the previous one had, centering on the Chancellery building. It demonstrated that the Russians might arrive at any moment, so the Führer assembled the second 'suicide council'. Again, all the plans to destroy the bodies of everyone in the bunker were repeated. It was decided that as the Russians entered the grounds of the Chancellery, the mass suicide would begin. The last instructions were given on how to extract the poison from the vials.

58. Everyone was in a kind of trance after this meeting about suicide, and a general discussion started on how to completely destroy human bodies. After that, some people made short speeches swearing allegiance to the Führer and Germany, which were repeated again and again. But there was still a glimmer of hope that **Wenck** would hold out long enough to let them escape. Even on the 27th, **Reitsch** says, they were only repeating this in imitation of the Führer. Almost all had lost their hope of salvation and they talked about it when **Hitler** was not around. Concluding their discussions on annihilation of the bodies, it was decided that the SS should receive orders to make sure there was no trace of them. All day on the 28th, the heavy shelling continued and discussions about suicide were held in the bunker to the accompaniment of exploding shells.

59. Himmler's betrayal.
Then, on the 29th, the heaviest blow fell. A telegram was received to the effect that **Hitler's** bulwark, **Himmler**, had joined **Göring** on the list of traitors. For everyone, it was like a deadly blow. **Reitsch** says that all the men and women cried and shouted in fury, fear and desperation, everything mixed up in one crazy convulsion. **Himmler**, the Protector of the Reich, is a traitor! It was impossible. The telegram said that **Himmler** had contacted the American and British authorities through Sweden and proposed surrender at the conference in San Francisco. **Hitler** raved like a man possessed. His face was red and virtually unrecognisable. The additional proof of **Himmler's** betrayal was that he had asked not to be named in connection with the proposal. They said that the American command was satisfied with this proposal but the British were not.

60. After a long paroxysm of rage, **Hitler** sank into a torpor and for the time being all in the bunker were silent.

61. Information arrived subsequently that the Russians would launch an all-out attack to take the Reich Chancellery on the morning of the 30th. At the same time, small-arms fire was heard above the bunker. According to reports, the Russians were approaching the Potsdamer Platz, killing thousands and fanatically preparing for the attack which was to start the next morning.

62. Reitsch says that everyone once again looked to their poison vials.

63. The order to evacuate the bunker.
At 1.30 in the morning of 30 April, **Hitler** entered **von Greim's** room, his face white as chalk, and sat heavily on the edge of his bed. He said: *'Our only hope is Wenck, and to make it possible for him to arrive we should summon the Air Force to protect his advance'.* Then Hitler

said he had been informed that **Wenck's** artillery was shelling the Russians in the Potsdamer Platz.

64. *'All available aircraft'*, Hitler said, *'should be summoned at daybreak, so I order you to return to Rechlin and to send your planes from there. The mission of your air force is to pound the positions from which the Russians want to start the attack on the Chancellery. With the help of the Air Force, Wenck will come. This is the first reason why you should leave the bunker. The second is that it is necessary to stop Himmler'.* And as he named the Führer of SS, his voice became less confident, and his hands and lips trembled. **Von Greim** was ordered to arrest **Himmler** immediately if he had really contacted the enemy and could be found.

65. 'Never should a traitor be my successor as Führer! You have to leave here to prevent it'.

66. Von Greim and **Reitsch** protested energetically, saying that the attempt would be fruitless, that it was impossible to reach Rechlin and that they preferred to die in the bunker, that the plan would fail and that it was crazy. ·

67. *'Your sacred duty as soldiers of the Reich'*, replied **Hitler,** *'is to do everything possible. This is the only chance for success. Your duty and mine is to take it'.*

68. Hanna was not convinced. *'No, no!'* she shouted. *'What can be done now even if we do break through? All is lost, it is crazy to try to change anything'.* But **von Greim** thought differently. *'Hanna, we are the only hope for those staying here, Even if there is only a tiny chance, we must take it. If we don't go, we'll deprive them of the only ray of hope left. Maybe Wenck is there. Maybe we can help. Whether we can help or not, we'll go'.*

69. Hanna, still convinced that the attempt was senseless, went alone to the Führer while von **Greim** was getting ready. Sobbing, she asked: *'My Führer, why, why don't you allow us to stay?'* He looked at her and said only: *'May God preserve you'.*

70. Parting.
All the preparations were made very quickly, and **Reitsch** describes their parting in every detail. **Göring's** former liaison officer to the Führer, now **von Greim's**, said: *'You should go. It is up to you to tell the truth to our people, to save the honour of the Air Force, to save the image of Germany for the world'.* Everyone gave them something to take away with them into the world they were about to leave. Everyone quickly wrote final short letters. **Reitsch** says that she and **von Greim** delivered all of them, except for two letters from

Goebbels and his wife to their eldest son by Frau Goebbels' first marriage, who was in an Allied prisoner-of-war camp. These letters were found with **Reitsch**. Frau **Goebbels** gave her a diamond ring from her finger to wear in remembrance of her.

71. Flying out of Berlin.

The whole city was engulfed in flames and rifle fire could be heard very close by. The SS troops who guarded **Hitler** until the end were being forced back into a circle. These soldiers provided a small armoured car to take **von Greim** and **Reitsch** to the Brandenburg Gate where an Arado-96 was hidden. The air was full of the sound of exploding shells, some of them falling so close that their car was damaged several yards from the shelter in which the Arado was hidden.

72. **Reitsch** says she is sure that it was the last plane available. She says the rumours that there was another airworthy plane available that could have flown **Hitler** out are highly improbable because **von Greim** would certainly have known about it. She knows that there was no such aircraft. She also knows that **von Greim** sent other planes but all of them were shot down. And because the city was already completely surrounded by the Russians, she is sure that **Hitler** remained in Berlin.

73. A wide street leading from the Brandenburg Gate was to be their runway. They had 400 metres of flat, undamaged road to use. They took off in a hail of bullets, and when the plane reached rooftop height it was caught by many searchlights and shot at. The plane was tossed about like a feather by the shell-bursts, but only a few splinters hit it. **Reitsch** circled up to an altitude of 20,000 feet, from which the city below looked like a sea of fire. From up there, the extent of the destruction seemed immense and fantastic. Heading north, they reached Rechlin in 50 minutes, again landing under fire from Russian fighters.

74. The Germans' last efforts.

Von Greim immediately ordered all available planes to be sent to help Berlin. Having fulfilled **Hitler's** first order, he decided to fly to Plön near Kiel to find out if Dönitz had any news about **Himmler**. He flew there in a Junkers 181. As they took off, German pilots were already arriving in response to von **Greim's** order. The skies were practically full of German and Russian aircraft. To escape detection, **Reitsch** flew as low as 1–2 metres above the ground, and even then they were attacked twice. After they landed in Lübeck, they had to go by car to Plön and again they were under constant Russian air attack. On arrival, they learned that **Dönitz** knew nothing about **Himmler's** activities. The next trip they made was to **Keitel** to organise any necessary changes in air tactics to support **Wenck's** entry into Berlin.

75. News that Wenck's army no longer exists.

They found **Keitel** early on the morning of 1 May and he told them that **Wenck's** army had already been defeated or captured and that he (**Keitel**) had sent a report about it to **Hitler** (on 30 April).

76. Now **von Greim** and **Reitsch** knew that **Hitler** had probably given up hope, and they were both sure that the well-laid plans for suicide had been put into effect.

77. A 'new' government.

The advance of the British troops forced **von Greim** and **Reitsch** to retreat to Schleswig on the evening of 1 May. Here, **Reitsch** and **von Greim** learned that **Hitler's** death had been announced and that his successor was **Dönitz**. On 2 May, a new government was to meet in Plön. **Von Greim** and **Reitsch** were supposed to receive **Dönitz's** orders as representatives of the Air Force. Besides, they wanted to confront **Himmler** and expose him as a traitor.

78. How Himmler explained the capitulation.

Himmler arrived late, when everyone was already in the conference hall, and **Reitsch** was alone when he came in.

'*One moment, Herr Reichsführer, I have a question of great importance. Do you have any time?*' **Reitsch** asked.

Himmler looked almost playful as he answered: '*Yes, sure*'.

'*Is it correct, that you, Herr Reichsführer, contacted the Allies offering peace without Hitler's orders?*'

'*Why, sure*'.

'*You betrayed your Führer and the people at the worst moment. It is high treason, Herr Reichsführer. You did it when your place was in the bunker with Hitler*'.

'*High treason? No! You'll see that History will see it in a proper perspective. Hitler wanted to go on with the struggle. He was driven mad by his arrogance and his sense of honour. He still wanted to shed German blood when there was no blood left. Hitler was crazy. This should have been stopped long ago*'.

'*Crazy? I left him less than 36 hours ago. He died for the cause he believed in. He died bravely and full of the honour you are talking about, and as for you, Göring and the others, you shall live branded as traitors and cowards*'.

'*What I did, I did to save German blood, to save what was left of our country*'.

'*You talk about German blood, Herr Reichsführer? You talk about it now? You should have thought about it years ago, before you were associated with this useless bloodshed*'.

A sudden air raid interrupted this conversation.

79. The final orders – to repulse the Russians.

Von Greim said that in the first war council at **Dönitz's** headquarters little was decided, but all agreed that it was possible to hold out for only a few days more, while the commanders on the Russian front were ordered to stand firm until the end so as to enable as many people as possible to escape. **Reitsch** says that **von Greim**, despite the deteriorating condition of his wounded leg, insisted on immediately flying to see Field-Marshal **Schörner**, commander of the forces in Silesia and Czechoslovakia, to instruct him to continue resistance, even after the order to surrender.

80. During the flight to **Schörner**, the pain of **von Greim's** wound was so bad that sometimes he lost consciousness. On arrival, **Schörner** informed them that he had already decided to hold out as long as possible and had already ordered this before **von Greim's** arrival.

81. It was then decided to fly to **Kesselring** with the same message, but **von Greim's** leg was in such a state that it was impossible to move him. From 3 to 7 May they had to stay at **Schörner's** headquarters in Königgratz where **Reitsch** cared for **von Greim** until he was able to be moved again.

82. On night of 7 May, they flew in a Dornier 217 to Graz, where **Kesselring** was reported to be. When they were directly over the airfield, German anti-aircraft guns damaged their plane and it crash-landed at the end of the runway. **Reitsch** and **von Greim** learnt that the capitulation would take place on the night of 9 May and hearing that **Kesselring** had left Graz for Zell-am-Zee, they flew there to give him his instructions.

83. The end in Zell-am-Zee.

They arrived at Zell-am-Zee in a Fieseler-Storch and reached General **Koller**, Chief of the General Staff of the Air Force, who could tell them where **Kesselring** was. Here, they learnt that the capitulation would take place on the 8th, not the 9th. They still wanted to see **Kesselring**, but **Koller** preferred not to say where he was, either because it was too late or he did not know that **Kesselring** was in the village of Almdorf, several miles to the north of Zell-am-Zee. On hearing this, **Reitsch** and **von Greim** decided that any further efforts on their part would be absolutely fruitless. Before the capitulation, they left Zell-am-Zee for Kitzbühl to see a famous doctor who had just opened a clinic there.

84. Reitsch says that if had not been for **von Greim's** weakened state, she would not have been be able to force him to save his leg. To the end, he wanted to support resistance against the Russians. ✓

85. Why the 'last redoubt' was not used.

In answer to the question why the 'last redoubt' in Austria and Southern Germany was not used, **Reitsch** has little to add to what is already known. She says that as early as 15 April it seemed that everything had been prepared to move the government and the military headquarters to Berchtesgaden. All the offices and headquarters in Berlin were on constant 2-hour alert at that time. It seems from the account of Colonel **Below** and others that the meeting mentioned above was intended to work out this proposal in detail. She says that the reports **Hitler** received were so dire that he was convinced it was impossible to complete the preparations for a successful defence from the 'redoubt' in time. It was believed that **Hitler's** loss of confidence was caused by the realisation that this 'redoubt' project, which had been expected to be so successful, had finally been abandoned. It was also said that **Göring** and **Hitler** had a serious argument about it. **Göring** insisted on an early evacuation to the 'redoubt', but **Hitler** refused, in the hope that the line on the Oder would hold. Supposedly, **Göring** argued that the 'redoubt' was completed while **Hitler** preferred to wait until its readiness was proved at the above-mentioned conference. Later, at a war council at **Dönitz's** headquarters, they said that **Göring's** departure could be explained by the fact that he knew that the Oder line would not hold and hoped in vain that only the partly-finished 'redoubt' would do so.

The failure of the 'redoubt' was due first to **Göring's** failure to complete it, and **Hitler's** belief that continued resistance in Berlin would be more effective than a retreat to a partially-completed 'redoubt'.

86. Surrendering to the Americans.

They arrived in Kitzbühl on the morning of the 9th and were brought before the American military authorities. **Von Greim** was under interrogation until 23 May and then brought to Salzburg before being sent to Germany as a prisoner-of-war. On the night of 24 May, he committed suicide in Salzburg, using the poison capsule **Hitler** had given him. Although he was far less well-known, both in Germany and abroad, than his corpulent predecessor, Hanna believes he should have had **Göring's** job years ago. She considers the fact that he disagreed with **Göring** about almost everything was sufficient proof of his abilities.

87. Appraisal of the evidence.

The investigator believes that the information presented above was given in good faith and with a sincere wish to speak correctly and accurately. The suicide of her family, the death of her closest friend, **von Greim**, the physical sufferings of Germany and all she experienced in the last days of the war led her to also seriously contemplate suicide. She says that she lives now only for the truth, to tell the truth about **Göring**, 'a petty showman', to tell the truth about **Hitler**, 'criminally incapable' and to tell the truth to the German people about that dangerous form of rule that created the Third Reich. She believes that by answering the investigator she has fulfilled a major part of her mission.

For this reason, we consider that her account can be taken as a profound effort to be truthful and honest. She is now experiencing a difficult inner struggle, trying to reconcile her understanding of 'honour' with her evidence concerning **Göring**, **Himmler** and **Hitler** himself. These difficulties, it seems, are not so great when she talks to the investigator as when she talks to private individuals. But according to information which the investigator has received from private individuals whom she has contacted and with whom she was not previously acquainted, it can be seen that she has tried to influence her compatriots in a more progressive and democratic way. ✓

Translated into Russian by M. **Goltz**

2 November, 1945

Ф. К-1 ос; оп. 4; д. 16; л. 2-25
(машинописная копия; перевод с английского)
(photocopy; translated from English)

✓ **Hanna Reitsch**, *born 29 March, 1912 in Hirschberg, famous test pilot with numerous flight records. Hitler's favourite pilot and one of only two women awarded the Iron Cross First Class during World War II. Held for 18 months by the American military. In 1952, she won third place in the world gliding championships in Spain (the only woman to compete). She subsequently founded a sports gliding network in India and a gliding school in Ghana. She broke many gliding records in the 1970s, several of which stand to this day. Reitsch died of a massive heart attack on 24 August, 1979 in Frankfurt-am-Main.*

✓ **Robert Ritter von Greim**, *born on 22 June, 1892 in Bayreuth, lawyer, World War I flying ace, the last German officer to achieve the rank of Field Marshal. Appointed Supreme Commander of the Luftwaffe on 26 April, 1945, captured by American soldiers on 8 May, 1945, the day the Third Reich surrendered. Committed suicide in Salzburg on 24 May, 1945.*

MANUSCRIPT TESTIMONY OF
GENERAL HELMUTH WEIDLING

4 January, 1946

The first time I met the Führer of Germany and Commander-in-Chief of the Armed Forces was on 13 April, 1944. With 12 other officers and generals I was summoned to Hitler's office at the Berghof near Berchtesgaden to receive a decoration – the Knight's Cross with Oak Leaves.

Hitler's senior aide-de-camp, General **Schmundt**, lined upC all 12 officers in a row in **Hitler's** large study and carefully instructed us that while being introduced to **Hitler** we should only give our name, rank and position, adding that if **Hitler** wanted to know more about us he would ask questions himself.

Hitler entered. His face was unhealthily pale, and he was bloated and bent over. Each of us gave his name as instructed. Handing over the decorations **Hitler** only shook hands, saying nothing, except to express sympathy to Lieutenant-General **Hauser**, who was on crutches.

After that, we all sat at the big round table in his study and **Hitler** addressed us for half an hour, in a low, monotonous voice. In the first part of his speech, Hitler touched upon the improvements in our weapons and those of the enemy, and the new tactics that resulted from this. **Hitler** interspersed his speech with detailed figures on the calibre and range of weapons, the thickness of armour and so on. One could see that **Hitler** had an outstanding memory. But it seemed to me that the matters touched on were of little importance.

In the second part of his speech, he touched upon political events. 'Co-operation between the Anglo-Americans and the Russians cannot last long', **Hitler** stated, '*because communism and capitalism are naturally incompatible*'. On this assumption, **Hitler** appeared to hope for a favourable outcome of the war.

Hitler finished his speech, stood up, shook hands with each of us again and we left.

I left the Berghof displeased and dissatisfied. A conversation I had subsequently with General **Martinek** is an example of my state of mind.

We asked ourselves why we were brought to Berchtesgaden from the front. The majority of those decorated had expected that **Hitler** would use this opportunity allow each of us to share our experiences with him of battle. These were experienced officers whom he had summoned directly from the front. A real general should be interested in their needs and requirements.

'*Now we can see what an invisible wall surrounds Hitler*', said **Martinek**.

'*Yes*', I answered, '*Hitler cannot and does not want to know what the reality is. This is the work* of the camarilla. Otherwise General **Schmundt** would not have instructed us so thoroughly in what we were to say during our meeting with Hitler'.

'It is obvious', **Martinek** added, 'that for the same reason Hitler has not been to the Front for the last year and a half, otherwise some brave man might have told him that with leadership like this we'll never win the war'.

I agreed absolutely with **Martinek** and added: 'I am bitterly disillusioned by Hitler's behaviour. He did not give us any guidance about how we should act in the heavy fighting we will obviously be facing this year. We have heard enough of his discourse, but it is hardly useful. How will it end?'

The following year, I met **Hitler** in an absolutely different situation.

The Russian spring offensive of 1945 on the Oder started on 14 April. The 56th Panzer Corps under my command was in the Seelow-Wolkow area, to the west of Kustrin – in the main path of the Russian offensive. Soon after it started, as a result of heavy fighting, there were deep penetrations of the left and right flanks of the sector I defended there as well as in the rear of the Corps. Communications with the two neighbouring Corps and with the Army were cut. But my Corps managed to fight a defensive battle and retreat to the west, to the outer Berlin defence perimeter.

On 21 April, I sent Lieutenant-General **Voigtsberger**, a former commander of the 'Berlin' Division, to establish communications with 9th Army. Two days later, Voigtsberger returned from Army headquarters and in great excitement reported to me as follows.

Information had been received by the army that supposedly I and my headquarters had moved to Döberitz, to the west of Berlin. For this reason, Hitler had ordered that I be arrested and shot. Voigtsberger insisted at 9th Army that such a movement would be impossible. The orders he brought with him from the 9th Army stated that the 56th Panzer Corps was to establish communication with the left flank of its neighbour to the right.

At first, I was unsure and unclear as to what to do, but the orders I received made our hearts beat faster because the idea of fighting in a ruined city had been demoralising us.

With my Chief-of-Staff Colonel **Dürfing**, I immediately started to prepare orders for the Corps to re-group on the night of 23/24 April. During this work, the Chief-of-Staff of the Berlin Defence Area, Colonel **Refior**, informed me by telephone of General **Krebs**' order to send a staff officer from the 56th Panzer Corps with a map of troop deployments to the Reich Chancellery.

Two reasons made me go to the Reich Chancellery personally. First, I wanted to know the reason for the order for my arrest and execution, and second I wanted, if possible, to ensure that my Corps avoided fighting in the ruined city.

Helmuth Weidling's soldier's book.

Accompanied by the Chief of Department-1 of the Corps Staff, Major **Knappe**, I reached the Reich Chancellery. From the pavement of the Vosstrasse, a staircase led down to an underground 'city', which had been built between the Wilhelmstrasse and the Göringstrasse. The size of this shelter is indicated by the fact that during heavy air-raids on Berlin 4000–5000 children were accommodated and fed down there every night as 'guests' of Hitler.

We were immediately led to the so-called aide-de-camp's bunker. I was received by the Chief of the General Staff General **Krebs** and Hitler's personal aide-de-camp General **Burgdorf**. The meeting was somewhat frigid, in spite of the fact that I knew **Krebs** well from the days of the Reichswehr and later when he was Chief-of-Staff of the 9th Army and the 'Centre' Army Group.

During our conversation, I was easily able to convince both generals that I had no intention of, and nor was there any sense in, relocating to Döberitz, considering the situation. They had to admit that they had taken mere rumour as fact and now, after my explanation, they regretted their credulousness. Nevertheless, it turned out that I had been dismissed but they did not tell me so.

Concerning the situation in eastern Berlin, **Krebs** told me that the deep Russian penetration was causing them considerable trouble. They wanted to discuss with me what counter-action could be taken by the 56th Panzer Corps. When I informed them of the order the Corps had received from the 9th Army, **Krebs** shouted: *'Impossible, absolutely impossible! I'll immediately report to the Führer about it'.* With these words, **Krebs** left me alone, and **Burgdorf** followed him like a shadow.

I ordered Major **Knappe**, who had accompanied me, to notify the Chief-of-Staff by telephone that the Corps might still be needed in eastern Berlin that night. During the telephone conversation, the Chief-of-Staff said that he had received a telegram from the Department of Personnel of the Army signed by **Burgdorf**, saying that: 'General **Weidling** is transferred to the reserve of command personnel of the General Command of the Wehrmacht. Lieutenant-General **Burmeister**, commander of 25th Panzer Division, is appointed as commander of 56th Panzer Corps'.

I was highly indignant. It was only by good luck that I had been able to rehabilitate myself here. But how many generals had suffered lately only because they had had no chance to disprove rumours about themselves!

While **Krebs** and **Burgdorf** were absent, one of **Krebs**' officers gave me a brief report on the situation in Berlin. **Hitler** was staying in Berlin with some of his staff to personally direct the defence of the capital. State officials had begun to flee Berlin on 15 April. The road to Munich was being called 'the Reich refugee road'. From the WSC and GCA, two General Staff branches were formed: the first, 'North' Staff under Field-Marshal **Keitel** and the second 'South' Staff under Field-Marshal **Kesselring**. General **Jodl** was attached as Chief-of-Staff.

One can judge how rapid and chaotic this reorganisation was by the fact that the two Staffs took all the radio sets in Berlin with them. General Command in Berlin had to be content with a single remaining SS radio unit, connected to **Himmler**'s headquarters.

I was briefly told about the following interesting event. On 23 April, a telegram from **Göring** in Berchtesgaden dropped like a bombshell on the Reich Chancellery. **Göring** demanded that **Hitler** hand over executive power to him because **Hitler**, surrounded in Berlin, was in no position to execute his official duties. Göring mentioned Hitler's speech in the Reichstag on 1 September, 1939 when he had supposedly appointed him as his successor.

Krebs and **Burgdorf** returned from their report to Hitler. **Krebs** said to me: *'You should immediately report to the Führer about the situation in your Corps. The order from the 9th Army is cancelled. Tonight the Corps will be used to the east of Berlin'.* Then I gave vent to my anger and said that the Corps' situation should be reported by its new commander – General **Burmeister**. Together, the two generals were just about able to calm me down and they said that **Hitler** would surely leave me in command of the Corps.

Notwithstanding the fact that I was accompanied to the Führer's bunker by both generals, my papers were most carefully checked three times. Finally, an SS Sturmbannführer took away my waist-belt and pistol.

From the so-called Kolenhof, we went deeper into the labyrinth of shelters. Through a small kitchen we went into a kind of officers' mess where a lot of officers were dining. Then we went down another floor and found ourselves in the reception room outside the Führer's study.

It contained many people in grey or brown uniforms. Walking around the reception room I recognised only the Foreign Minister, **Ribbentrop**. Then a door opened and I found myself before Adolf **Hitler**. He sat in a rather small room in an armchair near a big table. When I entered, Adolf **Hitler** rose with obvious difficulty, leaning on the table with both hands. His left leg was constantly trembling. From his puffy face, two feverishly bright eyes stared at me. His smile changed into a stiff mask. He extended his right hand to me, with both his hands shaking like his left leg.

'Do I know you?' he asked. I answered that two years ago I had received a decoration from him – the Knight's Cross with Oak Leaves. **Hitler** said that he easily remembered names, but not faces. After that greeting, **Hitler** sank back into the armchair again.

I reported about the situation of the Corps and said it had already begun to relocate south-east to regroup. If it were now ordered to about-face 180 degrees, there would be terrible confusion in the morning.

After a brief talk with **Krebs**, **Hitler** again confirmed to me the order to send the Corps to the eastern sector of Berlin.

At the end, **Hitler** expounded on his criminally amateurish plan of operations for the relief of Berlin. He spoke in a low voice, with long pauses, often repeating himself and suddenly turning to insignificant matters, that were strangely discussed at length.

Hitler's 'plan of operations' came to the following: from south of Brandenburg the 12th Assault Army under the command of Lieutenant-General **Wenck** would attack through Potsdam to the south-west sector of Berlin. Simultaneously, the 9th Army would receive an order to disengage from the enemy along the line of the Oder and advance into the south-east sector of Berlin. As a result of the joint action of the two armies, the Russian forces to the south of Berlin would be destroyed. To ensure freedom of manoeuvre of the 12th Assault Army and the 9th Army, the following German forces would be sent against the Russians to the north of Berlin: from the Nauen region, the 7th Panzer Division and the 'Steiner' SS Assault Group from south of Fürstenberg. Later, that is when the Russian forces to the south of Berlin had been destroyed, the Russians north of the city were to be destroyed also, by the joint action of all four attacking groups.

When **Hitler** finished, it seemed to me as if I had heard it all in a dream.

I had participated for several days and nights in heavy fighting and I knew only one thing: a few days more, and the final catastrophe would come, unless a miracle occurred at the last moment. There were only limited quantities of ammunition, almost no fuel and, above all, the troops fought without the will to resist because they had lost faith in victory and in the necessity to resist.

Was a miracle possible? Was **Wenck's** Assault Army, about which **Goebbels** had talked so much in the last few weeks, what Germany was holding in reserve? Or was it only a figment of the imagination of a fanatic who had lost touch with reality?

Struck by the sight of this human ruin who headed the German state, and badly affected by the amateurishness that reigned in ruling circles, I left **Hitler's** study. As I was leaving, **Hitler** rose, with obvious difficulty, and extended his hand to me. Nothing was said about my arrest, execution or dismissal.

In the aide-de-camps' bunker, **Krebs** explained my Corps' orders to me on the map of Berlin. I was to shoulder responsibility for four of the eastern and southern sectors of Berlin's defence area, out of the total of nine. Five sectors remained in the hands of the commander of the defence area. My Corps was under **Hitler's** direct command.

At that I did not hesitate to say to General **Krebs**: '*So, Hitler is really the commander of the Berlin defence area!*'

And I added some questions for him:

'*Can you believe that Hitler's plan of operations includes raising the siege of Berlin? For example, Hitler has simultaneously given the 9th Army defensive and offensive combat missions. Do you have any idea here in what state the army is now? The left flank of my Corps is completely destroyed, and what is left of it is with the "Weichsel" Army Group. As for the neighbouring Corps to the right, all I know is that it, too, has been in heavy combat and is now in the same state as we are, if not worse. The rest of the 9th Army cannot be that strong. And yet despite this, under constant Russian pressure, the troops are to be removed from the Oder in order to fight in the eastern part of Berlin. You know, Krebs, I cannot understand Hitler's orders*'.

Meanwhile, I issued combat orders to my divisions and chose the Tempelhof airfield for my command post.

About 22.00, I left the Reich Chancellery and went to the commanders of the defence sectors who had been newly placed under me to get information on the situation on the ground.

After speaking to the commanders, the situation was as follows:

Berlin was defended not by organised armies but by loosely-connected units and small groups. More-or-less suitable officers had been brought in as commanders, but the first thing they had to do was form their staffs. There were no means of communication. The infantry was made up of 'Volkssturm' battalions, artillerymen and Hitler Youth units. The only anti-tank weapons were grenade-launchers (Panzerfaust).

The artillery was equipped with captured trophies, and there was no centralised artillery command. The core of the defence was the anti-aircraft batteries, and although it had a centralised command, due to the scarcity of motor transport, the fixed batteries were rarely useful in ground combat.

The chain of command was confused. Orders came not only from the defence command, but also from many Party officials, such as the Defence Commissioner and the Deputy Gauleiter. Most of all, I was shocked by the fate of the civilian population, whose sufferings **Hitler** ignored. Any sensible person could easily imagine what a horrible drama was being prepared.

Late at night on 24 April, my Deputy Commander arrived at the Corps command post and informed me that the Corps' movements that night had generally gone according to plan. Soon after, I was again summoned to the Reich Chancellery. I arrived there about 12.00 at night.

Krebs informed me of the following: '*Due to the impression you made yesterday on the Führer, he appoints you the Commander of the Berlin fortified region. Go immediately to the command post of the fortified region in the Hohenzollerndam and report to me when you have taken command*'.

I only replied: '*It would be better if Hitler enforced the order for my execution, at least this chalice would pass me by*'.

But the real reason of my appointment was not the impression I had made on **Hitler**. The first commander of the fortified region, Lieutenant-General **Reymann** had been dismissed on 24 April after a confrontation with **Goebbels**, the Berlin Defence Commissioner. His immediate successor was Colonel **Kaether**, Chief-of-Staff to the Wehrmacht's Chief National-Socialist Officer, who, on being appointed to this position, was simultaneously promoted to Lieutenant-General. But because **Kaether** was not trained for this leading position, and I was the only commander of combat troops available, I was entrusted with this task.

Taking command of the defence area, I understood that the real commander was the Defence Commissioner of Berlin, Dr **Goebbels** and his retinue. The headquarters of the defence area region were used mainly as an inquiry office (due to contradictory orders) and that interfered considerably with the new commander's efforts to control the actual fighting.

I received no precise information on the strength of the defence forces, either at the moment of my appointment or later. I now believe it was between 80–100,000 men. Neither in numbers, training nor available ammunition was this force capable of defending a city several million strong from a modern army.

In mid-April, 30 well-armed 'Volkssturm' battalions had been formed in Berlin, which were attached to the 9th Army. The previous commander, Lieutenant-General

Reymann, had protested at this military absurdity, and was, as I have already mentioned, dismissed.

Gathering up the reins of this more-than-complicated command took me half the day of 24 April, and only at 19.00 was I able to report to **Krebs** that I had assumed command.

On 25 April, I was on the road almost all day, to see for myself the readiness of my sector for defence. I happened to discover some interesting details. First of all, no arrangements had been made to evacuate the civilian population from the central districts of the city, which might become a battlefield at any moment. The civilian population was left to itself to decide when to escape. Second, none of the bridges had been prepared for demolition. Goebbels had entrusted a 'Spur' company with this task, because demolition carried out by combat units damaged surrounding property. But it turned out that all the materials prepared for blowing up the bridges as well as explosives stored for that purpose had been removed from Berlin when the 'Spur' offices were evacuated.

In the evening, I was invited to the Reich Chancellery to discuss the situation. At 21.00, I met **Krebs**. Not long before, Air Force General Ritter **von Greim** had arrived at the Reich Chancellery on a stretcher. He had flown into Berlin with a woman pilot, Hanna **Reitsch**, and had been wounded in the leg while landing. Hitler appointed Ritter **von Greim** Supreme Commander of the German Air Force and gave him the rank of Field-Marshal. **Göring** was dismissed. Before the meeting, Hanna **Reitsch** passed by me several times, once walking arm-in-arm with Frau **Goebbels**. The rest of the time she was in **Hitler**'s private apartments. I heard that later Hanna **Reitsch** got Field-Marshal **von Greim** out of Berlin in an aeroplane.

As for Frau **Goebbels**, I later saw her every evening in **Hitler**'s bunker.

Almost all the officers had gathered in the Führer's reception-room. I was introduced to **Goebbels**, who greeted me with exceptional courtesy. He seemed to me to be Mephisto personified. **Goebbels**' aide-de-camp, State Secretary **Naumann**, was tall and thin, but in other respects resembled his master. Reichsleiter **Bormann**, as I was later told in the Reich Chancellery, was **Hitler**'s evil genius. With his close friend **Burgdorf**, he gave himself up to the earthly joys of life, the main ones being cognac and port. Ambassador **Hewel** hid himself in a corner and it seemed to me that he had renounced everything. I did not see **Ribbentrop** again; they said that he had left Berlin. The Deputy Gauleiter of Berlin, Dr **Schach**, almost grovelled before his master, **Goebbels**. The Reich Youth Leader **Axmann** looked modest and reserved. **Himmler**'s liaison officer, Gruppenführer **Fegelein**, was a typical arrogant, swaggering and self-assured SS officer. There were also Hitler's adjutants: Major **Johannmeier** from the Army, Colonel von **Below** from the Air Force and Sturmbannführer **Günsche** from the SS. There was only one Naval liaison officer, Vice-Admiral **Voss**.

When **Krebs** arrived with a battle map, we all entered the Führer's study. **Hitler** greeted me by shaking hands. **Goebbels** immediately occupied the place against the wall in front of **Hitler**, where he usually sat during meetings. Everyone else sat wherever they could.

Krebs stood at **Hitler's** right, with **Burgdorf** and **Bormann**, and myself on his left, ready to report. I had to make an effort not to stare at **Hitler**, bent over in his armchair, his arms and legs trembling constantly.

I began my report by describing the enemy's situation, illustrating it with a large map I had prepared with the enemy positions marked on it. Hitler showed particular interest in this map. Several times during my report, he asked **Krebs** if my data on the enemy's strength corresponded with reality. Each time, **Krebs** confirmed my information.

Then I reported on the situation of our forces. Apart from two deep penetrations, one near Spandau and the other in the northern sector of Berlin, we were nevertheless managing to hold the main front line. At the same time, I described the situation in the defence sectors to which my Corps was going to be sent. **Hitler** made me speak about it in detail.

Turning to the state of the civilian population, I immediately noticed that I had touched on a matter that disturbed them. **Goebbels** began to feel uneasy and took the floor without asking permission from Hitler.

According to **Goebbels**, everything was completely in order, and his deputy was keeping him informed about this in regular reports. I had to restrain my indignation. At the end of my report I pointed out the great threat to all our supply lines. All the depots were in the outer ring of the city and they were already in imminent danger. **Goebbels** again wanted to intervene, but here **Krebs** interrupted and started to report on the general situation.

It became evident to me how tightly this *camarilla* was bound up with each other. They ignored anything that was unpleasant to them. It seemed to me that **Hitler's** role was already finished. This physically and morally broken man was only an instrument in the hands of the *camarilla*.

I remember the following incident in **Krebs'** report of 25 April. From **Krebs'** speech on 25 April, I remember the following moment. **Krebs** said: '*The 9th Army reported that it is moving in the direction of Luckenewald, i.e. in a westerly direction*'. **Hitler** excitedly rapped on the table with the three pencils he constantly held in his left hand to stop his fingers trembling. Had he realised that his 'plan of operations' to relieve Berlin had gone off course? But **Krebs** was cleverly able to calm **Hitler**, despite it being obvious to any sensible man that after the withdrawal of the 56th Panzer Corps the 9th Army would be unable to attack the powerful Russian forces.

The 9th Army's real job was to avoid being encircled and to join up with General **Wenck's** 12th Assault Army, but **Krebs** reported: *'General Wenck's 12th Assault Army has begun an offensive to lift the blockade of Berlin'*.

These were what Germany was holding in reserve!

'Wide and deep penetrations by the Russian forces through the "Weichsel" Army Group would negatively influence the defence of Berlin', **Krebs** continued.

It was already 1.00 at night. After the meeting everyone, including the secretaries, had a brief conversation. Here I got to know some of the people better.

On 26 April, the situation of Berlin's defenders became more critical. Deep penetrations took place in all sectors. **Krebs** telephoned almost every hour and tried to present the general situation in a more favourable light. First of all, according to his information, the 12th Assault Army was advancing and its vanguard patrols were approaching Potsdam. Notwithstanding repeated requests, **Krebs** said nothing about the movements of the troops to the north of the city, whose attack was very necessary. In fact these two groups never even began to advance.

One more episode should be mentioned that is characteristic of the *camarilla's* behaviour. **Goebbels** telephoned me late at night. Most politely, he asked me to let one of the commanders of a sub-sector in northern Berlin – Lieutenant-Colonel **Bärenfänger** – go to the Reich Chancellery for several hours. Before my Corps arrived, **Bärenfänger** had been the independent commander of a defence sector, but later he was demoted to sub-sector command. As a former Hitler Youth leader, he was a staunch supporter of **Hitler**. His self-esteem having been wounded, he appealed to **Goebbels**, whom he knew well. Approximately 2 or 3 hours after my conversation with **Goebbels**, I was telephoned by General **Burgdorf** and informed that Lieutenant-Colonel **Bärenfänger** had been given the rank of Major-General and **Hitler** wanted to appoint him commander of an independent sector. It seemed to me that the fortified region had turned into a lunatic asylum!

I reported to **Krebs** daily. I was relieved of having to attend the nightly general situation conferences at the Reich Chancellery because of the amount of work I had to do.

On 27 April, the enemy's encirclement of Berlin was complete. In a concentrated attack, the Russian armoured and infantry divisions were moving closer and closer to the centre of the city. In those tragic days of April, the horrified civilian population saw everything that had managed to survive the Anglo-American bombing destroyed in heavy fighting. The inhabitants were hiding in bomb-shelters and in the underground like animals. Life had no meaning for them any more. There was no electricity, no gas, no water!

The most terrible thing was the situation in the hospitals. Professor **Sauerbruch**, in his letter to the Commandant of Berlin, described the terrible fate of the wounded.

Being a combat veteran I know how cruel modern warfare is, but what Berlin experienced surpassed everything.

In the early morning, our command post in the Hohenzollerndam came under fire, and we had to move to the Bendlerstrasse.

In the evening of 27 April, it became absolutely clear to me that there were only two options available: to surrender or break out. Further fighting in Berlin would be criminal.

During the next situation meeting at the Reich Chancellery, my task would be to portray to **Hitler** the senselessness of further fighting and to get permission to surrender Berlin.

The next situation conference took place in **Hitler**'s study at 22.00 on 27 April, 1945. I began by explaining the enemy's strategic situation. According to my Corps' intelligence, a Russian tank corps, which had been operating to the south of Berlin, had been relieved by an infantry corps. Presumably the Russian Command had thrown this tank corps against the 12th Assault Army. After his initial success, General **Wenck** was bogged down in heavy defensive fighting to the south-west of Potsdam. Berlin was surrounded, but one could not detect any diversion of the besieging forces in response to the four attacking groups. One could not depend on the siege of Berlin being lifted.

In this respect, I indicated a dangerous threat to the troops' morale, due to our own propaganda. Right up to the last, newspapers had been published in Berlin with the headlines 'Numerous armies are speeding to lift the blockade of Berlin'. Soon the troops would know what was true and what was false.

Goebbels interrupted, saying indignantly: *'You're going to blame me for this, aren't you?'* I had to control myself to answer quietly: *'Being the commander of the troops I consider it my duty to point this matter out'*. **Bormann** calmed **Goebbels**.

This confrontation took place in **Hitler**'s presence but he did not say anything.

At that moment, State Secretary **Naumann** burst into the room and, interrupting me, reported in great agitation: *'My Führer, a Stockholm radio station has broadcast that Himmler has made a proposal to the British and the Americans for the capitulation of Germany and received an answer from them that they would agree to hold talks as long as the third partner – Russia – were invited'*. There was silence in the room. **Hitler** was tapping on the table with his pencils. His face was distorted and there was fear and alarm in his eyes. Voicelessly he mouthed a word like 'traitor' to **Goebbels**.

For some time there was a heavy silence, then **Krebs** quietly advised me to continue with my report. I reported that both Berlin airfields – Templehof and Gatow – were lost. An emergency airstrip that had been built in the Tiergarten could only be partially used by single aircraft because it was so heavily cratered by enemy fire. Supplying Berlin was only possible now by air. Almost all of the large supply dumps, including that in the Western Port, had been captured by the enemy on 26 and 27 April. The shortage of ammunition was already being felt.

For several weeks previously, I had been experiencing the defeat of the whole army in a small area in East Prussia, so it was not difficult for me to picture what the next few days would be like. This time, the situation was even more terrible, because the civilian population would share the same fate as the troops. I pictured the terrible fate awaiting the wounded and read Professor **Sauerbruch**'s letter aloud. As I was about to sum up, I was interrupted by **Hitler**, who said '*I know what you are driving at*', and then delivered a lengthy explanation as to why it was necessary to defend Berlin to the last. His speech was punctuated by frequent pauses, during which **Goebbels** interrupted more than once, supporting what **Hitler** said.

All of **Hitler**'s speech could be summed up by the following: '*If Berlin falls into the hands of the enemy, the war will be lost. That is why I am here and why I firmly reject any capitulation*'.

I therefore decided not to propose a break-out from the encirclement at this time.

Because it was 02.00 at night, we were dismissed. **Goebbels** and **Bormann** stayed with **Hitler** in his study.

All of us sat in the next room and discussed **Himmler**'s betrayal. At the end of the conversation, I explained the plan for a break-out from Berlin. **Krebs** showed great interest in it. He entrusted me with the task of developing a plan for a break-out and to report on it at the next conference. His interest was so great that he asked for a draft of it to make his own amendments.

The plan was worked on in the morning of 28 April at the command post in the Bendlerstrasse. The break-out was to be in three waves from two sides.

Work on the plan was performed on the morning of 28 April at the command post in the Bendler Block. The breakthrough was to take place in three waves from two sides, using bridges over the Havel south of Spandau. **Hitler** and his headquarters would be in the third wave.

At noon, my Chief-of-Staff Colonel von **Dürfing** went to the Reich Chancellery and presented the plan to General **Krebs**. **Krebs** approved it.

Meanwhile the situation was getting more and more desperate. The ring around Berlin was getting tighter and tighter.

At 22.00 on 28 April, 1945 there was another situation meeting.

Fewer people were there this time. Two of the adjutants, Colonel **von Below** and Major **Johannmeier**, were absent. It was said that they had been sent out of Berlin with important documents. How and by what route they had left Berlin I was unable to discover. I cannot be sure if I saw Gruppenführer **Fegelein** on 28 and 29 April. I only heard about his execution on Hitler's orders several months later in Moscow.

This time, because of the increasing shortage of ammunition and the impossibility of aerial resupply, it was not difficult for me to propose a break-out.

Hitler thought for a very long time, then, in a tired, hopeless voice, he said:

'What good would this break-out do? We'd just go from one encirclement to another. Should I wander around, waiting for the end in some peasant's house or other such place? It is better for me to stay here'.

Now it was all clear. It was all about himself, about 'I, the ego'. **Goebbels'** interjection was the same: 'Certainly, my Führer, it is absolutely correct!'

I was prepared for anything but this. To give them the chance to be secure in the bunker for as long as possible, many thousands of people on both sides were to make the ultimate sacrifice in this criminal fighting.

I left the Reich Chancellery in an embittered mood.

The drama was swiftly coming to its end. The airborne supply on the night of 29 April had brought almost nothing: only 6 tons of supplies were delivered, including 8–10 boxes of small arms ammunition, 15–20 artillery rounds and a small quantity of medical supplies.

The troops' demands for ammunition became more and more insistent. Communication between the separate sectors was possible only by messengers, who had to go on foot because the Berlin streets were impassable to vehicles.

Inside the Reich Chancellery.

We, in our command post, were on the front line. Facing us, on the other side of the Landwehr canal, was the enemy. The Reichstag was lost. The enemy's machine-guns were concentrated on the Potsdammerplatz.

Under fire from machine-guns and grenade-launchers, I reached the Reich Chancellery covered in mud. It was 22.00 on 29 April. The atmosphere in the bunker was like that of a front-line command post. All who gathered there for the situation report were in despondent mood. **Hitler**, his face still more pinched, was looking fixedly at the map spread before him.

I persistently asked **Hitler** to permit a break-out as soon as possible, saying that, as was well known, no soldier can fight without weapons. I finished with the words: '*The break-out will be a success if an assault group comes to meet us*'.

Hitler, with bitter irony in his voice, said: '*Look at my map. Everything shown on it is not based on information from the Supreme Command, but from foreign radio station broadcasts. No one reports to us. I can order anything, but none of my orders is carried out any more*'.

Krebs supported me in my attempts to get permission for a break-out, but in very proper form.

At last it was decided that, as there were no airborne supplies, the troops could break out in small groups, but on the understanding that they should continue to resist wherever possible. Capitulation was out of the question.

Although I had failed to get **Hitler** to call a final halt to the bloodshed, I had managed to persuade him to end resistance in Berlin.

Where **Hitler** would be during this break-out was not mentioned. This struck me only when I got to my command post. But **Hitler**'s personal safety was outside my responsibility.

I ordered all the sector commanders to assemble at the Bendlerstrasse at 10.00 on 30 April. They were instructed as to what 'small groups' meant, and the time for the break-out was decided.

Because the previous night's airborne supply drop had almost completely ceased, I set the time for the break-out at 22.00 on 30 April.

The commanders agreed with me that the units under their command should remain under their command, and so 'small groups' was to mean their units. This was against **Hitler**'s orders but it was impossible to consult with **Krebs**, as all telephone communication had been cut since early that morning.

About 13.00, the commanders went to their units. They felt a sense of moral relief, because they would not have to continue senseless fighting in Berlin. The future did not seem so gloomy for them.

I tried to reach the Reich Chancellery in the afternoon. At 15.00, a Sturmführer arrived from there (I don't remember his name), having been ordered to deliver a personal letter from **Hitler** to me. It occurred to me that I was going to be held to account for disobeying **Hitler**'s orders as to the meaning of 'small groups'. My officers only let the Sturmführer come to my room alone after they had disarmed him.

Very tensely, I opened the letter. It was dated 30 April, 1945. **Hitler** repeated exactly what had been said at the last meeting: 'Due to continuing lack of airborne supplies, a break-out in small groups is permitted. These groups must continue fighting wherever possible. Any capitulation must be decisively rejected'. The letter was signed in pencil.

About 17.00, I was about to return to the Reich Chancellery, but the Sturmführer arrived again. He was brought to me and handed me a note with the following contents: 'General **Weidling** must come immediately to the Reich Chancellery to see **Krebs**. All actions planned for the evening of 30 April must be postponed'. The signature was illegible.

From the Sturmführer, I learned that this note had been signed by the aide-de-camp of Brigadenführer **Mohnke**, who commanded the defence of the government district and reported directly to **Hitler**.

Again, I was faced with a difficult decision. Was this all right? Was this order a trick by fanatics, who intended to fight in Berlin until the last bullet? Or maybe something had happened that put things in a completely different light? If I stayed here for one more night then there would be only one way out – surrender.

Taking all this into consideration, I decided to obey the order and go to the Reich Chancellery.

The Bendlerstrasse was some 1200 metres from the Reich Chancellery. Usually it took a quarter of an hour to walk there, now it took five times as long, as I had to make my way through debris, cellars and gardens. Sweating, I reached the Reich Chancellery some time around 18.00–19.00.

I was immediately taken to the Führer's study. **Goebbels, Bormann** and **Krebs** were already seated at the table. As I entered, they all stood up. **Krebs** solemnly stated the following:

1. **Hitler** had committed suicide at 15.00.

2. His death should be kept secret for the time being. Only a small circle of people knew about it. We were made to promise to keep the secret.

3. **Hitler**'s corpse, according to his last will, had been soaked with petrol and burnt in a shell-hole in the grounds of the Reich Chancellery.

4. In his last will, **Hitler** had appointed the following government:

Reichspresident – Grand-Admiral **Dönitz**

Reichschancellor – Reichsminister Dr **Goebbels**

Party Minister – Reichsleiter **Bormann**

Defence Minister – Field-Marshal **Schörner**

Interior Minister – **Seyss-Inquart**.

Other ministerial posts were unoccupied, because they had no significance.

5. Marshal **Stalin** had been informed of this by radio.

6. Attempts had been made for the last two hours to contact the Russian High Command to arrange for a cease-fire in Berlin. If these were successful, the German government legally appointed by **Hitler** would begin talks with Russia concerning surrender. I was to be sent as a messenger.

The mood of those present and the businesslike manner of **Krebs**' speech seemed strange. I had a feeling that all three of them were shaken by the death of **Hitler**, who had been their God until now. It seemed to me as if I were among a group of businessmen who were conferring after their boss had departed and despite myself I said: *'First I have to eat. Do any of you have a cigarette? Now one can finally smoke in this room'.*

Goebbels took out a pack of British cigarettes and offered them to all of us.

I used these few minutes to consider what **Krebs** had said. My first thought was: *'So we have been fighting for five-and-a half years for someone who committed suicide. Having drawn us into this terrible disaster, he himself chose the easy way out and left us to fend for ourselves. We must now end this madness as soon as possible'.*

I addressed **Krebs** as follows: *'Krebs, you lived in Moscow for a long time and should know the Russians better than anyone else. Do you believe they would agree to an armistice? Whatever happens, tomorrow or the day after, Berlin will fall into their hands like a ripe apple. The Russians know it as well as we do. In my opinion the Russians will only accept unconditional surrender. Shall we go on with this senseless fighting?'*

Instead of **Krebs**, **Goebbels** answered. In powerful words he insisted that any thought of Berlin's capitulation must be rejected: *'Hitler's will is still compulsory for us'.*

Then, having calmed down, he said the following: *'The traitor Himmler tried and failed to hold talks with the English and Americans. The Russians would sooner agree to negotiate with a legal government than with a traitor. It is possible that we shall succeed in reaching a separate peace with Russia. It all depends on the rapid formation of the legal government, and for that we need a cease-fire'.*

'Herr Reichsminister, do you really think that Russia will negotiate with a government in which you, the most prominent representative of National-Socialism, hold office?', was all I could say.

When **Goebbels**, looking offended, wanted to argue, **Krebs** and **Bormann** intervened. Both began to try to convince me to make every effort to reach a separate peace with Russia.

My opinion, which was that such talks could end only in unconditional surrender, was not supported.

As for **Krebs**, I felt that deep inside he agreed with me in many respects. Therefore, for example, he asked me: *'Can you name someone with whom the Russians would agree to hold talks?'*

It occurred to me somehow to name Professor **Sauerbruch**.

Krebs did not dare to come up with his own opinion, so like the other two he supported the idea of a cease-fire.

I was held in the Reich Chancellery. I had to wait for **Krebs'** return.

I managed to find out from **Burgdorf** and **Bormann** the details of **Hitler's** last hours. Lately, **Hitler's** fear of death had become stronger and stronger. If, for example, a shell hit his bunker, he gave orders to find out as soon as possible if anything was damaged. Generally, shells exploding above the bunker severely irritated **Hitler**.

On the night of 29/30 April, **Hitler** told those closest to him of his decision to commit suicide. Frau **Goebbels** supposedly went on her knees before him, begging him not to abandon his people in this trying time.

Hitler took poison and shot himself. His wife Eva **Braun** also poisoned herself.

According to **Hitler's** last will, the corpses were to be burnt. **Hitler** had apparently said that he didn't want his body put on show in Moscow.

That night of 30 April/1 May was the first time I had heard that **Hitler** had lived with Eva **Braun** for the past 15 years. On 28 April Hitler, wearing a Volkssturm uniform, married Eva **Braun** in the Reich Chancellery. Through this marriage, **Hitler** sought to legalise his 15-year cohabitation.

I did not see **Hitler's** last will, but I managed to find out what he had written.

At 13.00 on 1 May, General **Krebs** returned to the Reich Chancellery.

The Russians, as expected, had rejected the cease-fire proposal and demanded the unconditional surrender of Berlin.

My point of view again failed in the face of **Goebbels'** stubbornness, and the loyal **Krebs** and **Bormann** supported him. Capitulation was rejected. I received permission for the break-out I had planned earlier for the evening of 30 April. I was release from my promise to keep silent about Hitler's death.

Meanwhile, as could be expected, the situation became so bad that a break-out could no longer be contemplated. On the night of 1/2nd May, I surrendered to the Russians together with the units of which I was still in communication.

While in captivity, I heard that **Hitler's** body had not been found. This made me wonder whether Hitler's death was a sham.

I was badly shaken by the events of 30 April to 1 May, and I took the news of **Hitler's** death as the truth. At the time, it did not occur to me that **Hitler's** associates would abuse my trust and lie to me. I believed that **Hitler** was dead, and because of that, on the evening of 30 April, I had dared to tell **Goebbels**: '*Will History blame us, if we do not obey the will of a suicide?* (by this I meant Hitler's absolute refusal to surrender). *Hitler deserted us in a terrible situation and because of that we have the right to act as we see fit*'.

I cannot say whether **Hitler** really died, based only on what I have seen and heard. Going over in my mind all that **Hitler** said and did in his last days, I ask myself what evidence there is that **Hitler** is alive.

1. **Hitler**'s mortal fear of death and unconcealed self-interest.

2. The sending of the adjutants from Berlin on 28 April. They were said to have been entrusted with important documents that had to be taken out of Berlin. But they could have been sent on a special mission· to prepare a place for **Hitler** after a proposed escape.

In such a case, it would be very interesting to know the route taken by both adjutants when they left the Reich Chancellery and who accompanied them.

3. The businesslike manner, without a trace of mourning, of **Hitler**'s closest associates – **Krebs**, **Bormann** and **Goebbels** – when they informed me that **Hitler** was dead.

4. The fact that I was initially required to keep **Hitler**'s death a secret. This may have been for military considerations, so as not to demoralise the defenders of Berlin, but it might have been to buy time for those helping **Hitler** escape.

5. Many people were living in the numerous rooms of **Hitler**'s bunker at that time. It would hardly have been possible to keep the suicide, the removal of the bodies and their cremation in the garden a secret under those conditions.

After I was taken prisoner, I spoke to SS Gruppenführer **Rattenhuber** and Sturmbannführer **Günsche**, and both said they knew nothing about the details of **Hitler**'s death . . . I cannot leave this alone. Are all who know about this bound by an oath of silence, or aren't they?

In spite of these arguments which might make me doubt whether **Hitler** is dead, I continue to believe that he is dead, for the following reasons:

1. **Hitler**'s physical and mental state. I cannot imagine that a such a physical and mental wreck of a man could have made his way through the ruins of Berlin. It could still be argued, though, that he might have been helped to escape.

On the night of 29/30 April there were still opportunities to leave – through the Zoo underground station in western Berlin and through the Friedrichstrasse station in the north. One could have escaped relatively safely through the underground tunnels. But it should be remembered that **Hitler**'s escape, however clandestine, could not have been kept secret for long, even in the chaos of Germany in April, 1945.

2. It is absolutely out of the question that **Hitler** could have escaped from Berlin by air. The reserve airstrip in the Tiergarten was out of action after noon on the 28th. Cars could not even drive on it, the runway was so heavily damaged. **Hitler**'s escape from Berlin by aeroplane was absolutely out of question.

It would have been theoretically possible to fly out in an 'autogyro' (helicopter), but I never heard that the Reich Chancellery had such an aircraft. Furthermore, the landing and take-off of such an aircraft could hardly have escaped attention.

3. If **Hitler** had intended to continue the struggle elsewhere, his plans could hardly have been kept secret from his closest collaborators. If that was so, why, then, did those most loyal to him – **Goebbels, Krebs, Burgdorf** and others – commit suicide after **Hitler**'s supposed escape? Surely, if **Hitler** had escaped, they would have tried to escape too once the cease-fire negotiations had failed? ✔

Арх. H-21146; т. 1; л. 75-126
(ПОДЛИННИК)
(original)

Helmuth Weidling, *born 2 November, 1891, General of the Artillery. Ordered by Hitler to fight to the end to save Berlin, but surrendered the city to the Soviets on 2 May, 1945. Died as a Soviet prisoner of war on 17 November, 1955.*

RECORD OF INTERROGATION OF
FIELD-MARSHAL FERDINAND SCHÖRNER

10 May, 1947

Schörner, Ferdinand, born in 1892 in the city of Munich, German national, German citizen, from a police officer's family, higher education.

Question: Why were you appointed Commanding General of the German 'Centre' Army Group?

Answer: On 17 January, 1945 I was summoned from Kurland to **Hitler**'s Headquarters in Berlin. During this meeting **Hitler**, in the presence of the Chief of General Staff **Guderian**, told me that he was displeased with the Commander of the 'Centre' German Army Group, General **Harpe**, who, in his opinion, was not able to cope with the tasks entrusted to him.

Hitler expressed the hope that I, as a man who had frequently proved his loyalty to National-Socialist Germany, would be able to put this sector of the front in order, and this was of colossal significance in the future prosecution of the war, because it covered Silesia which at that time was the main industrial base of Germany.

Question: As is known, you were unable to complete this task. What instructions did you receive from **Hitler** later?

Answer: Being the Commanding General of the German 'Centre' Army Group I went to **Hitler**'s headquarters several times to receive the necessary instructions on the main military matters and to be briefed on the political situation.

In the middle of February, 1945, I visited **Hitler** in relation to further combat operations assigned to the army group under my command, whose task it was to defend the front-line along the Oder and the Neisse. I asked **Hitler** to place several armoured divisions under my command, with whose aid I considered it possible to recapture the Silesian industrial region. **Hitler** rejected my request, saying that at that moment all tank reserves should be concentrated around Budapest, because of the immense military and economic significance of the Hungarian bridgehead.

I also asked **Hitler** to allow me to surrender the fortress of Breslau, but he refused. **Hitler** pointed out that it was necessary to resist until a favourable political outcome of the war could be found.

At the time, in **Hitler**'s headquarters, I heard from **Guderian** and his deputy General **Krebs**, that there were plans to obtain a separate peace with England and that supposedly talks were being held with that aim in view in Spain, Switzerland and Sweden.

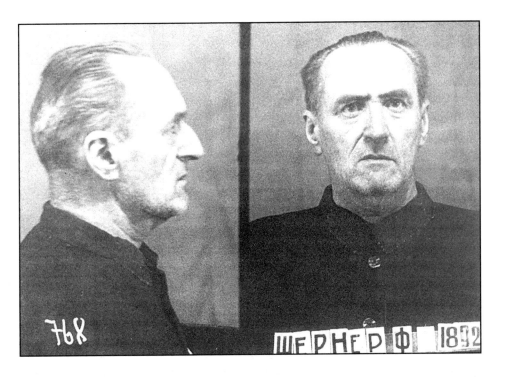

Photo from the investigation file.

'Schörner 1892.'

On 6 August, 1951 Schörner was arrested by the officers of the USSR MSS on charges that he 'occupied positions of command in the former German Army, actively participating in the preparation and carrying on of a criminal war against the USSR in violation of international law and treaties'. The troops under his command with his knowledge and on his orders carried out mass destruction, atrocities and brutality against the civilian population and prisoners-of-war in the temporarily occupied territory of the Soviet Union'. By the ruling of the Military Board of the USSR Supreme Court of 11 February, 1952 he was sentenced to 25 years' imprisonment. Under a decree of the Praesidium of the USSR Supreme Council of 12 April, 1952, his sentence was reduced to 12 years 6 months and in a decree dated 22 December, 1954 Schörner was released early and handed over to officials of the GDR. On his arrival in West Germany, Schörner was convicted of the manslaughter of Wehrmacht soldiers and served 4 ½ years in prison. Released from jail in 1963, he remained in Germany living in poverty and died from a heart attack on 6 July, 1973.

The Pope had also promised his mediation in this issue. At headquarters, I was told by **Ribbentrop**'s deputy **Weiszäcker** that as early as 1943 or 1944 that **Ribbentrop**, who was also the German ambassador to the Vatican, had had talks with the Pope on this issue on **Hitler**'s orders. The Pope had agreed to mediate in talks between the Germans and the British and Americans. This is proved, for example, by the fact that shortly thereafter, **Hitler** issued an order to place Vatican property in Germany and the occupied countries under special protection.

In mid-March, 1945, I was summoned to **Hitler**'s Headquarters for the second time, due to the obvious Soviet preparations for a major offensive aimed at Berlin and the northern flank of the German 'Centre' Army Group. It was then that I was able to obtain the additional men and equipment that I needed to hold off the possible Russian offensive.

Thanks to this, in March, 1945, I was able to recapture the city of Lauben in Silesia from the Russians. Then **Goebbels** came to visit me at the front and delivered a long propaganda speech to the assembled troops and the inhabitants of the city of Gerlitz.

On 5 April, 1945, I again flew to **Hitler**'s headquarters where I was informed that I was to be promoted to the rank of Field-Marshal.

This time, I participated in discussions of the plans for the defence of Berlin. **Hitler** expressed confidence that with the help of the newly-formed Hitler Youth divisions we would be able, not only to hold back the Russians, but to conduct a major counter-attack against the Soviet armies.

In presence of **Guderian**, **Krebs** and his aide-de-camp **Burgdorf**, **Hitler** informed me that a strong base of resistance was under construction in the Alps, the so-called 'Alpine Redoubt', and ordered me to send weapons and supplies there from Czechoslovakia.

I discovered that, at that time, hopes of a separate peace were mounting at **Hitler**'s headquarters. It is significant that **Himmler** was absent from the headquarters at that time. I was told that he was having talks elsewhere concerning a separate peace with the British and the Americans.

On Sunday 22 April, 1945, I was again unexpectedly summoned by **Hitler** to his headquarters in Berlin, that being my last meeting with him. On that day, I also met **Goebbels** for the last time.

Question: Recall your talks with **Hitler** during your last meeting with him on 22 April.

Answer: This, my last meeting with the Führer, took place in the Reich Chancellery in the presence of the newly-appointed Chief of the General Staff, **Krebs**, and Hitler's personal aide-de-camp, **Burgdorf**.

During this meeting, **Hitler** made a very bad impression on me, having the appearance of a sick man who was depressed by the course of events. His face was pale and swollen and his voice was weak. He began the meeting by asking for my opinion on the current situation.

I reported my concerns for the outer flanks of my armies – to the south of Brno (Brünn) and in the Kottbus area – and proposed to withdraw the troops from the Brno-Moravska Ostrava (Mährisch-Ostrau) salient, and also asked again to be permitted to surrender Breslau. I said that the situation in my Army Group was becoming more and more threatening every day, the morale of the troops was very low and they would not be able to withstand the evident threat of encirclement much longer.

In reply, **Hitler** told me categorically that the front must hold. Retaining Czechoslovakia, he said, with its industrial and economic potential was and would remain decisive. Czechoslovakia's material base was indispensable for resistance in the Alps, because it was not enough just to have ammunition depots and food provisions brought there. Besides, Czechoslovakia was a stronghold, defending the avenues of approach to the 'Alpine Redoubt'. Breslau, the Führer said, should hold also, otherwise the Russian forces tied up there would be released and present an additional threat.

In this discussion, **Hitler** said for the first time that he saw no way out of the war by military means, though he still cherished hopes for political opportunities. He believed it was necessary to keep fighting as long as possible in order for such political opportunities to present themselves.

In answer to my question as to whether there were any guarantees or clear signs that we had a chance of ending the war, **Hitler** said that, if we were able to slow down the Russian offensive, there were some indications that it might be possible to reach a partial political arrangement with the Western Allies, initially with the British, but that we would only have this chance if we went into the negotiations with sufficient remaining military strength.

Hitler continued, saying that he had decided to transfer German forces from the West to the East in order to shift the centre of combat towards the Russians, and **Krebs** added that the appropriate orders had already been given to the commanders of the 9th and 12th Armies on the western front, Generals **Busse** and **Wenck**. **Hitler** said that the passive behaviour of the Western Allies, especially of their Air Forces, which we had seen lately, justified that transfer. He expressed confidence that, as a result of such measures, the situation in the vicinity of Berlin would stabilise and our resistance in the south would be strengthened.

At the same time, **Hitler** informed me directly that he was going to take his own life at a suitable moment, so as not to be an obstacle in the talks concerning a separate peace with one of Germany's enemies.

I tried to convince **Hitler** of the necessity of leaving Berlin for Salzburg, saying that his death would make it impossible for any real resistance to continue. I told him that any successful resistance in the Alps required his presence and that his death would mean the end of Germany. Then all of us would have to decide whether to stay alive or commit suicide.

Hitler decisively rejected my proposal and said exactly the following: 'No, *not under any circumstances. With me, it is different. You must understand that. The generals must stay at their posts. I cannot leave Berlin. I swore before the troops that Berlin would remain German. If Berlin falls, I will not remain alive. I am also the main obstacle in the way of diplomatic talks. Let Göring, Himmler or someone else reach an agreement with the British'* . . .

Then **Hitler** informed me that he had compiled his political testament, which he was going to send to me by special messenger along with other instructions. He did not disclose the contents of this document to me at the time, saying only that among other things there were orders for me to organise and direct the resistance in the Alps.

Question: What was your reaction to these last statements of **Hitler**?

Answer: The last statements and outward appearance of **Hitler** deeply shocked me. It was clear to me that, in a military sense, we were facing a catastrophe and that the Führer had decided to commit suicide.

The only hope was the possibility of coming to an agreement with England and America; their inactivity at the front confirmed this possibility. **Hitler's** statement that such a hope existed if we could enter into talks with weapons still in our hands seemed convincing to me. For this reason, I took the decision, according to the Führer's order, to hold the front by any means.

Question: When did you receive **Hitler's** last will?

Answer: **Hitler's** last will never reached me. On 24 or 25 April, 1945, a message was transmitted to my Army Group by the telephone or telegraph from General **Krebs**, that Lieutenant-Colonel of the General Staff **Johannmeier** had been entrusted to hand me the Führer's last will and that he should be collected by a Fieseler-Storch aircraft from a command post in Berlin.

I ordered several Storch aircraft to be sent. This was done but none of the aircraft returned. I do not know why. I assume that Lieutenant-Colonel **Johannmeier** was killed on his journey.

Thus I am unaware of the contents of this document.

Question: By sending you his political testament, **Hitler** appointed you his executor. What place in the German leadership was assigned to you by **Hitler**?

Answer: I repeat that the details of **Hitler's** last will are unknown to me. I can only say that on 22 April, 1945, when I was in **Hitler's** Headquarters, his personal aide-de-camp, General **Burgdorf**, informed me that **Hitler** had chosen me for the post of Commander-in-Chief of the German Army.

Question: What was the subject of your last conversation with **Goebbels**?

Answer: **Goebbels** was waiting for me in a room adjacent to the Führer's. After I left **Hitler's** room, accompanied by General **Burgdorf**, State Secretary Dr **Naumann**, Dr **Morell** and Reichsleiter **Bormann** were also there.

At **Goebbels'** request, I repeated to him the report I had just made to the Führer and then turned to more general matters, focusing especially on the fighting for Berlin. In general, it was the same subject about which I had reported to the Führer.

I took this opportunity to find out from **Goebbels** his opinion of the foreign policy situation. He said the following about it: *'I can only confirm what the Führer has already told you. We need a stable front in the East to allow possible talks with the Western Powers, so we have an important factor that they will have to take into consideration . . . You are the only man who has risen to this task and the only one on whom we can rely. You can be sure that we, for our part, will do all we can to ensure that these further sacrifices will not be in vain . . . You may think that further resistance is futile, but I can assure you that your task is of immense importance. It will prevent us from losing this last chance'.*

As for the decision taken by the Führer to stay in Berlin and commit suicide, **Goebbels** told me: *'I am of exactly the same opinion as you. I have tried everything to save his life and I am still trying. But you know the Führer and I do not hope for success. The least that I can do is to ensure that the Führer's corpse does not fall into the hands of the enemy as a trophy'.*

Then, on the advice of **Burgdorf**, I proposed to **Goebbels** that, if he decided to stay on as well, to at least permit me to fly his children out of Berlin in my aircraft. To that **Goebbels** said something to the effect that: *'Neither I nor my family will survive the Führer. If the Führer falls, the National-Socialist State will fall, and then the Goebbels family will not live'.*

I had the impression that, at the time, **Goebbels** was the most energetic person in **Hitler's** entourage. He had foreseen everything and had prepared for any possible eventuality. **Goebbels** said nothing to me about **Hitler's** last will.

After that talk with **Goebbels**, I wanted to find out details about the 'redoubt' in the Alps from **Krebs**. He said that everything was being done according to plan and that he would give me the details in due course. But I never received this information.

After that, I wanted to talk to **Ribbentrop** to find out about the political possibilities of withdrawal from the war and the outcome of the talks with the British and the Americans, but he never came.

Due to the forthcoming difficult night flight I had to go to Staaken, to my plane.

Question: Did you receive any orders from **Hitler** after 22 April, 1945?

Answer: After the meeting of 22 April, 1945 I did not receive any important instructions from **Hitler**.

When I returned to the Headquarters of the Army Group, on my own initiative I sent the Führer a radio message, in which, in the name of the officers and men of German 'Centre' Army Group and myself, I asked **Hitler** to change his decision and to save himself in order to lead further fighting as head of state.

In this telegram, I also assured **Hitler** of my unquestioning loyalty and determination to carry on with the war to the last. Simultaneously, I pointed out that the troops under my command were quite efficient and ready to fulfil any order of his. The text of that telegram was agreed by me with my Chief-of-Staff, Lieutenant-General von **Natzmer** and the commanders of my Armies: 1st Panzer, General **Nering**, 4th Panzer, General **Gläser**, 7th Infantry, General **von Oberstfelder** and 17th Infantry, General **von Hasse**.

In his reply, Hitler informed me that he was not going to change the decision he had taken and called upon my troops to take part in the battle for Berlin. Simultaneously, he expressed his gratitude to me for my expressions of loyalty and devotion.

Question: Did you take part in the battle for Berlin because of **Hitler**'s order?

Answer: The German 'Centre' Army Group was to participate immediately in the fighting for Berlin, and all available forces were to move to Berlin along the Herlitz–Bautzen–Königsbruck line and simultaneously to tie down the enemy troops. However, the situation in the area of my Army Group prevented me from taking part in this battle.

Question: Why?

Answer: In late April, 1945, the situation on my right flank deteriorated (1st Panzer and part of the 17th Infantry Army); its integrity was threatened, which could have resulted in the loss of the important industrial area of Brno. It became necessary to change our battle plans. The necessary proposals were sent by me to the Army High Command, and these were the same as those I had reported to **Hitler** in mid-April, 1945, namely, a planned withdrawal, at least from the eastern Brno–Moravska-Ostrava salient, to shorten the front line, in accordance with the movements of Army Group 'South'.

My strategic plan was, while containing the swift thrust of the Soviet troops, to withdraw my troops to German territory to link up with other German forces in the defence of the so-called, 'inner German fortress'. Based on my opinion of the general situation, I sent my armies orders containing plans for a general offensive to the west. I received no confirmation from OKH as to the reaction of the High Command to my actions.

On 2 May, 1945, events in the area of Moravska-Ostrava-Troppa, where some units failed to withstand the continuous Russian attacks, made me immediately evacuate the Eastern salient. I ordered the 49th Jäger Corps to speedily retreat. As a result all this, that sector of the front went on the move.

At the same time, according to Army High Command orders, the 4th Panzer Army started a counter-attack to the north, in the direction of Berlin, but this counter-attack achieved only limited success. The Seventh Army confronting the Americans could not hold the Dresden–Chemnitz line.

On 2 May, 1945, after **Hitler**'s death was announced, the situation quickly deteriorated. If previously, both at the front and in the rear, the effectiveness of poorly-trained units was shaky, now the morale of tested and experienced troops was broken.

As a result, on 2 May, 1945, I issued an appeal to the troops. I called on the officers and myself to follow the Führer's example and to continue to fight against Bolshevism, which threatened the existence of National-Socialist Germany, to their last breath.

The position occupied by the German 'Centre' Army Group was very important, since unlike the 'South' Army Group, and particularly the 'North', my troops were still on foreign soil.

Our lines of communication with Germany were becoming less secure because of the uprising against the Germans that had begun in Czechoslovakia, and intense partisan activity was causing me a lot of trouble.

Question: Did you suppress the uprising and the partisan movement in Czechoslovakia?

Answer: Yes, I suppressed it, but it took quite a lot of troops. I had to act very severely against Czechoslovakia's guerrillas and rebels and I did it because they not only disrupted my communications with the Fatherland, but because of them communication between my Armies became almost impossible. The partisans cut wires, blew up bridges and killed messengers.

Besides, the rebels were demoralising my men. From Czech radio, they learnt of the impending surrender of Germany. I asked the Army High Command to request the Anglo-American Command to stop these Czech broadcasts, but this was not done.

Question: What was the situation of the German 'Centre' Army Group after the fall of Berlin?

Answer: After the fall of Berlin, events unfolded rapidly. There was one capitulation after another. After 2 May, 1945, information began to be received that the Russians had transferred powerful tank forces from the vicinity of Berlin to the south, against my left flank.

The soldiers and, regrettably, many officers, were afraid of being cut off from Germany.

As a result, instead of a planned withdrawal, there was a wild panic-stricken flight towards Germany. According to information from the Armies and Corps with which we were still in communication, everywhere one could see a picture of the complete disintegration of German forces. One of my Army Commanders characterised the flight of his soldiers as a 'mountain avalanche, which could not be stopped by mere paper orders'.

On 5 May, 1945, an order came from the Army High Command to begin withdrawal along the whole front, and it was pointed out that the withdrawal must begin immediately and be carried out in good order and according to the plan in 7 days.

After that, in my order to the troops that was sent to every unit, I called upon the officers and men to be disciplined and loyal in carrying out their last duty. In my order, I stressed that the war was coming to the end. I also pointed out that this order was, obviously, the last they would receive, as communications could be expected to break down completely.

The Armies were ready for an immediate withdrawal and, in part, a more-or-less planned retreat began.

On 7 May, 1945, the 1st Panzer Army, some units retreating in good order, others in full flight, withdrew from the Brno area and west of Olmutz. The 17th Army was crossing the mountains from the region of Friedenthal–Niesse–Waldenburg–Hirschberg. The 4th Panzer Army retreated from an intermediate position along the Gerlitz–Bautzen–Dresden line and was occupying previously fortified positions in the mountains (Erzgebirge). Substantial numbers of its troops were crossing the Elbe to counter-attack Russian tank units speeding south on a broad front. The 7th Army was engaged in hopeless fighting against those Russian tanks, its front facing the American 7th Army to the west that was occupying positions in the cities.

Question: On 7 May, 1945, the German Supreme Command Headquarters signed the Act and issued the Order of Unconditional Surrender of the German Armed Forces.

Did you know about this order?

Answer: Yes, I knew of it.

Question: When and under what conditions did you hear of the Order of General Capitulation?

Answer: On 7 May, 1945, in the evening, when I was at my headquarters near the city of Königgratz (Czechoslovakia), I received the order from the German Supreme Command Headquarters by radio that the troops under my command were to capitulate no later than 01.00 on 9 May, 1945. The order was signed by Grand-Admiral **Dönitz** or Field-Marshal **Keitel**, I do not remember exactly which.

On the morning of 8 May, 1945, a representative of the Supreme Command, General Staff Colonel **Maier-Detring**, arrived at Army Group Headquarters with American officers, and repeated the order orally.

Question: Give the precise wording of the order received by you.

Answer: The order I received was approximately as follows: 'The partial capitulation ordered previously must be cancelled. I order an announcement of general capitulation which must take place no later than 01.00 on 9 May, 1945'.

Question: After the capitulation of Germany, the troops under your command continued their resistance. Why didn't you give an order for a general cessation of fighting?

Answer: Despite the fact that the situation of my troops was desperate, I, being a National-Socialist general and a staunch supporter of the war started by **Hitler**, believed the Act of Capitulation to be disgraceful, and advocated the continuation of the war, at least against the Russians.

I was sure that, despite the surrender, some military or political leadership would survive in Germany that would be loyal to National-Socialism and would have some armed forces. I decided to put myself under the command of such a leadership and carry out my existing plan, which was to withdraw to Germany, while containing the Russian offensive, and link up with those armed forces defending the 'inner German redoubt'.

Furthermore, I considered the order for general capitulation to be unacceptable and contrary to the earlier Army High Command order for my troops to withdraw fighting into Germany and there to engage in active defence. I also considered it impossible to carry out, as my troops were already heading west and I would not be able to stop them and make them lay down their arms to the Russians, who were hated by both myself and them.

I had also promised to lead my officers and men home, and did not want to betray them.

Question: Did you inform the Supreme Command that you were not going to capitulate?

Answer: Yes, immediately upon receiving the order for capitulation I asked the General Command of the Army to tell Grand-Admiral **Dönitz** that I was not going to capitulate. I also said this to **Dönitz** and **Keitel**'s representative, Colonel **Maier-Detring**, who reached me on 8 May, 1945.

Question: By your criminal refusal to capitulate you increased the number of losses to both German and Soviet troops. Do you admit it?

Answer: Yes, I do not deny it.

Question: What was the reaction of the German Supreme Command to your refusal to capitulate?

Answer: The representative of the Headquarters, Colonel **Maier-Detring**, who had arrived at my headquarters on 8 May, 1945 and whom I personally informed that I was not going to capitulate, did not insist upon it. **Maier-Detring** had come to me as the representative of **Dönitz** and **Keitel**, so it was absolutely clear to me that **Dönitz** and **Keitel**, in their hearts, agreed with my decision to refuse to capitulate.

I was sure that **Dönitz** and **Keitel**, no less than myself, were interested in a more favourable withdrawal from the war instead of a shameful capitulation.

From the first days of his leadership of both the state and the army, **Dönitz**, who became **Hitler**'s successor, took active measures to fulfil **Hitler**'s order to preserve the German armed forces and the potential for resistance in the East as an indispensable factor in achieving positive results in the conclusion of a separate peace with the Western enemy.

They issued a number of orders to resist the Red Army before 7 May, 1945, i.e. before the General Capitulation Order. For example, in the above-mentioned Headquarters Order of 5 May of that year, it was proposed that the troops under my command withdraw to the German border and engage there in active defence against the Soviet forces.

Simultaneously, **Dönitz** and **Keitel** finally abandoned the western front to the British and the Americans, and moved all the troops to the East. The troops remaining in the West were to surrender to the Anglo-Americans without fighting and hand over their weapons and ammunition intact. In these orders, exactly as in **Dönitz's** Appeal to the Army of 2 May, 1945, it was stressed that we were continuing the war only against the Russians, and we engaged in combat against the Americans and the English only as far as they hindered our fighting against Bolshevism.

All that convinced me that the Supreme Command undoubtedly agreed with my position.

Question: What did you actually do after you received the General Capitulation Order?

Answer: On the morning of 8 May, 1945, I informed the commanders of 4th Panzer Army (General **Gläser**) and 17th Infantry Army (General **von Hasse**) that the General Capitulation Order had reached us and told them not to obey this order as it countermanded previous orders from Supreme Headquarters, and that they were to follow the directives laid down in the order for the withdrawal of the troops to the German border. At the same time, I asked them to inform me of the condition of the troops.

By the time the order arrived, I had lost communication with the commanders of the 1st Panzer Army (General **Nering**) and 7th Infantry Army (General **von Oberstfelder**) and never met up with them again. At this time, these armies were withdrawing to the German border, according to the order I had issued earlier.

At 09.00 on the morning of 8 May, 1945, I left my command post near the city of Königgratz (Czechoslovakia) and, accompanied by several officers of my Staff, including the Chief-of-Staff of German 'Centre' Army Group Lieutenant-General **Natzmer**, visited the positions of units of the 4th Panzer Army in order to inspect the state and effectiveness of the troops. I left the commander of the 17th Army, **Hasse**, as my deputy at the command post.

Besides, I hoped to establish contact with other armies.

But my hopes were not fulfilled. An absolutely unexpected thrust by Russian tanks over a wide front through the Erzgebirge mountains that was developed on the west bank of the Elbe scattered my staff column in the vicinity of the city of Salz (Czechoslovakia). From then on, it was impossible for me to command the troops. The hangars and barracks at Salz airfield, were already on fire. Many staff officers had probably died or been taken prisoner.

My Chief-of-Staff **Natzmer** and I left our armoured cars on the road and with the remaining staff officers made for the town of Salz. On that same day, 8 May, 1945, I entrusted **Natzmer** to establish contact with the American Command and to assess the current situation. He went to the Americans but never returned to me in Salz.

Being in such an uncertain position, on 9 May, 1945 I changed into civilian clothes to better escape from the pursuit of the Russian and the Allied authorities, and flew in a Storch aircraft that happened to have remained at the Salz airfield to the Kitzbühl (Austria) region. I took with me my loyal old messenger Warrant Officer Julius **Fuchs**, who found me civilian clothes from inhabitants of the city of Salz (I do not know their names). We landed near the village of Mittersill in the Tyrol where I lived in hiding from the American military authorities until 17 May, 1945.

Question: What was the purpose of your flight to the Kitzbühl region?

Answer: I believed this area to be the centre of the so-called 'Alpine Redoubt', and that it would be there that the surviving German Supreme Command would be stationed to lead the defence of the Inner German Redoubt'. I decided to place myself under the command of that headquarters.

During the last days before the German capitulation, the location of the Headquarters was generally unknown, and often there was no possibility of communicating with it by radio. It was also unclear who, in fact, commanded the army. Orders came from the OKW (**Keitel**), the OKH (**Krebs**, later **Vinter**), from Army Group 'South' (**Kesselring**) and, finally, from **Dönitz**.

As early as 29 April, 1945 I had heard at Headquarters that the OKH Headquarters were being moved from Berchtesgaden to the Tyrol, and I believed that by that time it was already there.

From the inhabitants of the village of Mittersill I learnt that there was no German Headquarters in this region and that a day or two previously, **Guderian** had been taken prisoner near the village by the Americans. I also learnt that nearby, in the city of Sankt-Johan, the staff of General **Ferch's** 1st Army had surrendered to the Americans. **Ferch's** army had earlier been part of Army Group 'G' under General **Schultz**.

When I concluded that there was no sense in my staying in hiding any longer, I decided to put myself in the hands of the American military authorities.

On 17 May, 1945, I arrived at the headquarters of the 1st Army and asked General **Ferch** to telephone the nearest American headquarters to send a representative to take me prisoner. On the same day, two American officers arrived at the Headquarters and took me to the Headquarters of the American 7th Division, which was situated in the vicinity of the health resort of Kitzbühl. The next day, i.e. 18 May, 1945, the commander of the American Division sent me to the prisoner-of-war camp near the city of Augsburg. Not long before my arrival, **Göring**, **Ley**, **Kesselring**, ministers, ambassadors and other military, political and diplomatic officials of Germany as well as prominent scientific researchers, including atomic weapon scientists and others had been held there.

I was held in that camp until 26 May, 1945, when I was handed over to the Soviet command at the demarcation line near the city of Ems.

Question: Were you questioned by the American authorities?

Answer: Yes, I was questioned both at the headquarters of the American 7th Division in Kitzbühl and in the camp near Augsburg.

Question: Who exactly questioned you and what evidence did you give to the Americans?

Answer: At the Headquarters of the 7th Division I was questioned by an American lieutenant-colonel or colonel, whose name and position were unknown to me, and who demanded my confession to my supposed participation in German underground resistance in Austria, set up to fight against the occupying forces. This colonel or lieutenant-colonel said to me that, in the Tyrol, they had discovered the underground organisation of Dr **Schäffer**, which was engaged in resistance against the American occupation forces and that I had come to this region not to surrender to the Americans but to establish contact with **Schäffer**, for underground work. He also said that **Schäffer** and other members of this organisation had been arrested by the Americans.

I flatly denied the American officer's accusations and gave no evidence on this matter and he did not ask me any further questions. About an hour-and-a-half to two hours later, the same officer summoned me again to the office, and this time said that his accusations against me should not be taken seriously and apologised.

In the Augsburg camp, I was questioned almost daily by one person with the rank of a senior lieutenant in the US Army, who I learnt worked for a major New York industrialist, but I do not know the name.

In every interrogation, he only questioned me about the Red Army, its strength, numbers and offensive capability. In particular, he asked how Russian artillery, tanks and anti-tank weapons could be combatted, and how Russian infantry attacks could be overcome. He also asked a lot of questions about the strategy and tactics of the Soviet Command, their combined arms tactics and so on. He asked me for my assessment of the Russians' role in the collective Allied victory if, in my opinion, war between Russia and America was possible and so on.

On a number of questions, for example, on the tactics of the Russian offensive, on Russian artillery and anti-tank weapons I gave written statements to the American officer.

Question: Speak about your role in setting-up underground organisations to resist the Allied Occupation Forces.

Answer: I was not involved in the formation of underground organisations to resist the Allied Occupation Forces and had no contacts with any such organisation.

I presume that the underground organisation about which I was informed by the American officer existed in Austria and that Dr **Schäffer** had played some role in it. But I state that I have no connection to this or any other German underground organisation.

Question: Do you know Dr **Schäffer**?

Answer: I know a medical officer **Schäffer** who served during the Balkan campaign as a doctor in my regiment. The same **Schäffer** recently served in the German mountain medical school in the city of Sankt-Johann in the Tyrol and he is obviously the same person who was described as a participant in an underground organisation by the American officer when he questioned me.

Question: You are one of the men who set up and led 'Werewolf' in Germany. Why do you hide it?

Answer: I ask you to believe that I also have no connection with 'Werewolf'.

As far as I remember, this organisation was set up as early as 1944 or the beginning of 1945 by **Bormann** and was a strictly Party affair. The leadership both at the top and at the grass-roots consisted solely of Party members.

In my Army Group's area, there was no 'Werewolf' organisation and I received no orders or information concerning it.

It is impossible that any 'Werewolf' activity could have taken place in my Army Group's area without my knowledge. Its activities were impossible without links with the Army command, because any sabotage or guerrilla activity could not have taken place without the support of the military.

For myself, I regarded 'Werewolf' negatively because of the inopportune nature of such a movement, its poor security, insufficient supply of weapons, and so on.

Question: When you left the German 'Centre' Army Group did you give the officers of your Headquarters any orders about underground activity?

Answer: On 7 May, 1945, before leaving the headquarters of the Army Group to go to the 4th Panzer Army, I ordered an officer of my staff, Captain Dr **Todenhäfer**, to collect the private addresses of the most reliable officers of the Army Group and to give each of them my address so we could remain in contact.

I meant to unite my like-minded comrades and carry on our work for National-Socialism in the future. Until a centre of resistance could be set up in the Alps, I still considered it possible to support military co-operation with my colleagues. Nothing was said about any underground resistance movement, sabotage or the like, neither to **Todenhäfer** nor to any other staff officers. Neither was anything said about plans for the future.

Concerning this matter, I believed that only the Führer's last will could give us the correct line of behaviour. I do not know if Todenhäfer carried out my orders, because I never saw him again.

Question: Who is this **Todenhäfer**, that you so confided in him?

Answer: **Todenhäfer** enjoyed my confidence. He is a fanatical National-Socialist. I met him in the summer of 1942 on the Murmansk front, when he served in the 14th Machine-Gun Battalion of my 19th Mountain Corps. After graduating in law, **Todenhäfer** worked for **Ribbentrop**, then he was transferred to State Secretary **Naumann**. For some time he was a Vice-Consul in Petsamo. **Todenhäfer** surpassed his comrades in his mental faculties, his erudition in various scientific fields as well as in his military achievements. When I was appointed the Commander of the Nickopol Army Group, I took **Todenhäfer** with me as a personal liaison officer. From then on, he belonged to my closest staff. In August, 1944, he was badly wounded and only returned to the front in February, 1945. On my staff, he was in charge of political education and, if necessary, household matters.

Question: What did you do while you were on the run between 9 and 17 May, 1945?

Answer: During that time, with the help of **Fuchs**, I tried to find out from the inhabitants of the Tyrol what was going on in Germany, because I was unaware of what had happened after the capitulation. I still hoped that there was some surviving military or political authority that could lead the continued resistance of the army. I wanted to place myself at its disposal. However, when I learnt that the Germans had capitulated everywhere, I also decided to surrender. I should add that, by chance, **Fuchs** had been born in the village of Mittersill near where we landed after crossing the Czech-Austrian border, and as a local, he was quickly able to ascertain the current situation. Through his relatives and acquaintances he provided me with food and hid me from the Americans during that time.

Question: Where are your Field-Marshal's uniform jacket, decorations and personal papers?

Answer: My uniform jacket had been left in the city of Salz after I changed into civilian clothes. My decorations and identification card were taken away from me by the Americans in the Augsburg camp and were not returned to me.

I should state that my wife **Schörner**, Liselotte, who lives in Upper Bavaria, Mittenwald, Vierspitzstrasse 4, keeps my personal archive, which is of some historical interest.

From about 1930 to Germany's surrender, every month I sent my wife the most important documents regarding my service as a general, for safe-keeping. In particular, they include copies of reports on the state of the Italian Army and various discussions with military Nazi personnel in Italy.

Of major importance is my archive from the start of World War II, especially from the time when I became commander of an Army Group. From that time, there are copies of my letters and telegrams to **Hitler**, his replies and major battle orders and instructions in my archive. I sent **Hitler** a telegram or a letter from the fighting in the Baltic States about once a week. But **Hitler's** replies came relatively rarely.

Also, the archive contains my private correspondence with my close friends from leading National-Socialist circles and the German Military Command.

Question: Who are your close friends among the National-Socialist leaders and the German Military Command?

Answer: I maintained close relations with **Goebbels**, with whom I exchanged letters and who helped me to provide National-Socialist literature for the troops.

I also had good relations with **Himmler**, whom I had known since 1923.

I established more intimate contact with him and maintained it during my work on the General Staff in 1935–7. **Himmler** was closely connected with Italian fascism, and because I worked a lot on the Italian question, we had much in common in this respect. In that period, I was often enlisted by **Hitler** for consultations on the question of bringing together German National-Socialism with Italian Fascism for joint participation in the war. During our work together, **Himmler** made sure of my loyalty to National-Socialism, and it also turned out that we both came from Munich which was the breeding-ground of National-Socialism. What's more, it turned out that my grandfather and **Himmler's** father served together in the Munich police. All these circumstances brought **Himmler** and I closer together.

Besides, I maintained personal friendly relations with Gauleiters **Rainer** and **Hizler**, with ministers **Speer**, **Todt** and others.

Of the German generals, I was especially close to Generals **Ritter**, **von Schobert** and **Dietl** who, like me, were among the first German officers to take an active part in the National-Socialist movement. I can also count among the generals close to me Field-Marshals **List** and **Guderian** as well as the former Chiefs of the General Staff Generals **Halder** and **Adam**.

Question: You, being among the closest of **Hitler's** helpers, participated in the planning, preparation and direction of the war against peace-loving countries and peoples. You committed war crimes against peace and humanity as a result of which the democratic nations sustained tremendous losses, and inflicted unmatched and countless suffering to those nations. Do you plead guilty to that?

Answer: Yes, I do.

Question: What do you plead guilty to exactly?

Answer: I plead guilty that, as a staunch adversary of Communism, as early as 1919, I participated in the liquidation of the Soviet Republic in Bavaria and in suppressing the revolutionary movement in the Rhineland.

I was among the first Reichswehr officers to join the National-Socialist movement at its dawn in 1920–3, and, being a convinced National-Socialist, actively participated in carrying out National-Socialist policy.

I also plead guilty to planning and preparing the aggressive wars unleashed by Germany against peace-loving nations. This mostly manifested itself in my active participation in the ideological and military preparation of German youth for these predatory wars. Throughout the period between the two World Wars, I constantly implanted revanchist sentiments in my subordinates, preparing them for future wars to conquer living space for Germany. I especially implanted this idea in German youth and stirred up its dreams of a Greater Germany while I worked as a lecturer at a military school in Dresden.

I also took an immediate part in the planning and preparation of the new world war during my service in the Department of Foreign Armies of the German General Staff where, under my command, the military potential of countries adjacent to Germany was studied.

Being an officer of this Department, I repeatedly went to Italy for talks with the Italian military and Fascist circles, to formulate joint preparatory measures for unleashing a predatory war against the democratic states.

I completely believed in **Hitler**'s political genius and approved and supported **Hitler**'s foreign policy, based on systematic breach of treaties. As early as 1939, I was completely aware that the Soviet-German Friendship and Non-Aggression Pact was a ploy by the National-Socialist leadership to conceal preparations for the war against the USSR and unexpectedly attack it. I was in complete agreement with this diplomatic trick of the Führer because the attack to the East which was being prepared, which was aimed at the conquest and colonisation of immense tracts of Russian territory, I considered to be the main means to fulfil the idea of creating of the Great National-Socialist Germany.

It is also my fault that, being a National-Socialist General, I actively participated in aggressive wars against Poland, the Netherlands, Belgium, France, Greece, Yugoslavia and especially against the USSR, which were also wars that breached international treaties, agreements and obligations.

Being guided by the idea of submissive obedience to the Führer, for a long time I presented this idea to the troops under my command and insisted on it, inspiring them to fight for the Great National-Socialist Germany to the last man.

Throughout World War II, I fanatically struggled with all my energy for the ideas of National-Socialism as laid down in Hitler's book *Mein Kampf*.

I was especially active and ardent in fighting against the USSR and in calling my troops to fight against it, understanding that Bolshevism was an irreconcilable

One of the photographs of Hitler which was used to identify his corpse.

ideological adversary of National-Socialism and that an occupation of immense tracts of Russian territory with their vast natural resources and food supplies was the best way to solve the problem of living space for Germany.

By my decisive actions as Commanding General of Army Groups 'South', 'Centre' and 'North', after these Army Groups had suffered heavy defeats at the hands of the Red Army, I was able each time to bring them back to combat readiness and prepared them for further losses.

I confess that these further losses inflicted on both the German and Russian sides were senseless.

I acted like this because I considered it to be my duty to hold the front until the Führer found the necessary political means to withdraw Germany from the war on favourable terms.

It is also my fault that my criminal refusal to capitulate increased the losses of troops on both sides.

I am also to blame because, in carrying out Hitler's will, I actively urged statesmen of Romania and Finland to maintain these countries as military allies of National-Socialist Germany, notwithstanding the fact that the hopeless military situation of Germany and its allies was absolutely clear to me.

In 1944, I headed the work of indoctrinating the German Army with a spirit of fanatical loyalty to the Führer and of savage hatred of the Russian people, helping in this way to prolong the war.

This propaganda also involved preparation for implementation of the principles of racial theory, resulting in the mass killing of civilians.

Question: You are guilty of more than the crimes mentioned by you. It is established by documents that on your order, the troops under your command in the Baltic States, the Ukraine, and Czechoslovakia killed and robbed civilians and prisoners-of-war and senselessly destroyed cities and villages as well as carrying out further devastation unjustified by military necessity.

Do you plead guilty to this?

Answer: I have no reason to doubt the correctness of the accusations brought against me, but I want to assure you that if such things took place they were done without my knowledge and not on my orders. As my only fault in this area, I confess that the troops of my Army Group, in the last days of its existence, on my orders, dealt brutally with the Czechs who rebelled against German rule.

Question: Did the German High Command issue orders concerning criminal methods of conducting the war?

Answer: Yes, it did.

Question: Which of these orders are you aware of?

Answer: As for criminal methods of war, I know of the following orders of the German Command, which defined the attitude of the German forces to prisoners-of-war and peaceful civilian populations.

At the beginning of the war against the Soviet Union, an order was issued by the Supreme Command of the German Armed Forces, signed by Field-Marshal **Keitel**, instructing that all commissars and political leaders of the Red Army who had been taken prisoner were to be shot.

In 1942 (I do not remember the exact date), an order of the Supreme Command of the German Armed Forces, also signed by **Keitel**, was published concerning the treatment of Soviet prisoners-of-war. It ordered that any Soviet prisoner-of-war who fell behind in the marching column for whatever reason was to be shot.

Another order, signed by **Keitel**, was issued in the winter of 1942 concerning punitive measures against the Soviet civilian population. In this order, **Keitel** required the commanders of military units to deal mercilessly with the civilian population in areas of partisan activity: to burn the villages and shoot all adult males.

In 1942, **Keitel**'s order was that all captured paratroopers, no matter whether they were in military uniform or not, must be shot, and this was also published.

As far as I know, this order applied not only to Russia, but to the West as well and was applied to the so-called commandos, who were regular British soldiers.

These orders detailed by me are not all the instructions of the German Military Command that authorised criminal methods of war, they are just the ones I can remember.

Question: Did you obey these orders of the Supreme Command?

Answer: Yes, I was obliged to obey the orders of the Supreme Command because I was under its command.

The Record is written down from my words correctly, translated for me into German.
Schörner.

Interrogator:
Deputy Chief of Sub-Section of 4th Section of the 3rd
General Department of Counter-Intelligence of the USSR MSS
Major **Maslennikov**

Translated by:
Interpreter of the 4th Section of the 3rd General
Department of Counter-Intelligence of the MSS
Lieutenant **Shilova**

Арх. Н-21138; т. 1; л. 167-195
(ПОДЛИННИК)
(original)

PART III

RUMOURS, FANTASIES, INVESTIGATIONS

'THE DEATH OF HITLER: ANALYSIS OF THE SOURCES'

Letter from Brian Conrad, Chief of the US Secret Service
1945

THE FORM OF THE EVIDENCE

1. The only decisive evidence of **Hitler**'s death would be the discovery and positive identification of the corpse. If such evidence is unavailable, all that remains are the detailed accounts of certain witnesses, who either knew of his intentions or were eye-witnesses to his fate.

THE SOURCES

2. The best witnesses would certainly be those who were close to **Hitler** during the last days of his life, who lived with him in the bunker and who ensured the implementation of his decisions, including the decision concerning the fate of his corpse. These people include Dr **Goebbels**, Martin **Bormann** and Dr Ludwig **Stumpfegger** (**Hitler**'s doctor and his staff). Of these, **Goebbels** is definitely dead; **Bormann**, according to the reliable evidence of two separate witnesses, was killed in the Friedrichstrasse on 2 May; as for **Stumpfegger**, he was seen last either dead (according to the evidence of one of the said witnesses) or seriously wounded, if not dead (according to the evidence of the other one) after the same incident.

Due to eye-witnesses being unavailable, we have to rely on other groups of witnesses. True, it has been established that both **Bormann** (generally speaking) and **Goebbels** (definitely) informed **Dönitz** on 1 May that **Hitler** had died, and the time of his death as indicated by **Goebbels** coincided with the evidence of the witnesses given below. It is also possible that **Bormann** or **Goebbels** officially informed General **Weidling** on 1 May that the Führer had performed hara-kiri and consequently **Weidling** released the soldiers from their oath of allegiance to him.

3. After **Goebbels**, **Bormann** and **Stumpfegger**, the probable witnesses sub-divide into the following groups:

4.(a) Certain politicians, generals and private individuals who were with **Hitler** at different periods between 22 and 30 April and were aware of his plans and intentions. There is substantial evidence from these sources, which include **Speer** (in the bunker on 23–29 April), **Gebhard** (there on 25 (?) April), Ritter **von Greim** (there on 26-29 April) and others. Substantial evidence can also be gathered from the others who were in the bunker on 30 April, including Hans **Baur**, **Hitler's** personal pilot, who is now in a Russian hospital as a prisoner-of-war. But it seems that none of them actually witnessed **Hitler's** death and burning or burial of the corpse, so they could only add some details at second hand.

5. (b) **Hitler's** and **Bormann's** personal secretaries, who were in the bunker on the last day and knew details of the events. At the time, two of **Hitler's** secretaries, Frau **Junge** and Frau **Christian** were there; Fraulein **Krüger** was **Bormann's** secretary. Of them, Frau **Junge** was last seen on 3 May in a village near Hafelberg, where she was left behind because she was not able to travel further; Frau **Christian**, according to trustworthy reports, was in the British zone and her tracks were uncovered; Fraulein **Krüger** was interrogated and she was one of the witnesses whose evidence was used below.

6. (c) **Hitler's** personal aides-de-camp and servants who were present at his death. The most significant of them are Sturmbannführer **Günsche** – his personal aide-de-camp, Sturmbannführer **Linge** – his personal servant and Sturmbannführer Erich **Kempka** – the officer who was in charge of his personal vehicles. In fact, they all took part in burning **Hitler's** and Eva **Braun's** corpses. Of them, **Günsche's** whereabouts are unknown, **Linge** is possibly held captive by the Russians (one witness believes she saw him among a group of German prisoners-of-war in the Müllerstrasse, Berlin-Wedding on 2 November); **Kempka** is in the hands of the Americans and has been interrogated.

7. (d) Officers of the SS guard command, who were on duty in **Hitler's** bunker on the last day. The guard was under the command of SS Sturmbannführer Franz **Schedle**, and its officers, obviously, had various duties connected with the destruction of **Hitler's** corpse. It is known that **Schedle** asked that his wife be told that he was not going to fall into the hands of the Russians alive. Of the other officers of the guard command, Hauptsturmführer Helmut **Beermann** is reported to have been arrested by the US 9th Army and will be interrogated as soon as his current whereabouts are known.

8.(e) The officers of the Reich Security Service (Sicherheitsdienst), who were responsible for **Hitler's** personal security. A detachment of these officers was on duty in the bunker during the last days. The chief of the Reich Security Service, SS Brigadeführer Johann or Hans **Rattenhuber** in the bunker himself and if he is alive, he could be a valuable witness because it is stated that he was the one who ordered that the remains of the bodies be buried (according to the Russian military communiqué of 7

May he was captured by the Russians). His deputy, Stafelführer **Hegl**, may be dead. Of the other RSD officers who stayed in Berlin, the following were on duty during this period:

Harry **Mengershausen**,
Hilco **Poppen**,
Herman **Karnau**,
Hans **Bergmüller**,
Max **Keltz**,
Erich **Mansfeld**,
Hans **Hofbeck**.

Of these, **Mengershausen** was seen in Bremen; **Karnau** and **Mansfeld** (in the hands of the British and the Americans) were interrogated and they happened to be accidental witnesses of the burning of the bodies. The whereabouts of **Keltz**, who is believed to have information about the burial of the remains, are unknown; the same applies to **Hofbeck** who is said to have been a witness to the burial.

Poppen is in the hands of the British and has been interrogated.

9. Aside from the well-differentiated categories of witnesses mentioned above, there are accidental witnesses who could add details to the known facts. One of them was a woman who was living in one of the bunkers thanks to her personal connection with an officer of the SS guard command and she used to come to Hitler's bunker for food. She gave valuable testimony. There are possibly other witnesses of that kind but they are hardly likely to be able to add important details to that part of the story which is still obscure.

EVIDENCE FROM RELIABLE SOURCES

Events in the bunker on 20–29 April

10. Evidence received from the currently available sources completely coincides in all the main points and this coincidence should be emphasised, because the groups of witnesses are totally disparate. Thus, top officials and intimate friends were kept informed of **Hitler**'s intentions and this definitely influenced the testimonies of the guards, who were at their posts outside the building and were soon incidental witnesses of the implementation of the plan. Similarly, the woman mentioned in paragraph 9 is personally unknown to all the other witnesses, nor were **Kempka** (paragraph 6) and Fraulein **Krüger** (paragraph 5) personally acquainted. The evidence received from these sources leads us to the following main conclusions, which were thoroughly verified and are beyond doubt.

11. Initially, **Hitler** wanted to fly to Berchtesgaden on 20 April, 1945, his birthday, and his servants were given orders to prepare for his arrival on that day. But when the day came, he postponed the decision. He appointed **Dönitz** the Commander of all the forces in the so-called 'Nordraum' with full authority to take any measures necessary for the defence of this zone. **Dönitz's** appointment reflected **Hitler's** growing distrust of the Army leadership and of **Himmler**.

As a regular officer, **Dönitz** was entrusted with the command of the armed forces and because being a naval officer, he avoided the distrust that **Hitler** had had of the Army since 20 July, 1944. Similar authority for the 'Südraum' was, however, not given. Possibly, **Hitler** had yet not finally decided that he would not go to the south himself.

12. On 21 April, **Hitler** ordered a massive counter-attack in Berlin. This was to be carried out under the command of SS General **Steiner**. Due to lack of equipment and communications, the necessary orders were not given and the attack never began.

13. On 22 April, during the daily situation conference, which started at about 16.30, **Hitler** learnt of the failure of **Steiner's** attack, and this together with general despair and fatigue caused **Hitler** to suffer a breakdown when he showed for the first time that he had lost all hope of victory. During a scene that shocked everyone, he accused the SS of treachery similar to that of the Army. **Hitler** also proclaimed his decision to stay in Berlin and, if the city fell, to die there. **Goebbels**, although he was trying to persuade **Hitler** not to be such a 'defeatist', took the same decision. The generals unanimously disapproved of this decision, which they believed to be low cowardice, but were unable to change it. Answering their question as to what their orders were, **Hitler** said he could not issue orders any longer and they could leave if they wanted, but as for him – he was staying.

According to **Jodl's** evidence, he said that **Göring** would give them further orders and when one general argued that the soldiers would not fight under **Göring's** command, **Hitler** said that there was no longer any question of fighting. There was only the question of negotiations and for that **Göring** was better than him. As a result of this statement, of which **Jodl** informed General **Koller** (the Air Force Chief of Staff), **Koller** flew to **Hitler's** Obersalzberg retreat and informed **Göring**. Thus, the ensuing episode with **Göring**.

14. The incident with **Hitler** on 22 April was, in many respects, the beginning of the end. After that, he never left the bunker and stayed there surrounded not by generals and politicians as before (when Berlin was surrounded, the OKH moved to Krampnitz and later to Fürstenberg), but by his 'family circle': **Goebbels** and his family, Eva **Braun**, **Bormann** and a few devoted flatterers – **Hewel** (**Ribbentrop's** liaison officer), **Burgdorf**

(Chief of the Personnel Department of the OKH), **Stumpfegger** (the staff doctor) and so on. The Army was represented by several officers, responsible for the defence of Berlin and the Reich Chancellery. Two of his secretaries and one of **Bormann's** stayed but the rest of the clerks of the Staff, his doctor and many of his followers left him on the night of 22/23 April. To demonstrate the strength of his decision, **Hitler** ordered **Goebbels** to broadcast it on Berlin radio. This was done at noon on 23 April.

15. After the crisis of 22 April, according to the reports of all who saw him, **Hitler's** mood became easier. The storm was over, the decision had been taken, and he was only waiting for further developments. He even renewed private talks about the battle for Berlin, though they were not based on any rational strategic plan.

This peace of mind was interrupted by occasional moments of low spirits, when he remembered old betrayals or discovered new ones (such as **Göring**, **Fegelein** and **Himmler's** 'treachery') but he never again experienced a crisis of hesitation. Obviously, in the last days, **Hitler's** general physical condition was not very good due to the nervous stress from which he suffered, the hours of eccentric behaviour and the unhealthy life in the underground bunker. It is not true, however, that he was slightly paralysed. He had long recovered completely from the consequences of the attempt on his life of 20 July, 1944. But he suffered from almost constant trembling of the hands (which dated from before the bomb plot) which was diagnosed by some of his doctors, though not all of them, as Parkinson's Disease. Except for this tremor and a general weakness, he was absolutely sane and in healthy spirits.

16. On the night of 23/24 April, **Hitler** was visited by Albert **Speer**, Minister of War Production, who came to explain his opposition to the proclaimed 'scorched earth' policy. There **Speer** met **Bormann**, who still insisted on flight to the south, but **Hitler** refused to agree and Eva **Braun** and **Goebbels** supported him.

Hitler told **Speer** that he had planned to commit suicide and the complete destruction of his corpse by burning. In the presence of **Speer**, a telegram was received from **Göring**, asking if it had been finally decided that he should succeed him as **Koller** had informed him. **Bormann**, **Göring's** greatest enemy, interpreted this telegram as a treacherous usurpation. **Hitler** agreed with **Bormann** and entrusted him to answer **Göring** by dismissing from all his posts.

17. On 24 April, **Wegener**, who was with **Dönitz**, telephoned **Hitler** and proposed to enter into armistice negotiations in the West with the aim of freeing the forces for the fight against the Russians. **Hitler** refused to take such a step until the battle for Berlin had been won.

18. At approximately the same time (the exact date is not known), **Himmler** sent **Gebhardt**, his personal doctor, to **Hitler** with instructions to persuade **Hitler** to leave Berlin while it was still possible to do so. **Himmler** also sent his guard battalion to accompany **Hitler**, if **Gebhardt's** persuasion were successful. **Gebhardt's** attempts were supported by **Stumpfegger** (who had been **Gebhardt's** assistant in Hohenlychen and was recommended by him for the post of physician to the Führer's Main Headquarters), but **Hitler** interrupted them impatiently, saying that he did not want to hear such proposals any more.

19. On the evening of 26 April, Field-Marshal Ritter **von Greim** arrived at the bunker to accept the post of the Commander of the Air Force in place of **Göring**. He was accompanied by Hanna **Reitsch** and they made a forced landing in a Fieseler Storch on the Charlottenburgerstrasse. **Von Greim** injured his leg and for three days he and **Reitsch** stayed in the bunker. That evening, **Hitler** told **Reitsch** he had taken measures for his and Eva **Braun's** bodies to be burnt so there would be nothing to identify them. He also gave poison pills to **Reitsch** and **von Greim**, which the latter later used. From this time on, due to increasingly intensive Russian shelling, suicides became the order of the day. Poison pills were given to everyone.

20. On 27 April, it was discovered that Obergruppenführer **Fegelein**, **Himmler's** liaison officer with **Hitler**, had disappeared from the bunker. **Fegelein** had hoped to secure his position at **Hitler's** court by marrying Greta **Braun**, Eva **Braun's** sister, but seeing that the privileges of being one of the family circle had by then dwindled to sharing in a family suicide, he escaped from the bunker.

Hitler sent his deputy pilot, SS Standartenführer **Beetz**, to search for **Fegelein** and he managed to find him in a private house in Berlin lying in bed in civilian clothes. Being unmasked, **Fegelein** tried to induce **Beetz** personally and Eva **Braun** by telephone not to give him up, but in vain. He was delivered back to the bunker under armed SS guard, tried for desertion under the chairmanship of Obergruppenführer **Müller**, the Gestapo chief, taken out in the garden of the Reichstag and shot on **Hitler's** order.

21. On 28 April, the residents of the bunker heard in disbelief mixed with disgust about the talks **Himmler** had started with Count **Bernadotte**. **Hitler** was outraged by this news and all his followers showed their disgust, considering it as one more act of treachery.

22. Early in the morning of 29 April, a report reached the bunker that Russian tanks had broken through to the Potsdamerplatz. **Hitler** therefore ordered **von Greim** to return to Rechlin and to arrange an air raid to support **Wenck's** army, which he still believed in, though in fact it had already been defeated. **Von Greim** and **Reitsch** took off from Charlottenburgerstrasse at about 02.00 in an Arado-96 (a training aircraft) which flew in to take them and descended on Charlottenburgerstrasse from 13,000 feet. They flew away with great reluctance, being sure that further operations were senseless and being afraid of losing their lives.

23. Aside from the orders for the air raid, **von Greim** was ordered to investigate **Himmler's** behaviour and, if the report was correct, to arrest him. The next day (30 April) **Bormann** telegraphed **Dönitz** to inform him that **Hitler** had appointed him as his successor, obviously to prevent **Himmler** from taking the post from which **Göring** had been removed.

24. On 29 April, **Hitler** received a report of the deaths of **Mussolini** and Clara **Pettacchi** in Milan. It is not known if the full details of their bodies being strung up and mocked by the crowd reached the bunker, because communications with the outside world were so difficult, but if they had, such news could only have fortified **Hitler's** and Eva **Braun's** decision to prevent the discovery of their bodies.

25. By that time, those still in the bunker had lost all hope that Berlin could be relieved. The news of the defeat of **Wenck's** army at last reached **Hitler** and the telegrams sent by the last defenders of Berlin to **Dönitz** were written in the manner of hysterical mutual reproaches, indicating total despair. On the evening of 29 April, **Hitler** either decided or agreed to marry Eva **Braun**. The idea obviously came from her. She had always dreamed of the fame of dying with **Hitler** and had used every opportunity to influence him to stay and die in Berlin. The last-minute marriage was what she wanted, so as to create the necessary position for her to fulfil her intention. The ceremony was performed by an official from the Ministry of Propaganda in a small conference room in the bunker with **Bormann** and **Goebbels** in attendance. After the ceremony, **Hitler** and Eva **Braun** went out into the corridor of the bunker, where the usual situation meetings were under way, and shook hands with all those present. The meaning of this was not understood immediately, but later Frau **Christian**, who accompanied **Hitler** and Eva **Braun** to their rooms for dinner, went out and explained that the atmosphere was so depressing that she couldn't stand it. She had expected a marriage celebration but all the talk was of suicide. The news of **Hitler's** marriage was very soon known everywhere in the bunker and was openly discussed, not like his death which was officially kept secret from the soldiers.

26. Approximately at the same time, **Hitler** killed his dog. The dog was poisoned by Dr **Haase**, formerly **Hitler's** Headquarters physician, who later became a professor at the

Institute in Rostock in the Pigelstrasse. Other dogs owned by the residents of the bunker were shot by the sergeant-major who looked after them.

27. The same night, at about 22.00, one of the SS guards was sent to the other bunkers under the old and the new Chancelleries to tell everyone not to go to sleep as **Hitler** wanted to say goodbye to the ladies. At about 02.30, those invited arrived and 20 of them, including 10 women, gathered in the corridor of the bunker that was usually used as a dining-room. **Hitler** entered, accompanied by **Bormann**, and shook hands with all the ladies, saying a few words to most of them, and then left. His eyes were sunken and had a vacant look about them, so that many of those present thought that he had poisoned himself, but in fact his hollow eyes were noted by all those close to **Hitler** in the last days (**Reitsch**, for example), and they were only the result of his eccentric and strained life. After the ceremony, the participants stayed for some time to discuss the meaning of what could be considered suicide, and then went to sleep.

THE DEATH

28. On 30 April, **Hitler** and Eva **Braun** appeared alive for the last time. They went around the bunker and shook hands with all the secretaries and assistants, then returned to their apartments, where both committed suicide, **Hitler** by shooting himself in the mouth, Eva **Braun** (though she had a revolver) by swallowing one of the poison pills that had been distributed to everyone in the bunker.

29. At approximately the same time (it is not established if it was before or after), an order was signed for the Department of Transport for 200 litres of petrol to be delivered to the bunker immediately. About 160–180 litres were collected and delivered to the garden, to be precise, to the emergency exit from the bunker. In the course of the delivery, there was an argument with one of the SD guards on duty near the bunker who had not been informed and who quite reasonably refused to believe that petrol had been sent to refuel the electricity and ventilation power-plant.

30. After the suicides, all the outside doors of the bunker were locked to avoid the subsequent events being witnessed. The SD guards had already been ordered to leave. The bodies of **Hitler** and Eva **Braun** were carried down the staircase from the bunker to the garden by **Goebbels, Bormann, Günsche** (**Hitler**'s SS aide-de-camp), **Linge** (**Hitler**'s personal bodyguard) and **Kempka** (a transportation officer), and perhaps **Stumpfegger** as well. **Hitler**'s corpse was wrapped in a blanket (possibly because it was covered with blood), Eva **Braun**'s was not. The corpses were laid side-by-side in the

garden, approximately three yards from the bunker's emergency exit, and petrol was poured over them from the cans already brought there. Then the people retired under the cover of the emergency exit, because the shelling of the Russian artillery was intensifying, and from this, less dangerous position, **Günsche** threw a burning petrol-soaked rag at the corpses. The corpses caught fire at once.

31. At that time, one of the guards, who had earlier been ordered to leave the bunker, decided to return, and when he found the door locked, turned around and went into the garden to the emergency exit. Going around the corner tower he saw and recognised the two corpses and saw them suddenly catch fire.

32. When the corpses caught fire, the group saluted **Hitler** and returned to the bunker. After that, the evidence becomes scarcer and less immediate. The majority of those present were busier saving their own lives than with carrying out the ritual, and one of the more devoted guards complained of everyone else's indifference. It is not known how much petrol was poured over the corpses nor for how long they burned, and though four SD guards accidentally saw them, one cannot rely on their timings. **Günsche** told one of the witnesses that the corpses had burned until there was nothing left. It is more likely that they burned until they were unrecognisable and it was possible to crush the bones and mix them with other corpses buried in the garden.

One of the guards later saw a newly-dug grave which, he believed, had been prepared for the corpses, but until now no one has been found who witnessed the burial. The names of the people who could either have personally participated in the burial or given orders for it are known, but they have not yet been found.

CONSEQUENCES

33. The immediate consequence of **Hitler**'s death was a relaxation of tension in the bunker. A tragic life was replaced with a more cheerful one. For the first time, there were cigarettes in the bunker (they had been always forbidden in **Hitler**'s time). Then plans were made – not for a mass suicide, as had been loyally promised when **Hitler** was alive, but for a mass escape. First, a mission headed by General **Krebs** was sent to General **Zhukov** to establish the date for an exchange of the wounded. This and the late return of General **Krebs** were the reasons why the escape was postponed until the next night – 1 May.

34. On the morning of 1 May, **Bormann** sent a telegram to **Dönitz**, which in short informed him that **Hitler**'s will had come into effect (i.e. that **Hitler** was dead) and that he, **Bormann**, would try to reach **Dönitz** and join him. This information was later

supplemented by a telegram from **Goebbels** who said that **Hitler** had died at 15.30 the day before (i.e. 30 April) and that, according to his last will of 29 April, **Dönitz** was appointed Reichspresident, **Goebbels** Reichschancellor, **Bormann** Party Minister and **Seyss-Inquart** Minister of Foreign Affairs.

Goebbels added that **Bormann** was trying to reach **Dönitz** to inform him about the situation. These two telegrams were the only information known to **Dönitz** about **Hitler's** death, and the statement broadcast by **Dönitz** on the radio on 1 May that **Hitler** had died leading his fighting armies was a fabrication.

35. On 1 May, General **Weidling** (the Commandant of Berlin) came to the bunker and there he was told (obviously by **Bormann** or **Goebbels**) that **Hitler** had committed hara-kiri. Like the other soldiers, **Weidling** considered it a base betrayal and released his men from their oath of allegiance.

36. In the evening of 1 May, the plans for a mass escape of all the inhabitants and defenders of the Reichstag were carried out. Everyone, except for **Goebbels**, who stayed to commit suicide, gathered in one of the bunkers and made their way in groups, first to the Wilhelmsplatz and then down to the underground station and along the tracks to the Friedrichstrasse, where they re-emerged. The plan was to break through the Russian lines in the wake of SS Brigadeführer **Mohnke's** battle group, but on leaving the underground at the Friedrichstrasse they faced such heavy fire that further movement was almost impossible. Only one group crossed the Weidammer Brücke, took shelter in a beer cellar and was later captured by the Russians. It included Hans **Baur**, **Hitler's** pilot, Johann **Rattenhuber**, the SD chief (who had joined them later), Walter **Hewel**, Sturmbannführer **Günsche**, **Hitler's** two secretaries (Frau **Christian** and Frau **Junge**), his cook (Fraulein **Manzialy**) and **Bormann's** secretary (Fraulein **Krüger**).

Some of them were captured by the Russians, some committed suicide and the four women were released.

Earlier, another group, including **Bormann**, **Stumpfegger**, **Rattenhuber** and **Kempka**, had tried to cross the Weidammer bridge in a German tank, but a grenade thrown from a window hit the tank, and both **Bormann** and **Stumpfegger**, who were on its left side, were hit by the blast.

According to **Rattenhuber's** evidence (who told the group he joined later in the cellar), both of them were killed.

According to the evidence of **Kempka** who was following the tank, **Bormann** was killed and **Stumpfegger** seriously wounded. Both **Rattenhuber** and **Kempka** were themselves injured by the blast, **Rattenhuber** rather seriously, and their evidence is possibly not very accurate. Neither **Rattenhuber** nor **Kempka** knew of each other's presence.

CONCLUSION

37. The aforesaid evidence is not complete, but it is positive, circumstantial, convincing and independent. There is no evidence to support the theories circulating that **Hitler** is still alive. All the reported theories were investigated and found to be baseless. The majority of them fell to pieces at first contact with the facts, and some turned out to be the pure invention of their authors.

It is impossible to refute the existing evidence summarised above. It is impossible to suppose that the versions of different witnesses present a prefabricated story. They were too preoccupied with their own safety to be able or inclined to memorise an invented enigma which they would persist in defending for five months in isolation from each other, in the course of detailed and persistent cross-examination.

It is hardly possible that the witnesses were mistaken as to **Hitler's** corpse (the identity of Eva **Braun's** corpse is beyond doubt – she was not wrapped in a blanket and was easy to recognise).

There was a theory that **Hitler** had fled on 30 April after 14.30 and Eva **Braun** was replaced by the corpse of a double, which was secretly delivered. But escape after 14.30 was almost impossible. Even if it had been possible to fly a training aircraft from the Charlottenburgerstrasse there was no pilot, because both **Hitler's** pilots who had been in the bunker on 30 April participated in the attempted escape in May. **Baur** is now in a Russian hospital, and **Beetz** was seen for the last time with serious head wounds in the Friedrichstrasse. In any case, there are no well-founded reasons for the construction of such theories that contradict positive evidence and they are not supported by any data.

Ф. К-1 ос; оп. 4; д. 16; л. 28-38
(копия)
(copy)

THE REPORT OF HITLER'S PERSONAL SECRETARY

One of **Hitler**'s personal [male] secretaries, **Gergezel** [the name was recorded incorrectly] stated in an interview to an American correspondent, that on 21 April **Hitler** confirmed for the first time that the German leaders had lost any faith in victory. This was the day when **Hitler** realised that Germany would be defeated. **Gergezel**, who was in **Hitler**'s headquarters until 22 April, said:

'On 21 April at 10.20 a.m., the Russians opened a hurricane of fire on the central street of the city, the Wilhelmstrasse, in which **Hitler**'s office was situated. The shelling did not stop for almost the whole day and sirens were going off constantly. In **Hitler**'s headquarters, along with him, there were a certain Eva **Braun**, **Keitel**, **Bormann** and **Jodl**. **Hitler** couldn't decide whether he should stay in Berlin or not.

At 5.30 p.m., a meeting was held at the headquarters, with the participation of **Keitel**, **Bormann** and **Jodl**. It was there that **Hitler** said for the first time that he had lost hope in the victory of Germany. '*We cannot win*', he said, '*this is the end of Germany. I do not believe in the strength of the Army, the Air Force and the SS forces any longer*'.

After that, **Hitler** ordered **Keitel**, **Jodl** and **Bormann** to leave Berlin immediately. He repeated this order no less than ten times. But **Bormann** and **Keitel** refused to obey. Only **Jodl** said he could not stay there any longer and left at once.

The telephone in the headquarters was ringing endlessly. **Dönitz** called. **Hitler** listened to him and, saying '*Thank you, Herr Gross-Admiral*', replaced the receiver.

Then **von Ribbentrop** telephoned, saying that a split between the Western powers and the East was expected very soon. **Hitler** also thanked him and ended the conversation.

Soon **Goebbels** arrived at the headquarters with his children. He said to **Hitler**: '*Maybe we should turn our backs on the West and go on fighting against the Russians*'.

'*There is no reason for it*', **Hitler** answered, '*we are lost*'.

On 22 April, at 1.45 p.m., **Gergezel** left Berlin by plane along with the wives of **Hitler**'s staff officers and **Hitler**'s physician **Morell**. What happened at the Headquarters after that he does not know.

Ф. К-1 ос; оп. 4; д. 17; л. 1
(машинописный экз.)
(retyped)

THE STENOGRAPHER'S EVIDENCE OF
HITLER'S LAST DAYS

Reuters' special correspondent Oakshott
reports from Berchtesgaden:

During his last hours in Berlin, **Hitler** was a sick and absolutely disillusioned man with trembling hands. Pacing from corner to corner in his bunker under the Reich Chancellery in Berlin on the night of 22 April, he shouted: *'I've lost confidence in the Army, in the Luftwaffe. I'll stay in Berlin until the end because, having killed so many generals during this retreat, I cannot retreat myself. If I leave Berlin it will be lost'*. He insisted on this despite the attempt of Field-Marshal **Keitel**, General **Jodl**, Martin **Bormann**, von **Ribbentrop** and **Goebbels** to persuade him otherwise. They tried to convince him to retreat to the south and to continue the fight for every piece of German land.

According to the official stenographers, who for many years had been writing down all the discussions between **Hitler** and his generals and from whom I learned all this information, **Hitler** was possibly killed by SS Sturmbannführer **Günsche**, who was in charge of the defence of the Reich Chancellery. This **Günsche** is a grim individual, who was entrusted to make sure that **Hitler** was really dead.

The last meeting between **Hitler** and his generals started at 15.00 and lasted until 19.30. During this meeting, **Hitler** kept on leaving the room, telephoning, reading situation reports and consulting. Pacing from corner to corner with disarranged, greying hair, he did not resemble the **Hitler** of earlier days. He was dressed in a field-grey uniform without badges of rank or a swastika on his sleeve, but with an Iron Cross. He looked morally and physically degenerate. He held his left arm behind his back and the arm seemed paralysed. His hair looked thicker than before and was combed back without the usual lock falling over one eye.

During this meeting **Hitler** repeated no less than 20 times: *'I am going to stay in Berlin, I shall not leave Berlin'*. And he went on repeating this phrase in different ways. He also said pathetically: *'I am going to die at the door to the Reich Chancellery'*.

At 17.00, he took **Keitel**, **Jodl**, **Bormann** and a stenographer, who told me all about this, into the next room, saying to all the others that he wanted to be alone with them for 15 minutes. Replying to his repeated statements that he was going to stay in Berlin, **Keitel**, supported by **Bormann**, said: *'My Führer, you told us something else several months ago when you said you were going to fight to the last piece of German land remaining. You said that you would sooner be killed three times over rather than give up this idea'*.

Keitel and **Bormann** told him if he went to the north, to the south or to the west he could get the situation under control because he had sufficient forces.

But **Hitler** made a dramatic gesture and said: *'There is no way back. If I leave Berlin it will fall. I have lost confidence in the Army, in the Air Force, I have also lost confidence in the SS'*.

One of the stenographers, who was present at the conversation, told me: *'He had been losing confidence in the Luftwaffe for a number of years and was very displeased with Göring'*.

SS Gruppenführer **Steiner** told him that he was going to counter-attack with two divisions in the north of Berlin, but when this counter-attack failed, **Hitler** was very disappointed. After that, **Hitler** ordered his generals to go to the south and set up a new government headed by **Göring**, saying: *'Göring will hold negotiations in future'*.

Some thought that **Hitler** said it sarcastically, but none of them could later believe that **Hitler** had ordered the arrest of **Göring**, as the latter asserted.

The meeting between **Hitler** and the three Nazis ended with **Hitler** rushing out of the room. **Keitel** said: *'It is impossible for Hitler to stay in Berlin. We should take him away by force'*.

Then the meeting was broken off.

Everyone was terribly frightened by the Russian shells, which began to fall in the next street; the Russian forces were already only 20 minutes' walk from the Reich Chancellery. **Goebbels** said to **Hitler** that it was silly to stay in Berlin any longer, adding: *'If you die then the whole war will be lost'*. He proposed moving the armies from the west to fight against the Russians, but **Hitler** exclaimed: *'No, it will be capitulation in the west and I reject it'*.

21 May, 1945 (TASS)

Ф. К-1 ос; оп. 4; д. 17; л. 2-2 об (машинописный экз.)
(retyped)

HITLER'S PERSONAL PHYSICIAN'S
EVIDENCE ABOUT THE FÜHRER

London, 21 May. Reuters' special correspondent reports from Berchtesgaden, with the story of Herr **Morell**, **Hitler**'s personal physician, about **Hitler**. 'Morell told me', the correspondent writes, 'that before the fall of Berlin, Hitler suffered fits of rage and he was afraid of being drugged and taken away from the capital by force. Morell does not believe that Hitler committed suicide because, according to him, Hitler did not have the attributes of a suicide. Morell, who had observed Hitler's health day-by-day for the last nine years, was dismissed by him in the last days as Hitler began to suspect that the doctor was going to give him morphine. 'Hitler's angry silence', Morell says, 'was more awful than his outbursts of angry verbosity. Hitler turned white as a sheet, his teeth clenched and his eyes opened wide. Everyone near him was panic-stricken because such fits usually ended with orders to dismiss or execute somebody'.

Ф. К-1 ос; оп. 4; д. 17; л. 3
(машинописный экз)

R. BELFORD'S ARTICLE:
'HITLER – A CORPSE OR A LEGEND?'

This is an article by Ronald Belford 'Hitler – Corpse or Legend?' provided by Reuters:

'In the silence of their laboratories, the pathologists of the Allied Nations are busy solving one of the greatest mysteries mankind has ever encountered, the mystery of the Führer of the German Reich, Adolf **Hitler**.

'The cool and systematic expertise which they use to examine four burnt and disfigured corpses, any of which could turn out to be **Hitler**'s body, is in dramatic contrast to the previous scene the last act of the drama that was played out in the underground fortress under the Reich Chancellery, enveloped in smoke and flames, that had been **Hitler**'s headquarters.

'Examination of these human remains is the culmination of a strenuous week-long search in the ruins of Berlin. The search was made by Red Army soldiers, seeking indisputable evidence of **Hitler**'s death.

'The events that led to the discovery of the four corpses were as dramatic as the discovery itself. The search started this May, after Marshal Stalin in his order quoted the statement of **Goebbels**' deputy Hans **Fritzsche** that **Hitler**, **Goebbels** and General **Krebs** had committed suicide. Stalin's words were followed by Truman's statement at the press-conference held the same day in Washington: *'Hitler is dead. This assertion is based on data from the most reliable sources currently available'*.

'It is said that the Führer's last residence was the Reich Chancellery, where he personally led resistance against the Russians. When the Reich Chancellery was enveloped in flames, caused by the massive fire of Russian artillery and machine-guns of the Red Army's infantry, **Hitler**, making a superhuman effort, cut his way through into the burning building.

'The Russian reporters following the troops after the barricades had been broken through made a thorough search. In one of the room of the headquarters, the reporters discovered that the windows were barricaded with the books praising the rise of the Nazi monster to power and the whole Nazi hierarchy. There were a lot of copies of **Hitler**'s *Mein Kampf* there. The machine-guns covering all the entrances to the building were concealed by books. Behind the books, thousands of small red boxes were concealed, each containing an Iron Cross. A lot of similar boxes were scattered all over the room. This proves that **Hitler** or someone else possessing supreme authority, at the last moment gave out the medals en masse in the hope of boosting the besieged garrison's morale and encouraging the soldiers to fight to the last drop of their blood.

'The Red Army soldiers, before the terrible heat made them leave the nerve-centre of Germany and the last symbol of **Hitler**'s collapsing empire, managed to find a number of bodies. Among them were German rank-and-file Army soldiers and high-ranking SS officers. The removal of the burnt corpses was an extraordinary scene. It was the fitting end for the madman who has led the world to the edge of hell. The corpse that might be that of **Hitler** was carried along streets through which once **Hitler** had been driven triumphantly grimacing and gesticulating before the adoring crowds of the 'Master Race'. But on the Red Army's route there were no rejoicing crowds. There were absolutely no buildings, and almost no streets.

'Soviet artillery fire and Anglo-American bombing had reduced Berlin to ashes. The buildings, which had echoed with the loud cries of Berlin's population, greeting **Hitler** as he passed by in triumph, had turned to ashes – there is not even wreckage.

'The Allied pathologists have an enormous responsibility: they must indisputably prove the death of Hitler.

'The Nazi fanatics who are still in hiding in hope of avoiding the impending justice of the Allied War Crimes Commission, pray that the pathologists' efforts will be futile. For the Nazis, there is nothing more desirable than unconvincing claims of the Führer's death. If the Führer's death is not finally verified then the 'cells' established long ago to preserve Nazi teaching in case of Germany's defeat would fan the flames of the **Hitler** myth. Proof of this can be found in the contradictory statements of **Fritzsche**, one of the Nazi leaders who was captured alive. At first, he said that **Hitler** and **Goebbels** committed suicide. Later, he said that they died in the Reich Chancellery and their corpses 'were probably destroyed' by the fire enveloping the underground corridors. Then, in the course of an interview with Russian reporters, **Fritzsche** said that 'the Führer's corpse is hidden in a place where it will never be found'.

'The Allies have some information about the fate of a number of Nazi leaders. The former Commander-in-Chief of the German Air Force, Germany's Falstaff, **Göring**, was captured by the American forces. **Himmler**, after **Hitler** had dismissed **Göring**, zealously exaggerated the rumours that the former Air Force Commander had gone completely mad. However, these rumours were refuted by American correspondents, who personally saw that **Göring** was far from mad but had not lost his former bombast. The corpses of **Goebbels**, his wife and children have already been identified by the Russians.

'**Himmler**'s whereabouts are still a matter for speculation in Allied circles. Some reports say that **Himmler** and his wife were heading for the Bavarian border. Others imply that the new Führer, Admiral **Dönitz**, is holding **Himmler**'s wife as a hostage.

If that is true, then **Himmler** cannot expect any pardon from **Dönitz** when he falls in his hands. The Nazi fanatic **Dönitz** will hardly make any allowances for the man who held talks with the Allies at the time when Germany was in its death throes.

Von Ribbentrop, the former German Ambassador to Great Britain and Minister of Foreign Affairs before he was fired by **Dönitz**, is said to be under observation.

'It is definitely known that after his dismissal from his post as Minister of Foreign Affairs, **Ribbentrop's** activities were enshrouded in mystery. There is also a theory that he was done away with by **Dönitz's** followers.

'To receive the correct picture of **Hitler's** and **Goebbels'** last hours it is necessary to return almost to the beginning of 1944. Starting from the conspiracy in July, 1944, different rumours about **Hitler** have constantly circulated. Photographs of him decorating members of the Hitler Youth, the SS and the German Army or receiving the Quislings from satellite countries have not lessened this speculation'.

Ф. К-1 ос; оп. 4; д. 17; л. 4-5 об.
(машинописный экз.)
(retyped)

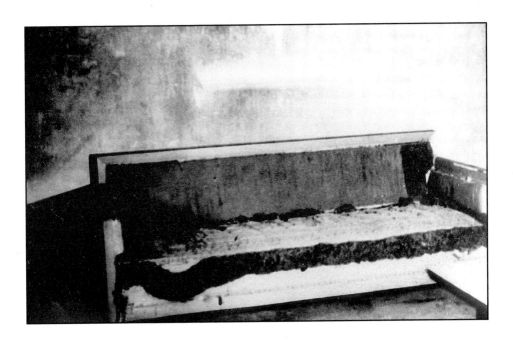

The sofa from the Reichs Chancellery on which Hitler died, and on which bloodstains were found (used for scientific evidence in 1946).

FOREIGN PRESS REPORTS CONCERNING HITLER'S FATE

A United Press Service correspondent reports from Berchtesgaden that **Hitler**'s private driver **Kempka**, recently arrested by the Americans, testified that **Hitler** and his mistress Eva **Braun** shot themselves in the underground rooms of the Reich Chancellery in Berlin on 30 April. Their bodies were burnt at night in the garden of the Chancellery. **Kempka** insists that he carried **Braun**'s body there himself and personally saw to the burning of **Hitler**'s and **Braun**'s corpses. He also said that **Goebbels** and his wife, who had committed suicide, were burned on 1 May.

* * *

A UPS reporter at the British 21st Army reports that a former officer of the Nazi criminal police testified that he witnessed the burning of **Hitler**'s and **Braun**'s corpses near the Reich Chancellery during daylight on 1 May.

* * *

An AP correspondent reports from Travemunde that it has become known that, during the last weeks of the war, the personnel of the local airfield received an order to keep ready a giant four-engine aircraft spacious enough to hold quantities of petrol. The aircraft was believed to be for **Hitler**'s flight to Japan.

The plane could carry only three passengers, all the remaining space was occupied with fuel. Also, three seaplanes were ready at a secret airfield for the flight of other Nazi officials from Germany.

20 June, 1945 (TASS)

Ф. К-1 ос; оп. 4; д. 17; л. 9.
(машинописный экз.)
(retyped)

THE EVIDENCE OF HITLER'S FORMER SECRETARY

Paris, German language,
21 June 12.30, for the record.

Hitler's secretary gave the following evidence concerning the meeting of 21 April this year on the second floor of the 'Braun House' in Berchtesgaden. Along with **Hitler**, there were **Keitel**, **Jodl**, **Dönitz**, **Goebbels** and **Bormann**.

At the meeting, it was decided that **Hitler** should assume supreme command in Berlin and stay there to the very last moment, until his death. **Hitler's** behaviour at the meeting gave the secretary the impression that **Hitler** was absolutely insane and didn't understand what was going on and passively reacted to all proposals and statements.

When the meeting was over, **Goebbels** rose, pushed away his chair and said that he would return to Berlin with **Hitler** and if necessary commit suicide there, together with his wife and children.

Keitel stated that he was not going to participate in this farce, which was unworthy of a soldier. In contrast, **Dönitz** said he was staying with **Hitler** to the end. **Göring** was not present at the meeting.

Keitel and **Jodl** left the meeting first. **Hitler** and **Goebbels** went by car to Salzburg, and then on by plane to Berlin. The authentic record of this meeting is available.

1 June, 1945 (TASS)

Ф. К-1 ос; оп. 4; д. 17; л. 10
(машинописный экз.)
(retyped)

THE EVIDENCE OF THE FÜHRER'S DRIVER AND
SECURITY OFFICER ON HITLER'S DEATH

Two Germans, who insist that they saw **Hitler**'s corpse, were interviewed by Allied reporters.

One of them, Erich **Kempka**, is supposed to be **Hitler**'s driver, the other, Hermann **Karnau**, says he was one of **Hitler**'s personal security officers.

The reporters spoke to **Karnau** at the headquarters of the 21st Army Group. He said that on 1 May, when Berlin was under heavy fire from Russian artillery, he saw **Hitler** sitting on a chair in his underground hiding-place. Later, he saw the bodies of **Hitler** and Eva **Braun**, lying at the emergency exit to the bunker.

Karnau says that the corpses were burning but were recognisable. Near the corpses, there were four empty petrol cans.

The other German, the driver **Kempka**, is at the headquarters of the 101st Airborne Division. He insists that it was he who carried the body of Eva **Braun** out of the bunker. Someone else carried out the corpse of Hitler, wrapped in a blanket. Five cans of petrol were emptied over the corpses and they were set on fire.

Both these stories are rather similar.

But none of these Germans saw how **Hitler** died and their evidence as to the cause of his death varies.

The driver Kempka says that **Hitler** and Eva **Braun** shot themselves but **Karnau** says that they were poisoned.

Ф. К-1 ос; оп. 4; д. 17; л. 11
(машинописный экз.)
(retyped)

Erich Kempka, *born 16 September, 1910 in Oberhausen. Hitler's chauffeur from 1936 onwards, he escaped from the bunker but was captured by the Americans on 20 June, 1945 and interned until 1947. He died on 24 January, 1975 in Freiburg.*

REPORTS ON THE EVIDENCE OF
HITLER' DEATH

According to Reuters special reporter Kerr, who is with the troops of the 21st Army Group, one of **Hitler's** personal guards recounted how **Hitler** died in the Reich Chancellery in Berlin with Eva **Braun**, who is supposed to have been either **Hitler's** wife or his mistress. Hermann **Karnau**, 32 years old, is a policeman from Wilhelmshafen. He recently escaped from the Russian occupation zone of Germany and turned himself over to the Canadian forces. He said that **Hitler** died on 1 May and that he married Eva **Braun** at the end of April.

Karnau said:'I arrived at Berchtesgaden in February, 1945. In Berchtesgaden, I saw the rooms in which **Hitler** and Eva **Braun** lived and I was told that these rooms were connected by a door. No one was allowed to call Eva "Fraulein **Braun**", it was ordered that she be called only by the initials, E.B. When I returned to Berlin, there were rumours among the guards that **Hitler** and Eva **Braun** had married at the end of April. On 30 April, I met Eva **Braun** in the underground bomb-shelter. She was alone and very sad. She said: *"I would like to die here. I don't want to leave"*. I tried to comfort her, calling her 'Fraulein Braun' and she answered: *"You may call me Frau Hitler now."* On 1 May, when I was passing the bunker to get my breakfast I saw **Hitler**, who was sitting in a wicker chair and nervously drumming with his fingers of the left hand. He stood up and went to meet Brigadeführer **Mohnke**, who greeted him with a **Hitler** salute and shook hands with him. **Hitler** asked him: *"What is the news?"* The other answered: *"Good news. The Silesian station is cleared of the enemy."* These were the last words I heard from **Hitler**. When in the afternoon, about 5 o'clock, I returned to the bunker, it was empty'.

Karnau stated that on 1 May he saw the corpses of **Hitler** and Eva **Braun** near the emergency exit from the bunker. Both corpses were burning. 'Looking around I saw Sturmbannführer **Schedle** – one of **Hitler's** personal staff, who was very upset and cried out to me: *"The Führer is dead and burning!"*

I walked out of the bunker and saw the corpses of **Hitler** and Eva **Braun** on the sandy soil, approximately three yards from the emergency exit. **Hitler** was lying on his back, knees slightly bent, Eva **Braun** was near him, face down. Both corpses were burning and spreading a ghastly odour'.

If **Karnau's** story is correct, it solves the puzzle of what actually happened to **Hitler**. They have been saying that he was poisoned by his personal physician, that he was burned in the Reich Chancellery, that he is still hiding in Germany or is living abroad under a false name.

On 25 April, when the Soviet armies were attacking Berlin, German radio announced that **Hitler** had gone to the most critical point of the fighting in Berlin. Next day,

Hamburg radio announced that **Hitler** would stay in Berlin and a report from Oslo said that he was leading the defence of the capital. The day after, German radio announced that **Hitler** had received the commanders of the sectors of the Berlin front. When the Russians were approaching Berlin, the torrent of rumours about **Hitler** grew still greater. On 28 April, a report from Stockholm said that **Hitler** had suffered a brain haemorrhage and, two days later, the same source announced that **Hitler** died in Berlin on 29 April. On 30 April, a telegram from Berlin said that **Hitler** died at 12.00 that day. Admiral Karl **Dönitz**, who came to power after **Hitler**, stated on 1 May: 'Our Führer Adolf **Hitler** is dead'. And on 2 May a German communiqué said that **Hitler** had died in battle leading the defenders of the capital of the German Reich. On 8 May, the Russians insisted that **Hitler** and **Göring** were in hiding. After this, the Red Army started an intensive search for the corpse though, according to a report, the remains uncovered in the building of Reich Chancellery were those of **Hitler**. According to information later discovered by the Russians, **Hitler** died as the result of an injection of poison administered by his private physician Dr **Morell** in a Berlin bomb-shelter on 1 May.

Count Folke **Bernadotte**, who held talks with **Himmler**, stated later that **Hitler** had been killed by his own subordinates.

Karnau went on: 'The corpses were easy to identify. I recognised **Braun** by her black boots with small heels, by her summer dress and dark coat, and **Hitler** by his brown uniform and by his face, though the lower parts of both corpses were heavily burnt. The four empty petrol cans, which I have already mentioned, had been taken to the bunker the same day. According to my theory, both **Hitler** and Eva **Braun** were poisoned by Professor **Stumpfegger** – the senior medical officer of the Chancellery. I met **Stumpfegger** immediately after I saw the burning corpses. He was walking through the cellars. The previous night, **Stumpfegger** had poisoned **Hitler**'s favourite pet, his dog Blondi. All the officers of **Hitler**'s personal guard believed that he would sooner take poison rather than fall into the hands of the Russians. His personal servant **Linge** received orders to make sure that his corpse would never fall into the hands of the enemy. When I saw the corpses, there was no one nearby. Probably, no funeral ceremony took place. Later that night, our chief **Kolke** gathered all the officers of the personal guard and addressed them: "It is sad that none of the officers is interested in where **Hitler**'s corpse is. I am proud that I am the only one who knows where he lies."'

Karnau told me that he saw **Goebbels**, whose room was next to that of the Führer. **Goebbels** was standing alone in the rooms next to those of **Hitler**. 'He looked shocked,' **Karnau** said. 'Soon after Hitler's death, his deputy Martin **Bormann** sent a telegram with the order to arrest **Göring**, who was accused of high treason, and I personally accompanied the officer who was ordered to give this telegram to the communications department'.

Another photograph of the bloodstained sofa in the Reichs Chancellery
that was used for scientific evidence in 1946).

Karnau was interrogated by a British intelligence officer. 'I am sure that **Karnau**'s report about **Hitler**'s death is authentic', he told Kerr. 'I have interrogated many German prisoners-of-war and I would call this man a reliable witness'.

The report about **Karnau**'s statement is being prepared for transfer to the Russian intelligence officers.

On 23 April, **Karnau** stated, a group of Nazi officials, including several officials of the Reich Chancellery, flew from Templehof airfield to Bavaria.

21 June, 1945 (TASS)

Ф. К-1 ос; оп. 4; д. 17; л. 12 об.-13 об.
(машинописный экз.)
(retyped)

FOREIGN PRESS REPORTS ABOUT HITLER'S LANDING IN ARGENTINA

Reuters' correspondent reports from Buenos Aires that the Argentinian evening newspaper *La Critica*, commenting on the mystery surrounding submarine *U-530*, which surrendered to Argentina seven days ago, advanced the theory that Adolf **Hitler** and his wife Eva **Braun** landed from the submarine on Queen Maude Island in the Antarctic near the South Pole. The newspaper says that 'a second Berchtesgaden' had been built on the island during the German expedition in 1938–9. The newspaper adds that *U-530* is possibly one of a group of submarines that left German ports heading for the Antarctic.

* * *

According to a Reuters' reporter in Buenos Aires, Argentinian radio announced on the evening of 17 July that the government of Argentina, in a session on 17 July, approved the decision to hand over the *U-530* submarine and its crew to the governments of the United States and Great Britain, along with the report of the Navy Ministry on the results of investigations connected with the arrival of the submarine.

* * *

According to the United Press Service agency's reporter in Buenos Aires, Mr. Ameguino, the Foreign Minister, stated that the government of Argentina had been informed about the possibility of **Hitler**'s landing in Argentina and are investigating, though there is no evidence supporting this report.

* * *

According to Reuters' correspondent in Buenos Aires, Mr. Ameguino denied the veracity of the report that **Hitler** and his wife Eva **Braun** landed on the Argentinean coast from a German submarine.

* * *

According to Reuters' Washington correspondent, a spokesman for the US State Department stated on 17 July that the US Embassy in Buenos Aires would clear up the circumstances connected with the report that **Hitler** and Eva **Braun** were in Argentina.

Reuters agency adds: 'After *La Critica* published reports in Buenos Aires that **Hitler** and Eva **Braun** might have landed from a submarine that had arrived in the Mar del Plata six days previously, another report was published about **Hitler** and Eva **Braun** landing in Argentina'.

The *El Tribuno* newspaper, published in the city of Dolores between Mar del Plata and Buenos Aires, published an unconfirmed report that two more submarines had been captured near the Argentinian coast. The newspaper adds that Argentinian Naval aircraft escorted the submarines.

17–18 July, 1945 (TASS)

Ф. К-1 ос; оп. 4; д. 17; л. 14-16
(машинописный экз.)
(retyped)

REPORTS FROM ABROAD ABOUT THE DISCOVERY OF
THE LAST WILLS OF HITLER AND GOEBBELS

London, 31 December. The personal and political testaments of **Hitler**, his marriage certificate as well as **Goebbels'** last will were discovered in a house in Tegernsee (Bavaria), according to Reuters' reporter Jack Edmond in Gerford (Westphalia). **Hitler's** political will was published in Nuremberg.

London, 31 December. (The beginning of the report was not received). 'For the past three decades I have expended all my time, all my energy and all my health. It is wrong that in 1939 I, or anyone else in Germany, wanted a war. It was desired and it was provoked exclusively by the international statesmen either of Jewish origin or by those working in the interests of the Jews.

'I made too many proposals on arms limitations and arms control for our descendants to be able to ignore them forever with the aim of placing all the responsibility for starting of this war on myself. Besides, I never wanted the terrible World War I to be followed by a second one, either against Britain or America.

'Centuries will pass, but the hatred for those who are really responsible will always grow and grow. Here are the people whom we should thank for all that: international Jewry and their assistants.

'Three days before the German-Polish war, I proposed a plan to the British Ambassador in Berlin for the settlement of the German-Polish problem under international control similar to that in the Saar.

'This proposal also cannot be ignored. It was rejected solely because the ruling political clique in Britain expected war, partly due to commercial considerations, partly because it was influenced by international Jewry's propaganda.

'I also specified quite clearly that if the peoples of Europe were again to be considered mere pawns in the game played by the international conspirators, the money magnates and financiers, that it would be on them, the Jews – the race which is the real culprit behind this deadly struggle – that all the blame for this would fall.

'I left no doubt that, although millions of European Aryan children would starve to death and hundreds of thousands of women and children would perish in deadly bombing of cities, this time the real culprits would pay for their guilt, though it would be done by more humane means than war.

'After six years of war which, despite all the failures, will one day take its place in history as the most glorious and courageous manifestation of the Nation's fight for survival, I cannot desert the city that was the capital of this state.

'Because our armed forces are too few to withstand further enemy attacks against this city, and because those defending us are increasingly exhausted by their struggle against those who are merely blind automata, I want to share the fate chosen by millions of other people in this city.

'Besides, I will not fall into the hands of the enemy, which only wants to stage a new entertainment directed by the Jews to distract the attention of their hysterical masses.

'That is why I have decided to stay in Berlin and to choose a voluntary death here at the moment when I conclude that the existence of the Führer and The Chancellor is no longer bearable.

'I will die with joy in my heart, being aware of the innumerable heroic deeds and achievements of our soldiers in the battlefields, our women on the home front, of the achievements of our peasants and workers and of the contribution, unique in History, made by our Youth movement, named after me.

'My gratitude to all of them from the bottom of my soul is as obvious as my wish that they do not abandon the struggle whatever the circumstances, that they continue with the struggle against the enemies of the Fatherland always whenever possible, upholding their allegiance to the principals of Clausewitz.

'The sacrifices of our soldiers and my comradeship with them until death itself will sow the seeds that sometime in the history of Germany will ensure the glorious rebirth of the National-Socialist Movement and a truly unified Nation.

'Many brave men and woman decided to tie their lives to mine until the very last moment.

'I have asked them, and finally I ordered them, not to do this but to continue with the struggle of the Nation.

'I request the Commanders of the Army, the Navy and the Air Force to fortify by all possible means our soldiers' spirit of resistance as well as their National-Socialist faith, especially stressing the fact that I, as a founder and creator of this movement, prefer death to cowardly submission and/or even surrender.

'In future, let German officers consider it a debt of honour not to even think of the capitulation of any district or city, similar to the practice of our Navy, and that the commanders first and foremost provide a shining example of faithfulness and loyalty to their duty until death itself.

'Before my death I expel the former Reichsmarshall of Germany **Göring** from the Party and strip him of all the prerogatives entrusted to him by the decree of 29 June, 1941 and by my speech in the Reichstag on 1 September, 1939.

'Before my death I expel the former Reichsführer and Minister of Interior Heinrich **Himmler** from the Party and from all positions of State.

'To say nothing of their disloyalty to me, **Göring** and **Himmler** indelibly disgraced the country and the whole Nation by negotiating with the enemy without my knowledge and against my will, and also illegitimately tried to seize control of the state'.

Another photograph of Hitler that was used to identify his corpse.

There follows a list of the new cabinet members appointed by **Hitler**, including Karl **Dönitz** as President, Josef **Goebbels** as Chancellor, Martin **Bormann** as Party Minister and **Seyss-Inquart** as Minister of Foreign Affairs.

Further, **Hitler** expresses the hope that 'My spirit will stay among them and will always be with them.

'Let them be strict', the last will continues 'but let them never be unjust; let them never be influenced by fear in their actions and let them put the honour of the Nation before anything else in the world.

'I request that all Germans, all National-Socialists, men and women and all the soldiers of the German army be loyal and obedient to the new government and President until death.

'Above all, I request the government of the Nation and the people to totally support the racial laws and mercilessly resist the poisoner of all nations – international Jewry'.

Berlin, 29 April, 1945, 04.00 a.m. (*signed*) A. **Hitler**.

Witnesses: Dr Josef **Goebbels**; Wilhelm **Burgdorf**; Martin **Bormann**; Hans **Krebs**.

London, 30 December. In his personal last will **Hitler** leaves 'all his property whatever its value' to the Nazi party, Reuters' reports from Nuremberg.

London, 30 December. According to Reuters' reporter Kerr in Nuremberg, **Goebbels'** last will was discovered along with that of **Hitler**. In it, **Goebbels** says that for the first time in his life he 'has to decisively refuse to obey the Führer's order'. 'The Führer', he says, 'ordered me, should the defence of the Reich capital collapse, to leave Berlin and join the government appointed by him as its leading member'.

'To say nothing of the fact that out of feelings of comradeship and personal fidelity we could never force ourselves to leave the Führer alone at the time of greatest disaster, I would be a dishonourable traitor and a coward for all my life and lose my self-respect as well as the respect of my fellow citizens, the respect I would need for any further work for the future reconstruction of the German nation and the German state'.

Further on, **Goebbels'** last will runs as follows: 'In the nightmare of treachery surrounding **Hitler** in these crucial days of the war, at least some men must stay with him unreservedly till death, even if it is against the formal and, from the practical point of view, quite justified order he issues in his political last testament. I believe that by doing this I best serve the future of the German people.

'In the forthcoming hard times examples will be of more significance than persons. There will always be persons to show the Nation the way out of trouble but the reconstruction of our Nation's life would be impossible if not inspired by clear and easily-understood examples.

'This consideration demonstrates why my wife and I, and in the name of our children, who are too young to speak.' (*the end of the communication was not received*).

London, 31 December. According to Reuters' reporter Edmond, **Goebbels** states in his last will: 'My wife and my children join in my refusal. I express my unshakeable decision not to leave the capital of the Reich, even if it falls and along with the Führer to put an end to my life which will not be of any further value for me personally'.

New York, 31 December. According to the Associated Press Agency's reporter from Nuremberg, American military intelligence officers stated that **Hitler**'s so-called political testament, found yesterday contains 'political dynamite'. The text will be kept secret while the search for all persons named in the last will is under way throughout Europe. The investigation will continue for several weeks. Many of those mentioned in the will are now outside Germany. American intelligence officers in Germany, Austria, Italy and other countries are co-operating closely with officers of the British intelligence service. The reporter says that the Allied authorities have discovered the codicil to **Hitler**'s last will, written by **Goebbels**.

30–31 December, 1945 (TASS)

Ф. К-1 ос; оп. 4; д. 17; л. 18 об.-23
(машинописный экз.)
(retyped)

THE STATEMENT BY A BRITISH COUNTER-ESPIONAGE OFFICER ON THE FATE OF THE CHIEF NAZIS WHO STAYED IN HITLER'S BUNKER

According to a Reuters' reporter in Gerford (Germany), a senior British counter-espionage officer who, with the assistance of the Americans, managed to discover Hitler's last will, stated that he believed it was now possible now to give an exact description of the last days of Hitler and Eva Braun's stay in the Reichstag bunker in Berlin.

The British officer said that the investigation undertaken by him presented the following picture of Hitler's last hours:

On the night of 29 April, Hitler came to the conclusion that the end was near and no help was possible for besieged Berlin.

At 2.00 or 3.00 o'clock in the morning of 29 April, Hitler presumably married Eva Braun. He dictated his last will at 4.00 in the morning.

At 10 a.m., Hitler took measures to ensure that his last will was taken out of Berlin with the assistance of three reliable couriers. These couriers were supposed to be men of determination who would be able to reach their destinations by any means. They were given instructions addressed to Admiral Dönitz (who was appointed in Hitler's last will to be the Reich's President and War Minister) and to Field-Marshal Schörner (appointed Supreme Commander of the German Army).

Another copy of the last will was to be saved in case the others didn't reach their destinations.

By the time these measures were taken, Berlin had already been surrounded by the Russians for two days.

Hitler's couriers travelled at night and rested during the day. By the time they reached Hanover, passing through territory occupied by the Russians, they had obviously decided to abandon any hope of delivering the documents to their destinations. They went their separate ways to their homes, keeping the documents.

But on 29 April, Dönitz received a telegram from Martin Bormann saying that Hitler had appointed Dönitz his successor and that the due written authorisations had been sent out.

On 1 May, Josef Goebbels (whom Hitler had appointed Chancellor) and Bormann telegraphed Dönitz that Hitler was dead and the 'government' of Dönitz (which did not include Göring or the others sacked by Hitler) was now in power.

The officer said that according to information received, Dönitz had refused to have any 'discredited Nazis' appointed by Hitler in the Reichstag bunker in his government.

Lorenz was arrested by chance due to the fact that he was carrying false papers. When he was searched (in the vicinity of Hanover), the wrinkles made by the papers in the shoulders of his coat made those searching him rip up his clothes, and the documents were discovered. Then **Lorenz** disclosed that other copies had been sent with other couriers.

The second courier (German Army Major Willi **Johannmeier**) was sent by **Hitler's** Chief of Staff. He was arrested in mid-December in his own house in Iserlohn (in the Ruhr).

The third one (**Bormann's** advisor Wilhelm **Zander**) was followed from Munich to Tegernsee in Bavaria (near the Austrian border) notwithstanding the plausible claims of his wife that he was dead.

In Tegernsee, he was hiding under the name of **Paustin**. He was arrested after Christmas in a village where he was staying with a girl named Ilsa **Unterholtzner** who had been a secretary before 20 April.

As far as is known, neither **Dönitz** nor the other Nazi leaders knew of these documents until they were discovered in the British zone.

The first courier to be arrested (Heinz **Lorenz**) was on **Goebbels'** staff, working there as a liaison officer with **Bormann**.

The British officer adds: 'Both the documents and the statements coincide with what we already know, based on telegrams sent to **Dönitz** from the Reichstag bunker. There is no reason to doubt their authenticity. If the Russians did not add anything, it is because they know nothing more. We now know what happened during the last hours of **Hitler** and Eva **Braun**, even if we do not take account of the witnesses' statements about burning their bodies'.

The British officer stated that there was some evidence that two women had been ordered to conceal the bodies of **Hitler** and Eva **Braun**, adding: 'In my opinion **Hitler** and Eva **Braun** were buried in the Reichstag garden'.

After their death, he added, there was probably a mass escape of the people in the bunker, with the exception of those who had decided to commit suicide along with **Hitler** and his wife.

Later it was assumed that **Bormann** had died in an armoured car explosion. There was only circumstantial evidence for this because the witnesses themselves had been wounded. 'I suppose', said the officer, 'though it is not final, that **Bormann** was killed'.

31 December, 1945 (TASS)

Ф. К-1 ос; оп. 4; д. 17; л. 26-27 об.
(машинописный экз.)
(retyped)

CONCERNING THE REPORT OF THE BRITISH
INTELLIGENCE SERVICE ABOUT HITLER'S LAST DAYS

The British Intelligence Service, after thorough examination of the materials, yesterday published a report about the events in the bomb-shelter of the Reichstag in the last days of the battle for Berlin. The report said that **Hitler** died at 3.00 p.m. on 30 April and not on the 29th as had previously been supposed. The report continued that on the night of 29 April, **Hitler** came to the conclusion that he couldn't expect help from anywhere and that the end was very near. He sent **Göring's** successor, Ritter **von Greim**, appointed Commander-in-Chief of the Air Force, together with the pilot Hanna **Reitsch**, with a letter to Admiral **Dönitz**. On 29 April, presumably, between 2.00 and 3.00 o'clock, **Hitler** married Eva **Braun**. The marriage ceremony was performed by an official of the Berlin citizens' register office, Walter **Wagner**. On the same day, at 4.00 a.m., **Hitler** dictated his private and political wills. Later, three couriers were sent out with copies of these documents to Admiral **Dönitz** and General **Schörner** in Prague, and the third courier had orders to conceal his copy in a secret place.

One of the couriers, Heinz **Lorenz**, of the Ministry of Propaganda, was arrested by the British authorities three weeks ago near Hanover. The documents were sewn into the lining of his coat. Another courier, Major Willi **Maier***, was arrested on 20 December in Iserlohn (in the Ruhr). He still refuses to reveal the location of the copy given to him. The third courier, Wilhelm **Zander**, an SS officer and formerly **Bormann's** secretary, was arrested last week at the Bavarian-Austrian border, where he was living under the name of **Paustin**. He testified that the copy was in a school in Tegernsee. The copy taken from him was published three days ago.

1 January, 1946 (TASS)

Ф. К-1 ос; оп. 4; д. 17; л. 24
(машинописный экз.)
(retyped)

---

* Sic.

RUMOURS CONCERNING THE EXISTENCE
OF HITLER'S SON

Reuters' special correspondent Kerr reports that along with **Hitler's** last will, the photograph of a 12-year-old boy was discovered, that made the American authorities suppose that perhaps the ex-Führer had a son. One can see a great resemblance between **Hitler's** features and the face of the boy in the photograph.

US security officers are checking all the materials connected with **Hitler's** private life in the hope of finding some hints about this mysterious boy.

One US 3rd Army officer stated: 'The resemblance between the boy and **Hitler** is striking. He has sharp features and black hair. The boy has the same angry expression that was characteristic of **Hitler** when in a pensive mood. There is also some resemblance to Eva **Braun** but it is not that evident'.

There are no signs or notes indicating where and by whom it was taken. The boy does not resemble the two little girls with Eva **Braun** in the photograph found earlier.

It is supposed that **Bormann's** aide-de-camp Friedrich Wilhelm **Paustin**, tried to deliver **Hitler's** last will and the boy's photograph to Eva **Braun's** family.

* * *

Reuters' own reporter in Nuremberg, Kerr, says that according to reports received there the Czechoslovak police have arrested a 12-year-old boy in Bohemia who is possibly **Hitler's** son.

The description of the arrested boy coincides with the photograph found by American intelligence officers at the end of the week, along with **Hitler's** marriage certificate and his last will.

False documents were found with the boy in which he was named as Friedrich **Schultz**. In Bohemia, 'Friedrich Schultz' is as common a name as 'John Smith' in Britain.

The arrested boy arrived in Bohemia from Berlin two months ago.

He is reported to strikingly resemble **Hitler**.

1 January, 1946 (TASS)

Ф. К-1 ос; оп. 4; д. 17; л. 25 об.-26
(машинописный экз.)
(retyped)

REUTERS' CONCERNING HITLER'S 'SON'

Reuters: Due to reports that the boy whose photograph was found along with **Hitler's** last will is now presumed to be **Bormann's** son and that **Hitler's** charred corpse was discovered and 'undoubtedly identified' by the Soviet authorities, both dead German leaders, **Hitler** and his deputy Martin **Bormann**, were back in the limelight once again.

Hitler's photographer Heinrich **Hoffmann**, when interrogated by Allied intelligence officers, said he believed that the 12-year-old boy in the photograph found along with **Hitler's** documents was **Bormann's** son.

Kerr, Reuters' special correspondent, reports from Nuremberg: 'Hoffmann said he is certain that Eva **Braun**, whom **Hitler** married on 29 April, 1945, had no children, but he added that **Bormann** had a son whose description coincides with that of the boy pictured in the photograph'.

It is also reported that a 12-year-old boy resembling the one in the photograph was arrested in Bohemia by Czechoslovak police, being in possession of false identity documents in the name of Friedrich Schultz.

The Paris *France-Soir* special correspondent reports in a telegram from Berlin that on 19 December, 1945 the Russians discovered **Hitler's** charred corpse in a hideout near the Reichstag.

The telegram says that on receiving information from a German woman, the Allied intelligence officers went to this hideout on 18 December, but failed to gain entry.

They informed the Allied Command about it, which next day sent a representative there. He was greeted by a Russian officer who stated that **Hitler's** body had already been exhumed by the Russian authorities.

The next day, the Russian Supreme Command informed the Allied Command that **Hitler's** corpse had been discovered in a hideout and definitely identified by **Hitler's** dentist, who had been detained by the Russians.

The Soviet Command asked that this be kept a secret to aid the search for the persons who had hidden **Hitler's** corpse.

According to this report, 'important arrests will soon be announced'.

This report was not confirmed.

2 January, 1946 (TASS)

Ф. К-1 ос; оп. 4; д. 17; л. 29-29 об.
(машинописный экз.)
(retyped)

DAILY EXPRESS REPORT OF THE FORGERY OF EVA BRAUN'S 'MARRIAGE CERTIFICATE'

Reuters', the *Daily Express* reporter in Germany, Selkirk Panton, is investigating a suggestion that Eva **Braun**'s marriage certificate was falsified to mislead Allied Intelligence.

He writes: 'The supposition that the marriage certificates created under fire in the Reichstag bunker are forgeries, because of the mistakes in German made in them, is mainly based on facsimiles of the document reproduced in the British press. I have examined these facsimiles and they substantially differ from the original.

'There are three mistakes common to all the facsimiles of this marriage certificate published in the British press. These mistakes could be explained by the haste of the person who wrote them, either due to his inability to use a typewriter or because the person who made three copies of the marriage certificate made mistakes or by garbling due to transatlantic transmission. The authentic photograph of the marriage certificate was transmitted by radio to London via America.

Other mistakes, especially in the signatures, must be proven before these documents can be presumed doubtful'.

2 January, 1946 (TASS)

Ф. К-1 ос; оп. 4; д. 17; л. 29-29 об.
(машинописный экз.)
(retyped)

FRANCE SOIR ON HITLER'S DEATH

The Agence France Press news agency repeats the report published in the newspaper *France Soir* that 'Hitler's corpse was allegedly discovered on 19 December by the Russian Command, but this fact has been kept secret so as not to interfere with the arrest of the Nazis who participated in the burial'.

The reports by the British and American Supreme Commands concerning the documents drawn up before Hitler's suicide, should be seen as an introduction to an official announcement of the evidence of the former Führer's death.

It is said that reports soon will be published about numerous arrests as a result of operations that have been undertaken in Germany, Italy and even in some of the liberated countries.

'Obviously, we cannot check this report immediately', the newspaper writes, 'which we are publishing as a document. We have received this report from a trustworthy correspondent, who in turn got it from a reliable source'.

2 January, 1946 (TASS)

Ф. К-1 ос; оп. 4; д. 17; л. 28
(машинописный экз.)
(retyped)

CONCERNING THE REPORT OF THE RITSAUS AGENCY ON HITLER'S ATTEMPT TO FLEE BY SUBMARINE

Copenhagen, 26 November. The Ritsaus Agency has reported the following sensational news.

Near Roskilde, a young Dane found a sealed bottle with a German label, that had a German sailor's letter inside saying that **Hitler** was taken on 10 November from Finland in a submarine bound for Fascist Spain. On the way, the submarine hit a ship and went down. **Hitler**, obviously, failed to survive. The letter is written in German Gothic letters. It has been forwarded to the police.

* * *

Copenhagen. On 27 November, details were published of the discovered letter, which presents a version of **Hitler**'s death. The sealed bottle was discovered by inhabitants of the small settlement of Solred, near the bay of Kege to the south of Copenhagen. The bottle itself had been made to order for one of the Holstein breweries. The letter is written on a German official military form, dated 9 November, 1945 and headed 'the *Nautilus* submarine'.

The letter says: 'These are the last words of one of the survivors of the *Nautilus* submarine in which the Führer of the German people, Adolf **Hitler**, was in hiding. The submarine was on its way from Finland to Franco's Spain when it collided with a ship near Gedser and went down. We could have survived approximately 15 and a half hours more under water and during that time I wrote this report, taking it with me in a sealed bottle when I and others [illegible] were saved. The Führer was, at the moment of the catastrophe in [illegible word, ending with '-kammer' room], which was sealed and because of this was separated from us, the others. Our shared opinion is that the submarine sank before the Führer could [illegible]. I publish this to discount the rumours that the Führer was burned in the Reichstag. His last great secret which was entrusted to us is safe here and we shall be able to save it. We understand our great mission: to return Germany to its former might and power. In the near future, the Army will co-operate with the Navy and the swastika will fly from the windows of the buildings. Germany will be free again [illegible words] together with the Allies and other predatory states. With a triple "Heil" for our beloved Führer I leave this ship. Soon we shall be free again'.

The letter is signed: Hans **Rutenburger**.

26–27 November,1946 (TASS)

Ф. К-1 ос; оп. 4; д. 17; л. 30-31
(машинописный экз.)
(retyped)

THE LAST DAYS OF HITLER

A SUMMARY OF THE BOOK BY BRITISH HISTORIAN HUGH TREVOR-ROPER

LIFE MAGAZINE, 17 March, 1947

'Rumours spreading through the world and the mystery surrounding the circumstances of **Hitler**'s death have paved the way for the growth of a dangerous myth about **Hitler**.

'Before this legend could pass for truth and possibly lead to the rebirth of German nationalism, the British government entrusted a young Oxford historian, H. R. Trevor-Roper, with the task of establishing the facts of the matter. Here we give a summary of H. R. Trevor-Roper's book, *The Last Days of Hitler* (published by Macmillan), which is to appear in early April.

For two years, Trevor-Roper collected and analysed statements from **Hitler**'s generals and from private soldiers, ministers and servants. He came to the conclusion that **Hitler** really did die and that in the last days of his life he was nothing like a new Siegfried, who could lead his nation even from the grave, but in fact he was a frightened, neurotic old man who was addicted to narcotics'.

In the spring of 1945, Adolf **Hitler** was preparing for the last decisive and desperate battle. The Western Allies had crossed the Rhine and the Russians were only 60 miles from Berlin. In his underground bunker under the Reichstag, **Hitler** directed the last operations.

The man in the bunker was not the **Hitler** of the pre-war period. At that time, he had found relaxation from the unbearable pressures of political life by visiting Obersalzsburg on weekends, watching motion pictures and dreaming. But in 1939, he became a great military leader and he had to alter the company he kept and his pastimes. His working routine became monotonous and rapidly changing events did not permit painless relaxation of his inner dynamism.

Notwithstanding the fact that the unsuccessful attempt on **Hitler**'s life in July, 1944 did not seriously affect his health, it nevertheless increased his paranoia and brought his fear of betrayal to a peak. He became a hermit, isolated from people and events. **Hitler** was sure that he was the only one who could save the German people from defeat and lead them to victory, and that therefore his own life had a crucial significance for the fate of Germany. **Hitler** was also sure that attempts on his life were waiting for him around every corner. As a result, it was quite logical that he rarely left his underground headquarters and the commonplace company of his charlatan-doctor, secretaries and a few close generals who still believed in his intuition. Only occasionally did he go to the front and he did not let himself go into details as to the real state of his defeated armies, his cities and industries. More and more, he dreamed of an elegant retirement in Linz. At the time when Germany was going to pieces, he was engaged in drawing architectural plans. His enemies were wrong to say he was planning the rebuilding of Buckingham Palace. No, he used his leisure time to work out the projects for an Opera House and a new Art Gallery for the city of Linz.

It can easily be imagined how such a life influenced **Hitler's** physical condition. '*Before 1940*', says **von Hasselbach**, the most competent of **Hitler's** doctors, '*he looked younger than his age (he was 51 years old). Later, he began to age very quickly. In 1940–3, Hitler's looks corresponded to his age. After 1943, he already looked much older than his age.*' In the last days of April, 1945, **Hitler** was ruined physically. **Hitler's** health was collapsing for two reasons – his way of life and his doctors' treatment. Whatever **Hitler's** physiological condition, his resilience could be considered to be exceptionally high. It is known that before the war he only once suffered serious illness, in his vocal chords. In 1935, **Hitler** was very concerned with the state of his health and called in a specialist, Professor **von Eicken**. **Von Eicken** diagnosed a tumour of the vocal chords which was removed.

After this operation, **Hitler's** voice returned and despite suffering from tinnitus as a result of overwork as well as a tendency to colic, he was in good health until 1943. **Hitler** himself believed that he had a weak heart and after 1938 he abandoned any physical exercise.

His doctors examined him for heart disease and came to the conclusion that the symptoms described by **Hitler**, as well as the pain in his stomach, were of a hysterical nature.

The most extraordinary of all the doctors who treated **Hitler** was 'Professor' Theodor **Morell**. It is hard to speak of him using professional medical terminology. Morell was a charlatan. Those who saw him after he was interned by the Americans describe him as a tall, thin old man with the manners of a sycophant, inarticulate speech and the hygiene habits of a pig.

Morell treated **Hitler** for nine years. The latter esteemed him more highly than all his other doctors and finally completely turned himself over to the deadly experiments of this charlatan. **Morell** was equally indifferent to science and to scientific truth. He prescribed instant remedies and quack potions. He even insisted that a British doctor had stolen the secret of penicillin from him. It should be noted that **Morell** could easily manage without such claims. **Hitler** deeply believed in alternative medicine as well as in magic and astrology. And when the former ship's doctor **Morell**, who made his name as a venerologist among Berlin's aristocratic demi-monde, was introduced to **Hitler** by his private photographer **Hoffmann**, **Morell's** career was secured.

HE STUFFED HITLER WITH MEDICINES

Morell's financial ambitions were considerable. He built factories and produced patent medicines. His position as 'court physician' assured official recognition of these products. Sometimes he managed to ensure compulsory distribution of his products all over Germany, or he secured the exclusive right to produce certain medicines. His 'vitamin chocolate' was especially profitable. On Hitler's order, 'the Russian powder' against lice, invented by Morell, was compulsory for use in the armed forces. The pharmaceutical faculty of Leipzig University found that 'Ultraseptil', a sulphonamide produced by Morell's company in Budapest, caused nerve damage. The faculty's findings were reported to Hitler, but in vain. Thus, Morell's product received political sanction which helped him to expand his ouput.

These medicines were not distributed so profitably by Morell without being experimentally tested. They were tested on Hitler. In the list of medicines used by Morell to treat Hitler, along with morphine and sleeping remedies, there were 28 different medications, fake balsams and 'aphrodisiacs' stimulating the organs of internal secretion. Morell's methodology was described by a very competent doctor named Brandt:

'Morell more and more frequently came to use treatment by injection and finally used this method of treatment exclusively. Thus, for example, even for a minor cold he used overdoses of sulphonamide. Later, he began using injections of dextrose, hormones, vitamins and so on, as a result of which the patient immediately felt better, which impressed a personality such as Hitler's. When he felt he had a cold, he was given from three to six injections a day.

If Hitler was supposed to deliver a speech in cold or rainy weather, he was given an injection the day before, on the day of the speech and the day after it. Thus, the normal resistance of the body was gradually replaced by an artificial medium. During the last two years of his life, injections were given to Hitler every day. Once I asked Morell what medicines he used but he refused to answer'.

To treat the stomach colic from which Hitler suffered, Morell prescribed a patent remedy called 'Dr Kester's Anti-flatulence pills'. Dr Kester's pills included strychnine and belladonna and the maximum dose was eight pills a day. Hitler took from two to four pills before every meal. Such was the combined pressure of his way of life and medical treatment. Only Hitler's strong constitution had prevented his health from collapsing earlier.

In 1943, the first symptoms of physical ageing became obvious. Hitler developed tremors in his extremities, especially in his left hand and leg; he dragged his left foot; he became round-shouldered.

The causes of such a physical condition were never reasonably explained. Some doctors were of the opinion that this condition was of a hysterical nature, but nobody could provide a firm diagnosis.

By the autumn of 1944, the latent symptoms of the deterioration in **Hitler's** health were evident and a number of specialists were engaged in his treatment. Notwithstanding all these efforts, **Hitler's** health grew worse and worse. All the witnesses of his last days unanimously note **Hitler's** exhausted face, his grey hair, rounded shoulders, trembling hands and legs, hoarse voice and lacklustre eyes.

Such was the state of the man in the bunker on the eve of the fall of Berlin. Among the sycophants, who still were with him 50 feet underground in the 18 cramped uncomfortable rooms of the bunker, there were only two creatures in whom he still believed – his dog Blondi and Eva **Braun**.

EVA ARRIVES FOR MARRIAGE AND DEATH

Eva **Braun** will be a disappointment to all connoisseurs of history because she did not possess any of the colourful characteristics of a typical tyrant's lover. It is also true that **Hitler** himself was not a typical tyrant. The underlying motive for his passion was not a wild desire to satisfy his sexual needs but a typical petty-bourgeois longing for home comforts. Eva **Braun** completely satisfied this constant, though secret, peculiarity of **Hitler's** nature and so as a personality she is of no interest.

Pretty rather than beautiful, with a youthful face and rather high cheekbones, placid, uninterested in political matters and eager to please, Eva **Braun** soon managed to assume influence over **Hitler**, corresponding to his idea of relaxation from his stormy political life. Eva presided at the tea-table, turning **Hitler's** attention away from politics.

Nothing is known of the more intimate side of their life. '*They slept separately,*' stated the already-mentioned Dr **Morell**. '*But still, I suppose . . .* '. But you cannot draw any conclusions based solely on Dr **Morell's** assumptions. In the relationship between Eva and **Hitler**, the latter was attracted by their idealistic nature. '*The long years of true friendship,*' as he wrote in his last will and testament.

Thus, when on 15 April, 1945 Eva **Braun** arrived in Berlin to share **Hitler's** fate, she was neither his wife nor his acknowledged lover. She came to the Reich Chancellery unbidden and thus she had no more right to symbolically die alongside **Hitler** then Fraulein **Manzialy**, who cooked vegetarian dishes for **Hitler** and who dined with him in the absence of Eva **Braun**. **Hitler** ordered Eva **Braun** to leave Berlin but she refused. She arrived for her marriage and her death.

However, **Hitler** did not take the decision to die yet. It seems impossible that in the last days of the Third Reich its Führer could still believe that either his star or the hand of Providence might save him. Nevertheless, witnesses unanimously claim that he was never able to understand the inevitability of his failure.

Hitler with his favourite German Shepherd dog, Blondi.

In the depths of the bunker, **Hitler** sought for support in horoscopes and in *A History of Frederick the Great* by Thomas Carlyle. One night, when **Goebbels** was reading this book aloud to him, they came to the passage describing how Frederick foresaw his inevitable defeat and decided to poison himself in case his misfortunes continued. This is how Carlyle addresses Frederick with the following words:

'Brave king! Wait a little and the days of your trouble will pass. The sun of your happiness is already hidden behind the clouds and very soon it will shine on you'.

After that, when **Goebbels** read how, at the last moment, Frederick was saved from suicide by the news of the death of his enemy, the Russian Empress Elisabeth, **Hitler** shed a few tears. Then **Hitler** and **Goebbels** discussed the circumstances of this miraculous salvation of Frederick and they sent for two horoscopes, which were carefully preserved in one of **Himmler's** 'scientific' departments, the horoscopes of **Hitler** and the Third Reich. These sacred documents were delivered and **Hitler** and **Goebbels** studied them together with hope.

They established that both horoscopes foretold the beginning of a war in 1939, German victories until 1941 and then a series of defeats culminating in the first half of April, 1945. Later, a stunning victory by the Germans in the second half of April would be followed by stability until August and by peace the same month. After the conclusion of peace, Germany would face hard times for three years, then starting from 1948, Germany would again triumph and become a great power.

'I SHALL NEVER LEAVE BERLIN'

The horoscopes, which were so accurate about the past, turned out to be unlikely for the future. Nevertheless, the story told by one of **Goebbels'** secretaries shows how seriously **Hitler** and **Goebbels** took such predictions.

'I remember Friday, 13 April very well', testifies this secretary. *'Every week Goebbels went to the Eastern front, where he addressed the troops and gave out cigarettes, cognac and books as presents. On that day, he returned late at night as usual. Berlin was under heavy bombing and the Adlon Hotel was engulfed in flames. We met Goebbels by the steps of the Ministry of Propaganda. One of the journalists told him: "Herr Reichsminister, Roosevelt is dead." Goebbels practically jumped out of the car and for a moment stood as if transfixed. I will never forget his face, lit up by the flames. "Well," he said to me, "bring the best champagne and we'll talk to the Führer on the telephone." We went to the office where champagne was served. Goebbels was put through to Hitler on a direct line and said: "My Führer, I congratulate you! Roosevelt is dead. It is written in the stars that the second part of April will be the turning point. Today is 13 April, Friday. The turning point has come."'*

These emotions soon evaporated. As before, the evacuation from Berlin of the Ministries continued, but **Hitler** stayed in the bunker and decided to make another attempt to repulse the Russians from the capital. On 21 April, **Hitler** ordered all the Berlin troops to start counter-attacking under the command of SS General **Steiner**. *'Any commander, who does not carry out the order,'* **Hitler** shouted, *'will pay with his life'*. That was **Hitler's** order but his orders already had no connection with reality. He moved imaginary battalions, formulated academic plans. **Steiner's** attack was the last, symbolic act of **Hitler's** strategy – it never took place.

These facts came to light during the meeting of the council of war on 22 April, which was opened by the usual reports from Generals **Krebs** and **Jodl**. Later, news came of the failure of **Steiner's** attack. Despite the plans and intimidation, the Air Force was never engaged in combat. At the same time, more unpleasant reports were received. When the troops were withdrawn to support **Steiner** in the south, the Russians penetrated the suburbs from the north and their vanguard tanks were already in Berlin.

This provoked the storm that was characteristic of **Hitler's** last days. **Hitler** fell into a rage. He screamed that he had been abandoned, he attacked the Army, cursed the traitors, talked of all-embracing treachery, corruption and deception, and finally broke down and said that it was the end. Finally, and for the first time, he lost faith in his historical mission. It was the end: the Third Reich had collapsed and the only thing left for its creator was to die. He refused to leave for south Germany. Anyone who wanted to, could leave. *'But as for me,'* **Hitler** said, *'I shall never leave Berlin, never'*.

On the night of 26 April, Air Force General Ritter **von Greim** flew to Berlin. He was accompanied by a heroine, the well-known test-pilot Hanna **Reitsch**. Impetuous, quick-tempered and, at the same time, a boastful woman, she, better than anyone, matched the atmosphere of this last underground lunatic asylum in Berlin. **Reitsch** was an ardent Nazi and a veteran admirer of **Hitler**.

The evidence of Hanna **Reitsch** about life in **Hitler's** bunker, despite a number of regrettable historical errors, should still be considered as a document of outstanding significance. According to her, she and **von Greim** managed to reach the suburban airfield of Gatow with a only a few holes shot in the wings of their plane, although several escort fighters were shot down.

Finding a training aircraft at the airfield, **von Greim** decided to fly to the centre of the city and land in a street near the Reich Chancellery. During take-off, the remaining fighters diverted the attention of the Russians away from them. They flew towards the Brandenburg Gate at treetop height.

'NOTHING HAS PASSED ME BY!'

Below them, fierce street fighting was going on; above them, the air was filled with Russian aircraft. Several moments later, the explosion of a heavy Russian shell tore out the belly of their plane and injured **von Greim** in the right leg. **Reitsch** reached over his shoulder, managed to get hold of the controls, and by dodging and keeping the plane close to the ground she managed to land it perfectly in the street. A passing car was stopped and **von Greim** was carried to the Reich Chancellery. On the way, he was given first aid and upon arrival at the bunker, he was taken to the operating-room where he was immediately visited by **Hitler**. His face, **Reitsch** says, expressed his gratitude for **von Greim**'s arrival. *'Even a soldier,'* **Hitler** said, *'has the right not to obey an order which seems to him useless and hopeless'.* He asked **von Greim** if he knew why he had been summoned. The latter answered in the negative.

'Because Hermann Göring betrayed me and the Fatherland,' **Hitler** explained. *'Behind my back he established relations with the enemy. It is cowardice! He sent me a disrespectful telegram in which he said that I had once called him my successor and that now, when I was no longer in a position to rule from Berlin, he was ready to succeed me in Berchtesgaden. The telegram ended with the words that if he did not get an answer, he would assume that I agreed!'*

During this conversation, **Hitler** had tears in his eyes. He hung his head, his face was deathly pale, and when he gave **Göring**'s fatal telegram to **von Greim** to read, the paper shook in his hand. While von **Greim** was reading the telegram, **Hitler** watched him, breathing heavily and convulsively. His cheek twitched. Suddenly he shouted:

'Ultimatum! A harsh ultimatum! There is nothing left! Nothing has passed me by! They know neither loyalty nor honour. There is no insult, no treachery left which I haven't experienced. And now this! This is the end! No blow has missed me!'

After some time, **Hitler** came to his senses and told **von Greim** that he had been summoned in order to be appointed Commander-in-Chief of the Air Force with the rank of Field Marshal to replace **Göring**. For this formality, the lives of German pilots had been sacrificed. A telegram would be quite enough, but **Hitler** preferred this dramatic though costly measure, as a result of which **von Greim** was bedridden for three days for nothing.

That night, **Hitler** summoned Hanna **Reitsch** to his room. He told her that it was all over and that he and Eva **Braun** had already prepared everything for their suicide and the subsequent burning of their corpses, giving Hanna **Reitsch** ampoules of poison for her and **von Greim** to use in case of capture.

That night, Russian shells were bursting in the grounds of the Reich Chancellery and the inhabitants of the bunker sat around in different tragi-comic poses, listening to the rumbling and cracking of the solid ceilings. Hanna **Reitsch** spent almost all night sitting at **von Greim**'s bedside, preparing for a joint suicide in case the Russians burst into the room in the morning. They agreed to swallow the poison given by **Hitler** and then immediately pull the pins on hand grenades pressed to their bodies.

'I AM AWAITING HELP FOR BERLIN'

On the night of 27 April, the Russian shelling of the Reich Chancellery reached its climax. For those sheltering in the bunker, the accuracy of the shells seemed deadly. At any moment, they were expecting to see Russian infantry marching into the grounds of the Reich Chancellery. According to Hanna **Reitsch**, on this night **Hitler** summoned his close assistants and this meeting of the doomed discussed in detail their plans for suicide and the disposal of the bodies. They agreed that the approach of the first Russian soldiers would be the signal for mass suicide. After that, each of them delivered a short speech of eternal loyalty to the Führer and Germany. Such was the atmosphere in the bunker.

But in fact all this was, of course, a sham. Very few of those who expressed their willingness to die fulfilled their heroic intention. It is interesting to note that quite a number of them are now in perfect health, assuring the Anglo-American authorities that in fact they never had any contacts with the Nazis.

As for **Hitler**, his intentions were sincere. He decided to die if Berlin fell. And at the same time – such was his unusual confidence, little by little changing into despair – that even now he still believed that the capital could be saved. He obviously considered himself as a kind of talisman whose presence made the city invulnerable.

'*If I leave East Prussia,*' he once said to Field-Marshal **Keitel**, '*then East Prussia will fall. If I stay it will be retained*'.

Keitel convinced him to leave East Prussia and consequently it fell. But **Hitler** decided not to leave Berlin and for this reason Berlin couldn't fall. He was racing hither and thither in the bunker, waving the map that was almost disintegrating in his sweaty hands as he explained complicated military operations which would save everyone to each and every passing visitor. Sometimes he shouted orders as if giving commands to the defenders of Berlin; at other times he spread a map on the table and bending over it he moved the counters representing the armies with trembling hands.

But even the most stubborn illusions were swept away by the facts. On 28 April, the Russians were already fighting in the centre of Berlin nearby. Hysterical telegrams were pouring out from the bunker. '*I am awaiting help for Berlin,*' **Hitler** telegraphed **Keitel**. Instead of help, the news came that **Himmler** was holding talks with the Allies. The scene which followed this news was terrible. '*He raved like one possessed,*' Hanna **Reitsch** testified. '*He turned so purple with rage that his face became unrecognisable*'. It was the last and the hardest blow: the faithful Heinrich had betrayed him.

ADOLF AND EVA ARE MARRIED

There is no doubt that **Himmler's** betrayal was the signal for the end. Early on the morning of 29 April, having said goodbye to Field-Marshal **von Greim** and Hanna **Reitsch**, both of whom managed to escape by plane, **Hitler** performed one of his last acts before death. He married Eva **Braun**. To perform this symbolic ceremony, **Goebbels** brought in a certain Walter **Wagner** to the bunker. Holding an honorary position in the Berlin municipal authority, he was to solemnise **Hitler's** marriage. **Wagner** arrived at the bunker, where nobody knew him except **Goebbels**, wearing an Nazi party uniform with a Volkssturm armband. The ceremony was held in a small conference room, next door to the Führer's private apartments.

Apart from **Hitler**, Eva **Braun** and Walter **Wagner**, **Goebbels** and Martin **Bormann** were present as witnesses. The formalities were very short. The bride and the groom announced that they were of pure Aryan descent and had no hereditary diseases. Due to martial law and other extraordinary circumstances, they concluded a wartime marriage without delay. In several minutes, the marriage certificate was signed and the ceremony was over. When the bride began to sign, she started to write the name 'Braun', but then crossed out the letter 'B' and signed 'Eva **Hitler**, *née* **Braun**'. After that the couple retreated to their room to have a wedding breakfast.

Soon **Bormann**, **Goebbels**, his wife and two of **Hitler's** secretaries – **Christian** and **Junge** – were invited to the Führer's room. There, they spent several hours drinking champagne and talking about the good old times and old friends, and about **Goebbels'** wedding, at which **Hitler** had been a witness. Then **Hitler** spoke of his suicide plans, and for some time everyone was absorbed in gloomy reflection. After that **Hitler**, dictated his last will to his secretary **Junge** in an adjacent room. From time to time, the others were called to this room by **Hitler**.

In the evening, **Hitler** ordered that his dog Blondi be killed. **Hitler's** former doctor, Professor **Haase**, killed her with poison. The other two dogs were shot by the SS officer who looked after them.

On the same evening, while the staff officers were having their supper in the passage used as a dining-room, one of the guards came and said that the Führer wanted to say goodbye to the ladies and asked everybody not to go to bed until ordered. About 2.30 in the morning, all the inhabitants of the bunker were summoned by telephone and they gathered in the same passage. There were as many as 20 officers and women. When all of them had assembled, **Hitler**, accompanied by **Bormann**, came out of his room. With a vacant look in his eyes, he silently went along the passage and shook hands with each of the women. Some spoke to him but he either did not answer or murmured something inaudible. After that, a ceremony of silent farewell became commonplace in the bunker.

Hitler's suicide was to follow. But something unexpected happened. It seems that the spirit of the bunker's inhabitants was freed from a heavy, pressing storm-cloud. Soon the terrible tyrant who had turned their lives into unbearable, melodramatic torment would be dead. Dancing started in the dining-room of the Reich Chancellery in which the soldiers and orderlies had their meals. The news reached the bunker but no-one there dared to interfere with their revelry. The dancing went on even when the order came from the Führer's bunker not to be so noisy.

The next day after breakfast Hitler, accompanied by Eva Braun, emerged from his apartment, and the second farewell ceremony took place. Bormann, Goebbels and the 12 officers and servants closest to Hitler were present. Again in silence, Hitler and Eva Braun shook hands with each of them and returned to their rooms. All the others, except Hitler's closest staff, went away. There was a shot. After some moments those entering the room saw Hitler lying on the sofa covered with blood. He had shot himself in the mouth. Eva Braun, also dead, was lying by his side. The gun had been dropped nearby. Eva Braun did not use it – she took poison. It was 3.30 in the morning.

THE BODIES WERE BURNT

Soon after that, two SS officers, one of them Hitler's servant Linge, entered the room. They wrapped Hitler's body in a bedsheet to cover his bloody head, and took it into the passage. Then two other SS officers carried the corpse upstairs and out through the emergency exit into the garden. After that, Bormann entered Hitler's room and carried Eva Braun's body upstairs.

In the garden, both corpses were laid side by side a few steps away from the bunker and petrol was poured over them. At that moment, the Russian bombardment intensified, and they had to take cover in the bunker for several minutes. When the shelling eased a little, Hitler's aide-de-camp, Günsche, set fire to a cloth soaked in petrol and threw it over the corpses. The bodies were immediately engulfed in flames. The SS officers saluted and returned to the bunker. Later, Günsche said that burning Hitler's corpse was the most horrible moment of his life.

The other witness at the scene was one of the guards, Hermann Karnau. At the time, being off duty, he went to the Reich Chancellery dining-room on his commander's orders. Some time later, he decided to return to the bunker, contrary to orders. Reaching the bunker, Karnau found the door closed and decided to go through the garden to reach the emergency exit. Turning the corner near the flak-tower, he suddenly saw two bodies engulfed in flames at the entrance to the bunker. Karnau watched the scene for a moment. He at once recognised the burning bodies as those of Hitler and Braun, in spite of the fact that Hitler's head was smashed. It was a 'sickening sight', as he testified later. After that, **Karnau** went down to the bunker through the emergency exit. There, he met the commander of the guard SS Sturmbannführer Franz **Schedle**. *'The Führer is dead,'* **Schedle** said, *'and his body is being burned in the garden'*.

Another guard, **Mansfeld**, was on duty in the flak-tower and also witnessed the burning of the bodies. He saw how SS officers came out of the bunker several times and poured more petrol over the corpses to feed the fire. Some time later, **Karnau** took over from **Mansfeld** and both of them approached the corpses. By that time, the corpses' extremities were burnt almost totally, so that one could see the bones of **Hitler's** legs. When, an hour later, **Mansfeld** went to the corpses again, they were still burning, but the fire had died down considerably.

Late at night, the commander of the police guard, Brigadeführer **Rattenhuber**, entered the bunker and ordered three reliable SS officers to be chosen to bury the bodies.

At close to midnight, **Mansfeld** returned to his post in the watchtower. The Russian bombardment was continuing, and the night sky was lit up with fires. **Mansfeld** noticed that a shell-hole near the emergency exit had been freshly filled in and that the corpses had disappeared. He had no doubt that the shell-hole had been turned into a grave for **Hitler** and **Braun**, because no shell could make a neat, square hole.

That is all that is known of the fate of **Hitler** and Eva **Braun's** remains. **Hitler's** servant, **Linge**, later told one of the secretaries that **Hitler's** order to 'burn the corpses to ashes' was carried out, but there were doubts that complete burning was possible. It is known that 180 litres of petrol were used to burn the bodies; burning, on the sandy soil, could certainly destroy the bodies, but the bones would withstand the fire.

It should be stressed that the bones were not discovered. Possibly, they were mixed up with those of soldiers killed during the defence of the Reich Chancellery which were also buried in the garden. The Russians made exploratory excavations in the garden, discovering up to 160 bodies. There is also some evidence that **Günsche** testified that the ashes of **Hitler** and his wife were collected and removed from the Reich Chancellery. It is possible that the investigation was not carried out carefully enough. People who could leave **Hitler's** office diary lying on a chair in the bunker for five months could easily have missed other, no less important evidence.

Either by this means or some other, **Hitler** managed to achieve his final aim. Like Alaric the Goth, who sacked Rome in 410 and who was secretly buried by his followers near the River Busento in Italy, this modern destroyer of mankind is forever hidden from people's eyes.

Translated [into Russian]:
Senior Interpreter of the Investigation Section
of the 2nd General Department

Major **Kopeliansky**

18 April, 1950

Ф. К-1 ос; оп. 4; д. 17; л. 41-62
(машинописный текст)
(text typed)

IS HITLER ALIVE?

This was the title of an article by Michael **Musmanno**, published in the Swiss newspaper *Die Nation* in issues 50, 51, 52 of 1948 and issue 1 of 1949. Here is the translation.

EDITORIAL INTRODUCTION

1 May, 1945. The news of **Hitler's** death spread all over the world with lightning speed. In the countries ravaged by war, people couldn't help rejoicing, but soon they began to doubt: what if it is not true?

Rumours circulated that **Hitler** had managed to escape at the last moment; that he is hiding in a cave somewhere in the Alps; that he flew away in a plane and that he was able to reach South America by submarine.

Over three years have passed since **Hitler** vanished from the face of the Earth. There have been numerous theories and rumours as to his fate.

Will the image of this man, who pushed the world into disaster, be surrounded with mystery, will a legend be built around him?

More than three years ago, a U.S. naval officer who witnessed the German forces' capitulation in Italy, understood how important it is to answer the question of whether **Hitler** is still alive. He was startled by the fact that after the news of **Hitler's** death, many German senior officers still hoped that he would reappear.

In search of the facts

The naval officer, Captain Michael **Musmanno**, decided to investigate the circumstances connected with **Hitler's** death so that any legends spread by his fanatical admirers could be refuted with undeniable facts and should **Hitler** really be alive, to bring him to well-deserved punishment.

Circumstances favoured **Musmanno** in the fulfilment of his purpose. In civilian life, he had been a long-serving judge and knew the law and methods of investigation. As a military man he occupied a high rank and later worked as a member of the War Crimes Tribunal in Nuremberg. Thus, he had more opportunity than anyone else to investigate the matter of **Hitler's** death.

Musmanno started his investigation at once. He flew to Berlin to examine the bunker in which **Hitler** spent the last days before his disappearance. He cross-examined those who had been in the bunker who were still alive. He visited prisons, prisoner-of-war camps and displaced persons centres, so he could speak to anyone who had knowledge of the system and the methods of the Nazi leadership.

As an observer for the US Navy, he attended the trial of **Hitler**'s successors, Admiral **Dönitz**, **Göring**, **Ribbentrop** and other prominent Nazis, and eventually he became a Judge at the Nuremberg War Crimes Tribunal. This gave him a new opportunity to collect material about **Hitler**, who was invisibly present at all these sessions as one of the accused. **Musmanno** was on the panel of judges at the trial of Field-Marshal **Milch** and General **Koller** and was presiding judge at the trial of members of the SS extermination units.

20 volumes of documents

During all this time, **Musmanno** never forgot his intention to investigate the circumstances of **Hitler**'s death. He travelled round Germany to see those who were in the Führer's bunker and interrogated more than 200 people from **Hitler**'s immediate circle: generals, ministers, secretaries, dentists, private individuals, aides-de-camp, doctors, servants, housekeepers, barbers and **Hitler**'s driver as well as the soldiers of his guard.

Besides, **Musmanno** had access to all of the case papers, which he studied thoroughly, such as diaries and notes made by **Hitler**'s aides-de-camp and his staff.

After three years' work, **Musmanno** had collected over 20 volumes of documents and witness statements and he completed his research. He returned home to Pittsburgh (USA) and there wrote the first complete and truthful report of the events that took place in the Reich Chancellery bunker in the fatal days before the end of World War II. He answered the question as to whether **Hitler** was still alive on the basis of the facts.

THE FÜHRER'S BIRTHDAY IN THE REICH CHANCELLERY BUNKER

It was 20 April, 1945. World War II in Europe was reaching its climax. The encirclement of the Allied Powers around Berlin was becoming tighter and tighter. Germany was defeated. But **Hitler** refused to see it.

Underground in the Reich Chancellery bunker, he celebrated his 56th birthday. 'Congratulations' from the American and British bombers were sounding like thunderbolts overhead, accompanied by Russian artillery.

All that went on then in the bunker was told to me by the surviving officers of **Hitler**'s headquarters who had participated in the celebration.

At this 'underground' jubilee, **Göring**, **Himmler**, **Dönitz**, **Jodl**, **Keitel** and other high officials of the Nazi hierarchy saw a man who had nothing in common with the one whose bombastic speeches had once provoked wild enthusiasm among the Germans, with that 'Führer' who was shown in magnificent sequences in the weekly newsreels. The growling and furiously gesticulating 'superman' of old had disappeared, and only a poor caricature was left. Deathly pale, hunched over, with shaking head and hands, he could hardly walk. His legs refused to serve him; he had to hold on to the furniture to be able to stand for a few minutes.

His generals understood that the war was lost, but to say it aloud meant not only a death sentence for oneself but possible arrest and an uncertain fate for one's whole family. The soldiers, who were tired of the war, knew that their sacrifices were already senseless, but also knew that at the same time deserters who were caught were hanged immediately. The lamp-posts and the branches of trees were the gallows, displaying the fate of these realists.

Allied armies were approaching from all directions. The Americans had already crossed the Elbe river, the Russians the Oder, and the French the Danube. The British were advancing from the North. In Italy, Anglo-American forces had already crossed the Po. Marshal **Zhukov** had cut off Berlin from the east and was about to close the western arm of his pincer movement.

With shaking fingers, **Hitler** traced an imaginary line on the map and murmured: '*Here in Berlin, the Russians will suffer their most bloody defeat*'. Hearing the congratulations, he hastily gave orders.

SS Obergruppenführer **Steiner**, who was 30km from Berlin on the other side of the northern arm of the Russian pincers, was to attack the enemy at dawn on 22 April to cut this salient off and to prevent the threatened encirclement. Everybody was to support him: pilots and ground staff of the Air Force, the Hermann Göring Division, any available unit, every soldier, every functioning weapon, every tank still able to move.

On 22 April, **Hitler** sat all morning, bent over his table. Generals, adjutants and liaison officers were gathering in the bunker, shouting into telephone receivers and desperately flicking radio switches, trying to find any news.

The truth could not be concealed any longer. Through a veil of anger and despair, **Hitler** started to understand that total defeat, in which he had never wanted to believe, was a fact. It broke him. Almost inaudibly, he whispered that everything was over, that the war was lost and there was nothing left for him to do except shoot himself. He sent for his personal aide-de-camp, SS Obergruppenführer Julius **Schaub**. **Schaub** gathered **Hitler**'s documents that were in the shelter and burnt them. After that, he flew to Munich and Berchtesgaden and did the same thing there.

Hitler stated that he would remain and die in Berlin. Whoever wanted to could go to Berchtesgaden, which was to be the headquarters of his last line of defence, i.e. 'The Alpine Redoubt'.

Two secretaries, Johanna **Wolf** and Krista **Schröder**, and two stenographers, Ludwig

Krieger and Gerhard **Herzegel**, left for Berchtesgaden. All four told me they left the bunker certain that they would never see **Hitler** again. Another two of **Hitler's** secretaries, Frau Gerda **Christian** and Frau Gertrud **Junge**, stayed behind.

The air in the bunker was full of smoke and the smell of gunpowder. Those participating in meetings in the map room often lost consciousness, and **Hitler's** personal physician, Dr **Stumpfegger**, had to provide them with medical aid. His second physician, **Morell**, left for Berchtesgaden with a group of approximately 80 people.

Though at the time **Hitler** had approved the departure of this section of his closest circle, he was angry with some of them as he had assumed that they would stay with him in these last days. He was especially angry that Hermann **Göring**, his deputy, showed such unseemly haste in his attempt to save his own life and to shake the dust off his decorated full-dress uniform coat.

On 22 April, **Hitler** told General **Jodl** and Field-Marshal **Keitel** of his intention to commit suicide. Both tried to persuade him to abandon this idea and asked what would happen if there were a chance to make peace with the Western Powers. **Hitler** answered that **Göring** would be a better mediator than himself.

Göring heard about this from General Karl **Koller**, Commander of the Air Force Staff. On 23 April, **Hitler** received a telegram from **Göring**, saying that if he did not receive an answer to this telegram by 22.00, he would have to consider that **Hitler** had lost his freedom of action and, according to the law of 1941 about the succession, he would immediately assume power.

Göring was going to fly to Eisenhower and start negotiations on capitulation. His telegram struck the bunker like a bombshell. **Göring** was stripped of his rank and was to be immediately arrested and executed. **Hitler** described **Göring's** act as treachery. When I talked to **Göring** in Nuremberg, I asked him, why he, who was considered to be a man of political insight, sent such a provocative telegram. **Göring** answered that having seen **Hitler** for the last time on 20 April in such poor physical condition, it was not illogical to suppose the possibility of paralysis, which would disable him completely or at least cause a lack of interest in the question of a successor.

Hitler's complete breakdown could be attributed not so much to his passionate nature, extreme nervous strain and pressure of events, but to the harmful medicines he was being given. To treat overwork, depression and nervous fits, Dr **Morell**, also having it in mind to improve his circulation, prescribed him 28 different medicines, including strychnine. To make **Hitler** feel better, he administered one or two injections a day, even when he was not ill.

After the attempt on his life on 20 July, 1944, **Hitler** suffered concussion which, together with chronic poisoning by Dr **Morell** and the stressful life in the bunker, resulted in an inevitable physical collapse.

Up to 20 July, 1944, **Hitler** had placed the blame for defeat on his 'incompetent generals', but since that day he had poured out his wrath upon all Germans.

Now, he stated, all the German people would pay for their disloyalty: they would be left by **Hitler** to face their own destiny.

When it became obvious that **Steiner**'s attack had failed, **Hitler** grasped the depth of the catastrophe. The Soviet pincers around Berlin had closed.

THE FINAL PLANS

Hitler had an almost hypnotic influence upon his followers, and when it was clear to him that the war was lost, his generals, in their attempts to save themselves, were still clutching at straws.

Major von **Freytag-Loringhoven**, adjutant of General **Krebs**, the Chief of the General Staff, told me of their last plans, born out of despair. General **Jodl**, Field-Marshal **Keitel** and General **Krebs** decided that General **Wenck**'s 12th Army should be moved to the bank the Elbe so as not to be encircled by the Americans and to break through to Berlin. To free the Berlin 'Vistula' Army Group under General **Stumm von Bordwehr**, he was to begin an offensive from the north, General **Busse**'s 9th Army from the south-west and General **Schörner**'s Army Group 'A' from Czechoslovakia.

But the Russians were already in the suburbs of Berlin, and the American, British and French divisions were inflicting defeats on the German armies everywhere. On 25 April, the American and Soviet forces met on the river Mulde. On 26 April, General **Wenck**, despite heavy losses, fought his way forward but 15km from Potsdam he was forced to fall back to the Elbe. His army was annihilated.

After **Wenck**'s defeat, the gleam of hope aroused by these offensives initiated by an exhausted army finally disappeared. I asked **Loringhoven** what they could have expected had **Wenck** really managed to enter Berlin and reach the Reich Chancellery. Wasn't the war lost anyway? *'Of course it was lost,'* **Loringhoven** said, *'but Hitler's influence on the generals in the bunker was so great that in despair they wracked their brains to find a way to help him in those last hours. They refused to think of anything else'.*

Conversations with the surviving inhabitants of this underground world made me understand that all of them thought highly of **Goebbels**, who stated that he would die with **Hitler** and brought his wife and six children to the shelter. The children were not supposed to outlive **Hitler**. **Goebbels**' wife also wanted to die with the Führer. At first she objected to her husband's plans to commit suicide and to kill the children, but in the end she also fell victim to that 'influence' mentioned by **Loringhoven**, and ceased resisting.

And certainly Eva **Braun** was there. She arrived from Munich in an elegant dress with a large supply of expensive toiletries and declared her resolve to die with her beloved man.

On 26 April, through smoke and flame, an aeroplane landed in Berlin. **Hitler**, learning of **Göring's** 'betrayal', decided to appoint General **von Greim** as his successor. **Von Greim**, who had to land in one of the streets, managed to get into the bunker to accept the already futile command of the Air Force, which did not exist any longer. The woman accompanying him turned out to be the well-known pilot Hanna **Reitsch**.

Thus, there were now two more people in the bunker. But soon their numbers dropped again. SS General **Fegelein**, **Hitler's** brother-in-law (he had married Eva **Braun's** sister Gretl), couldn't stand life in the bunker and notwithstanding his 'family relations' was not inclined to die 'a heroic death' there. He disappeared on 27 April. **Hitler** ordered him to be found. He was discovered in his own flat in Berlin, wearing civilian clothes. In vain, he begged Eva **Braun** to plead for him. **Hitler** called a court-martial consisting of his officers and ordered **Fegelein** to be sentenced to death. He was taken out of the bunker, put up against a wall and shot.

Fegelein's execution was possibly also caused by the suspicion that he was involved in a more serious betrayal than **Göring's**. A report was received that caused another nervous breakdown: Heinrich **Himmler**, known as 'faithful Heinrich', had made peace proposals to the enemy, and furthermore promised to give **Hitler** up to the victors. **Hitler** thought in horror of **Mussolini's** death or of an even more terrible end, i.e. humiliation, which he would probably have to suffer before death. He could already see himself displayed to the public in a crowded square in Russia. He took a handful of small brass ampoules that looked like lipsticks from a drawer and distributed them among his closest friends. They contained the strongest poison – potassium cyanide.

It was presumed that not all of them would commit suicide at once. And furthermore, **Hitler** ordered **von Greim** to postpone his suicide until he had organised an air attack on the Russian forces in Berlin. **Von Greim** argued that there was no Air Force any longer to carry out such an attack and he would rather stay and die with his commander, but **Hitler** insisted. He had one more reason for this. '*A traitor cannot be allowed to become my successor*'. he said to **von Greim**. '*Himmler must be stopped by any means*'.

The only aircraft left was the small two-seater in which **von Greim** had arrived two days previously. By the light of the huge fires, Hanna **Reitsch** took off. Soon both of them were far away from the ruins of Berlin.

In Berlin, the fighting continued, not for the streets but for every small garden, for every house, for every room. The Germans barricaded themselves into the underground railway stations and tunnels, where they also put the wounded, and also used the tunnels to move around the city. But the Russians started to infiltrate this underground labyrinth. Captain **Boldt** told me about this war in the tunnels: 'Hitler ordered the underground locks of the Spree to be opened to flood the city's underground railway tunnels on the south side of the Reich Chancellery. Thousands of the wounded who were in there drowned'.

Hitler was convinced it was important to have poison with him at all times. His stenographer, Ludwig **Krieger**, described to me how **Hitler** compared himself with Frederick the Great, who always had poison to hand.

At the beginning of April, **Goebbels** read to **Hitler** about the period in Frederick the Great's life when, following the death of the Russian Empress, his lucky stars again began to shine for him. **Hitler** had absolutely no chance, but then on 12 April, news suddenly came of Roosevelt's death. For **Hitler** that meant that the miracle had been repeated.

According to General Erhard **Engel**, who witnessed it, **Hitler** lost control. '*You see, you, unbelievers!*', he exclaimed. '*This is again the sign of Providence!*' An unhealthy colour came into his cheeks. '*Roosevelt obviously wanted to outlive me, but died! His death means that in America the isolationists will come to power!*'

But **Hitler's** hopes were not realised and he wanted to know if the dose of cyanide he had was enough. There could be no doubts about that.

At first, he wanted his SS adjutant Otto **Günsche** to shoot him, but later he decided that it would be better to take poison first and then to shoot himself. But how quickly would the poison act and was it fatal?

Hitler settled all doubts himself. He needed a subject for his test. For this experiment he chose his only constant companion, his dog. In the afternoon, the inhabitants of the bomb-shelter heard the dog's painful howl. The experiment was successful.

THE MARRIAGE OF THE DEAD

The women in the bunker asked once again about the horrible 'lipstick'. Did its terrible contents cause pain and if so, how much pain? **Hitler** was ready to answer, going into excruciating detail. He explained that the poison immediately paralysed the respiratory organs and then the heart. Death comes only after several minutes, but pain ceases in several seconds because convulsions begin.

Hitler's secretary, Frau **Junge**, told me: '*I remember Eva Braun asking: "Isn't it painful? I have nothing against dying a heroic death but it mustn't be painful." Everybody laughed, but the laughter was not happy*'.

On 28 April, sensational news spread through the bunker, which excited its inhabitants more than the bombing raids: Adolf **Hitler** and Eva **Braun** were getting married.

Hitler announced his intention officially in the most unusual marriage announcement that there has ever been. It was contained in his last will, which he dictated to Frau **Junge** and which ended with his instructions for their burial: 'My wife and I choose death instead of the dishonour of defeat and capitulation. We wish our corpses to be burnt immediately'.

After that, he dictated his political will, which Frau **Junge** characterised as having no importance. '*He only repeated the things that he always said in his speeches and proclamations*'.

In between the dictation of the first and second wills, **Hitler** married Eva **Braun**. I asked Gerda **Christian**, the other secretary, who had attended the marriage ceremony, if she had congratulated the newlyweds. 'No,' she replied. '*I said nothing, because the day of his marriage was in fact the day of his death. I couldn't tell him: "With all my heart I wish you all the best", because I knew what was going to happen. It was really the marriage of the dead*'.

And yet . . . champagne was served and with the champagne there came some animation. It was not cheerful, but nevertheless the sounds of shelling and explosions were from time to time accompanied by light laughter.

At 2.30a.m. on 29 April, the 20–25 people, the servants, cooks and clerks who attended **Hitler** and his followers in those last days, gathered in the dining-room as if for a major sermon. Erwin **Jakubeck**, who for a long time had served **Hitler** on his private train and followed him to the bunker, told me that **Hitler** was walking with slow, unsteady steps. In a low and trembling voice, to the horror of those present, he said that he had decided to end his life by suicide and wanted to say goodbye to them. He thanked them for their service. His head and hands were shaking and his body was bent like that of an 80-year-old man. He could hardly move from one to the other and extended to everyone a lifeless hand.

After this, **Hitler** signed both his wills and withdrew with his wife.

In the new government, Admiral **Dönitz** was to become the President and **Goebbels** the Reich Chancellor. When the Nuremberg Court passed sentence in its first session, I asked **Dönitz** why he, an officer, had become involved in politics. He told me that he was not a politician, and because he was in Plön at the time he had no idea he had been appointed head of state.

On 29 April, the situation in the bunker became critical. Russian snipers were shooting at the Reich Chancellery from the opposite side of the street, from the roof of the Kaiserhof Hotel and from the Ministry of Propaganda.

Three 'brave men' – **Krebs**, **Burgdorf** and **Bormann** – tried to ease their despair with drink. The first two had no more battle plans to work out, and **Bormann**, the tyrant of the Party, had no Party left to dominate.

They were lying drunk in the reception room and there was no one to say one word of reproach. Even **Hitler** himself stepped carefully over the legs of the sleeping men so as not to disturb them. The concrete roof of the bunker was damaged in several places but the sound of the falling fragments did not wake them.

There was nothing left to do, no reports came in from anywhere, **Hitler** had no decisions to take. Like an old man, he dragged himself from one room to another, exchanged a few words with someone, and played with **Goebbels'** children. Most of all, he was troubled by the thought that somehow he would be taken out of there and handed over to the enemy. Several days previously, he had even dismissed Dr **Morell** who had previously enjoyed his special confidence. When **Morell** wanted to give him an injection as usual, he refused, saying: *'Stop it, Morell. You want to give me morphine and take me out of here when I lose consciousness'*.

He talked about death constantly. Frau **Junge** told him she believed the leader should die fighting alongside his troops, but he answered that the risk was too great: he could be wounded and taken prisoner, and later paraded in disgrace and humiliation. He repeatedly said that his suicide could be excused, for *'there were no chances left'*.

Suddenly everyone noticed a smell of tobacco. For 12 years, no one had dared to smoke a cigarette, cigar or pipe in the presence of **Hitler**, but now it didn't matter. Even Eva **Braun**, who had not smoked before, lit a cigarette, and the Führer did not object. No-one was afraid of the Führer any more. Artur **Axmann** came and stayed for an hour with him but they were not discussing military matters. **Hitler** no longer thought of the soldiers parading past him. He felt abandoned. Those in whom he had believed most of all had abandoned him: **Fegelein, Göring, Himmler, Speer.**

'He understood absolutely clearly that the catastrophe for everyone had come'. **Axmann** told me. *'One thing was evident: Hitler knew it was time for him to depart this life'*.

The same night, **von Loringhoven** and **Boldt** left the bunker as if to join **Wenck's** army. In fact, they wanted to escape from the repressive atmosphere and the inevitable destruction of the bunker.

THE LAST HOUR STRIKES

On 30 April, 1945, **Hitler** sat at the table with his wife, the secretaries and his vegetarian cook, Fraulein **Manzialy**, for the last time. The thoughts of everyone were overshadowed by the invisible guest who was present at the table. The conversation did not go well.

About 3 o'clock in the afternoon, **Hitler** entered the reception room arm-in-arm with his wife. Her face was especially pale, emphasised by her black dress. **Hitler** was dressed as usual in black trousers and a field-grey uniform jacket.

Although no one had said it was the last farewell, the room at once filled with people. On the night of the 28th, **Hitler** had said good-bye to his servants. Now he was parting from his immediate assistants. He was going round, shaking hands with everyone and almost inaudibly murmuring several words that were almost impossible to understand.

Goebbels' wife suddenly threw herself on her knees and begged him to abandon his decision. *'There is no other way out'*, **Hitler** answered. After that, he addressed Goebbels: *'I entrust you with the responsibility to see that our corpses are burned immediately'*. Everyone stood frozen as **Hitler** left arm-in-arm with his wife, dragging his feet. Frau **Junge** suddenly noticed **Goebbels'** children. They were standing on the staircase leading to rest of the bunker that was situated higher up. She rushed to them. For the children, life in the bunker was a most exciting experience. They amused themselves by counting the explosions and tried to guess where a bomb or a shell would fall before it exploded. Later, they told **Hitler** about the results of their monitoring. Could they have come to see 'Uncle Adolf', as they called him?

Suddenly, a loud shot was heard and its sound reverberated around the arch of the ceiling. One of the children shouted: *'That's a direct hit!'* This shot ended **Hitler's** life. The echo had hardly ceased before Artur **Axmann** and **Goebbels** were at the door to **Hitler's** room. They burst into the room but involuntarily recoiled from the horrible sight. **Hitler** and Eva **Braun** were dead. She had taken poison. Hitler had shot himself in the mouth.

Sturmbannführer **Linge** wrapped **Hitler's** blood-soaked head and upper body in a blanket, and with the assistance of Dr **Stumpfegger** carried the body up the stairs to the garden of the Reich Chancellery.

Eva **Braun** also wanted to shoot herself but after she took poison the revolver dropped from her hand. It lay on the floor. It turned out that the poison was quite enough.

The gigantic Otto **Günsche**, whom **Hitler** had entrusted with the task of burning their corpses, carried Eva **Braun** out and laid her near **Hitler**.

Günsche and **Hitler's** driver, Erich **Kempka**, poured the contents of five petrol cans over the bodies and returned to the entrance to the bunker.

Several members of **Hitler's** personal guard stood in the room next to bedroom. At approximately 3 o'clock, **Günsche** lead them out of there. One of the soldiers, Hermann **Karnau**, of the Criminal Police Unit assigned to the Headquarters, left the shelter and reached the entrance to the Reich Chancellery. He handed over the order he had just received to his colleague, Hilco **Poppen**, and returned through the garden to the emergency exit of the bunker. There he froze with fear.

Before him, lay the bodies of **Hitler** and Eva **Braun**. The blanket covering **Hitler's** body had fallen away a little and the bloody face could be seen. At that moment, a burning rag was thrown on to the corpses and they immediately caught fire.

Karnau rushed to his friend **Poppen** and told him that *'The Führer is dead and his body is being burned in the garden'*. Then **Karnau** returned to the garden where the fire was still burning. When the fire died down, **Karnau** touched the corpses with his foot and the ashes fell to pieces.

At about 10.30, Gruppenführer **Rattenhuber** entered the guardroom and called for several reliable men to bury the remains of **Hitler** and Eva **Braun**. In 20 minutes, Hauptscharführer **Kolke** returned and reported that the order had been carried out.

At approximately the same time, **Goebbels** dictated a letter to Gerda **Christian** which was signed by **Krebs, Burgdorf** and himself. The letter announcing Hitler's death was intended for the Russian Supreme Command and contained a request for a cease-fire. General **Krebs**, who had been the German military attaché in Russia before the war, went with a white flag to the Russian frontline and returned the next day, 1 May at 9 a.m. The cease-fire was rejected, the fighting continued.

When **Hitler** died, **Goebbels** began to make preparations for the annihilation of his family, which was to take place the next morning.

To prepare the children for an injection that they were to be given before they were poisoned, Mrs **Goebbels** told them that after Uncle Adolf's death they would return to Schwanenwerder and, because the trip was dangerous, Dr **Stumpfegger** would give them an injection. When they woke up they would be back again in their nice house.

The youngest might possibly believe this tale, but Helga the eldest knew what was going to happen and said so. To avoid problems, she was given the injection first, followed by the others.

On 1 May, at about 7.30 p.m. **Goebbels** called his adjutant, Günther **Schwägermann**, to his room and gave him orders concerning the burning of the corpses. When **Goebbels** shot himself, **Schwägermann** was to shoot him again to be sure that he was really dead before the body was burned.

At about 8.15p.m., **Goebbels** rose from the table, put on his hat, coat and gloves and, taking his wife's arm, went upstairs to the garden. While **Schwägermann** was preparing the petrol he heard a shot. In the garden, he found the lifeless bodies of **Goebbels** and his wife. **Goebbels** had shot himself and his wife took poison.

Schwägermann ordered one of the soldiers to shoot **Goebbels** again because he was unable to do it himself.

Then the corpses were soaked in petrol and set alight. Before they had burned to ashes, **Schwägermann** received an order from the Commandant of the Reich Chancellery, General **Mohnke**, to set fire to the bunker. With the help of several soldiers, he poured petrol over the furniture and threw a burning match into the room.

In a moment, they were engulfed by flames because the fire had caused a strong draught that slammed the steel entrance doors shut. **Schwägermann** rushed to the entrance and with relief found that the mechanical locks had not engaged. They were forced to leave the bunker immediately.

FACTS AS OPPOSED TO SUPPOSITIONS

Hitler is dead. It is known who was with him in the bomb-shelter. Many of them died. Some managed to escape, but were later captured by the Allies. Others were taken prisoner at once. The corpses of **Goebbels**, his wife and six children were found by the Russians who identified them.

Speculation that **Hitler** is alive lacks any foundation. The statement of Artur **Axmann** should be considered the most important evidence, because he heard the shot and saw the corpses of Adolf **Hitler** and Eva **Braun**. **Axmann** was interrogated several times. In six months, I talked with him no less than ten times. There were never any contradictions in his testimony. I am absolutely confident that his statement is true and correct.

Then, we have the statement of **Hitler's** driver Erich **Kempka**, who burned the corpses. Over a period of four months, I interrogated **Kempka** four or five times on different occasions, including cross-examination. **Kempka** said: *'If you had someone sitting next to you for 14 years, you would not make a mistake identifying him'.*

Goebbels' aide-de-camp, Gunter **Schwägermann**, made a written statement about **Hitler's** death. The guard, Hermann **Karnau**, who saw **Hitler's** corpse on the ground in the garden, told me: *'Let me not live in this world if there is someone who can show me Hitler dead or alive'.*

Of those who were close to **Hitler** in the last month of his life, I met all those who are still alive. I talked to them in court-rooms, prisons, internment camps and their homes, and they told me about **Hitler's** last days and his death in such detail that it is absurd to speak of any 'mystery' surrounding **Hitler's** death.

Apart from oral testimony, we have documents and diaries throwing light on this period. The diary of **Linge**, **Hitler's** servant, is a very valuable source for the reconstruction of the events of those days. The same could be said of General **Koller's** diary. No one can claim that there is insufficient material concerning **Hitler's** last days.

Some, including the writer Emil **Ludwig**, think it possible that **Hitler** had a double, and that he was killed and his body burnt.

There is not the slightest evidence that **Hitler** ever had a double. Such an idea requires the double to have met the inhabitants of the bunker, then been killed and his body carried out into the garden – all without arousing the least suspicion.

Furthermore, it means that the real **Hitler** left the bunker alone, got through the Russian lines and has now been living somewhere for three years and without anyone recognising him.

It was impossible for anyone to enter or leave the bunker without being thoroughly checked. To believe that two different men could appear to the guards claiming to be Adolf **Hitler** and that the guards did not notice is as absurd as to believe that Eva

Braun could be so deceived as to marry a stranger, spend several days and nights with him and die with him.

Equally, no sane person could entertain the idea that all those who were cross-examined arranged to give the same testimony without it being discovered because of differences or contradictions between them. Furthermore, the witnesses had next to no opportunity to meet and co-ordinate their stories.

I spoke to Hanna **Reitsch** several times at her home in Oberursel. She describes the belief that Hitler might still be alive as absurd. **Hitler's** physical condition, she said, made it impossible for him to have left the bunker. The Arado-96 in which she flew out of Berlin was the last available aircraft. She had the last chance to fly out of Berlin, as soon after that all possible airstrips were in Russian hands, and, even if they had not been, it would have been impossible to take off. This is proved by the fact that **Hitler's** two pilots Oberführer Hans **Baur** and Standartenführer **Beetz**, who were still in the bunker when **Hitler** died, would surely have tried to escape by air rather than overland, had it still been possible to do so.

Therefore, since it was impossible to flee by plane after 29 April, and on 30 April **Hitler** was still in the bunker, the best he could have done would be to get out by car. **Kempka**, who was not only **Hitler's** driver but also responsible for the whole Reich Chancellery, insists that all the cars had been destroyed by the bombing and shelling. But even if there had been a car left, escape would have been impossible because all the streets leading away from the Reich Chancellery were occupied by the Russians.

Hitler was too weak to leave on foot. The likelihood of him being carried out and hidden in a safe place is also very improbable because of the heavy shelling. Besides, in that case, what **Hitler** most feared might have happened, i.e. he might have been captured and dragged in humiliation through the streets of Berlin.

THE LEGEND DISPROVED

To insist that **Hitler** is still alive means to close one's eyes to the facts. A substantial number of these suppositions come from authors who have obviously not studied the facts thoroughly before they sit down to write.

Thus, for example, in May, 1948 Emil **Ludwig** wrote in the Italian magazine *Tempo*: 'Suicide without spectators and without theatrical effects contradicts the nature of this personality'. But Ludwig mentions neither **Axmann** nor **Mansfeld** nor **Schwägermann**. He, obviously, did not meet **Karnau** and **Kempka** or talk to them.

How far Ludwig's article can be trusted is shown by his calling **Herzegel** the 'Chief of the German General Staff'. In fact this man, with whom I have had extensive conversations, was one of **Hitler's** stenographers!

If **Ludwig** thought that **Hitler**'s death lacked 'theatrical effects' and was thus improbable, he obviously did not realise that such 'effects' would be precisely what **Hitler** and his officials would want had they been staging a fake suicide to deceive the public. In such a case, fireworks, music and theatricals, thousands of spectators would have been inevitable, but that could not have taken place in Berlin under massive bombing and shelling.

The British writer, Hugh **Trevor-Roper**, states in his book, *The Last Days of Hitler*: 'Hitler's last wish came true. Like Alaric whose body was secretly laid at the bottom of the River Busento, the corpse of this modern tyrant of mankind would never be discovered'.

But **Hitler** had no such intentions. He gave strict orders not to hide but to destroy his body. If it had been concealed, there was always a chance it might be found, and **Hitler** could never forget what happened to **Mussolini**'s corpse. He could not hope for better treatment.

Like others, **Trevor-Roper** insists that 180 litres of petrol would not be enough to completely destroy a body. But it has not been proved that only 180 litres were used. **Kempka** said that he poured five cans on the corpses, but he did not claim that only five cans were used to burn them. It has been repeated said that those 180 litres were the last supply of petrol remaining in the garage of the Reich Chancellery. But it is known that, the next day petrol, was available to burn the bodies of **Goebbels**' family and for the attempt to set fire to the bunker.

Notwithstanding all these facts, which deprive all these suppositions of any foundation, there are still rumours circulating that **Hitler** is alive. They are spreading because people are fond of mystery. But these rumours turn out to be false and absurd as soon as one starts to think about them logically and reasonably.

On 1 May of last year, a report was published in the newspapers that a Mrs Dora May of Wiesbaden saw **Hitler** in Magdeburg in July, 1947. According to this report, he was posing as a lieutenant in the Polish Army, speaks 'fluent Polish and Russian' to the Poles and is inviting them to join a new party.

In answer to this it must be said, firstly, if Mrs May saw **Hitler** in July, 1947, why did she conceal this interesting news from the public for 10 months? Secondly, if **Hitler** was still alive in July, 1947 he must have been 58 years old. A 58-year-old lieutenant with trembling hands and a bent back serving in the Army inevitably had to raise questions as to why he had not been promoted for such a long time.

If, as is claimed, he speaks fluent Polish and Russian to the Poles, one can object that **Hitler**'s lack of talent for languages was well known.

During the three years that I was investigating the circumstances of **Hitler**'s death, I checked all reports that **Hitler** was still alive. In the end they always turned to be beneath serious consideration. In March, 1948, the world's press published the story of a former lieutenant, Arthur Friedrich **Mackensen**, 28, who claimed that he saw how **Hitler** and Eva **Braun** left Berlin while the Russians were making their way to the Reich Chancellery. He, **Mackensen**, took them by aeroplane to Tondern in Denmark and there they separated. I contacted **Mackensen** and talked to him. He told me a fantastic story. In three minutes, it was clear to me that I was dealing with a psychotic. Notwithstanding that, I interrogated him for three hours in the presence of a court stenographer.

(Since then **Musmanno**'s guess has proved to be true. As reported on 24 June, 1948 by the DENA agency, 'Count **Mackensen-Agnelotti**' turned out to be a man named Valentine **Gerlach**, an employee of a firm in Cologne. After confrontation with his mother, it was clear that **Gerlach**, who said that he was a disabled veteran, was neither wounded nor paralysed nor blind. Psychiatrists considered him a clear fantasist and a pathological liar.)

All this proves absolutely clearly and in the most unambiguous manner that there is not the slightest reason for doubt about **Hitler**'s death.

Ф. К-1 ос; оп. 4; д. 2; т. 2; л. 120-140

AFTERWORD

OPERATION 'ARCHIVE':
THE KGB SECRET OPERATION

March–April, 1970
Report of Y.V. Andropov to CPSU
Of Special Importance
Top secret
Series 'K'
copy No.2
13 March, 1970 CPSU CC

In February, 1946, in Magdeburg (GDR) in the grounds of a military base which is now occupied by KGB Special Department of the 3rd Army of the GSFG, the corpses of **Hitler**, Eva **Braun**, **Goebbels**, his wife and children were buried (10 corpses altogether).

At present, the above-mentioned military base, being surplus to our requirements, is being turned over to the German authorities by the Army Command.

Taking into consideration the possibility of construction or other excavations on the site, which could result in the discovery of the burial place, I would consider it advisable to conduct the exhumation of the remains and cause their complete destruction by burning.

This would be undertaken in strict secrecy by the operative group of the KGB Special Department of 3rd Army of the Group of Soviet Forces in Germany and documented in due form.

Chairman of the State Security

Committee

Andropov

On the document there is a note: 'Agreement of CPSU CC received'.

Reported from the 1 Section of the General Department of the CPSU CC comrade SOLOVIEV N.A.

Ф. К-1 ос; оп. 4; д. 98
(заверенная копия отпуска)
(certified copy)

Strictly personal. Do not open in the office
A copy
Top secret
copy No.2
Seria 'K'

The letter of 3rd Department of KGB attached at the USSR
CM to SS of KGB attached at the USSR CM m/p p/b 92626
26 March, 1970

TO THE CHIEF OF THE SPECIAL SECTION OF THE KGB attached at the
USSR CM military unit army post 92626 to Colonel Comr. **Kovalenko N.G.**

Attached herewith an execution copy of the order approved by the Command of the
KGB attached at the USSR CM.

Enclosed: 2nd copy of the plan in 2 pages, our No. 3/C/ 143

CHIEF OF 3 KGB DEPARTMENT
Lieutenant General **Fedorchuk**

Ф. К-1 ос; оп. 4; д. 98; л. 1
(заверенная копия отпуска)

Top Secret
Copy No____
Series 'K'
'APPROVED'
CHAIRMAN OF THE COMMITTEE OF STATE SECURITY
ATTACHED AT THE USSR COUNCIL OF MINISTERS
Y. V. ANDROPOV.
26 March, 1970

PLAN FOR CARRYING OUT OPERATION 'ARCHIVE'

The aim of the operation: To exhume and physically annihilate the remains of the war criminals buried in Magdeburg on 21 February, 1946 in the military base in the Westendestrasse, near building no 36 (now Klausenerstrasse).

Participants in the realisation of the said operation to include: Chief of Special Section of KGB m/u 92626 Colonel KOVALENKO N.G., operatives of the Section . . .

To carry out the operation:
1. Two to three days before the start of the work, a tent is to be erected over the place of burial by a platoon of guards of Sp. Sec., its size to be sufficient to conceal the work taking place under it, as required by the plan.

2. The approaches to the tent to be guarded by soldiers, and during the works by operatives assigned to Operation 'Archive'.

3. To set up a secret counter-observation post overlooking the nearest house, inhabited by local civilians, to discover whether the site is open to possible observation. In case of such observation, to take the appropriate measures to stop it as the situation requires.

4. The excavation to be performed at night, the discovered remains to put in specially-prepared boxes and taken to the vicinity of the training fields of engineer and tank regiments of the GSFG near the Faulsee (Magdeburg district, GDR) where they are to be burned, and then thrown into the lake.

5. Execution of these actions according to the prepared plan of action is to be confirmed

by compiling the appropriate Reports:
a) the Report on uncovering the burial site (the Report is to indicate the condition of the boxes and their contents, and their being put into the specially prepared boxes);
b) the Report on the burning of the remains.
The Reports to be signed by all officers of Spec. Sec. m/u 92626 named here.

6. After exhumation of the remains, the place of burial is to be put back in order. The tent is to be taken down 2–3 days after the main work has been completed.

7. The cover story: because the operation is to be undertaken on a military base, approach to which is forbidden for the local population, the necessity to explain the cause and nature of the work performed would arise only in respect to the Army officers, members of their families and non-commissioned officers living on the base.

The essence of the cover story: the works (erection of the tent, the excavations) are being performed in order to check the evidence of a criminal arrested in the USSR, according to whom important archive documents might be buried in this place.

8. In case the first excavation turns out to be futile due to inaccurate information as to the place of the 'Archive', a trip to the site is to be arranged by Major General com. **Gorbushin** V.N., retired, living in Leningrad, and with his help to perform the actions for execution under this Plan.

CHIEF OF 3 KGB DEPARTMENT
Lieutenant-General **Fedorchuk**

20 March, 1970

Ф. К-1 ос; оп. 4; д. 98; л. 2–3
(подлинник)

inc. no 1758

    10.4.70

    Top Secret

    The only copy

    Series 'K'

the city of Magdeburg

m/u p/b 92626

4 April, 1970

THE REPORT

(OF EXCAVATION OF THE REMAINS OF THE WAR CRIMINALS)

According to the 'Archive' plan of operation, approved by the Chairman of the KSS (KGB translator) attached to the USSR Council of Ministers on 26 March, 1970, an operative group, consisting of Chief of Special Section of KGB m/u 92626 Colonel **Kovalenko N.G.** and operatives of the Section, performed the excavation of the remains of the war criminals on a military base in the Westendestrasse, near building no 36 (now Klausenerstrasse).

The excavation discovered that the alleged remains of the war criminals were buried in five wooden boxes, placed one over the other in a form of a cross, three of them from north to south, the two others from east to west. The boxes had decomposed and turned into rotten wood, the remains mixing with the soil.

Having been dug up, the soil was thoroughly examined and the remains (skulls, shin-bones, ribs, vertebrae and so on) were placed in a box.

The remains were in an advanced state of decay, especially those of the children, which prevented the exact count of how many had been discovered. According to an examination of the shin-bones and skulls, the remains could belong to between 10 and 11 bodies.

After the excavation, the place was put back in proper order. The excavation was performed during the night and morning of 4 April, 1970.

Observation of the nearest house, where local German civilians live, did not detect any suspicious actions on their part.

The Soviet citizens living on the base showed no direct interest in the works or the tent erected over the place of work.

The box containing the remains of the war criminals was under guard by the operatives until the morning of 5 April, when physical annihilation was performed.

Chef of Special Section of KGB m/u p/b 92626 Colonel KOVALENKO N.G.
Operatives of the Special Section KGB m/u p/b 92626 (signatures)

Ф. К-1 ос; оп. 4; д. 98; л. 4-6
(ПОДЛИННИК)

Inc.no 1759
    10.4.70
    Top secret
    The only copy
    Seria 'K'
The city of Magdeburg (GDR)
m/u p/b 92626
5 April, 1970

THE REPORT

(OF PHYSICAL ANNIHILATION OF THE REMAINS OF THE WAR CRIMINALS)

According to the 'Archive' plan of operation, the operative group consisting of Chief of Special Section of KGB m/u p/b 92626 Colonel Kovalenko N.G. and operatives of the Section . . . performed the burning of the remains of the war criminals exhumed from the burial site on the military base in the Westendestrasse near building no 36 (now Klausenerstrasse).

Annihilation of the remains was performed by burning on the waste ground in the vicinity of the city of Schönebeck, 11km from Magdeburg.

The remains, burned with charcoal, were crushed to dust, collected and thrown into the river at Bideritz, as confirmed by this Report.

Chief of Special Section of KGB m/u p/b 92626
Colonel **Kovalenko** N.G.
Operatives of the Special Section KGB m/u p/b 92626
(signatures)

5 April, 1970

Ф. К-1 ос; оп. 4; д. 98; л. 7-8
(ПОДЛИННИК)

Facsimile of the Report, hand-written by General Kovalenko.

APPENDICES

THE ACT OF UNCONDITIONAL SURRENDER OF NAZI GERMANY

8 May, 1945

The Act of Military Capitulation

1. We, the undersigned, acting in the name of the German Supreme Command, agree to an unconditional capitulation of all our Armed Forces on land and sea and in the air as well as the Forces that are now under German Command – to the Supreme Command of the Red Army and simultaneously to the Supreme Command of the Allied Expeditionary Forces.

2. The German Supreme Command will immediately issue orders to all German Commanders of Land, Sea and Air Forces, and to all Forces under German Command to stop combat actions at 23.00 – 01.00 Central European time – on 8 May, 1945, to stay where they are and to disarm completely, handing over all arms and military equipment to local Allied commanders or officers, assigned by the representatives of the Allied Supreme Command, not to destroy and not to inflict any damage to the ships, vehicles and aircraft, their engines, hulls and equipment, apparatus and to any technological means of waging war in general.

3. The German Supreme Command shall immediately assign special commanders and execute all further orders issued by the Supreme Command of the Red Army and the Supreme Command of the Allied Expeditionary Forces.

4. This Act shall not constitute a hindrance to its replacement by any other general document on capitulation concluded by the United Nations or in their name concerning Germany and the German Armed Forces as a whole.

5. Should the German Supreme Command or any Armed Forces under its command fail to act in accordance with this Act of Capitulation, the Supreme Command of the Red Army as well as the Supreme Command of the Allied Expeditionary Forces shall undertake such punitive or other measures as they consider necessary.

6. This Act is compiled in the Russian, English and German languages, with only the Russian and English texts being authentic.

Signed on 8 May, 1945, in the city of Berlin.

In the name of the German Supreme Command:
Keitel, Friedeburg, Stumpf

In the presence of:

On the authority of the Supreme
Command of the Allied
Expeditionary Forces
Air Chief Marshal
Tedder

On the authority of the Supreme
Command of the Red Army
Marshal of
the Soviet Union
Zhukov

As witnesses to the signing there were also present:

Commander of Strategic
Air Force of the USA
General **Spaatz**

Commanding General
of the French Army
General **Delattre de Tassigny**

The Foreign Policy of the Soviet Union
during the Great Patriotic War,
v. III, Moscow, 1947, p.p./ 261-261

THE VERDICT OF THE INTERNATIONAL
WAR CRIMES TRIBUNAL IN NUREMBERG

30 September–1 October, 1946

'The reading of the verdict to the main German war criminals' – under this headline on 2 October, 1946, *Pravda* published a collection of TASS News Agency reports from Nuremberg where the trial of the chieftains of the Third Reich took place.

NUREMBERG, 30 September (TASS). Today, after a one-month adjournment, the International War Crimes Tribunal resumed its sessions to read the sentences in the case of the main German war criminals.

At 10.00 a.m., the prosecutors took their seats in the hall of sessions of the Tribunal. They were, fom the USSR, Comr. Rudenko, from the USA, Mr. Jackson, from Great Britain, Mr. Shawcross and from France, Mr. Champetier de Ribes.

Other prosecutors from the Allied countries were also present who supported the accusations against the 22 main German war criminals throughout the case. The press seats were fully occupied by media representatives from many countries of the world.

At 10.00 a.m. sharp, the Tribunal session began. The presiding judge, Lord Justice Lawrence, started to read the verdict.

'The government of the United Kingdom of Great Britain and Northern Ireland, the government of the United States of America, the interim government of the French Republic and the government of the Union of the Soviet Socialist Republics', the verdict ran, 'have come to an agreement whereby this Tribunal was established to try the war criminals whose crimes are not connected to any particular geographical area.

The governments of the United Nations: Greece, Denmark, Yugoslavia, the Netherlands, Czechoslovakia, Poland, Belgium, Ethiopia, Australia, Honduras, Norway, Panama, Luxembourg, Haiti, New Zealand, India, Venezuela, Uruguay and Paraguay have joined the agreement of the four Allied powers.

Starting the trial on 20 November, 1945, the Tribunal, in its 403 open sessions, heard oral evidence from 33 witnesses for the prosecution. Aside from the 19 defendants, 61 witnesses for the defence were questioned. One hundred and forty-three witnesses for the defence gave their evidence by submitting written answers to lists of questions. In the case of the criminal organisations, 101 witnesses for the defence gave evidence to the commissioner. Other witnesses presented 1,809 written items of evidence. Six reports were also presented, summing up a great amount of other written evidence. Thirty-eight thousand written items of evidence signed by 155,000 persons were presented in the case of the political leaders, 136,213 in the case of the SS, 10,000 in the case of the SA, 7,000 in the case of the SD, 3,000 in the case of the General Staff and OKW (the Supreme Command of the former German Army) and 2,000 in the case of the Gestapo.

The Tribunal has heard 22 witnesses in respect of the criminal organisations. The documents produced as evidence on the charges against individual defendants and organisations number several thousands.

Turning to the consideration of the crimes against peace as listed in the indictment, the Tribunal, in its verdict, first and foremost dwells on the general plan for and waging of aggressive wars as the gravest international crime. In this count, the verdict analyses in detail the question of preparing for Hitler's aggression, and assesses the planning of the aggression as being connected to two meetings at Hitler's office to which he summoned his top commanders, sketching out political events from 1919, reminding them of Germany's walking out of the League of Nations, its leaving the Disarmament Conference, of its re-arming, of introducing compulsory military service, of the occupation of the Rhineland and operations against Czechoslovakia. The main thrust of Hitler's speeches at these two meetings was the question of conquering "living space" (*Lebensraum*) on the continent of Europe.'

After a short break during the morning session, the Member of the Tribunal from the French Republic Donnedieu de Vabres read out the counts of the verdict which established the crimes of the Nazi conspirators connected with the seizure of Austria, Czechoslovakia and the aggression against Poland.

Two counts of the verdict, read out by the French alternate André Falco, concentrated on the question of the German invasion of Denmark, Norway, Belgium, the Netherlands and Luxembourg. The following counts, concerning the waging of aggressive wars by Hitler's conspirators, analyse the criminal actions of the conspirators while they were conducting their aggression against Yugoslavia and Greece.

Further on, a count of the verdict provides the appraisal of the aggressive war against the Union of Soviet Socialist Republics.

In the late summer of 1940, the verdict states, Germany started to prepare the aggression against the USSR. This operation was planned in secrecy under the cover name of 'The Barbarossa Plan'. Former Field-Marshal Paulus testified that on 3 September, 1940 when he became an officer of the German General Staff, he carried on working out the 'Barbarossa Plan', which was completed by November, 1940.

Further, the verdict presents Hitler's Directive No. 21 of 18 December, 1940, demanding the completion of all the preparations connected with the implementation of 'The Barbarossa Plan'.

This directive, that bears the initials of Keitel and Jodl, runs as follows: 'The German Armed Forces must be prepared to defeat Soviet Russia in a speedy campaign before the end of the war against England. Special security measures must be taken to make it impossible to discover the intention of aggression . . .'

After the meetings, with the help of the defendants Keitel, Jodl, Raeder, Funk, Göring, Ribbentrop, Frick, Schirach and Fritzsche or their representatives, the verdict continues, the defendant Rosenberg spent three months working out the basis for the future political and economic organisation of the occupied territories. This was the subject of a highly detailed report, compiled immediately following the invasion. These plans provided for the destruction of the Soviet Union as an independent state, its breaking-up and the setting up of so-called Reich Commissariats as well as the turning of Latvia, Lithuania, Belorussia and other territories into German colonies. On 22 June, 1941, without a formal declaration of war, Germany invaded Soviet territory in accordance with the plans prepared beforehand.

The final aims of the aggression against the Soviet Union, as it is stated in the verdict, were formulated at Hitler's meeting on 16 July, 1941, in which the defendants Göring, Keitel, Rosenberg and Bormann participated.

'The setting up of a military power,' as the minutes of the meeting record, 'to the West of the Urals will not be on the agenda, even if we have to fight for as long as 100 years . . . All the Baltic states are to become a part of the Reich. The Crimea and the neighbouring areas (to the north of the Crimea) must be included in the Reich as well. The Volga regions as well as the area of Baku must be included in the Reich. The Finns want to acquire Eastern Karelia; but because of its vast deposits of nickel the Kola peninsula must go to Germany.'

The German plans for economic exploitation of the USSR, the mass expulsion of the population, the murders of commissars and political leaders, were all part of the thoroughly developed plan, which began be fulfilled on 22 June without any public announcement and with no trace of any lawful definition. This was, as is stated in the verdict, obvious aggression.

The verdict continues with a count on the war of Japan and Germany against the United States of America. This count analyses in detail the events connected with these acts of aggression since the Japanese attack on the US Navy at Pearl Harbor.

NUREMBERG, 30 September (TASS). In the evening session of the Tribunal, the reading of the verdict on the case of the main German war criminals continued.

In the count of the verdict concerning the breach of international treaties by the German conspirators, which was read out by the member of the Tribunal from the United States of America Francis Biddle, it is stated that some of the accused planned and waged aggressive wars against 12 states and they are guilty of committing these crimes.

The verdict details the breach of the Hague Conventions, of the Versailles Treaty, of treaties on mutual guarantees, arbitration and non-aggression and the breach of the

Briand-Kellogg Pact by the German conspirators.

It is quite obvious, the verdict states, that the plans for war were being worked out as early as 5 November, 1937, possibly even earlier. The fact that Germany was speedily moving in the direction of an absolute dictatorship from the very moment of the seizure of power by Hitler's supporters and was constantly moving in the direction of war, is indisputably proven by its successive aggressive acts and wars.

The Tribunal considers that the evidence clearly establishes the fact of general planning, preparation and waging of war by the defendants.

Hitler, the verdict states, could not wage aggressive wars on his own. He needed co-operation on the part of the statesmen, military leaders, diplomats and businessmen. And when they, being aware of his aims, started to co-operate with him, they made themselves participants in the plan he created.

The count 'War Crimes against Humanity' is extensively covered in the verdict, which was read by the Alternate Member of the Tribunal from the United States of America, John Parker. This count comprehensively reveals the war crimes committed by the Nazi conspirators.

It is true, the verdict says, that war crimes were committed on such a wide scale and accompanied by such atrocities and terrorism as to be unequalled in the history of war. There is absolutely no doubt that the majority of these crimes originated from Hitler's idea of a 'total war'.

The verdict states that these war crimes were planned in advance, which is proved by the activities of the conspirators in the temporarily-occupied territories of the Soviet Union, where they practised plunder of the occupied territories and the most cruel treatment of the civilian population.

The conspirators planned the widest use of the population of the occupied countries as slave labour. The German Government considered these measures to be part of the war economy, and planned and organised this particular war crime down to the last detail. On the basis of the evidence of multiple witnesses and the documents, the verdict establishes the facts of killings of Soviet prisoners-of-war, their branding, death by hunger and epidemic diseases as well as those Soviet prisoners-of-war who were used for medical experiments, which were performed in the most cruel and inhumane ways.

The verdict refers to numerous directives, cites extracts from orders and decrees of Hitler and Hitler's co-conspirators on mass killings of the civilian population in the occupied territories of Western Europe and the Soviet Union.

The verdict establishes the guilt of these crimes by the defendant Keitel, who issued the corresponding orders and instructions aimed at the annihilation of the civilian population, and the defendant Rosenberg as the Reichskommissar of the Eastern Territories.

In Poland and the Soviet Union, the verdict continues, these crimes were part of the plan to drive out and annihilate all of the indigenous population in order vacate the area for German settlers.

The same fate was prepared for Czechoslovakia by the defendant Neurath.

In the West, the population of Alsace fell victim to the German 'expulsion operation'.

Along with the war crimes and the crimes against humanity, as well as the cruel treatment and killing of civilian populations, this special count of the verdict gives details of the plundering of public and private property in the territory occupied by Germany. This count of the verdict was read out by the Tribunal member from the Union of Soviet Socialist Republics, Comr. Nikitchenko.

Along with the seizure of natural resources and manufactured goods, the verdict emphasises, massive plunder of art objects was carried out in all the countries occupied by Germany. The plunder of valuables was performed by a special organisation, known by the name of the Rosenberg Einsatz-Staff, which carried out its operations on a very large scale. Ribbentrop's Special Battalions, the Reich Commissars and representatives of the military command in certain places acted similarly, looting cultural and historical treasures which belonged to the peoples of the Soviet Union.

Comrade Nikitchenko continued to read the count on 'Slave Labour'.

The verdict stresses that Hitler's followers used prisoners-of-war in labour directly connected with military activities, practised mass killings of prisoners-of-war as well as the tremendous crimes of the Nazis against the Jews.

Then the Alternate Member of the Tribunal from the Union of the Soviet Socialist Republics Volchikov began to read out the count of the verdict on the criminal organisations.

This count of the verdict dealt with the primary organisation accused – Hitler's Party leadership – exposing the actual crimes committed by the members of this organisation. These crimes manifested themselves in the carrying-out of the conspiracy to wage aggressive war, in the persecution of the Jews, in the realisation of the programme of slave labour, in the brutal treatment of prisoners-of-war and the killing of Allied pilots.

Analysing the structure and the departments of the Gestapo and the SD and their criminal activity, the Tribunal states in the verdict that they are guilty of the extermination of the Jews, brutalities and killings in concentration camps and in the occupied territories, in the implementation of the slave labour programme and the brutal treatment and killing of prisoners of war. The defendant Kaltenbrunner, who was the leader of this organisation, was found guilty of all these crimes.

The verdict further stresses that the Tribunal recognised the SS as a criminal organisation.

As for the SA, the verdict states that this organisation is not proclaimed criminal in the sense provided for under Article 9 of the Charter of the Tribunal.

The verdict states that the Prosecution called the Reich Government a criminal organisation. The Tribunal considered that the Reich Government should not be declared a criminal organisation for two reasons: firstly, because it had not been proved that after 1937 it, in fact, acted as a group or an organisation; and secondly, because the group of persons charged is so small that its members could appear individually before the court without difficulty, without requiring a ruling that the cabinet of ministers, of which they were members, is a criminal organisation.

At the end of the evening session, the Tribunal read out its verdict in the case of the final organisation accused – the General Staff and the Supreme Command of the German Armed Forces. The Tribunal considered that no such ruling could be passed as to the criminal nature of the General Staff and the Supreme Command.

The verdict stated that better results would be reached by holding separate trials of individual officers. Though they did not form a group as defined by the Charter, they undoubtedly formed a pitiless military caste.

NUREMBERG. 1 October (TASS). In the morning session, the count of the Tribunal's verdict was read out which determined the individual guilt of every defendant.

The defendant Göring, it says, stood accused on all four counts of the indictment (general planning or conspiracy, crimes against peace, war crimes, crimes against humanity). There were no extenuating circumstances in the case of Göring, because for almost the entire time, Göring was the 'driving force', leaving first place only to Hitler. He was the main initiator of the aggressive war, both as a political and military leader. He lead the programme of slave labour and initiated the programme of persecution of the Jews and other races at home and abroad.

Göring's crimes were unsurpassed in their terrible cruelty. No circumstances were discovered that could justify this man. The tribunal found the defendant Göring guilty on all four counts of the indictment.

Hess was accused under all four counts of the indictment. In the verdict, Hess' activities were specified over the many years of his membership of Hitler's Party and as Hitler's closest confidant. Hess actively supported preparation for the war. His signature is on the law that introduced compulsory military service. He supported Hitler's policy of intensive re-armament and was a participant in the German aggression against Austria, Czechoslovakia and Poland.

The Tribunal, nevertheless, did not consider the evidence produced to be sufficient to indicate Hess' participation in war crimes and crimes against humanity.

The editorial in 'Pravda' on 2 October, 1946 with the story of the German capitulation.

ИЗВЕСТИЯ

СОВЕТО
ДЕПУТАТО
ТРУДЯЩИХ
СССР

Приговор гитлеризму

Заседания Международного военного трибунала в Нюрнберге пришли к концу. Приговор вынесен. Международное правосудие наказало главарей преступной гитлеровской шайки.

Этого приговора с нетерпением ждало человечество. Фашистские агрессоры разожгли мировую войну, они залили кровью земной шар, покрыли развалинами обширные пространства Европы. Чудовищные преступления фашизма на временно оккупированных территориях потрясли мир. Миллионы людей пали на полях войны, погибли в застенках от рук фашистских палачей. Миллионы человеческих жизней искалечены, исковерканы.

Советский народ, вынесший на своих плечах основную тяжесть великой освободительной войны против фашизма, знает преступления фашистских извергов не по-наслышке, не по одним лишь газетным сообщениям. Своими глазами видели советские люди развалины городов и пепелища деревень, своими руками они хоронили трупы убитых и замученных. В минувшие тяжелые годы советские люди говорили себе: фашистские преступники не уйдут от заслуженной кары. Наш народ твердо знал, что день возмездия наступит. Порукой тому была решимость всего нашего народа. Порукой тому было слово великого Сталина.

И день возмездия наступил. В зале суда в Нюрнберге зачитан приговор. Двенадцать главарей немецкого фашизма из числа тех, кто вместе с Гитлером замышлял и творил кровавые преступления против человечества; узнали вчера, что их ждет позорная смерть. Перед другими преступниками раскроются тюремные двери.

Подобного суда, как и подобного приговора, еще не знала история. После первой мировой войны немецкие военные преступники во главе с кайзером

осуждение агрессии нашло воплощение в судебном приговоре. Правосудие свершилось: банде агрессоров — поджигателей войны предстоит взойти на эшафот.

Отчеты о заседаниях Нюрнбергского суда навсегда останутся беспощадным обличительным документом против фашизма и агрессии. Самые сильные и убедительные страницы этого документа являются вкладом советского правосудия. Устами его представителей в Нюрнберге говорил советский народ.

Более десяти месяцев в зале суда в Нюрнберге и далеко за его стенами шла борьба за справедливый приговор преступным гитлеровским главарям. Защитники упорно пытались укрыть подсудимых за частоколы юридической казуистики. Разношерстные покровители фашизма — от обитателей Ватикана до наемников пера из газетного концерна Херста — мобилизовали все свои силы в защиту подсудимых. Но правосудие одержало верх над беззаконием, правое дело победило.

Силы реакции хотят сейчас похоронить содружество Об'единенных наций, проявившее себя в годы войны на службе человечеству. Определенные реакционные круги стремятся расшатать основы сотрудничества между народами. Деятельность Международного военного трибунала в Нюрнберге показала, что жизнь сильнее этих интриг и происков.

В то же время все те, кто считает, что справедливость должна быть твердой и последовательной, не смогут согласиться с той частью приговора Международного военного трибунала, которая смягчила наказание Гессу и оправдала Шахта, Папена, Фриче. Такая снисходительность судей вызовет недоумение и сожаление в самых широких кругах. Роль этих четырех подсудимых в преступлениях гитлеровского режима известна достаточно хорошо — ее нельзя отрицать, невоз-

В от

Разв

П

Хотя лето
знойное, а в
лялись сухове
ли имени Ста
урожай. Высок
вый уход за п
леть трудности
ра по девянос
мых и более
колосовых кул
ко на участке
тридцать гекта
десят пудов зе

Урожай над
без потерь. Ко
ботали безотка
ли и перевыпо
колхозники, ч
пустили в ход
полную нагруз

Сложно и
передовой арте
рабочих рук. В
щадь на триста
вышала довоен
яно две тысячи
таров.

Обязавшись
года новой п
потерь, колхоз
самоотвержен
сили все хлеба
кончили скирд

Но затем не

Омски

The editorial in 'Izvestia' on 2 October, 1946 with the story of the German capitulation.

347

The Tribunal found the defendant Hess guilty on counts 1 and 2 and not guilty on counts 3 and 4 of the indictment.

Ribbentrop was accused of all four counts of the bill of indictment. There is considerable evidence, according to the verdict, establishing Ribbentrop's co-operation with Hitler and the other defendants in this case in committing crimes against peace, war crimes and crimes against humanity and that this co-operation was sincere and voluntary. Ribbentrop served Hitler of his own free will and to the end, precisely because Hitler's policy and plans coincided with his own convictions.

The Tribunal found Ribbentrop guilty on all four counts of the indictment.

Keitel was charged on all four counts of the indictment.

The verdict, on the basis of various documents, established Keitel's guilt in carrying out German aggression against Austria, Czechoslovakia, Poland, Belgium and the Netherlands. He signed various directives and orders to German Armed Forces concerning the aggression against these countries. Keitel was aware of the precise plans of action against Greece and Yugoslavia. He put his initials on the plan of aggression against the USSR ('The Barbarossa Plan').

There are no extenuating circumstances concerning Keitel, according to the verdict.

The Tribunal found Keitel guilty on all four counts of the indictment.

Kaltenbrunner was charged under counts 1, 3 and 4 of the bill of indictment. Stressing Kaltenbrunner's guilt in committing war crimes [and crimes] against humanity, the verdict pointed out that as Chief of the Security Police and SD, Kaltenbrunner gave orders for preventive detention in concentration camps, the executions of inmates, and the purges and brutal killings of the population of the territories occupied by Germany.

The Tribunal found Kaltenbrunner not guilty on count 1 and guilty on count 3 and 4 of the bill of indictment.

Rosenberg was charged on all four counts of the indictment. Establishing Rosenberg's guilt in the crimes against peace, the verdict describes in detail all of Rosenberg's criminal activities.

Rosenberg, the verdict runs, bears the main responsibility for the formulation and introduction of a criminal policy of occupation in the Eastern territories occupied by Germany.

The Tribunal found Rosenberg guilty on all four counts of the indictment.

Frank was charged under the first, third and fourth counts of the indictment. The verdict of the Tribunal emphasised Frank's war crimes and crimes against humanity, especially during the period when he was Gauleiter of the territory of Poland occupied by the Nazis.

The Tribunal found Frank not guilty on count 1 and guilty on counts 3 and 4 of the indictment.

Frick was charged on all four counts of the indictment. He was the Minister of the Interior in Hitler's Cabinet and stayed in this important post until August, 1943, when he was appointed to the post of the Reich Protector of Bohemia and Moravia.

The verdict says that the evidence provided by the prosecution does not indicate that Frick was a participant of the general plan or conspiracy to wage aggressive war, and for this reason, the Tribunal found Frick not guilty on count 1 of the bill of indictment and guilty on counts 2, 3 and 4.

Streicher was charged on counts 1 and 4 of the indictment. He was a convinced Nazi and supported the main political intentions of Hitler. However, the verdict says, during this activity he was closely connected with the formulation of the programme which lead to the war. On the basis of this, the Tribunal found that Streicher was not guilty on count 1, but guilty on count 4 of the bill of indictment.

Funk was charged on all four counts of the indictment. The verdict established that, notwithstanding the fact that Funk occupied important official posts, he did not play a leading role in conducting the different programmes in which he participated. For that reason, the Tribunal did not find Funk guilty on count 1, but found him guilty on counts 2, 3 and 4 of the bill of indictment.

Schacht was charged under the first and second counts of the indictment. As the verdict recognises, Schacht actively supported Hitler's Party before it came to power in 1933 and supported Hitler's appointment to the post of Chancellor. He played an important role in an intensive programme of re-armament, which was accepted, and used the potential of the Reichsbank to the greatest extent for German efforts to re-arm.

In the final appraisal of Schacht's activities that was given in the verdict, a number of circumstances were pointed out which, according to the Tribunal, justified the actions of the defendant.

The Tribunal found Schacht not guilty of the crimes named in the bill of indictment.

Dönitz was charged on counts 1, 2 and 3 of the bill of indictment. The verdict says that Dönitz set up and trained the German submarine fleet, but that the evidence does not establish his participation in a conspiracy to wage aggressive war, nor did the fact of his participation make him guilty of preparation for and unleashing of such wars. For that reason, the Tribunal found Dönitz not guilty on count 1 of the bill of indictment and guilty on counts 2 and 3.

Raeder was charged on counts 1, 2 and 3 of the bill of indictment. On the basis of the evidence provided, the Tribunal found that Raeder took part in the planning and waging of aggressive war and was guilty of war crimes committed on the high seas.

The Tribunal found Raeder guilty on counts 1, 2 and 3 of the bill of indictment.

Von Schirach was charged on counts 1 and 4 of the bill of indictment. The verdict stated that, despite the military character of the Hitler Youth, it may not be said that von Schirach participated in the planning or preparation of aggressive warfare. Schirach was convicted under the verdict in connection with his activities as Gauleiter of Vienna.

The Tribunal found von Schirach not guilty on count 1 of the bill of indictment and guilty on count 4.

Sauckel was charged on all four counts of the indictment. The verdict did not consider that Sauckel was connected sufficiently closely with the general plan for waging aggressive war, nor that he had a significant relationship to the planning and waging of any of the aggressive wars. For that reason the Tribunal found Sauckel not guilty on counts 1 and 2 of the bill of indictment and guilty on counts 3 and 4.

Jodl was charged on all four counts of the indictment.

The verdict stated that there were no extenuating circumstances in defence of Jodl. For that reason the Tribunal found Jodl guilty on the four counts of the indictment.

Von Papen was charged on counts 1 and 2 of the bill of indictment. However, the Tribunal did not consider that von Papen took part in the general planning, charged in count 1 or participated in planning of any of the individual aggressive wars, as in count 2 of the bill of indictment.

The Tribunal found von Papen not guilty.

Seyss-Inquart was charged on all four counts of the indictment.

The verdict details the criminal activities of Seyss-Inquart in Austria, Poland and the Netherlands. The verdict establishes that Seyss-Inquart was a well-informed and voluntary participant in war crimes and crimes against humanity.

The Tribunal found Seyss-Inquart guilty on counts 2, 3 and 4 of the bill of indictment and not guilty on count 1.

Speer was charged on all four counts of the indictment. The Tribunal was of the opinion that Speer's activities could not be classified as the unleashing, planning or preparation for aggressive wars nor conspiracy to that end. Proceeding from this, the Tribunal found Speer not guilty on counts 1 and 2 and guilty on counts 3 and 4 of the bill of indictment.

Von Neurath was charged on all four counts of the indictment. The verdict provided details of von Neurath's crimes and pointed out some extenuating circumstances.

The Tribunal found von Neurath guilty on all four counts of the verdict.

Fritzsche was charged on counts 1, 3 and 4 of indictment. However, the Tribunal considered the evidence provided to have been insufficient and found Fritzsche not guilty.

Bormann (tried *in absentia*) was charged on counts 1, 3 and 4 of the bill of indictment. On the basis of the evidence provided, the tribunal did not find Bormann guilty on count 1 of the bill of indictment. The Tribunal established that Bormann must take responsibility for the crimes and crimes against humanity, i.e. on counts 3 and 4.

After reading out the main part of the verdict and the part that established the responsibility of each of the defendants separately, the Chairman of the Tribunal

Lawrence made the following statement: 'Before reading out the sentences, the Tribunal, using the occasion of having all of the defendants present at the session, announces that if the defendants want to appeal against the verdict to the Control Council, they are allowed to do so within four days after the reading of the verdict through the Secretary General of the Tribunal.'

The morning session adjourned and an hour-long break was announced.

At 3.00 p.m. sharp, the Tribunal began reading that part of the verdict which stated the sentence for each of the defendants separately.

The defendants' seats were unoccupied. The first defendant, Göring, was brought in under guard.

The sentence, in accordance with the counts of the indictment, was read out by the Chairman of the Tribunal Lord Justice Geoffrey Lawrence.

Göring, in accordance with the counts of the indictment, under which he was found guilty, was sentenced by the International War Crimes Tribunal to death by hanging; Hess – to life imprisonment; Ribbentrop – to death by hanging; Keitel – to death by hanging; Kaltenbrunner – to death by hanging; Rosenberg – to death by hanging; Frank – to death by hanging; Frick – to death by hanging; Streicher – to death by hanging; Funk – to life imprisonment; Schacht – acquitted; Dönitz – to 10 years, imprisonment; Raeder – to life imprisonment; Schirach – to 20 years, imprisonment; Sauckel – to death by hanging; Jodl – to death by hanging; Seyss-Inquart – to death by hanging; Von Papen – acquitted; Speer – to 20 years, imprisonment; Neurath – to 15 years, imprisonment; Fritzsche – acquitted; Bormann, who was tried *in absentia* – to death by hanging.

After reading the sentence, which ended at 3.40 p.m., the Chairman of the Tribunal made the following statement:

'The Member of the Tribunal from the Union of the Soviet Socialist Republics wishes to record in the protocol his disagreement with the sentence of the Tribunal in the cases of the defendants Schacht, von Papen and Fritzsche. He is of the opinion that they must be convicted and not acquitted. He also disagrees with the ruling concerning the Reich Cabinet of Ministers, the General Staff and the Supreme Command, being of the opinion that they should be proclaimed criminal organisations.

He also does not agree with the ruling concerning the defendant Hess's punishment and considers that the sentence should be death and not life imprisonment.

This special opinion will be put in written form and attached to the sentence. It is to be published, as soon as possible.'

The session of the International War Crimes Tribunal in Nuremberg ended.

This is taken from the publication in the *Pravda* and *Izvestia* newspapers of 2 October, 1946.

FROM THE OFFICIAL GAZETTE OF THE CONTROL COUNCIL FOR GERMANY, NO.11, 1946. (12 October, 1946)

ARREST AND PUNISHMENT OF WAR CRIMINALS, NAZIS AND MILITARISTS: INTERNMENT, CONTROL AND SUPERVISION OF POTENTIALLY DANGEROUS GERMANS

Instruction no 38

The Control Council states the following:

PART I

1. The aim.

The aim of this document is to establish the general course of action for Germany, which shall include:

a) punishment of war criminals, Nazis, militarists and industrialists who encouraged and supported the Nazi regime;

b) complete and total annihilation of Nazism and militarism by means of isolation of prominent participants or supporters of their ideas and by the restriction of the activities of these people;

c) internment of Germans who, while not being guilty of actual crimes, are considered to be dangerous to Allied aims and control, and also the control and supervision of others who are considered to be potentially dangerous.

2. References.

a) The Potsdam Agreement, Section III, paragraph 3 (I a).

b) The Potsdam Agreement, Section III, paragraph 3 (III).

c) The Potsdam Agreement, Section III, paragraph 5.

d) Instruction no. 24 of the Control Council.

e) Act no. 10 of the Control Council, Article II, paragraph 3, Article III, paragraphs 1 and 2.

3. The problem and general principles.

It is considered that in order to be able to implement the principles stated at Potsdam, it is necessary to classify war criminals and those who present a potential danger into five general categories and to state for each of the categories the due punishment and penalties. We believe that some details must also be co-ordinated concerning certain categories, as well the nature of punitive measures and penalties, which would in no way restrict the prerogatives of the Commanders of the zones, accorded them under Act no. 10 of the Control Council.

4. A clear definition of Allied policy towards obviously dangerous, as well as potentially dangerous, Germans is now necessary in order to be able to establish uniform conditions of treatment of these people in the various occupation zones of Germany.

5. Categories and penalties.

A definition of categories and penalties is provided in detail in the second part of this document. They are to be applied in accordance with the following general principles:

a) There should be a difference between the imprisonment of war criminals and the like for their criminal acts and the internment of potentially dangerous people who could be isolated because the fact that they are at liberty might present a threat to the Allies' aims.

b) The Commanders of the zones may, if they wish, move a person to a lower category with the aim of testing him, excluding those persons convicted as principal criminals due to their being guilty of actual crimes.

c) Within the categories, the Commanders of the zones have the right to alter the penalties, if necessary, applying them to certain cases within the framework of this Instruction.

d) Classification of all criminals and potentially dangerous persons, defining the penalties and re-consideration of cases will be undertaken by the institutions appointed by the Commanders of the zones as the persons responsible for implementation of this Instruction.

e) Commanders of the zones and tribunals shall have the right to place certain persons in higher or lower categories. Commanders of the zones may, if they wish, use German tribunals for the classification of criminals and re-consideration of cases.

f) Persons liable for responsibility under this Instruction cannot avoid the implementation of this Instruction by moving from one zone to another, each zone Commander ensuring that the other zones are aware of and understand the methods used by him to mark the identity cards of persons included in one of the categories.

g) For the purpose of this Instruction, it is recommended that every Commander issue a law or zone regulation in compliance with the meaning, provisions and principles of this Instruction. The Commanders of the zones shall exchange copies of these laws and orders.

h) If these zone laws are in complete compliance with the principles stated here, the Commander of a zone shall be free to implement them according to the local situation in his zone.

i) In Berlin, the Allied Commandant's office shall be responsible for the implementation of the principles and provisions of this Instruction. It shall issue such regulations and orders as are necessary for this aim. The Commandant's office in Berlin shall have the same rights as the Commanders of the zones in implementing this Instruction.

j) Irrespective of the categories and penalties stated in Part II of the Instruction, persons who have committed war crimes or crimes against peace and humanity, stated in Law no. 10 of the Control Council, are liable to the provisions and procedures stated in the said Law.

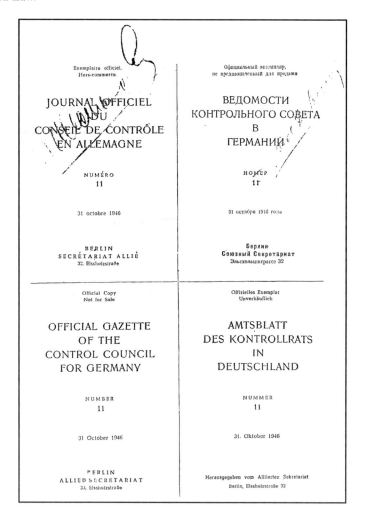

Facsimile of the title page of the Official Gazette of the Control Council for Germany No 11 dated 31 October, 1946 (in French, Russian, English and German).

PART II

Article I
Groups of Persons to be held liable.

To give a fair definition of responsibility and to ensure the provisions for penalties (excluding paragraph 5 below) the persons liable for war crimes shall be classified as follows:

1. Main criminals.
2. Criminals (activists, militarists and speculators).
3. Minor criminals (put on probation).
4. Fellow-travellers.
5. Rehabilitated persons (persons in the categories established above, who may prove their innocence before the courts).

Article II
The Main Criminals.

The main criminals are:

1. All persons who committed crimes out of political conviction against the victims or opponents of National-Socialism.
2. All persons who, in Germany or in the occupied territories, mistreated the population or prisoners-of-war in breach of international law.
3. All persons who have been responsible for gross breaches of the law, looting, deportation and other atrocities, even if they were committed in the struggle against the resistance movements.
4. All persons who took an active, leading part in the activities of the NSDAP, one of its groups or branches or in any other National-Socialist or military organisation.
5. All persons who held a leading position in the governments of the Reich, the federal lands or in the governments of the former occupied territories, such as could only have been held by a leading National-Socialist or a leading supporter of the National-Socialist tyranny.
6. All persons who gave significant political, economic, propaganda or other support to the National-Socialist tyranny, or those who, thanks to their relationship with National-Socialist tyranny, extracted huge profits for themselves or others.
7. All persons who were actively involved, for the benefit of the National-Socialist tyranny, in the Gestapo, SD, SS, secret field or border police (Geheime Feldpolizei or Grenzpolizei).

8. All persons who participated in different ways in killing, torture or any other atrocities in the concentration camps, labour camps or hospitals and psychoneurological institutions.

9. All persons, who for their own profit or benefit, actively co-operated with the Gestapo, SD, SS or other similar organisations, providing information or helping in other ways to purge the opponents of the National-Socialist tyranny.

10. All members of the High Command of the German Armed Forces, identified as the main criminals.

11. Part I of Appendix 'A' provides a list of the categories of persons who, depending on the nature of crimes supposedly committed by them, as stated in paragraphs 1–10 of this Article, and according to the positions they occupied, shall be thoroughly investigated and, should the results of such investigations call for consideration by the courts, they should be brought to trial as main criminals and punished if found guilty.

Article III
The Criminals.

A. The Activists.
I. The activists are:
1. All persons who, thanks to their position or activities, directly assisted the development of the National-Socialist tyranny.
2. All persons who used their position, influence or their connections for compulsion and threats, for brutality and for oppression and other unjust means.
3. All persons who manifested themselves as open supporters of the National-Socialist tyranny, including its racial ideas.

II. The activists include, in part, the following persons, because they are not included in the category of the main criminals:
1. All persons who significantly encouraged the establishment or support of the National-Socialist tyranny by word or deed, especially in public, by means of speeches or literature or by voluntary donations from their own or someone else's property or by use of their own reputation or position in political, economic or cultural life.
2. All persons who, because of National-Socialist ideas or education, poisoned the morals and ethics of youth.
3. All persons who, for the purpose of strengthening of the National-Socialist tyranny, demoralised the family and marriage with no respect to the common principles of morality.
4. All persons who, in the service of National-Socialism, unlawfully prevented the administration of justice, or politically abused their official position as a judge or a public prosecutor.

JOURNAL OFFICIEL DU CONSEIL DE CONTRÔLE EN ALLEMAGNE	ВЕДОМОСТИ КОНТРОЛЬНОГО СОВЕТА В ГЕРМАНИИ
Numero 11	Номер 11
31 octobre 1946	31 октября 1946 года

Facsimile of the contents of the Official Gazette of the Control Council for Germany, No 11 dated 31 October, 1946 (in French and Russian).

OFFICIAL GAZETTE OF THE CONTROL COUNCIL FOR GERMANY	AMTSBLATT DES KONTROLLRATS IN DEUTSCHLAND
Number 11	Nr. 11
31 October 1946	31. Oktober 1946

CONTENTS

INHALTSVERZEICHNIS

Facsimile of the contents of the Official Gazette of the Control Council for Germany, No 11 of 31 October, 1946 (in English and German).

5. All persons who, in the service of National-Socialism, used or instigated the use of force against the church, religious communities or ideological associations.

6. All persons who, in the service of National-Socialism, ridiculed, damaged and dictated the values of culture and the sciences.

7. All persons who took a leading and active part in the abolition of trade unions, in suppressing labour and the appropriation of labour union property.

8. All persons, who acting as provocateurs, agents or informants, caused or tried to cause damage to other persons due to their race, religion or political opposition to National-Socialism or due to any breach of National-Socialist rules.

9. All persons who used their position or power during the National-Socialist tyranny to commit crimes, including blackmail, embezzlement and fraud.

10. All persons, who, by word or deed, expressed hatred towards the NSDAP's opponents in Germany or abroad, towards prisoners-of-war, towards the population of the former occupied territories, foreign workers, prisoners and others.

11. All persons who encouraged the sending to the Front of those opposed to National-Socialism.

III. The activists shall also include persons who, after 8 May, 1945, endangered or might have endangered the peace of the German people or the whole world by National-Socialist or militarist propaganda, or by inventing and disseminating harmful rumours.

B. Militarists.

I. The militarists are:

1. All persons who tried to lead German people into a life that complied with the policy of military violence.

2. All persons who advocated or were responsible for domination over foreign peoples, their exploitation or deportation.

3. All persons who supported the development of armaments for these aims.

II. The militarists are, in part, the following persons, as long as they are not main criminals:

1. All who by word or deed introduced or disseminated military doctrines or programmes or were an active member of an organisation (excluding the Wehrmacht), which encouraged the dissemination of militaristic ideas.

2. All who, until 1935, organised or participated in the organisation of a systematic preparation of youth for war.

3. All who, in positions of command, were responsible for the senseless devastation of cities and villages after the invasion of Germany.

4. All who, notwithstanding their rank, as members of the Armed Forces (the Wehrmacht), the Reich Labour Office (Reichsarbeitsdienst), the Organisation Todt or the Transport Group Speer, misused their official position for private gain or for brutal treatment of employees.

5. All those whose previous training or activity in the ranks of the General Staff or in any other organisation, according to the Commander of the zone, helped to foster militarism, as well as persons whom the Commander of the zone considers to be dangerous to Allied aims.

C. Speculators.

I. The speculators are:

1. All who, used their political position or contacts to extract personal or economic profits for themselves and others belonging to the National-Socialist tyranny, for re-arming and war.

II. The speculators, in particular, are the following persons, as long as they are not main criminals:

1. All who, merely because of membership of the NSDAP, occupied a certain post or position or were given preference for a post because of it.

2. All who received substantial gifts of money from the NSDAP or from their units and supporting organisations.

3. All who received or obtained benefits for themselves and others at the expense of those who were purged for political, religious or racial reasons, directly or indirectly, especially in connection with expropriations, forced sales and other, similar actions.

4. All who gained huge profits from armaments and military trade in wartime, including the black market.

5. All, who unlawfully enriched themselves through governing the occupied territories.

D. Part II of Appendix 'A' provides the list of categories of persons who, according to the character of crimes supposedly committed by them, as stated in paragraphs 'A', 'B' and 'C' of Article III, will be thoroughly investigated and, should the results of such investigations call for consideration by the courts, they are to be brought to trial as criminals and punished if found guilty.

Article IV
Minor Criminals (put on probation).

I. The minor criminals are:
1. All those, including the former members of the Armed Forces, who belong to the general group of criminals, who thanks to special circumstances, seem to deserve lesser punishment and who, due to their character, are able to assume the duties of citizens of a peaceful democratic state after they have proved themselves worthy during the probation period.
2. All those who belong to the group of 'fellow-travellers' but because of their character and behaviour have first to rehabilitate themselves.

II. The minor criminals in particular are:
1. All persons born after 1 January, 1919 who, though they do not belong to the group of main criminals, are suspected of crimes but at the same time did not manifest reprehensible behaviour or cruelty and who might be expected to reform.
2. All who are not main criminals, but are suspected of crimes and who unquestionably and openly long ago abandoned Nazism and its methods.
3. Part III of Appendix 'A' gives the list of categories of persons who will be thoroughly investigated, and if their guilt is confirmed, they will be accused of being minor criminals and punished according to the provisions of paragraphs 1 and 2 of this Article.

Article V
Fellow-Travellers.

I. Fellow-travellers are:
All who were no more than nominal participants or adherents of the National-Socialist tyranny.

II. Consequently, fellow travellers, in particular, are:
1. All who, as members of NSDAP or one of its organizations, excluding HJ and BDM, only paid membership dues, attended meetings when necessary or fulfilled important or simply superficial duties necessary for all members.
2. All those who, not being main criminals, criminals or minor criminals, were candidates for membership of the NSDAP, but were eventually not accepted as full-time members.
3. All former members of the Armed Forces who, according to the Commander of the zone, are by their nature dangerous to Allied aims.

Article VI
Rehabilitated Persons.

The rehabilitated persons are:
Those persons who, notwithstanding their formal membership or candidacy or any other superficial indications, not only occupied a passive position but actively resisted National-Socialist tyranny as much as they could and suffered disadvantages as a result.

Article VII
Penalties.

The penalties, as stated in Articles VIII–XI, shall be carried out in accordance with the degree of their responsibility, with the intention of eradicating Nazism and militarism from the life of the German people and to exact compensation for the losses inflicted.

Article VIII
Penalties for the Main Criminals.

I. The main criminals, who committed military war crimes, shall be liable to the following penalties:
a) capital punishment;
b) life imprisonment or imprisonment for a term of between 5 to 15 years with or without penal servitude;
c) additionally, any of the penalties in paragraph II of this Article may be applied.

II. The following penalties may be applied to other main criminals:
a) they will be imprisoned or interned for a period of no longer than 10 years; internment after 8 May, 1945 may be taken into account; disabled persons shall be required to do special work depending on their abilities;
b) their property may be confiscated, but some means shall be left to them to secure a minimal standard of living with regard to their family status and possible earnings;
c) they shall be deprived of the right to occupy any official posts, including that of a notary and attorney;
d) they shall be deprived of the right to receive a pension or allowance payable from public funds;
e) they shall be deprived of the right to vote and to be elected, the right to political activity in any sphere and the right to be a member of a political party;

f) they shall not be permitted to be members of labour unions, business or professional associations;

g) they shall be prohibited from the following activities for a period of no less than 10 years after serving their sentence:

    1) to be engaged in independent professions or in business of any kind, to own shares in a business, or to manage or control a business;

    2) to apply for any position except a lowly one;

    3) to work as a teacher, preacher, editor, writer or radio reporter;

h) they shall be required to accept restrictions on their living space and dwelling place and may be enlisted for public works;

i) they shall be deprived of all licences, concessions and privileges given to them previously as well as the right to own a car.

Article IX
Penalties for the Criminals.

1. They may be imprisoned or interned for a period of 10 years to perform reconstruction and reparations work. Internment for political reasons after 8 May, 1945 may be taken into account.

2. Their property may be partially or totally confiscated (to be used for reparations). Where property is partially confiscated, preference shall be given to the confiscation of capital property. The necessary means of everyday life shall be left to them.

3. They shall be deprived of the right to occupy any official posts, including those of a notary and attorney.

4. They shall be deprived of the right to receive pensions and allowances from public funds.

5. They shall be deprived of the right to vote and to be elected, the right to political activity in any sphere and the right to be a member of a political party.

6. They shall not be allowed to become members of labour unions, business or professional associations

7. They shall be prohibited from the following for a period of no less than 5 years after serving their sentence:

    a) to be engaged in independent professions or in a business of any kind, to possess shares in it, to manage it or to control it;

    b) to apply for any position except a lowly one.

    c) to work as a teacher, preacher, editor, writer or radio reporter.

8. They shall be obliged to accept limitations on their living space and dwelling place and may be enlisted for public works;

9. They shall be deprived of all licences, concessions and privileges granted to them previously as well as the right to own a car.

10. On the consideration of the Commanders of the zones, the zone regulations may include penalties that forbid the criminals to leave the zone without permission.

Article X
The Penalties for Minor Criminals.

If according to the tribunal investigation, a person has been classified as belonging to the category of minor criminals, he may be put on probation. The probation period shall be no less than 2 years, but, as a rule, shall not exceed 3 years. The final definition of the category of such persons, making them liable to these penalties, shall be dependent upon their behaviour during the probation period. During the probation period the following penalties shall be applied:

1. They shall be forbidden for the period of probation:

   a) to conduct a business as an owner, a co-owner, manager or administrator, to supervise or control a business, to acquire a business completely or partially, to have a share in or to participate in it either in full or in part;

   b) to work as a teacher, preacher, writer, editor or radio reporter.

2. If at the time his category is being defined, a minor criminal is the owner of a independent business or owns shares in an independent business, his participation in such a business may be blocked.

3. The term 'business' used in paragraphs 1a and 2 of this article shall not include small handicraft shops, retail shops, farms and other businesses employing less than 20 persons.

4. Material valuables acquired by the use of political connections or special National-Socialist measures such as aryanisation and armaments production, shall be confiscated.

5. During the probation period, penalties additional to those stated in Article XI may be applied, suitably chosen and modified and, in particular:

   a) limitation on independent professions and teaching students;

   b) concerning civilian officials: the reduction of a pension, retirement or demotion in post or lower salary, cancelling of promotion, transfer from the position of a salaried to that of a wage-earning employee.

6. Internment in a labour camp or confiscation of all property shall not be necessary.

7. On the consideration of the Commanders of the zones, the zone laws may include penalties forbidding minor criminals to leave the zone without permission.

8. On the consideration of the Commanders of the zones, the zone laws may include penalties forbidding them to be elected, to be engaged in any political activity or to be members of political parties. They may be also deprived of the right to vote.

9. They may be obliged to report periodically to the local police.

Article XI
Penalties for Fellow-Travellers.

The following penalties may be applied to fellow-travellers on the consideration of the Commanders of the zones:
1. They may be obliged to report periodically to the local police.
2. They shall be forbidden to leave the zone or Germany without permission.
3. Civilians in this category may not stand as candidates for election on any level, but they may vote.
4. Furthermore, as regards civilian officials, they may be ordered to retire or transfer to a lower post or to a job with lower salary or have any promotion received while that person was a member of the NSDAP cancelled.
   Similar measures may be applied to persons working in business enterprises, including agriculture and forestry.
5. They may be ordered to pay, on a single occasion or repeatedly, a payment on account of reparations. When the sum of the payment has been decided, account shall be taken of the period of membership of the followers, their membership and occasional payments, their wealth and income, family situation and other relevant factors.

Article XII
Rehabilitated Persons.

No penalties shall be applied to persons rehabilitated by the Tribunal.

Article XIII
Persons belonging to the categories defined by Articles II–VI above who are guilty of certain military or other crimes may be prosecuted, irrespective of their classification in accordance with this Instruction. Application of the penalties in accordance with this Instruction shall not exclude criminal prosecution for the same crime.

Issued in Berlin, 12 October, 1946
Major-General R. Noiret
Colonel-General P. A. Kurochkin
Lieutenant-General Lucius D. Clay
Major-General G. W. E. D. Erskine
for Lieutenant-General B. G. Robertson

APPENDIX 'A'
PART I

The following is a list of the categories of persons who, due to the nature of the crimes allegedly committed by them, as stated in paragraphs 1–10 of Article II of Part II of this Instruction, as well as the posts they occupied, shall be thoroughly investigated, and should the results of these investigations call for consideration by the courts, they should be prosecuted as main criminals, and punished if found guilty.

A. The German Secret Service, including Intelligence (Abwehrbeamter):
1. All executive officials of the National Department of Security (Reichssicherheitshauptamt or RSHA), its organisations and offices under its immediate control.
2. All officials of the Secret Field Police (Geheime Feldpolizei or GFP) from the post of Director (Feldpolizedirektor) and above.
3. All executive officials of the experimental bureau of the Reich Aviation Ministry.

B. Security Police (SIPO):
1. All members of the Secret State Police (Geheime Staatspolizei or Gestapo).
2. The executive officials of the Border Control Police Komissariats (Grenzpolizei-Komissariats or Greko).
3. All executive officials of the main departments (Leitstellen) and departments (Stellen) of the Criminal Police (Kriminalpolizei).

C. Order Police (Ordnungpolizei or Orpo).
All officials of the following police departments who since 1935 held the rank of Colonel or equivalent and above:
   a) guard police (Schutzpolizei or Schupo),
   b) village police (Gendarmerie or Gend),
   c) waterways police (Wasserschutzpolizei or SW),
   d) anti-aircraft police (Luftschutzpolizei or L. Schupo),
   e) technical assistants (technische Nothilfe).

D. NSDAP:
1. All officials of NSDAP from a Section Head of a Kreis (Area) and above (Amtsleiter der Kreisleitung).
2. All members of the corps of the political leaders of the Party with the rank of political chief (Einsatzleiter) and above and all members of Ordensburgen school staff

(school guarantor), Schulungsburgen (school councillor) of Adolf Hitler Schools and National-Socialist training institutes (Nationalpolitische Erziehungsanstalten).

3. All members of the NSDAP faction in the Reichstag (Reichstagfakzione) prior to January, 1933.

4. The following leaders of the offices of the Reich Foodstuffs Department (Reichsnerschtand):

a) all agricultural Land leaders and their deputies (Landesbauernhohre);

b) all leaders of central and district trade offices (Hauptvereinigungen and Wirtschaftsvferbände);

c) all agricultural Kreis leaders (Kreisbauernführer);

d) all leaders of a Land Department of forestry (Landesforstamter)

5. All officials of a district chamber of commerce (Gauwirtschaftskammern), which were empowered to give guidance for the benefit of the Party.

6. Economic Gau advisors (Gauwirtschaftsberäter).

E. NSDAP Organisations:

1. Armed (Waffen) SS – all officers of the rank of major (Sturmbannführer) and above, all members of the SS Death's-Head Formations (Totenkopfverbände) and all SS auxiliary women's detachments during the war in the concentration camps (SS-Helferinen, SS-Kriegshelferinen in Konzentrazionslagern).

2. General (Allgemeine) SS – all officers of the rank of Untersturmführer and above.

3. SA – all officers of the rank of Sturmbannführer and above.

4. GU – all officers of the rank of Bannführer and its equivalent in the BDM (Bund Deutsche Mädel) and above and all members of 'Mobile Commands' (G.U. – Patrol Service) under SS control ('Schnelkommandos' – G.U. Streifendienst), who were born before 1 January, 1919.

5. NSKK – all officers of the rank of Standartenführer and above.

6. NSFK – all officers of the rank of Standartenführer and above.

7. NS – The Union of German Students (Deutscher Studentenbund) – all executive officials in the State and district offices (Reichsstudentenführung and Gaustudentenführungen).

8. NS – Union of Assistant Professors (Dozentenbund) – all executives of the level of the Reich and Gau.

9. NS – Womens' Organisation (Frauenschaft) – all executive officials at the level of the Reich and Gau.

F. Associated NSDAP Organisations:

1. German Labour Front (Deutsche Arbeitsfront):

a) all executive officials of German Labour Front (DAF) in the Central Department of DAF;

b) all executive officials of DAF in General military labour districts I, II, III, IV (Kriegshauptarbeitsgebieten);

c) all members of the High Chamber of Honour and Discipline (Ober Ehren- und Disziplinärhof);

d) all executive officials of the DAF in district departments of foreign organisations (Gauwaltung Auslandsorganisation).

2. NS-Charitable organisations (Volkswolfahrt) – all executive officials from chief of a department at the Reich level and above.

3. NS-Organisations for providing for the victims of war (Kriegsopferverzorgung or NSKOV) – all executive officials from chief of a department at the level of the Reich and above.

4. NS- The Union of German Technology (Bund Deutscher Technik) – all executive officials from chief of a department at the Reich level and above.

5. NS-The Reich Union of German Employees (Reichsbund der Deutsche Beamten) – all employees from head of a department at Reich or Gau level and above.

6. NS-German Union of Doctors (Deutscher Ärtzebund) – all executive officials from chief of a department at Reich and Gau level and above.

7. NS-Union of Teachers (Lehrerbund) – all executive officials from chief of a department at Reich and Gau level and above.

8. NS-Reich Union of Lawyers (Reichtsvorärebund) – all employees from chief of a department at Reich and Gau level and above.

G. Organisations under the Control of the NSDAP:

1. NS- German Alumni Association (Alterherrenbund) – all members of the circle of leaders at Gau level and above.

2. The Reich Union of The German Family (Reichsbund deutscher Familie) – all executive officials at Reich level.

3. The Organisation of The German Community (deutscher Gemeindetag) – all employees of the organisation of The German Community.

4. NS-Reich Sports Union (Reichsbund fur Leibensübungen) – all sports leaders at Reich level and all the chiefs of district sports groups (Reichssportführer and Sportbereichsführer).

H. Other Nazi organisations:

1. The Reich Labour Service (Reichsarbeitsdienst or RAD) – all male employees from senior labour leader and above (Oberarbeitführer), and all women of the rank of senior

staff leader (Stabssoberführerin) and above.

The Reich Union for the Colonies (Reichskolonialbund) – all officials in a colonial-political department attached to the Reich Leadership of NSDAP.

3. The Union of Germans Abroad (Volksbund fur das Deutschentum im Ausland or VDA) – all officials in departments of the Reich and Gau, who had worked since 1935 inside Germany and all the leaders of peoples and Land groups (Volksgruppenführer and Landesgruppenführer) outside Germany.

4. NS-Union of Veterans (Reichskriegerbund) – all officials of the rank of district leader of veterans (Gaukriegerführer) and above.

5. All the Reich Chambers of Culture (Reichskulturkammern) – all presidents, vice-presidents and managers; all members of the State Cultural Council (Reichskulturrat), the State Cultural Senate (Reichskultursenat) and presiding senators (Presidialrete).

6. Fichte German Union (Deutscher Fichtebund) – all executive officials.

7. The Reich Security Service (Reichssicherheitsdienst) – all officials from chief of a department (Dienststellenleiter) and above

I – J. Nazi Party Orders:

1. NS – Order of Blood (Blutorden) of 9 November, 1923 – all those so decorated.

2. Honorary badge for the first 100,000 members (The Golden Party Badge) – all those so decorated.

3. The medal for prolonged meritorious membership of the NSDAP – all who have had 1st class medals for 25 years.

K. Government Officials:

A Note. This classification applies only to persons who were appointed to one of the posts listed after 30 January, 1933 or who occupied those posts at that time and stayed in them in spite of the subsequent purges that were performed by the Nazis.

1. All politicians, including the Reich Minister (Reichsminister), the State Minister (Staatsminister), the State Secretary (Staatssekretär), the Reich Vice-Regent (Reichsstaathalter), the President of a Province (Oberpresident) and officials, heads of bureaux, deputies or commissioners of the corresponding rank.

2. All former German Ambassadors since 30 January, 1933.

3. All officials of the rank of Director of a Ministry (Ministerialdirektor) in departments of the Reich or the equivalent rank in the government offices, that existed before 30 January, 1933; all officials of the rank of Ministerial Councillor (Ministerialrat) in Reich or Government offices, that were set up after 30 January, 1933 for new purposes as well as in the offices in the countries and territories occupied or ruled by Germany.

4. All officials who since 1934 occupied one of the following posts:

a) Reich or Special Commissioner (Reichsbevollmächtigter or Sondervollmächtigter);

b) Reich Commissioner (Reichskomissar);

c) General Commissioner (Generalkomissar);

d) General Inspector (Generalinspektor);

e) Representative and Representative of the Military District (Beauftragter and Verkreichsbeauftragter);

f) Reich and Special Commissioner on Labour (Reichs- and Sonderträghänder der Arbeit).

L. German Armed Forces and Militarists:

1. NS-leading officers (Führungsofizierer) – all regular NS Führungsofiziere of departments in the OKW – The Supreme General Command of the Armed Forces, OKH – The Supreme General Command of the Army, OKM – the Supreme General Command of the Navy, OKL – the Supreme General Command of the Luftwaffe and above.

2. Officers of the General Staff – all the officers of the German General Staff, who since 4 February, 1938 belonged to the General Staff of the Armed Forces (Wehrmachtsführungssstab), in OKW – Supreme General Command of the Army, OKH – Supreme General Command of the Army, OKM – Supreme General Command of the Navy or OKL – Supreme General Command of Luftwaffe.

3. Leaders, and deputies of the leaders of military and civil administration in the countries and territories formerly occupied by Germany.

4. All former officers of a Freikorps and 'the Black Reichswehr' (Freikorps, 'Schwarze Reichswehr').

M. Members of Independent Professions and Local Enterprises:

1. All leaders of the military economy (Vehrwirtschaftsführer), who were appointed after 1 January, 1942.

2. Chambers of Commerce (Wirtschaftskammern) – all executive officials and their deputies in Wirtschaftskammern at Reich and Gau level.

3. Reich groups of commerce and industry (Reichsgruppen der gewerblichen Wirtschaft) – all the chairmen, presidents and their deputies.

4. Reich transport groups (Reichsverkehrsgruppen) – all the chairmen, presidents and their deputies.

5. Economic groups Wirtschaftsgruppen – all the chairmen, presidents and their deputies.

6. Reich Associations (Reichsvereinigungen) – all the chairmen, presidents and their

deputies at Reich level.

7. Advertisement Council of the German Economy (Verberat der deutschen Wirtschaft) – all presidents and president's managers.

8. Reich Commissioners (Reichskomissars) – all commissioners responsible for shipment of raw materials and supplying industry.

N. Lawyers:

1. The President and Vice-President of the German Academy of Law (Academy fur Deutsche Recht).

2. Chiefs and permanent officials of the Hans Kerrl Germeinschaftslager.

3. All judges, general prosecutors (Oberrechtsanwalt) and all public prosecutors as well as managers of people's courts (Volksgerichtshof).

4. All judges, public prosecutors and officials of the Party, SS- and SA-courts.

5. The President and Vice-President of the Reich Judicial Control Department (Reichsjustizprüfungamt).

6. The presidents of the courts:

   a) the Reich Court (Reichsgericht);

   b) the Reich Labour Court (Reichsarbeitsgericht);

   c) the Reich Court on Land Succession (Reichserbhofgericht);

   d) the Reich Court on Succession (Reichsergesundheitsgericht);

   e) the Reich Financial Court (Reichsfinanzhof);

   f) the Reich Administrative Court (Reichsverwaltungsgericht);

   g) the Reich Court of Honour (Reichsehrengerichtshof);

   h) the Reich College of Court Advocates (Reichsrechtsanwaltskammer);

   i) the Reich College of Notaries (Reichsnotärkammer);

   j) the Reich Patent Bureau (Reichspatentanwaltskammer);

   k) the Reich Chamber of Economic Control (Reichskammer der Wirschaftsprüfer).

7. The Presidents of High Provincial Courts (Oberlandesgerichte), who were appointed after 31 December, 1938.

8. The Prosecutors, Senior Prosecutors and General Prosecutors of High Provincial Courts (Rechtsanwälte, Oberreichsanwälte and Generalstatsanwälte), appointed after 31 March, 1933.

9. Vice-Presidents of the Courts:

   a) the Reich Labour Court (Reichsarbeitsgericht);

   b) the Reich Court on Land Succession (Reichserbhofgericht);

   c) the Reich Court on Inheritance (Reichserbhofegericht);

   d) the Reich Administrative Court (Reichsverwaltungsgericht).

10. Chairmen:

a) of the Special Senate of the Reich Court (Sondersenat Reichsgericht);

b) Administrative assistants of the Reich Ministry of Justice (Personalreferenten Reichsjustizministerium).

O. Other Groups of Persons:

1. War criminals.

2. All persons, who informed on opponents of National-Socialism or in some other way encouraged their arrest, or called for or used force against political or religious opponents of the National-Socialist tyranny.

3. Officers of shock brigades and factory units (Stosstruppen and Werkscharen) in the production plants.

4. Rectors of universities, chairmen of trustees councils, heads of teacher's colleges and heads of institutions equivalent to universities, who worked after 1934 if they were the members of NSDAP or its groups, as well as all those who were appointed after 1938, irrespective of their Party membership.

PART II

The following is a list of the categories of persons, who, by the nature of their alleged crimes, as stated in paragraphs 'A', 'B', and 'C' of Article 3 of Part II of this Instruction, shall be thoroughly investigated and, should the results of the investigations call for consideration by the courts, they should be prosecuted as criminals, and punished if found guilty.

A. German Secret Service, including Intelligence (Abwehrämter):

1. All officers and other staff of the RSGA (the State General Department of Security), its organisations and the agencies under its direct control not included in the category of main criminals.

2. All persons who served in the German intelligence service abroad after 30 January, 1933, including those persons who served in the military intelligence service or in organisations and units under the control of or dependent upon the German Secret Service.

B. Security Police (Sipo):

1. All persons who were officers of the Border Police since 1937 and not included in the category of main criminals.

2. All officials of the Criminal Police, starting of the rank of Commissioner of the Criminal Police and above, and not included in the category of main criminals.

3. All officials of the postal censorship service (Briefprüfungstellen), not included in the category of the main criminals.

C. Order Police (Orpo):
1. All police officers of the guard police, gendarmerie, waterways police, anti-aircraft police, technical emergency police, fire police, administrative police, special police, colonial police and auxiliary police, who were promoted after 30 January, 1938 or who remained in the service after 31 December, 1937, despite repeated purges.
2. All police officers who have ever served as such in the territories formerly occupied by Germany, in any military formations or in special military units (Einsatzgruppe) or in guard police or security police (SD).
3. All officials of the administrative police, attached to the Gestapo or SD.

D. NSDAP:
1. All salaried and honorary responsible officials and staff, starting at the lowest rank in the Party structures (main and subordinate), and in institutions and academies set up by the NSDAP.
2. All members of the corps of political leaders, not included in the category of main criminals.
3. All members of the NSDAP faction in the Reichstag, not included in the category of main criminals.
4. All members of the NSDAP who joined the Party before 1 May, 1937.
5. All members of NSDAP, who after four years' service in the Hitler Youth and upon reaching the age of 18 were selected to join the Party.
6. All members of NSDAP, notwithstanding their time of joining, in the following organisations;
  a) the Reich Press Chamber (Reichspressekammer);
  b) the Reich Radio Chamber (Reichsrundfunkkammer);
  c) German Academy in Munich (Deutsche Akademie Munich);
  d) German Christian Movement (Deutsche Kristenbevegung);
  e) German Religious Movement (Deutsche Glaubensbevegung);
  f) Research Institute on the Jewish Question (Institut zu Erforschung der Jüdenfrage);
  g) USA Friendship (Kameradschaft USA);
  h) Eastern-European Institute from 1935;
  i) The State Academy of Race and Hygiene (Staatsakademie für Rassen und Gesundheitspflege).
7. All regular officers of the Armed Forces (Wehrmacht), who joined the NSDAP and officers who, before joining the Wehrmacht, were members of the NSDAP and did not sever their contacts with the NSDAP thereafter.

8. All executive officials of the Reich Ration Food Supply Department not included in the category of main criminals as well as the officials of the Forestry Department (Regierungsvorstämter).

E. NSDAP Organisations:

1.Waffen SS – all members not included in the category of main criminals, excluding those recruited to the organisation and not promoted after being recruited, up to the rank of warrant officer; all personnel of concentration camps not included in the category of main criminals.

2. Algemeine SS and other organisations – all members not included in the category of main criminals, including the so-called 'supporting members', who joined the organisation after 31 December, 1938 or, if they joined earlier, those who paid more than 10 reichsmarks monthly, or those who made other sizable payments to the SS.

3. SA – all officers, not included in the category of main criminals, from warrant officer and above, because they fulfilled the duties of such in the SA, as well as members who joined the SA before 1 April, 1933.

4. HJ and BDM (Hitler Youth) – all officers, not included in the category of main criminals, of the rank of permanent warrant officer and above. All officers of HJ and Deutsche Jungvolk, who worked in the field of education and information and all members of 'movable commands' (HJ patrol service), which were placed under the control of the SS, and who were born after 1 January, 1919.

Note. See Appendix 'A', Part I, Section E, Paragraph 4 concerning the main criminals to compare with this section on the criminals.

5. NSKK – all officers of the rank of Sturmführer and above, if not included in the category of main criminals.

6. NSFK – all officers of the rank of Sturmführer and above, if not included in the category of main criminals.

7. NS-Union of German Students – all officials not included in the category of main criminals.

8. NS-Council of University Teachers – all officials not included in the category of main criminals.

9. NS-Women's Organisation – all officials of the rank of Blockfrauenschaftsleiterin and above, if not included in the category of main criminals.

F. NSDAP Branches:

1. German Labour Front or DAF, including 'Kraft dürch Freude' (Strength through Joy) union:
   a) all officials not included in the category of main criminals;
   b) all executives of the Research Institute of Labour (Arbeitswissenschaftlichesinstitut);
   c) all managers (Betriebsobmänner) and their deputies (Betriebswalter, Betriebswarte) of DAF enterprises.
2. NSV – all officials not included in the category of main criminals.
3. NSKOV – all officials not included in the category of main criminals.
4. NSBDT – all officials not included in the category of main criminals.
5. RDB – all officials not included in the category of main criminals.
6. NSDAB – all officials not included in the category of main criminals.
7. NS-Union of German Sisters of Charity (Reichsbund deutscher Schwestern) – all officials.
8. NSLB – all officials not included in the category of main criminals.
9. NS-Reich Union of Lawyers – all officials not included in the category of the main criminals.

G. Organisations that were under NSDAP Control:

1. NS-German Alumni Union – all officials not included in the category of main criminals.
2. The Reich 'German Family' Union – all officials not included in the category of main criminals.
3. The 'German Community' organisation – all officials not included in the category of main criminals.
4. NS-Reich Sports Union – all officials, not included in the category of main criminals.
5. All officials of the following organisations:
   a) German Women's Labour Organisation (Deutsches Frauenwerk);
   b) German Students' Organisation (Deutsche Studentenschaft);
   c) German Union of University Teachers (Deutscher Dozentenbund);
   d) the Reich Union of Teachers of the German Universities (Reichsdozentenschaft);
   e) the Union of German Hunters (Deutsche Jägerschaft).

H. Other Nazi Organisations:

I. The Reich Office of Labour (RAD) – all officers of the rank of Feldmeister for men and Mädenführrerinen for women, not included in the category of main criminals.

2. The Reich Council of Colonies – all officials who joined the service after 1 January, 1935, if not included in the category of main criminals.

3. The Union of Germans Abroad – all officials, appointed after 1 January, 1935, not included in the category of main criminals.

4. NS-Union of Veterans – all executive officials from the level of kreis and above.

5. The Reich Chamber of Culture and its affiliated bodies, such as the Reich Chamber of Writers, the Reich Press Service and the Reich Radio Chamber – all officials not included in the category of main criminals.

6. The German Fichte Union – all members not included in the category of main criminals.

7. The Reich Security Service – all members not included in the category of main criminals.

8. All officials of the following institutions:

    a) Research Institute on the Jewish Question;

    b) International institution (Weltdienst);

    c) German Academy in Munich;

    d) State Academy of Race and Health;

    e) American Institute (Amerika-Institut);

    f) Eastern-European Institute;

    g) Ibero-American Institute (Ibero-Amerikanisches Institut);

    h) German Foreign Institute (Deutsches Ausland-Institut).

I.–J. Nazi Party Orders:

1. Koburg Badge – all holders.

2. The 'Nuremberg's Party convention' of 1929 Badge– all holders.

3. The 'SA convention in Braunschweig' in 1931 Badge – all holders.

4. Gold Hitler Youth badge – all bearers.

5. The medal for prolonged meritorious service in the NSDAP – all holders not included in the category of the main criminals.

6. Honorary badge of Gau NSDAP (Gau Erenzaihen) – all holders.

K. The State Officials:

1. All officials of the Ministry of Foreign Affairs, Embassies, Representatives, General Consulates, Missions, of the rank of ministerial counsellor (Ministerialrat) or the rank of attaché.

2. All officials in high positions, promoted to these posts after 1 April, 1933 not as part of a routine career, and without professional qualifications.

3. All officials who occupied the following official posts after 1934:

a) commissioner (Bevollmechtiger);

b) inspector;

c) commissioner of labour and other fields as well as their deputies;

d) commissar;

e) deputies of the persons of these ranks and who occupied the posts listed under the category of main criminals;

f) Reich Engineer (Reichseinsatzingenieur and Arbeitseinsatzingenieur);

g) a commissioner, including an armaments commissioner (Obmann and Rüstungsobmann).

4. All members of the German Reichstag or the Prussian State Council (Staatsrat) from 1 January, 1934.

5. All officials of the Reich Ministry of People's Information and Propaganda and leaders of its regional and affiliated bodies from *kreis* level and above as well as all employees of the Nazi bodies that participated in political propaganda in an oral or written form.

6. All high-ranking officials of the civil service of the Reich Ministry of Armaments and Military Production, Ministry of Church Affairs; Gau commissioners on housing and their deputies.

7. Senior financial presidents (Oberfinanzpräsidenten).

8. Chairmen of [regional] governments, Landraten, Burgermeistern.

L. The German Armed Forces and Militarists:

1. NS-leading officers – all officers, regular or reserve, not included in the category of the criminals.

2. Officers of the General Staff, who worked there since 4 February, 1938 and not included in the category of main criminals.

3. All military and civilian officials empowered with special authority, including the leaders and their deputies of any functional and territorial department of a military or civilian administration in the occupied countries and territories as well as the officials of RUKA (armaments and military production), excluding those who are already included in the category of main criminals.

4. All officials of the Raw Materials Association.

5. All military commandants and their deputies in the cities and settlements.

6. Werhmacht – all permanent officers of the German Armed Forces of the rank of Major-General and its equivalents and above, on the condition that they were promoted to these ranks after 1 June, 1936, as well as the specialist officers of the Armed Forces of the rank of Colonel and above.

7. The Organisation Todt (OT) and the Transport Group Speer – all officers from the

post of the chief of a unit (Einsatzleiter) and above.

8. All members of training staffs and administrative officials of military academies and officers' schools (Kadetenanstalten).

9. All professors, lecturers and writers in the field of military research since 1933.

10. All members of the Black Reichswehr and all members of the Freikorps, who became members of NSDAP, not included in the category of main criminals.

M. Members of Independent Professions and Private Entrepreneurs:

1. Verwirtschaftsführer – all Verwirtschaftsführern appointed by the Ministry of Economics and not included in the category of main criminals.

2. The Chamber of Commerce – all officials of chambers of commerce, excluding those already included in the category of main criminals.

3. The Reich Groups of Trade and Commerce – all responsible officials of the groups, high committees, special committees, general bodies and special bodies.

4. The Reich transportation groups – all officials of the transportation groups.

5. Economic groups – all officials of economic groups.

6. Reich associations – all officials of the state associations, including heads of departments and chairmen, their deputies, directors of main committees, special committees, main and special units.

7. The Advertising Council of the German Economy – all officials, not included in the category of main criminals.

8. The leading officials of the Reich distribution organisations (Reichsstellen) and subordinate distribution organisations (Bewirtschaftungsstellen).

9. Business institutions, including financial institutions, that had an interest in, and were controlled by the Reich, NSDAP or any of its bodies or branches since 1 April, 1933, – all presidents, members of supervisory boards of and directors, director's managers and managers.

10–I. Private entrepreneurs in industry, commerce, crafts, agriculture and forestry, insurance institutions, transport, banks, and so on. Enterprises which, based on their capital, number of workers, the kind of product or for any other reasons are important and significant:

All owners, proprietors, tenants, companions, including the owners of more than 25% of shares, the chairmen of executive boards and supervisory boards and other persons with a decisive influence on management, as far as these persons were the members of the NSDAP or its bodies, or not being a NSDAP member, acquired their position thanks to their connections with the NSDAP.

10–II. Non-profit enterprises and charitable institutions; enterprises that are important due to their range of their activity:

All executive officials, managers, members of board of directors, and boards of supervision, councillors and other persons, who had decisive influence on the management or performed a function of supervision, because they were the members of the NSDAP or any of its bodies, or, not being members, acquired them due to their connections with the NSDAP.

11. Independent professions (doctors, lawyers, pharmacists, architects, engineers, actors, writers, journalists and others):

a) all administrators, members of boards of directors, managers, executive officials and members of the boards of professional and social bodies, including the courts of honour, and all advocates, who practiced in the Party's courts, SA and SS courts;

b) other representatives of the liberal professions who, due to their membership in the NSDAP or in any other of its bodies, gained special benefits.

N. Lawyers:

1. Candidates for the ranks of the German Law Academy.

2. Presidents and other permanent judges and permanent chiefs of departments of the prosecutor's office and special courts.

3. Chairmen, judges and public prosecutors of the military courts (Standgerichte).

4. Presidents and Vice-Presidents of:

a) the Reich patent bureau;

b) the Reich insurance department and Reich Court of Veterans (Reichsversicherungsamt and Reichsversorgunsgericht);

c) a provincial court on land inheritance (Landeserbhofgericht).

5. Vice-presidents and presidents of the Senate of the Reich Court who were appointed after 31 December, 1938 and the constant members of the High Disciplinary Senate attached to the Reich Court.

6. Vice-Presidents of:

a) the Reich Court of Health Protection (Reichserbgszundheitsgericht);

b) the Reich Financial Court;

c) the Reich Board of Attorneys (Reichsrechtssanwaltkammer);

d) the Reich Board of Notaries (Reichsnotärkammer);

e) the Reich Board of Patent Attorneys (Reichspatentanwaltskammer);

f) the Reich Board of Economic Supervisors (Reichskammer fur Wirtschaftsprüfer) as well as all permanent members of high courts of honour for lawyers, patent attorneys, notaries and economic supervisors.

7. Presidents of a High Regional Court and Prosecutors-General, excluding those who are included in the category of main criminals, as well as Vice-Presidents of Main Regional Courts

8. Presidents of Disciplinary Boards for Justice officials.

9. Presidents of the Regional Courts (Landgerichte).

10. Prosecutors (Oberstaatsanwalt) in the Landgericht.

11. Administrative Assistants (Personalreferenten) in Courts.

12. Permanent executive officers and permanent members of the Reich Office of Judicial Investigations (Reichsjustitzprufungamt).

13. Presidents of Boards of Attorneys, the Board of Notaries and the Board of Patent Attorneys in High Region Courts (Oberlandesgerichte).

14. Presidents and Vice-Presidents in:

  a) the Court of Property Inheritance (Fideikommisgericht);

  b) High Court on Navigation (Schiffartsobergericht);

  c) High Prize Court (Oberpreisenhof).

15. Presidents, vice-presidents and permanent members of the courts of honour for independent professions at Reich and Gau level.

O. Other groups of persons:

1. Warrant officers of the storm troop brigades and factory groups.

2. Persons who occupy the post of an authorised instructor (Vertraunsleiter) or the head of a youth group (Jungenwalter) in schools of any type.

3. The Rectors of Universities and Chairmen of Boards of Trustees, heads of teachers' colleges and institutes of university level, who were appointed after 1934 and are not included in the category of main criminals.

4. All other persons who disseminated Nazi and Hitler's ideology.

5. Persons, who after 1 April, 1933 applied for or were granted German citizenship or acquired it outside the lawful procedure of marriage or adoption.

PART III

The following is a list of the categories of people who shall be thoroughly investigated, and if their guilt is proved, according to paragraphs 1 and 2 of Article 4, Part II of this Instruction, they shall be prosecuted as minor criminals and punished if they are guilty.

1. Those who applied for membership in the organisations of the SS and its bodies.

2. Persons who joined the SA after 1 April, 1933.

3. Persons who were members of the HJ and BDM before 25 March, 1939.

4. Warrant-officers of RAD of the rank of field commander (Feldmeister) or a commander of a women's group (Mädenführerin) and below.

5. Persons who joined the NSDAP after 1 May, 1937 as well as all who applied for membership of the NSDAP.

6. Persons who, being civil servants in educational institutions or the press, were promoted unusually quickly after 1 May, 1933.

7. Persons who profited from the transfer of the property received by plunder of the former occupied territories by aryanisation or confiscation on political, religious or racial grounds.

8. Persons who occupied leading or administrative posts in the military or civilian administration of the former occupied territories.

9. Persons who made valuable donations to the Party.

10. Members of political parties or organisations in Germany that encouraged the NSDAP's seizure of power such as, for example, the Tannenbergbund and the AltDeutscher verband.

11. Leading officials of the German Red Cross, especially appointed after 1 January, 1933.

12. Members of the German Christian Movement and the German Religious Movement.

13. Members of NSKK, HSFK, NSDSTB, NSDOB, and NSF.

14. Holders of the Spanish Cross, of the Austrian, Sudeten, or Memel medals, Danzig Cross, the SA military-sports badge and the RAD medal for merit.

15. Parents or trustees who agreed to bring up their children in National-Socialist education institutions, schools of different orders (Ordensschulen) or in Adolf Hitler schools.

16. Persons who received financial reward through the NSDAP.

17. Persons who, due to National-Socialist influence, managed to avoid military service or service at the Front.

18. Employees of important commercial, industrial, agricultural and financial institutions who hold the post of managing director, director, president, vice-president, manager (Geschäftsführer), production manager and all members of a board, chairmen of control commissions and their deputies, general engineers, as long as they decided the technical policy of a production plant and had the right to hire and fire employees.

12 October, 1946

Ф. 46; оп. 5; д. 194; л. 77 об.-104 об. Типографский экз.

SOVIET COUNTER-ESPIONAGE OFFICERS

Arkhipenkov, Alexei Vasilievitch – born in 1912 in the settlement of Yasnaya Poliyana in the Spas-Dieminsky district of the Kaluga region, joined the State Security Service in 1938. During the Great Patriotic War [World War II] was the Chief of NKVD Special Section of 49th Armoured Brigade in the Briansk and Kalinin Fronts, the Chief of 'Smersh' CES of 1st Tank Army of the Voronezh Front, Deputy Chief of 'Smersh' CES of 1st Guards Tank Army of 1st Ukrainian and later of 1st Byelorussian Fronts. In 1945, assigned to the command of NKVD of the USSR and appointed Chief of Operational Section in Germany. In 1947, assigned to work at the Leningrad District Department of the Ministry of State Security. In May the same year, retired at his own request.

Bandasov, Dmitri Petrovitch – born in 1916 in the village of Berestok in the Sievsk region of the Briansk district, joined the Security Service in March, 1939. Investigator, then senior investigator, of the Briansk General Department of the NKVD, then in the NKVD Special Department of the north-western front, 5th Army of the 1st Byelorussian Front. From March, 1944 to June, 1945, Deputy Chief of 1st Sub-Section of 4th Section of 'Smersh' CES of the 1st Byelorussian Front. Retired from the State Security Service in 1963.

Barsukov, Vladimir Konstantinovitch – born in 1907 in the settlement of Avdeevka in the Avdeev region of the Stalin district (Ukranian SSR), joined the Security Service in April, 1936. Served in different posts in the military counter-espionage service. From 1 April, 1944, Chief of 3rd Section of the 'Smersh' CES of the 1st Byelorussian Front. Retired from the Security Service of the Soviet Army in 1955. Died on 9 December, 1969 in the city of Gorky.

Bystrov, Boris Alexandrovitch – born in 1907 in the city of Gorky, in the Security Service since 1941. Served in different posts in special departments of the Briansk, Byelorussian, and 2nd Baltic Fronts. From 3 February to 24 October, 1945, Chief of the 4th Sub-Section of the 'Smersh' CES of 3rd Assault Army of the 1st Byelorussian Front. On 1 November, demobilised and transferred to the staff register of the USSR Interior Ministry. Died in 1967.

Chernykh, Nikolai Aleksandrovitch – born in 1904 in the city of Perm, in the Security Service since 1928. Served in various posts in the OGPU Department in the Perm region, then in the special NKVD Section in the Sverdlovsk District. From 18 November, 1944 to 13 November, 1945, Deputy Chief of the 4th Section of the 'Smersh' CED of the 1st Byelorussian Front. On 14 January, 1955, demobilised to the KGB Reserve attached at the USSR Council of Ministers.

Deriabin, Anatoly Georgievitch – born in 1904 in the village of Zapolskaya in the Verchotursky region of the Urals district, in the State Security Service since September, 1930. Served in various posts in SS of OGPU-NKVD of the Urals Military Region. From July, 1943 to January, 1946, Deputy Chief of the 'Smersh' CED of the 76th Infantry Corps of the 3rd Assault Army of the 1st Byelorussian Front. On 18 November, 1947 assigned to CED of the Urals Military District.

Dubrovsky, Konstantin Vasilievitch – born in 1904 in the village of Dugna in the Dugna region of the Tula district, in the Security Service since December, 1929. Served in various command posts in special secions of the NKVD Departments in the Moscow, Tula, Kalinin districts and the Baltic and Western Military Districts, later the Briansk, South-Western, Southern and Ukrainian Fronts. In 1945–6, Deputy Chief of the Operative Section of the NKVD of the Group of the Soviet Forces in Germany. On 4 June, 1949 demobilised to the reserve of the USSR MSS.

Gershgorin, Nohim Nahmonovich – born in 1913 in the town of Dobrusz in the Gomel District (Byelorussian Soviet Socialist Republic), in the Security Service since April, 1938. Served in various posts in the NKVD Department of the Vitebsk District. During the war, in the military counter-espionage service of the Briansk, Central and Byelorussian Fronts. From 3 May to 15 August, 1945, Chief of 2nd Sub-Section of 4th Section of 'Smersh' CED of the 1st Byelorussian Front. In 1952, demobilised to the reserve of the USSR Ministry of Defence.

Hazin, Isaak Grigorievich – born in 1910. Served in various posts in the NKVD Department in the Kamienietz-Podolsk region, Special NKVD Department of the Moscow Military District, of the 60th Reserve Army (from January, 1942, the 3rd Assault Army). From 20 September, 1944 to August, 1945, Deputy Chief of the 'Smersh' CED of the 207th Infantry Division. After the war, served in the office of the Commissioner of the USSR MGB in Germany, then assigned to territorial militia. In 1958, demobilised from the Ministry of Interior due to illness.

Helimsky, Grigory Abramovitch – born in 1912 in the city of Odessa, in Security Service since June, 1938. Occupied different positions in departments of NKVD in the Kievsky and Cherepovetsky districts, in special departments of the Kievsky Special and Leningradsky Military Districts, then the South-Western, Stalingrad, Central and 1st Byelorussian Fronts. From 1 April, 1944 to 5 October, 1945, a senior operative officer of the 3rd Section of the 'Smersh' CED of the 1st Byelorussian Front. On 29 June, 1955, demobilised due to age to the reserve of the KGB attached at the USSR CM from the Department of KGB in the Kirov district.

Karpenko, Nikolai Matveevitch – born in 1904 in the city of Moscow, in the Security Service since February, 1929. Served in various posts in EKU OGPU, in special departments of NKVD of the Ministry of Interior. During the war, in military intelligence of the Southern and the 3rd Ukrainian Fronts. From November, 1944 to 25 April, 1946, the Chief of 'Smersh' CED of the 5th Assault Army of the 1st Byelorussian Front. On 18 May, 1951 demobilised from the post of the Chief of D MSS of the Altai region.

Katyshev, Nikolai Aleksandrovitch – born in 1916 in the village of Bieriezniki in the Solnietchnogorsky region of the Moscow district. Served in the Security Service from 1941. Served in military counter-espionage service of the Western and 2nd Baltic Fronts. From 9 February to 3 October, 1945, senior investigator of the 'Smersh' CED of the 1st Byelorussian Front. On 15 April, 1946 demobilised to the reserve.

Klimenko, Ivan Isayevitch – born in 1914 in the Fiodorovsky region of the Kustanai district (Kazakh SSR), in the Security Service since 1939. Served in the NKVD departments of the Central Asian and Carpathian Military Districts. During the war, in counter-espionage service of the Briansky, Baltic and Zabaikalsky Fronts. From 9 February to 8 August, 1945, the Chief of 'Smersh' CED of the 79th Infantry Corps of the 1st Byelorussian Front. On 1 August, 1971 demobilised to the KGB attached to the USSR Council of Ministers reserve.

Kopeliansky, Daneel Grigorievitch – born in 1918, in Security Service since 1941. Served in different posts in the 'Smersh' General Counter-Espionage Department of NKO, in 3rd General Department of the USSR MGB. From 15 March, 1944 to 22 May, 1946, operations officer of the 1st Sub-Section of the 2nd Section of the 'Smersh' General Counter-Espionage Department of the Peoples Commissariat of Defence. On 3 March, 1951 demobilised with transfer to the general military registration.

Kovalienko, Nikolai Grigoryevitch – born in 1917 in the city of Kiev, in the Security Service since February, 1939. In 1970, he was Head of the Special Department of the Soviet Forces Group in Germany. Decorated with combat orders and medals. In 1974, demobilised due to age with the rank of Colonel to the reserve of the KGB attached to the USSR CM.

Kush, Lidia Maximovna – born in 1917 in the settlement of Ramienskoye in the Smolienskaya District. Worked as a teacher of German in NKVD training schools, an interpreter in the military censorship section of the Briansk Front, 'Smersh' CED of the Briansk and 2nd Baltic Fronts. From 1 May, 1945 to 22 June, 1946, operations officer of the 4th Section of the General Counter-Espionage Department of the People's Commissariat of Defence. Retired in August, 1970.

Melnikov, Grigory Alexandrovitch – born in 1898 in the village of Selderevo in the Tutaev region of the Yaroslav District, in the Security Service since August, 1919. Served in different posts in the special departments of VCHK – OGPU-NKVD of Byelorussia. During the war, in military counter-espionage service of the Briansk and South-western Fronts. From 21 February, 1944 to 4 August, 1945, Deputy Chief of the 'Smersh' CED of the Byelorussian Front. On 29 July, retired to the KGB attached to the USSR CM. Died 17 July, 1972.

Miroshnichenko, Andrey Seliverstovich – born in 1904 in the Chertkov region of the Rostov district, in the Security Service since 1930. Served in command positions in OGPU-NKVD for the Rostov District. During the war, in military counter-intelligence of the Southern and Leningrad Fronts. From 1944 to 1946, Chief of 'Smersh' CED of the 3rd Assault Army of the 1st Byelorussian Front. On 3 January, 1956 demobilised to the reserve of the KGB attached to the USSR Council of Ministers. Died in 1970.

Potapova, Maria Afanasievna – born in 1916 in the village of Rozhnova in the Zaraisky region of the Riazan district, in the Security Service since 1938. Served as an interpreter in special departments of NKVD of the Volchov, 3rd Byelorussian, 'Smersh' General Counter-Intelligence Department. From 15 January to 15 July, 1945, an interpreter of the operations group of General Department of Counter Espionage Department of the 'Smersh' SED of the 3rd Byelorussian Front. In October, 1971, retired because she had completed her compulsory military service.

Sidnev, Alexey Matveevich – born in 1907 in the city of Saratov, in the Security Service since 1939. Served in command posts in special departments of the Leningrad Military District, Leningrad, and Karelian Fronts. From 6 July, 1944 to 10 November, 1945, Deputy Chief of 'Smersh' CED of the 1st Byelorussian Front. Demobilised from the Ministry of Interior in 1951. Died in 1958.

Terioshin, Nikolai Nikolaevich – born in 1916 in the city of Leningrad, in Security Service since 1939. An NKVD investigator in the Estonian SSR and NKVD Department in the Kirov district, since the beginning of the war in the Special Department of the Voronezh Front. From 10 May, 1943 to 8 February, 1947, senior investigator of 'Smersh' CED of the Central and Byelorussian Fronts and GSF in Germany. In 1950, assigned to work at the command of MSS of the USSR. On 21 June, 1960 demobilised from the KGB attached at the USSR Council of Ministers.

Vadis, Alexandr Anatolyevitch – born in 1906 in the village of Tripolye in the Obukhov region of the Kiev district, in the State Security Service since 1931. Served as an officer in the GPU-NKVD of the Zhitomir, Kamenietsk-Podolsk, and Ternopol districts. From 8 July, 1944 to 25 June, 1945, Chief of 'Smersh' CES of the 1st Byelorussian Front. Demobilised from the USSR Interior Ministry on 25 December, 1951.

Vasiliev, Sergei Semenovitch – born in 1901 in the village of Sapov in the Mosal region of the Smolensk District, in the Security Service since 1928. Served in various posts in the special and transport sections of the GPU-NKVD Departments of the Chiernigovskaya, Vologodskaya, and Bielostokskaya Districts. During the war, served in the military counter-espionage service of the Central, South-western and Briansk Fronts. From 30 August, 1944 to 22 October, 1945, was Chief of 4th Section of the 'Smersh' CED of the 1st Byelorussian Front. On 3 January, 1947 removed from the list of the staff following his death.

Vlasov, Nikolai Alekseevich – born in 1922 in the city of Novosibirsk, in the Security Service since November, 1941. An investigator of the special departments of the Briansk, Kalinin, and 1st Byelorussian Fronts, from February, 1944 to April, 1946, investigator of the 4th Section of CED of MSS of the GSF in Germany. In 1958, demobilised to the reserve of the MSS due to illness, and died in 1960.

Zelenin, Pavel Vasilievich – born in 1902 in the village of Kitchkas in the Zaporozhsky region of the Dniepropetrovsky district, in the State Security Service since March, 1920. Served in various posts in transport departments of OGPU-NKVD of the town of Alexandrovka of the South Don Railway and Southern Railway. During the war, in the military counter-espionage service of the Western, Zakavkazsky, South-western, and 3rd Byelorussian Fronts. From 15 August, 1945, Chief of 'Smersh' CED of the GSF in Germany. Demobilised to the reserve of the USSR MSS on 6 December, 1948.

TABLE OF MILITARY AND SPECIAL RANKS IN THE USSR
AND GERMANY DURING WORLD WAR II

NKVD-NKGB	RKKA	WEHRMACHT	SS
		Reichsmarschal*	Reichsführer**
———	———		
State Security Commissar General	Marshal of the Soviet Union	Feldmarschal (Generalfeldmarschal)	
			———
State Security Commissar First Rank	Marshal of . . . General of the Army	Generaloberst	SS-Oberst-gruppenführer. 1942 on
State Security Commissar Second Rank	Colonel General	General***	SS-Ober-gruppenführer
State Security Commissar Third Rank	Lieutenant-General	Generalleutnant	SS-Gruppenführer
State Security Senior Major	Major-General	Generalmajor	SS-Brigadeführer
State Security Major	Colonel	Oberst	SS-Standarten-führer
			SS-Oberführer
———	———	———	
State Security Captain	Lieutenant-Colonel	Oberstleutnant	SS-Obersturm-bannführer
State Security Senior Lieutenant	Major	Major	SS-Sturm-bannführer
State Security Lieutenant	Captain	Hauptmann	SS-Hauptsturmführer
State Security Lieutenant	Senior Lieutenant	Oberleutnant	SS-Obersturmführer
State Security Sergeant	Lieutenant	Leutnant	SS-Untersturmführer

* There was only one person who held the rank of 'Reichsmarschal' in the Luftwaffe – Hermann Göring.

** There was also only one person who held the rank of 'Reichsführer-SS' – Heinrich Himmler. SS high command officers, as a rule, also had a military rank with the same structure as that of the Waffen-SS.

*** In the German Armed Forces the rank of 'General' was followed by the arm of service, for example: General, Infantry, and so on.

ABBREVIATIONS

'Smersh' CED– 'Smersh' Counter-Espionage Department (may be translated from Russian as 'Smert' shpionam' = 'death to spies').

Frau – Mrs.

Fraulein – Miss.

Gen. – General.

Gestapo (German) – Geheimestaatspolizei – Secret State Police.

GPU (Russian) – The General Political Department.

GRU (Russian) – General Intelligence Department of the Red Army General Staff.

GFP (German) – Geheime Feldpolizei – Secret field police.

GSFG (Russian) – Group of Soviet Forces Germany.

HF – High Frequency transmitter.

Ju-52 – a German military transport aeroplane and bomber, manufactured by the Junkers company.

Me-109, Me-110 – German fighters produced by the Messerschmidt company.

MD – Military District.

MS – Medical Service.

MVO (Russian) – MMD – Moscow Military District.

MVS (Russian) – The USSR DM – the USSR Ministry of Defence.

NKO (Russian) – the People's Commissariat of Defence.

NKVD (Russian) – The People's Commissariat of Interior.

NSDAP (German) – Nationalsozialistisch Deutsche Arbeiterpartei – the National-Socialist Workers' Party of Germany (Nazi Party).

OGPU (Russian) – United State Political Department attached to the Council of People's Commissariat of the Soviet Union.

OK (Russian) – SD – Staff Department.

OKW (German) – Oberkommando der Wehrmacht – High Command of the Armed Forces of Nazi Germany.

p./b. – post box, p.o.b..

RSFSR (Russian) – The Russian Soviet Federal Socialist Republic.

SD (German) – Sicherheitsdienst – Security Service.

SD (Russian) – Special Department.

SS (German) –Schutzstaffel – political police.

EPILOGUE

What you have just read are the most important documents concerning Hitler's last days extracted from the strictly secret file about him that was compiled on the orders of Stalin and preserved in the Russian Federal Archives. These are the verbatim record of interviews, conducted in German by Russian counter-intelligence specialists and translated into Russian contemporaneously, with virtually all of Hitler's closest circle who were identified and captured immediately after his death. Other relevant reports and important documents are included, such as the account for the benefit of their superiors by those who disposed of the remains of Hitler and Goebbels. The photographs include vital pieces of evidence, such as the bloodstained sofa found in Hitler's room in the Bunker and, above all, the dental records that proved that the bodies found were unquestionably those of Hitler and Eva Braun, as confirmed through the interrogations of Hitler's dentist and the dental technician who made the distinctive crowns and bridges.

Hitler's Death was originally published under the name of *Agonia i Smert' Adolfa Gitlera [The Death Throes and Death of Adolf Hitler]* in Moscow in 2000, the year in which a four-inch fragment of Hitler's skull, showing the controversial bullet hole, was displayed under glass at Russia's Federal Archives Service as part of an exhibition called "The Death Throes of the Third Reich: The Retribution", timed to mark the 55th anniversary of the defeat of Nazi Germany.

The piece of skull and the jaw of which photographs appear in *Hitler's Death* were not displayed in the exhibition. They are the only parts of Hitler's remains not buried by the Russians in the Mageburg barracks and subsequently pulverised with the remains of Goebbels and his family and thrown into the river Bideriz in East Germany.

Anecdotal evidence of Hitler's demise has since been widely reported in other books, notably *The Death of Hitler* by Ada Petrova and Peter Watson, published in 1995 by Richard Cohen Books and the film entitled *Downfall*, directed by Oliver Hirschbiegel which was released in February, 2005. Leading historians, such as Hugh Trevor-Roper, in his *Last Days of Hitler* (originally published in 1947) who tried to piece together what happened to Hitler and his closest entourage, had no access to most of the physical evidence, since it had been removed and concealed by the Russians. Key eye-witness accounts were also missing (this was remedied in subsequent editions of Trevor-Roper's book, in which the testimony of Linge and Baur was included), since those who could have provided it languished in Russian labour camps. Yet Trevor-Roper and other historians, such as Walter Warlimont, came extremely close to the truth, sometimes with the help of the few eye-witnesses who had avoided captivity.

Only one enigma remained, that none could not have guessed at – the fact that the top of Hitler's skull, which had been concealed immediately the Russians found it some time later, contained a bullet hole. *Hitler's Death* explains why the wound was in a position which, according to some forensic experts, would have been difficult, if not impossible, to reach by a person committing suicide.

Hitler's Death is the final word on the subject, the sort of material that any lawyer would want to see as conclusive evidence when preparing a case. It has taken 60 years to uncover the truth.

Josephine Bacon

BIBLIOGRAPHY

Bernadotte, Count Folke, *The Curtain Falls*, New York, Alfred A. Knopf, 1945

Beevor, Antony, *The Fall of Berlin 1945*, London, Penguin, 2002

Beevor, Antony, *Stalingrad*, London, Penguin, 1998

Bezymenski, Lev, *The Death of Adolf Hitler: Unknown documents from Soviet Archives*, New York, Jove/HBJ, 1978

Byford-Jones, W, *Berlin Twilight*, London, Hutchinson, 1963

Dietrich, Otto, *The Hitler I Knew*, London, Methuen K, 1957

Fest, Joachim, *Inside Hitler's Bunker: The Last Days of the Third Reich*, New York, Pan, 2005

Joachimsthaler, Anton, *The Last Days of Hitler: The Legends, the Evidence, the Truth*, London, Weidenfeld & Nicolson, 1998

Kershaw, Ian, *Hitler 1936-1945: Nemesis*, London, Penguin, 2000

Leahy, William D, *I was There*, New York, Arno Press, 1979

Maser, Werner, *Hitler, Legend, Myth and Reality*, London, HarperCollins, 1975

Maser, Werner, *Hitler's Letters and Notes*, London, Bantam Books, 1983

McKenzie, F.C, *Greatest Illusion: the Death? of Adolf Hitler*, Beaver Publishing House, 1995

Montefiore, Simon Sebag, *Stalin: The Court of the Red Tsar*, London, Weidenfeld & Nicolson, 2003

O'Donnell, James, *The Bunker*, New York, Da Capo Press, 2001

Payne, Robert, *The life and Death of Adolf Hitler*, London, Jonathan Cape, 1979

Petrova, Ada and Watson, Peter, *The Death of Hitler: The Full Story with new Evidence from the Secret Russian Archives*, London, Richard Cohen Books, 1995

Pipes, Richard, *Russia Under the Bolshevik Regime*, New York, Vintage, 1995

Roberts, Andrew, *Hitler and Churchill: Secrets of Leadership*, London, Weidenfeld & Nicolson, 2003

Stone, Norman, *Hitler*, London, Little Brown, 1980

Toland, John, *Adolf Hitler*, London, Wordsworth Editions, 1997

Trevor-Roper, Hugh, *The Last Days of Hitler*, New York, Pan, 2002

Warlimont, Walter, *Inside Hitler's Headquarters, 1939-45*, New York, Presidio Press, 1997

Werth, Alexander, *Russia: The Post-War Years*, London, Robert Hale, 1971

INDEX